Brief Contents

Contents

List of Illustrations

Figures

Tables

Boxes

Preface

[Carnal sociology] aims to provide a demonstration in action of the fruitfulness of an approach that takes seriously, at the theoretical, methodological, and rhetorical levels, the fact that the social agent is before anything else a being of flesh, nerves, and senses . . . a 'suffering being' . . . who partakes of the universe that makes him, and that he in turn contributes to making, with every fiber of his body and his heart.

(Wacquant 2006: vii)

We have been conducting studies for a number of years on diversity and equality in the workplace. What Wacquant describes above as carnal sociology speaks well to our experiences as researchers in this discipline of the social sciences. The interpretation and narration of the evidence that we have collected during the research projects that we present in this book reflect our personal and professional experience, which has evolved with our interaction with large numbers of research participants in the diversity and equality industry in the US, Mexico, the UK, Continental Europe and Japan.

This book presents a collection of seven separate research projects that we have conducted between 2004 and 2007. The first research project involved an investigation of the diversity management industry and processes, particularly focusing on a global automobile manufacturing industry in Japan. This project was funded by the Japan Institute of Labour Policy and Training. The second study that we report in this book is a national survey of diversity management policies, practices and professionals in the UK. The study was commissioned by the Chartered Institute of Personnel and Development (CIPD). The third study is a set of in-depth interviews with diversity professionals in domestic and international employers in Britain. This study was supported by the CIPD contacts. Diagnostic equality check is the focus of our fourth study, funded by the Equal Opportunities Commission (EOC) in the UK. It involved interviews with stakeholders across the diversity industry as well as a comparative review of the international policies and practices of diagnostic checks. The fifth project was also commissioned by the EOC. It investigates equality and diversity across the private recruitment sector in the UK, through a number of interviews with key actors and agencies in the field. Arts Council England has funded the sixth project that we report. The project focused on work placement models and practices which provide employment to a broadly international group of students in the creative and cultural industry in London. We have conducted interviews in workplaces and higher education establishments. The seventh study concerns the case of a global automobile manufacturing company, which involved interviews with diversity managers in the US, Mexico, the UK and Europe, as well as documentary analysis.

We have decided to assign the title Global Diversity Management to this book in recognition of the urgent need for attention to concerns of diversity and equality beyond the narrow considerations at the national, organizational and intergroup levels. Our conception of global, in the context of global diversity management, embraces both international aspects of diversity management from cross-national perspectives as well as domestic diversity management practices which increasingly operate within the international workforce. We provide analyses of two under-researched domains of diversity management: global and agentic domains. At the global domain, we reveal that the North American origins of this concept deem it unsuitable for other national contexts. Therefore, there is a need for context specific frames to understand how diversity management may work across different cultural and economic settings. Furthermore, the analyses of diversity management processes demand the attention of individual professionals who carry out the daily activities of diversity management. By bringing in these two macro and micro- perspectives, we believe that this book will provide a comprehensive understanding of diversity management.

In this book we have adopted a relational perspective which requires the examination of all constituent groups and individuals that characterize a field of study. Therefore, we have utilized multilayered and multilevel analysis. Our approach is multilayered insofar as we bring in both structural considerations, such as the organization of diversity activities at global, national, sectoral and organizational levels, and also agentic considerations that permeate the process of managing diversity. This approach also involves recognition of history and context as being important considerations in situating diversity management activities across these layers of structure and agency. Our approach is multilevel insofar as it provides, through each field study analysis, recognition of macro-social, meso-organizational and micro-individual level dynamics.

It is our contention that diversity management activities and activism requires attention to multiple constituencies, which we will term in this book as stakeholders or actors. We have integrated a broad range of actors in our field studies: as participants. Our attention to the stakeholder groups was not only limited to the variation across their discourses and approaches. We have indeed investigated differentials in their power and influence across a range of diversity management activities. The stakeholders that we have incorporated in our studies include diversity and equality professionals; legislators; consultancies; trade union representatives; representatives from employers' organizations; professional bodies; public, private and voluntary sector equality and diversity bodies; academics; publishers; specialists; and people who are recipients of diversity policies and programmes.

This stakeholder approach has enabled us to conceive the diversity management field as an industry with a coherent discourse with dissonant voices. Whilst we recognize that there are certain dominant discourses in the industry, our research has revealed multiple discourses, some of which are marginalized. However, we have also paid particular attention to the material bases of these discursive struggles in the field. Analysis of power and politics are therefore integral elements in our approach to diversity management, as we consider rhetoric, theory, method and practice of diversity and equality as essentially political domains. Drawing attention to the key actors in the diversity industry, we demonstrate in this book that any analysis of diversity management requires a keen attention to power relations which are inherent in the negotiated nature of diversity management processes.

Rather than offering quick-fix solutions to diversity management problems, we will argue that the unique configurations of the organization, the sector and the society should be explored. This requires us also to take into consideration the power and resources of professionals who design and implement diversity management policies. We achieve this in our text by identifying parameters and models of diversity which are sensitive to social and organizational contexts, including the primacy of politics, history and economy.

The book frames diversity management in a way that reconciles disparate and contradictory beliefs about diversity and equality in order to overcome the problems associated with binary oppositional conceptions of diversity management. We believe that binary thinking in the field, which traditionally referred to superficial differences between diversity and equality, and business case and legal case arguments, are counterproductive, as they ultimately lead to essentialist and partisan attitudes, and to schism in the equality and diversity industry, which already lacks resources and influence to affect change. We have sought to transcend binary oppositions not only in our conception of diversity and equality, but also in our methodological choices. This has prompted us to combine qualitative and quantitative insights as well as extensive documentary and historical analyses. Following the path that Paulo Freire has mapped out in his magnum opus, *Pedagogy of the Oppressed*, we also have tried to overcome the extreme versions of verbalism (sacrifice of action) and activism (sacrifice of reflection) which serve as common traps for studies in the field. Similar to Freire, we advocate reflexive action and actionable knowledge, since we provide an assessment of diversity management practices with a view to improving them.

Our theoretical and empirical approach to social research allows for multi-disciplinary perspectives to be integrated. This requires us to blend theory and empirical evidence, with a view to grounding rhetoric in social reality. This approach is sometimes called evidence-based theorization or evidence based policy-making. In engaging with both theory and research, we have operational-ized key frames, concepts and theories for understanding diversity management.

In writing this book, we have taken special care to offer accessibility to our readers who may come from different walks of life. The text provides definitions of key concepts and gradually introduces the reader to a more complex set of ideas and political processes with the support of up-to-date insights in the field. Therefore, this book is suitable for study at the advanced undergraduate and postgraduate levels, and it also provides a useful resource for practitioners, researchers and scholars in the field.

MUSTAFA F. ÖZBILGIN
AHU TATLI

Introduction

In this introduction we will focus on the contested definition and scope of diversity management, and trace its historical development. Subsequently we will introduce our global diversity management framework and identify the divergent development of the practice and theory of global diversity management. The theoretical framework that is presented is a multilevel framework, which is constructed on evidence generated through seven research projects at all levels of global diversity management practice. Therefore, this introduction provides an overarching framework that illustrates the respective position of the levels and dimensions of global diversity management, which are then fully explored in Chapter Two. An overview of the structure of the book is provided at the end of this introduction.

1.1 Diversity management debate: definition, dissent and development

It is difficult to identify an aspect of diversity management that remains to be explored. There have been studies focusing on the interplay between the discourses, practices, rhetoric, myths, policies, reality, perceptions, antecedents, correlates and consequences of diversity in organizational settings. However, much of the work on diversity management has been carried out either in domestic settings, with little attention to diversity management in a global context, or drawn on a single-level analysis, focusing either on managerial or trade union dimensions of diversity. This book examines global diversity management. It explores key drivers for the take-up of diversity initiatives at global, regional and national, sectoral, discursive, organizational and individual levels.

We first unpack the diversity management debate, in terms of the way it has been defined, contested and developed in the mainstream literature. These elaborations then lead to a discussion of how global diversity management is different from its domestic counterpart. Subsequently, a conceptual model of key influences on appropriation and development of a global diversity management approach is offered. The model is illustrated with its key components.

Defining and interpreting diversity management has been a tall order. Although diversity management can be defined simply as a management philosophy that seeks to recognize and value heterogeneity in organizations, the key difficulty has been in interpreting this definition, due to the multiplicity of vested interests by multiple stakeholder groups over the aims, processes and proposed outcomes of diversity management, as well as what constitutes legitimate, assumed and real forms of heterogeneity in organizational settings.

Whilst there has been dissent amongst scholars in terms of authenticity and legitimacy of diversity management in contrast to earlier equal opportunities activities in organizations (see Agocs and Burr 1996), the concept of diversity management has been attributed multiple meanings (Jenner 1994) by public and private sector practitioners, consultants, trade unionists, employers' association representatives, the law and policy-makers. Furthermore, much of the diversity management research in the early 1990s suffered from the absence of a posteriori insights. Claims of unidirectional causal relationships between workforce or cultural diversity and improved business performance were not often substantiated by empirical evidence. Absence of empirical evidence in early pieces of diversity management writing is partly responsible for the poor reputation of the subject in management scholarship (see for example Gatley and Lessem 1995).

Two distinct camps have emerged as a result. Whilst a group of consultants and employers in Western Europe and North America hastily embraced and advocated the concept of diversity management as a new method for increasing organizational competitiveness and performance, this has been received with much scepticism by a number of trade unionists and by scholars from critical management and industrial relations disciplines, regarding the adequacy of the concept in addressing their traditional concerns over social and workplace inequalities. According to Cassell and Biswas (2000), the shift from equal opportunities to diversity management was marked by a move away from the emotive discourse and the moral case of equality such as elimination of discrimination and inequality by gender, ethnicity and disability, towards the individualized and performance-driven business case arguments which were advocated by diversity management scholars. The shift of emphasis from group-based inequalities to individual-level differences in the diversity management discourse was starkly evident in some papers in the field. For example, Neck *et al.* (1997) formulated a model of self-thought management of diversity, which involves a set of individual prescriptions for ways of thinking that welcome diversity, shifting the focus of diversity from social group membership to an individual-level concern.

The shift from embedded, situated and path-dependent understandings of inequality in organizational settings towards individualized and meritocratic formulations of diversity management is congruent with other reflections of neo-liberal ideology in management studies. Humphries and Grice (1995) critique diversity management discourse, arguing that it is closely allied with other neo-liberal ideologies of globalization, individualization and de-collectivization. They note that the change from equal opportunities and affirmative action came at a time of political transformation in industrialized economies and that diversity management has been instrumental as a tool for neo-liberal ideology.

Other scholars have also adopted critical approaches to diversity management. Kersten (2000) criticizes diversity management on three main accounts: (a) its discourse fails to take note of structural and institutional forms of racism; (b) it silences the identity politics surrounding sex and race relations, reducing such differences to one among many; and (c) it fails to offer prescriptions that address these key social concerns and diverts attention to surface-level issues.

However, it is important to recognize numerous attempts by scholars to incorporate social and structural equality concerns in diversity management literature and not to tar the whole breadth of the diversity management literature with the same broad brush, viewing it as a homogeneous management discourse. The diversity management, which has emerged as a management discourse and practice in the 1990s in the US, now receives a warmer reception even in more critical circles, due to the development of its discourse in a way that reconciles its polarized interpretations. Whilst diversity management was initially offered as an alternative approach to equal opportunities (Kandola and Fullerton 1994), it was reformulated as a complementary approach to equality of opportunity work which characterized the initiatives that have sought to eradicate discrimination and inequalities in the second half of the 20th century. Other scholars have also expressed concern over polarization of diversity and equality efforts, arguing that diversity management approach could be improved to embrace equality issues (Kirton and Greene 2000) and ethical considerations (Gilbert *et al*. 1999).

Moreover, there have been recent attempts at improving the vision of diversity through the critical lenses of management and industrial relations scholarship. For example, Lorbiecki and Jack (2000) review changes in the diversity discourse, identifying a need for more critical perspectives. The post-colonial literature, they argue, may provide such a critical perspective for the diversity management, if post-colonial literature's conceptualization of domination is incorporated in political and historical analyses of diversity management perspectives. Kirton and Greene (2000) warn about the limitations of the individualized focus of diversity management in addressing inequalities that manifest themselves at a collective level, and argue that diversity management rhetoric can be revised to capture a more critical perspective. Similarly, Mor Barak (2000) argues for a more inclusive definition of diversity management. This entails aligning diversities at the level of the local, national and international communities to organizational diversity by inclusive practices. The proposed conceptual framework draws on an ecosystems approach and provides evidence for the benefits of increased diversity for the workplace.

There were also calls for legal reforms to address the critique of the gap between the legal compliance case for equal opportunities and the voluntaristic case for the diversity management approach: some commentators argue that diversity management dilutes equality efforts and diverts attention from the legal and social obligations of employers (Dickens 1999; Kirton and Greene 2000) to provide equality of opportunity and to eliminate discrimination by gender, race, disability and sexual orientation, among other arbitrary factors. Barmes and Ashtiany (2003) call for legal reforms to capture this diversion and seek to address the loopholes that diversity discourse brought about in management practice. They argue that the current legislation on elimination of sex, race and disability discrimination are limited in scope to offer effective means to eliminate the range of unfair inequalities that are experienced. In the same vein, aligning the law to combat wider range of inequalities may also help eradicate the schism between the proponents of equality and diversity, the former emphasizing the legal and the latter the voluntary case for action.

Improvements to the substantive interpretation of diversity management aside, diversity management typologies and perspectives have also promulgated in the last decade. For example, Ashkanasy *et al*. (2002) review the use of typologies in defining diversity. They refer to Jehn *et al*.'s (1999) work on diversity, which includes three different types of diversity: informational diversity, social category diversity and value diversity. They also seek to offer a framework which bridges the divide between utilitarian and socially responsible perspectives on diversity, noting that diversity definitions should not be limited to the social diversity categories such as gender and race but could be more directly related to work performance, such as diversity in terms of skills, abilities and knowledge.

One of the most significant works that embrace both social category and other forms of difference is offered by Harrison *et al.* (1998). The authors make a distinction between deep and surface level diversity. The term surface level diversity refers to the forms of heterogeneity that can be detected by observing the physical qualities of a person. These include observable forms of difference by sex, race and age. Deep level diversity relates to divisions between individuals by belief, values and norms, which are observable only through time-intensive encounters and exchanges between people. The authors hypothesize that surface level diversity will become less important as deep level heterogeneities become more prevalent with the moderating influence of time. They identify that information rather than time is responsible for the acculturation process in which deep level diversities are shaped. As individuals gain information about others the significance of shallow level differences diminish before the deep level diversities crystallize. However, the authors caution that this may not be the case when the surface level differences are also associated with differences in status. The deep and shallow diversity model is very useful for broadening our understanding of diversity from its limited scope of classical categories such as gender and ethnicity that are often used for proxies for difference in a style which borders essentialism. The deep and shallow level diversity model makes it possible to view difference in organizational settings as a socially constructed phenomenon that can manifest in variable degrees of impact and visibility.

Bhadury *et al.* (2000) also offer a method in which the dynamics of multiple forms of diversity can be measured. They cluster groups of individuals with similar traits into 'families' and using an experimental design offer an 'optimal' way for managers to form diverse teams. The study uses educational background and gender as a proxy for diversity and in order to define 'families' with similar attributes. The experiment uses three decision variables: a diversity index, the number of tables, and the maximum number of family members to be seated at each table. Family analysis of heterogeneity in groups provides a useful means of exploring group level diversity issues.

Diversity management research has also evolved to explore the gaps between the rhetoric and the reality, the reality and the perceptions, and the policy and the practice of diversity management. For example, Harrison *et al.* (2002) identify a difference between perceived and actual diversity. Their research reveals that social interaction and time are important moderating influences on overcoming the negative consequences of perceived and actual diversity, and the creating of cohesion and improving performance. Despite evidence of elaborate policy statements and theoretical and conceptual constructs of diversity management, the evidence suggests that the practice and implementation of diversity management incorporate only very few of the promised forms of inclusiveness (see for example Groschl and Doherty 1999) or achieve levels of effectiveness (D'Netto and Sohal 1999) that is strong enough to generate the desired outcomes.

Contributing to the gap-analysis literature in diversity management, Barry and Bateman (1996) define social traps as the gap between consequences of short term individual choices and the longer term outcomes of those individual choices for the social group or the collective to which the member belongs. They link social trap theory to diversity management practices, examining evidence for the consequences of diversity management practices. Their paper also provides a set of trap solutions which seek to redress the imbalances between individual and collective outcomes of diversity management. Their review points to the significance of the individual efforts in achieving diversity goals. However, the authors also note that such changes, even if they constitute small steps, may result in sizeable changes if they are cultivated and accumulated.

Ivancevich and Gilbert (2000) refer to rhetoric, discourse and reality of diversity. However, they note a convergence of discourse and reality, illustrating that there is a growing body of evidence in support of positive individual and organizational consequences of carefully crafted diversity management initiatives. The evidence presented comes from research studies, field surveys, case studies and consultancy reports. The authors contend that diversity management research suffers from some rhetorical debates that are not fully substantiated with field work and empirical evidence. Managers have a range of strategies that they can adopt in relation to diversity management from exclusion of diversity to full recognition and mutual adaptation. The authors suggest that any strategic choice between these alternatives should be examined in terms of its ethicality, best value, legality and accountability.

Despite these developments in the diversity management literature, there are still outstanding concerns. Although diversity management scholars converge on the idea that differences should be recognized and valued, there is little other than general stereotypes about what constitutes a real, and what would be an imagined, difference, as well as how different forms of difference should be treated, for example valued, ignored, discouraged or eliminated. The philosophical issue of the essence versus construction of sameness and difference needs to be explored. Is individual difference an essential quality, an indelible mark that resides at the level of the individual? Or, is difference a quality which is imbued on us in our situated activities of social and economic kind, and hence a quality that is bound by time, space and relationships? At this point resides our primary concern on diversity management and its treatment of difference. Rigidly defining legitimate forms of difference in a way which only focuses on social group membership and equality concerns fails to recognize the heterogeneity within those social groups, essentializing their imagined difference. A similar rigidity in focusing on legitimate forms of difference through the lens of organizational performance runs the risk of diluting the work on anti-discriminatory action, by reducing sex and race equality concerns to one of a multitude of diversity issues. Furthermore, suggesting that all forms of difference should be valued would lack pragmatic sense in a world of competing priorities. Nevertheless, we contend that organizations can arrive at reconciled interpretations of diversity by adopting a multistakeholder and multidimensional diversity perspective that allows for different constituent groups' and actors' views to be reflected in the formulation of their diversity management approaches. Feminists have long questioned the issue of difference and sameness by gender, proposing liberal, radical and transformational agendas of change for gender equality (Jewson and Mason 1986; Cockburn 1989). Transformational change agenda (Cockburn 1989) suggests that organizations in the short term should try to eradicate inequalities by gender, but in the long term the role is to transform organizations in a way which will make their structures and cultures more egalitarian. Diversity management discourse, on the other hand, often views valuing of diversity as a means to other organizational ends, rather than as an end in itself. The main concern then becomes: when is a form of assumed and imagined difference legitimately reified? In the absence of an equality discourse, diversity management does little more than exploit the heterogeneity in the current supply and demand of the labour market. It fails to aspire to a transformation of some of the inequalities inherent in those supply and demand dynamics. If the woman's disproportionate share of domestic duties, or the supply of cheap labour of an ethnic group, are recognized as legitimate differences that should be accommodated and exploited, then by definition diversity management, unlike equality efforts, does little to transform gender and racial disadvantage, but rather serves to retain the status quo in the labour markets. So, what is required is to have a definition and approach to diversity that does not only state what kind of difference is valued, but also states how it is valued and in what ways. With such a recognition and valuing process, the organization commits to a transforming of social and economic inequalities that reinforce imagined differences which keep women, minority ethnic groups, disabled workers and sexual orientation minorities firmly in their place.

1.2 Global diversity management: from practice to theory

Most aspects of diversity management at the domestic level have been widely studied. However, the same cannot be said of global diversity management.

Global diversity management can be defined as planning, coordination and implementation of a set of management strategies, policies, initiatives, and training and development activities that seek to accommodate diverse sets of social and individual backgrounds, interests, beliefs, values and ways of work in organizations with international, multinational, global and transnational workforces and operations. Some scholars attempt to explain the differences between global diversity management and its domestic counterpart. Stumpf *et al.* (1994) argue that management of diversity in global organization is not about making effective use of individual differences but about creating an organizational culture which transcends these differences.

It is a truism to state that the growing number of international, multinational and global organizations have now offices and departments which specialize on global diversity management. These offices have a different function when compared to their domestic diversity management offices. Whilst the former seek to issue global diversity management policies and coordinate international and global operations with a view to foster organizational cultures and structures that are conducive to effective operation of diverse groups, the domestic diversity management function has a more traditional role of constructing a national policy and supporting the effective implementation of the policy in a specific country. Differentiation of global and domestic diversity management activities is particularly observable in the case of North American and Western European global organizations.

Furthermore, scholars in progressive higher education institutions conduct field studies and organize seminars, conferences and other knowledge dissemination activities on diversity management (Freeman-Evans 1994), whilst some institutions now offer courses on diversity management at both undergraduate and postgraduate levels. Despite clear lines of differentiation between global and domestic diversity management, as explained above, knowledge acquisition and dissemination activities have predominantly focused on domestic diversity management issues.

Therefore a gap between the practice and theorization of global diversity management has emerged. This sometimes means that global diversity managers have taken on their job roles with little or no training on specific global diversity management issues. The skills gap that can be identified in the global diversity management market serves as a point of reflection for academic research and dissemination activities. Doktor *et al.* (1991: 363) explain why globalization requires new ways of thinking and new approaches to management:

> As multicultural organizations become more global in their operations, difficulties arising out of the cultural diversity of the organization's members and clients become more apparent to the managers of these diverse organizations. Management behaviours are based upon cultural assumptions.

As organizations operate across multiple cultures, these assumptions vary. Managerial behaviours that are appropriate under certain cultural assumptions may become dysfunctional under other cultural assumptions.

In order to address these considerations, Doktor *et al.* (1991: 363) propose that management theorists should develop methods that capture these realities. In terms of global diversity management, there is a need for new conceptual frameworks, methods for research and new programmes for training and educating the new cohort of global diversity managers.

If global diversity management is a new field of practice and study, ideally where should global diversity management activities reside in organizational structures? The choices of where domestic diversity management practices should reside are wide and the choices for global diversity management activities are even wider. Global diversity management may be centralized through a common policy which is then translated and implemented in the branch network or localized with each domestic branch identifying its own diversity management approach and priorities. The latter practice resembles practices in multinational and international companies which seek to localize their practices. Global organizations, on the other hand, seek to centralize their activities as their practices are supposed to transcend national variations. In terms of diversity and globalization, one of the key markers of a global organization is its treatment of diversity, thus argue Hordes *et al.* (1995: 7–8). They explain the main differences between multinational organizations – which have operations across a wide range of countries, managed through much localization – and global organizations – which have centralized policies that transcend national differences – in the following way:

> the truly global enterprise operates very differently from both the international or the multinational enterprises. While it may have roots in one culture, it has created an organizational culture that values diversity. A few core values are its unifying force. Although it has headquarters, the global enterprise is often managed by a team of managers from diverse locations. Its business processes, policies, and technologies are often diverse with the exception of a few rigidly standardized policies, often centered around communication technologies and training of the workforce.

The location of the global diversity management activities may also depend on the professionalization of diversity management function within the organization. Global diversity management may be located in a separate department or office, or it can be a subfunction of a larger department situated at various levels of the organizational hierarchy with a wide spectrum of choices of reporting, monitoring, training and implementation methods. Diversity management activities may also be mainstreamed or devolved to one functional area, most frequently to the human resource management, or to the line management in one, or across a number of, sections, or even the whole of the organization. Therefore the choices of where global diversity management activities may reside are wide. However, it is hypothesized that in global organizations global diversity management activities should be centralized, as other diffuse methods resemble multinational management models more than the global management model.

If there are several choices in location of global diversity management activities, what are the factors that shape the global diversity management approach that the global organizations will take? Diversity management is a North American concept which has found acceptance in the rest of the industrialized world. Despite transfer of knowledge through multinationals, diversity management approaches have evolved to differentiate when they cross borders. Whilst there are global drivers due to changing demographics, and economic and legal forces at the international level encourage the adoption of diversity management principles, legal, social, economic and cultural conditions of the countries account for some of the variation in adoption of practices and implementation. There are also sectoral and organizational effects, particularly in relation to structures and systems of organizations being amenable to diversity concerns, and dependencies to the time and context of organizations. Furthermore the diversity management office at the national level also plays a role in raising awareness and in campaigning for global coordination of activities. Last but by no means the least significant issue is the role of the individual agency in promoting the case for global diversity management offices. Opinion and decision leaders as well as individuals in strategic positions may see the significance of global coordination in diversity management issues. The link between global diversity initiatives and its positive impact on individual and group performance may also persuade senior managers to pay attention to global diversity management concerns. **Figure 1.1** illustrates the key influences on global diversity management approaches as outlined here.

1.3 Organization of the book

The book is organized into five parts and 13 chapters. This chapter has introduced the text and its key concepts and has elaborated our particular theoretical and empirical approach. Part I brings together chapters which frame global diversity management. Chapter 2 is on the theory of global diversity management. It presents a theoretical model for investigating global diversity management in terms of five key effects on the dynamics of diversity at the global level, drawing on the international literature in the field. Chapter 3 presents a study of global diversity management in the automobile manufacturing sector in Japan, based on the model introduced in Chapter 2.

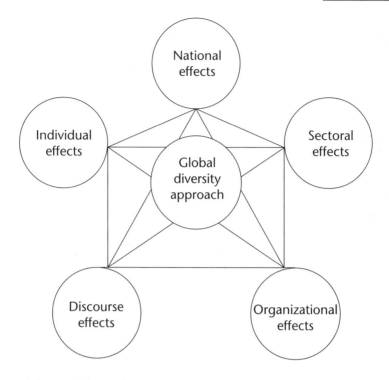

Figure 1.1   Main drivers for setting up a global diversity management initiative

Parts II, III and IV present different dimensions of global diversity management as outlined in **Figure 1.1**. All parts of the book present theory and practice and they are based on broadly international studies. Part II presents chapters which explore the national and discursive effects of diversity management. Chapter 4 presents the findings of a questionnaire survey on diversity management at the national level. A three-level framework is utilized in order to analyse antecedents, processes and outcomes of diversity management at the national level.

Deepening our analysis at the national level, the book then focuses on the policy and practice of diversity management in Chapter 5. This is achieved through an investigation of the case of tackling gender pay gap through equal pay reviews and diagnostic equality checks. Chapter 6 presents the findings of the field study, which was framed in-line with the theoretical considerations in Chapter 5, and which is based on a multistakeholder research on an assessment of diagnostic equality checks. Chapter 7 supplements Chapters 4, 5 and 6 with a qualitative study that focuses on discourses of diversity management as a process of storytelling.

Part III examines the sectoral effects on diversity management. Chapter 8 includes a survey of equality and diversity management practices and policies in private sector recruitment agencies. Chapter 9 presents the findings of a scoping study on work placements in the creative and cultural industry through participation of host organizations, higher education institutions and placement students.

Part IV narrows down the level of analysis to organizational and individual effects on global diversity management. Chapter 10 explores organizational level dynamics of diversity management in a global automobile manufacturing company through interviews with diversity managers in the US, the UK, Mexico and Europe. The chapter involves exploration of the organizational culture and objective organizational structures which impact upon choices of diversity management.

Chapter 11 offers a model for understanding the power, influence and resources of diversity managers, through a three-pronged framework of situatedness, relationality and performativity. Chapter 12 offers reflections on this framework and provides an analysis of different forms of capital and strategies of diversity managers in the context of a global automobile manufacturing organization. Part V (Chapter 13) presents a summary, conclusions and an outline of the challenges of the future and possible new directions.

Further reading

Agocs, C. and Burr, C. (1996) 'Employment Equity Affirmative Action and Managing Diversity: Assessing the Differences', *International Journal of Manpower*, vol. 17, pp. 30–45.

Barmes, L. and Ashtiany, S. (2003) 'The Diversity Approach to Achieving Equality: Potential and Pitfalls', *The Industrial Law Journal*, vol. 32, pp. 274–96.

Barry, B. and Bateman, T.S. (1996) 'A Social Trap Analysis of the Management of Diversity', *Academy of Management Review*, vol. 21, pp. 757–90.

Benschop, Y. (2001) 'Pride, Prejudice and Performance: Relations between HRM Diversity and Performance', *International Journal of Human Resources Management*, vol. 12, pp. 1166–81.

Bergen, C.W.V., Soper, B. and Foster, T. (2002) 'Unintended Negative Effects of Diversity Management, *Public Personnel Management*, vol. 31, pp. 239–51.

Cassell, C. and Biswas, R. (2000) 'Managing Diversity in the New Millennium', *Personnel Review*, vol. 29, pp. 268–73.

Fernandez, J.P. (1991) *Managing a Diverse Work Force*. Lexington: Lexington Books.

Gilbert, J.A. and Ivancevich, J.M. (2000) 'Valuing Diversity: A Tale of Two Organizations', *Academy of Management Executive*, vol. 14, no. 1, pp. 93–105.

Hays-Thomas, R. (2003) 'Why Now? The Contemporary Focus on Managing Diversity', in M.S. Stockdale and F.J. Crosby (eds), *The Psychology and Management of Workplace Diversity*. Malden: Blackwell, pp. 1–30.

Ivancevich, J.M. and Gilbert, J.A. (2000) 'Diversity Management Time for New Approach', *Public Personnel Management*, vol. 29, pp. 75–92.

▶

Joplin, J.R.W. and Daus, C.S. (1997) 'Challenges of Leading a Diverse Workforce', *Academy of Management Executive*, vol. 11, no. 3, pp. 32–47.

Kandola, R. and Fullerton, J. (1998) *Managing the Mosaic: Diversity in Action*, 2nd edn. London: Institute of Personnel Development.

Kersten, A. (2000) 'Diversity Management, Dialogue, Dialects and Diversion', *Journal of Organizational Change Management*, vol. 13, pp. 235–48.

Lorbiecki, A. (2001) 'Changing Views on Diversity Management: The Rise of Learning Perspective and the Need to Recognise Social and Political Contradictions', *Management Learning*, vol. 32, no. 3, pp. 345–61.

Nishii, L.H. and Özbilgin, M.F. (2007) 'Global Diversity Management: Towards Conceptual Framework', *International Journal of Human Resource Management*, vol. 18, no. 11, pp. 1883–94.

Thomas, A.D. (2004) 'Diversity as Strategy', *Harvard Business Review*, September, pp. 98–108.

Framing Global Diversity
Management

Theory of Global Diversity Management

2.1 Introduction

The aim of this chapter is to provide a theoretical framework for global diversity management. In order to achieve this we explain the main theories and define important concepts. The purpose of this chapter is neither to discuss whether globalization is a shameless myth (Spich 1995), nor to argue that it is an undeniable reality (Blake and Walters 1976), nor to suggest that it is a mixture of both, as a half-truth (Steingard and Fitzgibbons 1995). Instead, we examine the interplay of globalization with the management of diversity. Arguing that national and domestic considerations of diversity management are insufficient to explain the challenges that face individuals, organizations and countries in terms of their efforts to manage diversity in today's global context, we set out to explain the key global influences on the choice of mode in global diversity initiatives. This is presented across five dimensions of diversity management at national, discursive, sectoral, organizational and individual levels. Therefore, what we offer is a definition of global diversity management, and we provide an overarching theoretical framework for its study and practice.

2.2   What is global diversity management?

Global diversity management is recognized as a key strategic asset in several pieces of research on global organizations. For example Srinivas (1995) argues that one of the key strategic survival and growth assets of global organizations would be their global mindsets, which includes skills such as curiosity and concern, complexity acceptance, diversity consciousness, opportunity seeking, faith in process, continuous improvement, long-term perspective and systems thinking. In the same vein, Barkema *et al.* (2002), in their paper 'Management Challenges in a New Time', highlight diversity management as one of the main management challenges of our times. They note that organizations may benefit from multinational diversity if they manage to counter its undesirable outcomes such as interpersonal conflicts.

Diversity management is an expressly American concept. Can it be easily transferred and grafted onto management systems of other countries? Dass and Parker (1999) argue that there is not a best way to manage diversity. The approach that each organization will take will depend on the pressures for diversity management that they experience. They hypothesize that there are internal and external pressures for diversity management approaches to be adopted. The authors identify a typology of diversity perspectives: (a) resistance; (b) discrimination and fairness; (c) access and legitimacy; and (d) learning perspective. They note that each approach has its associated prescriptions respectively arranged as (a) sustaining homogeneity; (b) assimilating individuals; (c) celebrating difference; and (d) acculturation and pluralism. They propose that the higher the pressures for and priority of diversity in an organization, the better the organization will integrate diversity concerns in its other activities.

At the level of international management pressures, as well as urgency of diversity management, interventions vary more extensively than at the level of domestic operations. This means that global diversity approaches are informed by the pressures both at the domestic and international level. The international level pressures are the increased convergence of legal pressures to combat different forms of inequality; the regional influences are those such as the case of the Social Charter of the European Union and the influence of incipient international campaigns and organizations.

What is the significance of global dynamics of convergence and divergence on adoption of global diversity management approaches? The answer to this question may lie in our understanding of convergence and divergence of institutions across national borders. The evidence suggests that despite arguments of technological convergence, divergence in institutional forms is likely to continue. Aguilera and Jackson (2003: 461) examine the cross-national diversity of corporate governance systems. They conclude that hybridization, rather than convergence and divergence, is responsible for the changes in the global variation of corporate governance approaches. They also note that the interplay of international, national and subnational level influences can explain why path dependence of, or convergence towards, best practices were not in evidence.

In most agency theory literature, internationalization is seen as increasing competition over 'best practices', thereby leading to a convergence on an Anglo-American model, whereas institutionalists suggest countries will continue to diverge along stable, path-dependent trajectories. We claim that examining internationalization in terms of national models is becoming institutionally 'incomplete' because of the multilevel interactions spanning from international to national and subnational policies, most strikingly through the European Union. Furthermore, interactions between stakeholders are increasingly taking a cross-border dimension, exemplified by the pressures of US institutional investors in Continental Europe. Convergence and path dependence, thus, may be false theoretical alternatives in trying to understand simultaneous processes of continuity and change across national boundaries. Institutional change tends to occur in a slow, piecemeal fashion, rather than as a big bang. Where international pressures may lead to similar changes in one institutional domain, these effects may be mediated by the wider configuration of national institutions. This explains why internationalization has not led to quick convergence on national corporate governance models.

The lesson inherent in the debate over convergence and divergence for management of global diversity is that there is a need to recognize that continued divergence of national practices will deem global diversity management approaches, that require rigid observance of an inflexible set of rules across national branches, ineffectual. Although this may suggest that localization appears as a viable alternative, global diversity offices should indeed serve a more considered function, facilitating knowledge creation and dissemination activities across domestic diversity management offices, equipping them with skills to move their diversity initiatives forward, based on shared experiences in the branch network. It is also the role of the global diversity manager to develop global strategies that can transcend limited perspectives that emanate from their domestic networks. There is also a role for scholars. In the main, most North American and Western European research on domestic diversity management are presented without reference to national specificity of context, assuming a pseudo-global applicability. This approach has caused research from other parts of the world to be siloed into an 'international' category, where their contexts are made more explicit.

Absence of contextual elaborations, combined with over-confidence in global applicability of findings of domestic research across national borders without translation or tampering, has been the cause for some concern. The role for scholarship on diversity management is to make more explicit the context specificity of their findings as well as appropriateness of methodological approaches for cross-border appropriation of diversity management approaches. However, variations in cultural norms do not only manifest themselves in cross-national form, the intranational variation also needs to be taken into consideration when exploring internationally comparative data. Au and Cheung (2004) examine intranational variation of cultural norms across 42 countries revealing that such variation has greater explanatory power than the cultural means from these countries. This suggests that the studies which explore national cultures as monolithic entities are indeed failing to see evidence of cultural diversity within countries.

The interplay of global convergence and divergence with formulation of global management approaches is not straightforward. For example, in the wake of proposals to converge public management across OECD countries, Mathiasen (1999) explains that there are tensions inherent due to divergence of systems across these countries, as well as the variations in the interpretation of proposed policies. Geppert *et al.* (2003) present taxonomy of internationalization ranging from full convergence of national systems around a global ideal to predominance of national systems and cultures that deem such claims of globalization redundant. Reflecting on case studies in the international lift and escalator industry, they conclude that the more globalized the strategy of an organization, the more likely for it to draw on subsidiaries to bring in their national knowledge and approaches. This analysis suggests that national divergences are likely to resist or even be utilized in the process of globalization. A reflection of this in terms of diversity initiatives is the paradoxical situation of availability of global diversity statements and policies, and contradictory and divergent diversity management policies and practices at the level of national branch networks. Hence, it may be premature to expect that it will be easy to transcend cross-border variations with considered formulations of global management approaches.

Calori *et al.* (1995) are not very hopeful about the possibility of transcending cross-cultural differences. Based on interviews with American, Japanese and European managers, they map out the identity of the European managers from both 'insider' and 'outsider' (American and Japanese) perspectives. Their findings reveal the subjective, relative and socially constructed nature of the European management identity. The outsider perspective of European management style and identity suggests a poor recognition of customers. The findings of the study also highlight the primacy of the ways of thinking in managers' understanding of others' culture and ways of work. Based on this, the authors argue that although there was belief in learning from diversity across national borders, this remains a distant goal given the divergent ways of cross-border understanding of management practices in each country.

Nevertheless, global diversity management scholars may turn to cross-cultural studies in search for ways of formulating their global diversity management approaches. Using a number of qualitative study techniques, such as interviews, attendance to meetings, work observation and informal discussions, Chevrier (2003) studied three international project teams. The study identifies three distinct approaches to management of cultural diversity in teams. These are respectively termed as 'drawing upon individual tolerance and self-control', 'trial-and-error processes coupled with personal relationships' and 'setting up transnational cultures'. The author acknowledges the assimilationist or integrationist values that underpin the former three approaches and argues that a fourth method, which is based on the use of sense making techniques on a case-by-case basis, would be more productive for a longer-term solution to identifying and tackling cultural dilemmas and conflicts. This method is termed as 'ad hoc cross-cultural management'.

The global forces that encourage multinational organizations to take up global diversity management approaches are manifold. One of the main influences has been the expansion of the national laws and international policies on elimination of discrimination. Globally, there is extensive legalization of protections offered against discrimination by sex. There is also promulgation of forms of discrimination that are considered unlawful in North America, Europe and other industrialized regions. What remains divergent though are the forms of discrimination that are considered unlawful and the way these are identified. Furthermore, there is extensive national variation in interpretation and implementation of equal opportunities laws (Özbilgin 2002). Exponential spread and conceptual expansion of the legal frameworks for equal opportunities, coupled with increased numbers of high profile litigations against global organizations, introduced inequality as a potentially significant cost item for global organizations. There was an increase in the number of categories of discrimination that are considered unlawful. Whilst traditionally sex, race and disability discrimination were targeted by law, current legal frameworks are more complex, offering protection against age, sexual orientation, nationality, social background and many other arbitrary forms of discrimination in the workplaces.

The challenge of establishing workplace diversity policies that are relevant in a multinational organizational setting is demonstrated in the case of Colgate-Palmolive, a New York based company operating in 170 countries. The company, which receives 70 per cent of its $7 billion revenue from overseas markets, has grappled with the challenge of translating its US-based agenda of valuing diversity to the international arena. The concept of equal treatment and opportunity across race, gender, sexual orientation and disability does not readily translate into other cultures where the racial mix is rather homogeneous (for example in Japan) or where the gender divisions are clear and rigid (for example in Saudi Arabia). Through the office of the director of global employee relations, the company has redefined its diversity principles globally. The company addressed its mission in a training programme called 'Valuing Colgate People', in which all managers participated worldwide. Instead of exporting the US approach, the company examined what kind of training was needed in each country. It attempted to blend cultures and teach its managers how to collaborate across cultural boundaries. Although respecting other cultures was a central element of this policy, the company made a conscious decision not to override the essential policies of banning discrimination and sexual harassment (Mor Barak 2000: 349–50).

Adopting a global diversity approach presents challenges for global organizations. Adoption and diffusion of diversity management approaches of US companies in Europe has been explored through two contrasting case studies by Egan and Bendick (2003) whose research has revealed that the choice between adopting global or multidomestic approaches to diversity management yields different outcomes. They argue that although the European operations of US companies are likely to be exposed to diversity ideas, the organizations strategic objectives as well as their organizational structures will have an influence on their choice of diversity management approaches. Although the significance of the diversity issues in Europe is likely to increase, it is unlikely that the European branches of US organizations will directly adopt diversity management approaches of their host companies. Authors also identify that due to fundamental differences between economic, social and political business environments of the US and the European organizations, diversity initiatives may not also be directly transferred from the US to the European operations.

There are other arguments, such as the increased heterogeneity of world class employees and increased competition for human resources, as well as the shortages of supply in traditional recruitment pools, for adoption of global diversity management principles, despite problems of appropriateness and pragmatism, as outlined above. Global companies engage in benchmarking activities, as a result of which initiatives and programmes that prove successful in one organization are often appropriated by others in the same industry. What remains largely absent, however, from the literature is a recognition of the influence of key actors in the global scene on adoption of global diversity management approaches. The International Labour Organization, alongside other national bodies, asserts global labour standards. Further, there is diffusion of knowledge and sharing of best practice between national trade unions, employers' associations, as well as government agencies of equality and diversity, on the international stage. These linkages present themselves as possible sources of influence on adoption of global diversity management approaches.

2.3   National effects

Despite the possibility of global diversity management approaches in global organizations, these approaches are ultimately implemented at the level of domestic operations. Therefore the significance of national effects cannot be overstated. Research suggests that diversity management is a well recognized management function in the US, the country from which much of the discourse on diversity management originates. The Society for Human Resource Management (SHRM) surveyed its 60,000 members in 1993 and found out that diversity management was not a choice but a necessity for over 60 per cent of the respondents. Whilst diversity is a national concern in the US, the same may not be true in other national contexts. Indeed, variations in workforce heterogeneity in labour markets place pressures on global organizations to localize their diversity management approaches and diversity management discourses in order to capture different issues of diversity in each country. For example, in the case of Australia, the main diversity management effort has been on multiethnic diversity due to its ethnically heterogeneous labour force. D'Netto and Sohal (1999) surveyed 500 Australian organizations, revealing that the diversity management efforts concentrating on ethnicity have been nominally successful. They also explain that although the organizations are reaping the benefits of diversity, this is rarely reciprocated with proactive diversity approaches that seek to address inequalities. Exploring the case of Korean human resource management practices and the industrial relations system, Lee (2001) argues that the mainstream theories fail to account for the historical and contextual specificity of Korean employment relations. The author goes on to explain what makes Korea unique and identifies that dominance of paternalistic practices are the reason for its difference. The main characteristics of paternalism are given as (a) implicit nature of employment contracts and informality in personal relations at work; (b) different understandings and prioritization of familism, collectivism and loyalty; and (c) seniority based HR systems. The ultimate disadvantage of the paternalistic system is the fact that its practices reside at what constitutes the Western understanding of rationality, transparency and logic. Lee (2001) argues that if Korea is to survive global competition it needs to revise its human resource management system to recognize global diversity.

Heijltjes *et al.* (2003) study heterogeneity in top management teams of companies from the Netherlands and Sweden. Their study reveals that despite internationalization of the Dutch and Swedish companies to the levels of 'statelessness', the top management teams have remained largely homogeneous with there being only a few managers from other countries. However, they also indicate a steady increase in the number of foreign managers over the years. Therefore, internationalization, even if it has a slow pace, is taking course at the level of senior management teams as well.

In a world of extensive cross-national variations in forms of workforce heterogeneity, regional influences become increasingly important if the density of regional alliances and networks between countries and organizations increases. This hypothesis would be supported by a number of national cases.

For example, whilst diversity management has traditionally covered issues of gender, ethnicity and disability concerns in the UK, with the adoption of progressive European Union legislation, the number of categories which are considered as an unlawful basis of employment discrimination has increased to 13, including new aspects such as national origin, age, sexual orientation, social background, and so on. In the case of Japan, the US, Europe and the Asian countries are known to place political and economic pressure on Japan to reform its employment relations system.

National and regional level actors, by the virtue of their power of association in a networked world, may place pressures on global organizations to adopt global diversity management programmes in order to level cross-national variations and act on their pronounced commitments. Moreover, as most global organizations continue to retain organization footings in their countries of origin, they remain more perceptive to demands placed on them from their home countries.

Chapters 4, 5 and 6 explore national effects on global diversity management. Chapter 4 provides an account of a national survey which illustrates the state of macro-social, meso-organizational and micro-individual dynamics of diversity management at the national level. Chapter 5 provides a review of national policy and practice of diversity management through an assessment of diagnostic checks from cross-national comparative perspectives. Chapter 6 presents the findings of a national field study which operationalizes the concepts developed in Chapter 5.

2.4 Discourse effects

There are also discourse level reasons for adoption of different diversity management approaches. Debating the usefulness of the US diversity management approach in other national contexts, Agocs and Burr (1996) identify that the diversity management rhetoric in the US is based on the metaphor of melting pot, rather than the mosaic metaphor of the employment equity programmes in Canada. Whilst the former was associated with assimilation of group based differences for the sake of individual recognition, the latter metaphor refers to recognition of social identity differences and protections offered against discrimination of certain groups in society. The authors also note the dangers of liberally transferring diversity management approaches across national borders. They argue that the usefulness and appropriateness of diversity management should be considered in the light of key national concerns, assessed in terms of its contribution to core business objectives and overall fit with the systems and structures in the workplace.

Chapter 7 of this book illustrates the importance of discourses of diversity on practice of diversity management. The chapter examines storytelling as a means to reveal discursive aspects of organizational life in which diversity management practices are enacted. It brings out the power of discourse making and dissemination, and presents the findings of an empirical field study which reveals how diversity discourses are mainstreamed, marginalized or transformed.

2.5 Sectoral effects

Diversity management practices display variation by sector. Sectoral dynamics in terms of demographic profiles of workers, employer relations traditions, supply and demand for labour, stakeholder configurations, as well as customer demand, shape the way diversity management initiatives are prioritized. Furthermore, some sectors have stronger traditions of compliance and regulation in terms of equal opportunities, whilst others have less regulated, more liberal dynamics.

Part III of this book will examine sectoral variations in diversity management practices. Chapters 8 and 9 elaborate on diversity management practices in the recruitment sector and the creative and cultural industries, respectively. These two chapters show that diversity concerns, processes and outcomes vary by sectoral dynamics. Both chapters provide theoretical as well as empirical insights into diversity management.

2.6 Organizational effects

Diversity management literature suggests strong organizational reasons for adoption of diversity management philosophy and approaches. Empirical evidence of a positive correlation between effective management of diversity and improved organizational performance has been overwhelming in recent years. For example, Barkema *et al.* (2002) note that diversity is one of the challenges facing management in the 21st century. They highlight the evidence that suggests a clear link between positive organizational outcomes and effective management of diversity. They also mention studies which examine the negative outcomes of diversity, arguing that the effective management of diversity promises both positive outcomes and also a way to eliminate the possible negative consequences of diversity, such as conflict in teams. Similarly, Raatikainen (2002) reviews case study evidence in support of the interplay between diversity management and business performance, revealing a number of advantages such as improved creativity and customer focus through competitive practice of multiculturalism in the workplace. Complementing this, Harvey and Buckley (1997) argue that impatriation, the employment of foreign nationals in the headquarters of the global organization, is an important strategy through which global companies can gain strategic advantages of utilizing their local competencies in coordinating international operations.

Current research also identifies the differentiated impact of the type of diversity as well as the moderating impact of time on consequences of diversity in organizations: Govindarajan and Gupta (2001) propose an optimum level of diversity in global teams. They suggest that the difference between cognitive and behavioural diversity should be examined. Whilst cognitive diversity is about the substantive differences in how individual members perceive the challenges facing the teams, the behavioural diversity is about differences in language and culture. The authors argue that cognitive diversity presents a strength for global teams, whereas behavioural diversity is a challenge, a necessary evil, the impact of which should be minimized. Watson *et al.* (1993) examined the impact of diversity on interaction process and performance. The research reveals that although homogeneous teams perform better in the short term, heterogeneous teams start performing after a 17-week interval. The authors underline the significance of time in moderating team performance in diverse teams. Combining different types of diversity management approaches with the moderating influence of time, Svyantek *et al.* (2002) identify that diversity management may be practised from exclusionary and inclusionary perspectives. Based on a case study of two historical empires and their management of diversity, the authors argue that time moderates the impact of these two different forms of diversity management. Inclusionary perspectives secure better performance in the longer term if they are complemented by meritocratic systems.

Larkey (1996) identifies two processes by which individual differences may be recognized. These are categorization and specification. Categorization process takes place when the individuals refer to pre-assigned categorizations in relation to their colleagues. So, the categories of gender and ethnicity may be used to assign certain attributes to individuals before an interaction alters these mental schemas. However, the process of specification takes place during interactions where individuals assign piecemeal attributes to their colleagues based on the content and substance of their interactions. The difference between the two is that the categorization process allows for greater errors in recognizing individual differences, using broad-brush categories of social group memberships. The author suggests that the latter process of specification promises a more positive approach to recognizing diversity.

Other forms of diversity have also been linked to increased performance. Cummings (2004) has studied 182 work groups in the list of Fortune 500 companies in terms of value of knowledge sharing and structural diversity. His research reveals that the value of knowledge sharing for the organization increases if the work groups are structurally diverse and if the members have different affiliations, roles and positions in an organization. The author then argues for management to induce and support greater structural diversity in recognition of performance benefits identified in the study.

However, not all authors agree that the evidence on the usefulness of diversity management is immediate. Dadfar and Gustavsson (1992) argue that cultural diversity serves as an advantage at the level of the project management team, namely in the management workforce, in their study of the international construction industry. However, the same advantage of diversity was not identified at the workgroup level. The authors suggest use of homogeneous teams in competition against one another, in order to benefit from the construct of national pride. They also suggest the use of bicultural individuals as cultural moderators between groups with different cultures. In their conceptual paper, Agocs and Burr (1996) explore the differences between the terms 'employment equity', 'affirmative action' and 'managing diversity'. They illustrate the differences between the context, historical development, content and outcomes of these different initiatives (1996: 33). They argue that despite scant evidence for positive outcomes of diversity management, nevertheless it may promote awareness of difference and development of cultural sensitivity in communication. Indeed, there has been extensive research highlighting that diversity may jeopardize workplace harmony and interactive processes.

However, more recently based on a review of empirical evidence in the literature, Hopkins and Hopkins (2002) reveal that cultural recomposition, the process by which the homogeneity of a team alters through integration of new culturally different members, can be effectively managed without damage to the processes of interaction in the team. This is a significant proposition in the light of the earlier work which suggests that team heterogeneity may jeopardize team harmony and employment relations. Hopkins and Hopkins identify that the process of cultural recomposition may indeed be managed in order to engender positive outcomes. In the same vein, Mannix (2003) points out studies that demonstrate linkages between different types of diversity and conflict, explaining that further research is crucial if we are to make use of positive conflict and tackle negative conflict associated with diversity, and that exploring diversity and conflict in multiple forms is more productive then seeking tenuous linkages between their combined forms.

'Diversity means many things to many people' is now a common caveat that precedes many discussions on the topic. This is one of the main stumbling blocks on the way to effective management of diversity. At the organizational level, diversity management suffers from individualization of its definition, with different organizations adopting diversity initiatives in a pick-and-mix fashion, selecting aspects of diversity, management of which is too ambiguous to monitor and review and which present the organization in a positive light, such as valuing diversity of opinions and deselecting others that require capital investment or significant changes in their corporate practices, such as ethnic and gender diversity.

There is also extensive variation regarding where diversity management belongs in the functional and operational hierarchy and organization of workplace activities. Diversity management is traditionally viewed as the domain of human resource management practitioners. This has also been evident in scholarly circles. For example, Gilbert and Ivancevich (2000) review a number of company case studies and the literature for evidence of a business case for diversity management. They identify both individual and organizational level positive outcomes which require individual and management changes, drawing an explicit link between diversity management and human resource management function. Furthermore, McMahan *et al.* (1998) argued that the theory of strategic human resource management (SHRM) has failed to recognize the significance of diversity and how diversity can be turned into strategic advantage, even though diversity management has much to offer SHRM. Nevertheless, since the publication of their paper, there has been an increase of interest on diversity management from other fields of management, such as strategy (Kaplan and Norton 2000), finance, marketing, customer relations, information technology and operations management. This is a positive development in the sense that it elevates its strategic significance from the human resource management field to the level of strategic management. The use of the balanced score card approach (Kaplan and Norton 2000) and the development of other measurement and performance tools in Europe (Tatlı *et al.* 2007) has allowed for diversity management to gain strategic significance in the US and Europe.

However, multiple meanings that diversity management gains across organizations, sectors and countries brings forth certain paradoxes. Lindsay (1993) identifies three paradoxes of diversity management at the organizational level. These are the paradox of values, the paradox of fit and the paradox of categories. Organizational behaviour literature refers to creating and sustaining an organization with strong cultural values. Whilst the general trend is to achieve organizations with strong values, allowing for difference and diversity, presents a paradox of values. A paradox of fit takes place as organizations seek to create strong ties between their members, whilst diversity management requires organizations and teams to become more welcoming of outsiders and individuals with different attributes to the in-group members. The paradox of categories is about the socially constructed nature of social group categories such as gender and ethnicity. Whilst these are socially constructed, and by definition constitute perceived rather than real differences between individuals, espousing them as evidence of individual difference presents a paradox of categories. Unpacking the paradoxes of diversity management is essential in order for diversity management to be adopted as an overarching philosophy. Despite evidence that diversity management works to the advantage of organizations, presented with these paradoxes, there is a need for new formulations of diversity management that capture and addresses the tensions between individual differences and their incorporation into rather rigid organizational systems.

In order to tackle the challenge of diversity in organizational settings, some researchers attempt at identifying best practice approaches to diversity management, whilst others have cautioned that prescriptive approaches are insensitive to contextual conditions across national borders. They suggest that diversity management approaches should be carefully crafted to identify country, sector and organization specific strategies that reflect the unique characteristics of the targeted context. For example, Cox (1991) provides a set of prescriptions on how to create multicultural organizations. He proposes a six-pronged model which sets out the priorities that need to be addressed in order to achieve multicultural organizations: (a) pluralism; (b) full structural integration; (c) integration in informal networks; (d) cultural bias; (e) organizational identification; (f) intergroup conflict. The tools for dealing with these issues range from training and education activities to setting up committees, and from cultural research to changes in human resource management systems to value diversity. The evidence of prescriptive models can also be found in Thomas (1996; 1999), who identifies six barriers to effective management of diversity and six strategies to overcome them. The model draws on earlier cultural and structural works. Bergen et al. (2002) also attempt to reveal the factors that foster successful diversity management programmes. Their paper explains that there should be a broad diversity management policy and the diversity management initiatives should be supported by top level management. They should be concentrating on pragmatic solutions and goals in the short term, while having a broader range of goals for the long term. However, the prescriptive models of diversity management referred to domestic diversity management practices without making this assumption explicit in their assertions. Instead of offering prescriptive models, some researchers suggest that in order for diversity initiatives to be successful, there are certain preconditions. Identifying a number of conducive factors for management of diversity, research from Australia suggests that openness of an organization or a team to diversity has a positive impact on diversity related outcomes (Hartel 2004). Hartel tests the model of perceived dissimilarity and openness and identifies that there are affective, cognitive and behavioural consequences of diversity and these are partly explained by perception of difference and the size and scope of the response to this difference.

There are also tools available for measuring different aspects of cultural diversity and propositions as to how they may be managed. Gatley and Lessem (1995) propose a tool for measuring the intercultural and intracultural resources of organizations. Hofstede (1989) identifies how cultural diversity can be fostered in organizations and how managers can identify workers that will bring cultural added value to the workplace. He suggests a shift away from classical selection methods to incorporate more culturally aware approaches to selection. Based on a case study of two organizations, Gilbert and Ivancevich (2000) explain that diversity management initiatives that have senior management support, accountability, backing of an overarching corporate philosophy, multiple measures of success and that allow for changes in human resource management practices, employee involvement and buy–in, as well as improvements to diversity climate, are likely to be more effective than the initiatives that lack these key ingredients.

Two pressing diversity issues for global organizations have been the employment of women and minority ethnic workers. In most countries the gender equality debate has prepared the groundwork for extension of diversity considerations. Levy (2002) presents a resource-based argument in support for a utilization of the female workforce by multinational companies. Presenting evidence for increased competition, he explains why women are now an indispensable resource, exclusion of which would be a huge cost for multinational companies. The organizations which manage to offer work–life balance programmes, targeted recruitment and promotion activities, as well as training to make workplaces more welcoming, will benefit from a growth in numbers of talented workers. Sanchez and Brock (1996) studied the impact of perceived discrimination on Hispanic employees. Their study has revealed that perceived discrimination moderates levels of commitment, job satisfaction and work tension, and causes reduced levels of commitment and job satisfaction and increased levels of work tension. The results also suggest that there is an intergenerational difference between first and second generation Hispanic participants, as the impact of perceived discrimination on these workplace outcomes is considerably less for second generation workers, due to the fact that they are better integrated and have more resources to tackle the adverse impacts of discrimination. Both studies suggest that effective management of social group diversity is significant in terms of cost avoidance, compliance and more importantly for business performance reasons.

Another framework that has the analytical power of exploring multiple forms of inequality, such as by sex and race, is offered by Lau and Murnighan (1998). Fault lines are metaphorical lines that separate individuals into two or more groups. While sex presents a fault line between women and men, race presents fault lines between a larger number of racial subcategories. Lau and Murnighan argue that fault lines present the most serious problems at the group formation stage. If the groups are formed along fault lines, they are more likely to experience conflict. They propose that exchange of a wider range of personal information during group formation and at later stages may have a moderating impact on the levels of conflict, as this approach would give individuals an opportunity to form alliances across categories which are less arbitrary and more occupationally relevant.

Despite growing evidence of positive organizational outcomes and availability of some prescriptive models, scholars also identify a gap in implementation of diversity management in global organizations. Appelbaum and Fewster (2002) have completed 13 interviews with senior managers and conducted documentary analysis of policies from global aviation organizations. Their findings suggest a general weakness in adoption of equality and diversity perspectives in their global industry. They identify that, despite overwhelming evidence of the commercial success and reported significance of diversity and equality initiatives, the practice in the sector in terms of policy initiatives on equality and diversity and how these are disseminated is not widespread, as only 60 per cent of the organizations report policy and an even lower proportion of the workplaces engage in dissemination and monitoring activities. The authors argue that the industry would benefit from closely matching their internal workforce demographics to that of their external customer profile. They demonstrate this with company examples. The authors also argue that effective management of diversity and equality is imperative for the global aviation industry to break out of the vicious cycle of its current management approach, which is driven by cost cutting strategies that jeopardize its employment relations.

Furthermore, there are reports of a backlash against the fledgling diversity management initiatives. Backlashes against equal opportunities (Faludi 1991) and more recently against diversity initiatives have been extensively reported. In their scenario design study, Kidder *et al.* (2004) examine the backlash against diversity management versus affirmative action logics. They identify that the diversity management arguments engender less backlash than affirmative action scenarios. This signifies that different arguments used to achieve buy-in for diversity initiatives from organizational stakeholders will receive different responses. The study identifies that business case arguments are better received than fairness arguments. In addition, Nemetz and Christensen (1996) note that the backlash against the promulgating diversity and equality training programmes can be managed. An understanding of backlashes is possible through an ideological understanding of diversity management approaches. Such an understanding is achieved through recognition of the tensions between idealistic world views, between groups and individuals, and between smaller groups and larger and stronger ones. The authors also warn of the possibility of the ideal rhetoric of diversity management to turn into a tyranny if it is pursued too rigorously.

Global organizations introduce offices for diversity management in order to address the effects that are explored here. However, a diversity office is often a necessary but not a sufficient condition for a strong stance on diversity management on the part of organizations. Once established, a diversity office may serve to inform the direction of diversity management efforts. Although diversity offices may have an effect in terms of initiating diversity programmes and suggesting diversity management measures, these programmes need to receive top level management support either through the positioning of the diversity office as a high status department within the organization or with the solid commitment of the Chief Executive Officer to diversity issues.

As explained earlier, diversity management can be perceived as either a domain for employment relations (see for example Gilbert and Ivancevich 2000) or from a wider perspective as an issue for all sections of the organization, from finance and accounting to customer relations (Thorne and Davig 1999), and from strategy to marketing (Mulholland *et al.* 2005). As Thorne and Davig so succinctly express it, toppling disciplinary silos has been a significant achievement of diversity management scholars, who have attempted to demonstrate the significance of diversity management to a wider selection of functions within organizations, elevating its strategic significance. Where a diversity office is positioned, and whether it carries out functions other than ones that are human resource management related, exposes the influence and the status of the office. In some progressive companies, diversity management offices are located in higher echelons of the organizational hierarchies, and positioned to report directly to the executive committee, contributing to strategic decisions in the organization. However, this is not a general pattern, as diversity management departments reportedly lack status, authority and voice in strategic matters in the mainstream.

Diversity management offices, like any other functional area in the organization, need to negotiate their power and status. The negotiating power of the diversity office emanates from both the senior management support it receives, as well as the way diversity officers can achieve buy-in from senior executives. Cox and Blake (1991) identify six commonly used explanations to achieve buy-in for diversity management programmes and initiatives. First, there is a *resource argument*: as organizations need human resources that are competent and skilled, discrimination of any form other than by merit hinders successful recruitment and retention of human resources. Second, there is a *marketing argument*: organizations that have diverse workforces would be more receptive to market demand due to their shared attributes with their target markets. Therefore an organization that replicates the distributive attributes of its customers would benefit from better insights into their needs. Third, there is *flexibility*. Organizations that respond to diverse needs and the changes in labour market heterogeneities will benefit from the flexibility that inclusion of such diverse populations would require. Fourth, heterogeneity between workers encourages *creativity*. Creative individuals are often individuals who are different to the mainstream. Fifth, *problem solving* skills of a group is enhanced when the group is diverse, as this allows for multiple perspectives and critical reviewing of decisions. Sixth, an organization enjoys *cost-cutting benefits* if it integrates a diverse number of individuals. Ignoring diversity and allowing it to become a source of conflict can lead to absenteeism and a decline in workplace employment relations, which ultimately have cost implications for organizations. Kirby and Richard (2000) note that these arguments by Cox and Blake are not received with the same positive response in every organization. Their research identifies that the resource acquisition, marketing, flexibility and creativity arguments rank higher than other arguments between their study participants.

Strategies that diversity managers adopt in order to attend to cultural differences may vary extensively. Chevrier (2003) has studied multinational project teams and has identified four strategies which managers adopt in order to reconcile cultural diversity within their teams. First, individual tolerance and self-control may be applied by managers when faced with cultural differences with the idea that such differences are legitimate and should be merely ignored. A second way of handling such difference is through trial-and-error processes, coupled with personal relationships, where the parties engage in exploration activities with a view to understand and make sense of each other's point of views. Frequent encounters in this form are likely to result in negative stereotypes being formed if the normative and subjective nature of culture is not recognized. The third approach is forming transnational cultures. When the leaders cannot make use of shared cultural constructs they may opt to refer instead to other international cultural norms, such as professional cultures or corporate cultures. However, Chevrier argues that even in this case the conflict is likely to occur. Whilst the French may adopt a strong professional culture, this may not have supremacy over corporate culture, such as in the case of Japan. A fourth strategy is *ad hoc* cross-cultural management strategy. This involves personal engagement within the team, with the specific purpose of building shared understandings in a process facilitated by a cultural moderator, who actively engages with the team to increase cross-cultural learning and avoid polarization of the workers along negative stereotypes.

Diversity offices may play a key role in effecting change and informing the direction that diversity management approach of organizations should take. However, they also have to compete with other functional areas for resources, power and authority. Ultimate effectiveness of the diversity office, in impacting on organizational change and the adoption of an appropriate diversity philosophy, rests with its strategic position, its resources, as well as the skills and conviction of its key members of staff in shaping organizational opinion. However, a well resourced diversity office does not necessarily guarantee effective management of diversity either. Although diversity management may be centralized or professionalized, its effectiveness will ultimately rests with the effectiveness of its implementation at the level of line management.

Chapter 10 focuses on the organizational effects on diversity management, through an investigation of organizational culture, policies and programmes in the context of a global organization. The chapter also takes into consideration the historical dimension of diversity management.

2.7 Individual effects

Diversity management is not an activity that can be limited to the functioning of a diversity office. The significance of the individual workers and managers in championing and implementing diversity programmes cannot be overstated. Holger Kluge (1997), the president of Personal and Commercial Bank CIBC, explains that the line managers have a large responsibility in implementation of diversity management. Individual effects are cited as very significant in the shaping of diversity management approaches. For example, Roper *et al.* (1997) work on international hotel groups reveals that the organizational culture and structure of these organizations are highly bound by the culture and values of their founders and key decision makers. Although the groups are international in outlook, the values that drive them are informed by the founder and the strategic decision leaders' own personal cultures.

If organizational leaders and senior executives champion the cause of diversity management, diversity management may achieve a strategic position. However, some scholars warn of negative consequences of strong leadership that may contravene the philosophy that the diversity management approach hopes to bring to bear. Welch and Welch (1997) argue that strong corporate cultures and managers who advocate them contradict the requirements of flexibility, responsiveness and creativity in global enterprises, unless these are the very values which they advocate. Therefore they argue for a managerial and organizational model that is conducive to recognizing multiple voices. The model is akin to the university system in which critique and dissent are key constructs for advancement and adoption of knowledge.

However, absence of support from senior executives and managers would not help the cause of diversity management either. Indeed lack of support from management may be the most significant stumbling block on the way of introducing diversity management programmes. The support of senior executives and managers alone may also not be sufficient for the effective operation of a diversity programme. Workers may also resist diversity management programmes, display backlash behaviour or ignore the message of the programme. Several studies have explored the reception that diversity management receives when introduced to different groups. Smith *et al.* (2004) have studied the preference of a student population, who were exposed to training on the subject, between affirmative action and diversity management approaches. The study confirms the hypothesis that despite the current controversy, students find diversity management programmes less appealing than affirmative action ones, which they find more relevant to the legal concerns of corporate social responsibility. The study implies that the choice of equality and diversity programme will have a differentiated impact on the recipients. The study identified a clear support for the affirmative action over and above the support afforded to diversity management programmes.

Joplin and Daus's (1997) interviews with senior managers highlight a number of diversity management challenges, including the challenge of sharing power, emergence of deeper level divisions, such as differences of opinion, perceived lack of empathy, tokenistic practices, complexities of employee participation and overcoming of organizational resistance to change. James and Wooten (2001) argue that overcoming the reactive stance is necessary in order to achieve a reflective learning on diversity issues. The reflective perspective makes it possible for organizations to transform to meet the challenges of diversity. The way to overcome these challenges, the authors argue, is to move away from the one-size-fits-all approach that characterizes some diversity management initiatives that seek to offer standardized diversity training to all sections of the organization in a sheep dipping fashion. Standardized training activities, Joplin and Daus explain, are responsible for some of the backlash in organizations.

Individual workers' attitudes towards diversity management initiatives will have an impact on the choice of method and design. An extensive range of studies locate the issue of diversity management at the level of individual learning, implicitly suggesting that this is key to transforming homophily and homo-social individual behaviours to the ones that welcome diversity and difference. Cross-cultural disagreements require a recognition of the national context. The disagreements would be exacerbated should each manager retain his or her own approach to management, which is informed merely by their own cultural reference group. The conclusions suggest that a change in managerial behaviour is contingent upon their learning to let go of their own cultural references in preference for mutual understanding.

Similarly, based on a review of literature on cultural diversity in management of cross-border careers, Fish (1999) notes that there is need for a change in management mindsets from ethnocentric approaches to more sophisticated approaches that are informed by cross-border differences in values and cultural norms. Iles (1995) refers to the necessity of developing intercultural competence in making effective use of diversity at multiple levels. However, the theorizations of such idealistic competence measures lead to a priori suggestions of training and awareness raising programmes. Similarly, Flood and Romm (1996) elaborate a number of learning techniques associated with diversity. Ashkanasy *et al.* (2002) suggest that diversity in organizational settings generates emotional engagement, and that this should be managed. Noting the move from separation of rational and emotional in organization studies, the authors seek to demonstrate the relevance of emotional intelligence for effective management of diversity.

Skills, competence and learning-based approaches naively assume that the inequalities that are inherent in work practices can be overcome and the benefits of diversity can be realized if individuals are trained to gain skills to value diversity. The social traps literature makes a serious attempt at addressing the weakness in the skills/competence formulations of diversity management by highlighting the often conflicting difference between short-term individual and longer-term group outcomes. Lorbiecki (2001) also notes that without addressing the power imbalances in the workplace, it is rather simplistic to expect a learning perspective to facilitate successful incorporation of diversity problems.

What remains largely unexplored in the literature on diversity management is the role that diversity managers and diversity champions play in shaping organizational approaches to diversity management. Kirton *et al.* (2007) study of diversity managers in Britain points out that they act as tempered radicals in organizational settings, pursuing agendas of organizational change that often contravene the conventions of their workplaces. Tatlı (2008) reveals that indeed the outcome of the personal strategies employed by individual diversity officers is contingent upon the different forms of capital that they deploy in the situated context of the diversity management field.

There are two chapters that focus on the individual level of analysis. Chapters 11 and 12 examine the role and agency of individuals in the process of change that diversity management entails. Chapter 11 presents a fresh conceptual framework which aids the conceptualization of the role of individual managers in the process of diversity management. Chapter 12 looks at the agency of diversity managers at the actual setting of a global company.

2.8   Conclusion

In this chapter, we have offered a theoretical framework through which global diversity management can be studied. The framework brings together five different effects that shape global diversity management practices. The global diversity management practices are shaped by multilevel influences that manifest at national, sectoral, discursive, organizational and individual levels. By examining the extant literature, we have revealed the significance of spatial, temporal, social and relational contexts in which global diversity practices are shaped. Although the framework we present here involves a wide range of influences, it is important to prioritize them according to the specific circumstances of the organization and the global diversity initiatives in question. The framework that we provide in this chapter, nevertheless, serves as a sensitizing device which can allow students, global diversity managers and scholars to flesh out key issues that should be attended in the process of research, policy-making and implementation. The next chapter offers a case study of global diversity management which operationalizes the framework presented in this chapter.

Further reading

Appelbaum, S.H. and Fewster, B.M. (2002) 'Global Aviation Human Resource Management: Contemporary Recruitment and Selection and Diversity and Equal Opportunity Practices', *Equal Opportunities International*, vol. 21, pp. 66–80.

Brimm, L. and Arora, M. (2001) 'Diversity Management at Hewlett-Packard, Europe', in M.A. Albrecht (ed.), *International HRM: Managing Diversity in the Workplace*. Oxford: Blackwell, 108–24.

Calori, R., Steele, M. and Yoneyama, E. (1995) 'Management in Europe: Learning from Different Perspectives', *European Management Journal*, vol. 3, pp. 58–66.

Iles, P. and Hayers, P.K. (1997) 'Managing Diversity in Transnational Project Teams: A Tentative Model and Case Study', *Journal of Managerial Psychology*, vol. 12, pp. 95–117.

Keller, R.T. (2001) 'Cross-functional Project Groups, in Research and New Product Development: Diversity, Communications, Job Stress and Outcomes', *Academy of Management Journal*, vol. 44, pp. 547–55.

Lampel, J. (2001) 'The Core Competencies of Project Execution: The Challenge of Diversity', *International Journal of Project Management*, vol. 19, pp. 471–83.

McMahan, G.C., Bell, M.P. and Virick, M. (1998) 'Strategic Human Resource Management: Employee Involvement, Diversity and International Issues', *Human Resource Management Review*, vol. 8, pp. 193–214.

Nemetz, P.L. and Christensen, S.L. (1996) 'The Challenge of Cultural Diversity: Harnessing a Diversity of Views to Understand Multiculturalism', *Academy Management Review*, vol. 21, pp. 434–62.

Nishii, L. and Özbilgin, M.F. (2007) 'Global Diversity Management: Towards a Conceptual Framework', *International Journal of Human Resource Management*, vol. 18, no. 11, pp. 1883–94.

O'hara, S.U. (1995) 'Valuing Socio-diversity', *International Journal of Social Economics*, vol. 22, pp. 31–49.

Prasad, P., Mills, A.J., Elmes, M. and Prasad, A. (eds) (1997) *Managing the Organizational Melting Pot: Dilemmas of Workplace Diversity*. Thousand Oaks, CA: Sage.

Robinson, G. and Decant, K. (1997) 'Building a Business Case for Diversity', *Academy of Management Executive*, vol. 11, pp. 21–31.

Spich, S. (1995) 'Globalisation Folklore: Problems of Myth and Ideology in the Discourse of Globalisation', *Journal of Organizational Change Management*, vol. 8, pp. 6–29.

Woods, R.H. and Sciriani, M.P. (1995) 'Diversity Programs in Chain Restaurants', *Cornell Hotel and Restaurant Administration Quarterly*, June, pp. 18–23.

3 Global Diversity Management: The Case of Japan

3.1 Introduction

In this chapter, we present a case study of global diversity management, drawing on a study conducted in Japan. This study involved a large number of interviews with stakeholder groups, including diversity managers, trade union and employers' association specialists, and scholars who study various aspects of diversity in Japanese contexts, as well as documentary analysis of policies and company data. With this study, we will provide the answers to three key questions:

1 Who are the key actors who inform a global diversity management perspective to global car manufacturing firms in Japan?
2 Why and how do global automotive firms in Japan develop their global diversity management approaches?
3 What are the key influences and drivers in the adoption and diffusion of diversity management approaches in global organizations in Japan?

Section 3.2 includes an overview of the research design, methods and techniques used during the field study. Section 3.3 presents the findings of the field study conducted in Japan, and relates these back to the conceptual model which was introduced in Chapter 2. The concluding section contains a debate on the current state of global diversity management in global car manufacturing firms in Japan. The chapter also provides a set of recommendations for key actors, and identifies venues for further research on the subject.

Two appendices are presented in order to facilitate future discussion and research on the topic. Appendix A presents excerpts from speeches by the officers of the Japan Business Federation (Nikkeiren). Appendix B is the set of interview questions which were used in conducting the study.

3.2 The case study methods

This chapter uses a case study method (Yin 2002), which is a part of a global diversity management research project that started in 2005 with a visiting fellowship at the School of Industrial and Labor Relations (ILR) at Cornell University. The initial phase of the study involved the collection of an extensive range of academic sources on the issue of domestic and global diversity management. The field study that is reported here commenced on 10 August 2005 and was supported with a visiting fellowship offered by the Japan Institute for Labour Policy and Training (JILPT).

Cheng (1997) argues that the reduction of diversity to single level issues, such as micro-level analysis of discrimination – when this resides at the level of institutional history – and single category studies – such as work solely on women when women's heterogeneity is evident – have been effective strategies to retain the status quo of white, male, patriarchal domination and supremacy through academic research. Reflecting on bell hooks's feminist writings, Cheng (1997: 553) writes: 'Although women-in-management research has become mainstream, other diversity issues are almost entirely ignored, particularly racism, patriarchy, class, heterosexism, sexuality, sexual identity, religion, postcolonial issues, physical ability, and so on'. Congruent with Cheng's argument, the field study presented here involved a layered and multiparty approach to the study of key influences on global diversity management approaches in the Japanese automotive manufacturing sector. The literature review also has a layered framework which incorporated a wide range of diversity concerns as well as global, regional, national, organizational, diversity-office and individual-level effects on the global diversity management approaches of firms. The research techniques assumed a multiparty perspective, as the study contains interviews with key actors that influence diversity management approaches in organizations, including members from organizations, trade union and employers' unions, as well as academic experts. Furthermore the study involved a review of an extensive range of academic sources and company and union documentation and data. The model that is presented here involves a range of effects on the global firms' choice of diversity management approach. Although the effects are presented separately for pragmatic reasons, there are, indeed, relational dynamics that cross these effects and their respective levels of analysis.

The research project observes the conventions of a relational method tradition (Özbilgin 2005), which allows for a research design that captures the space and the interplay between layered social phenomena, ranging from objective organizational structures to subjective individual experience. One of the key tenets of relational methodology is that it seeks to transcend the objective–subjective divide, providing a reading of organizational phenomena in a way that is true to its real form, constituted through an interplay of individual agency in the context of organizational structures.

The field study of this project involved a total of 15 interviews. The interviews ranged between one and a half hours to two hours in length and focused on different aspects of diversity management, based on the expertise and position of the interviewee. Three interviews were conducted with officials, who assume responsibility on diversity related matters, from a global car manufacturing company in Tokyo, Rengo (Japanese Trade Union Confederation) and Nikkeiren (Japan Federation of Employers' Associations). The latter two interviews were conducted in the Japanese language with the help of an interpreter. The other interview was conducted in English. The three interviews largely focused on the diversity management approach that has been adopted and the activities that are carried out in these respective organizations. In order to supplement the interview data, we have also collected documentary resources and data from each organization. Another set of interviews were conducted with three professors from Keio University's economics department – highlighting issues of supply-and-demand-side economic changes that engender suitable conditions for the uptake of diversity management initiatives – and with scholars from Rikkyo, Tokyo, Senshu, Yamaguchi, Yamagata, Waseda and Tohoku Universities. These meetings have generated academic insights into issues of equality, disadvantage and diversity in Japanese workplaces, and have allowed for some of the pertinent issues to be discussed. Furthermore, the meetings were instrumental in gathering relevant academic works and in collecting Japanese and English language sources that are not easily accessible. Various experts at the JILPT were also consulted on diversity issues, and the library facilities of the Institute were utilized. Some of the Japanese language sources were translated into English in abstract form by the JILPT staff.

The interviewees were sent a letter outlining the content of the interview process, as well as the conditions of anonymity and confidentiality. Interview participants were promised full anonymity in order to protect their identity. All meetings were tape recorded when this was allowed by the participants. Otherwise, extensive notes were taken during the interviews. August is often a period of holiday in the academic calendar. Despite this, access to relevant officials and organizational data were gained with relative ease. The Japanese term the ease of access, which is afforded to foreign nationals, as 'foreigner's advantage', a uniquely Japanese phenomenon, where the foreign nationals are freed from the stringent rules of social exchange and are allowed greater liberty in their social interactions. The specific 'foreigner's advantage' that marked this research project was in making appointments, arranging interviews and asking politically charged and value laden questions to the interview participants. For example, it was possible to make cold calls to companies and universities, with only brief introductions in order to request interviews. Similar exchanges between Japanese nationals, however, would require introduction through a third person or a more formal way of contacting organizations with letters or faxes.

All forms of data that were collected were subject to two forms of qualitative data coding protocols: axial- and open-coding techniques (Charmaz 2000) were applied. Data were arranged into different predetermined themes in axial-coding technique. Open-coding technique involves identification of themes that emerge from the data itself, rather than categorization of data along predetermined themes. The data was analysed using a critical realist approach (Layder 1993): data from different sources and parties were juxtaposed in order to reveal the interplay between the seemingly objective statements of diversity management and subjective variations in evaluation and interpretation between these stakeholder parties.

3.3 The case of a global car manufacturing company

The range of actors and effects that shape the choice of diversity management approaches in Japan yields well to comparative analysis with other industrial countries of North America and Western Europe. However, the macro-, meso- and micro-pressures for the management of diversity, and the respective positions that key actors take in the Japanese context as well as in Japanese global companies, are so markedly unique that Japan provides an excellent example through which 'global diversity management' can be explored in a comparative context. This section presents the findings of the study in the thematic order in which the literature review of Chapter 2 was structured.

The expansion of the legal protections to a wider range of categories of workers and the divergence of diversity concerns across national borders calls for coordination of equal opportunities activities in global organizations which do not only employ home and host country nationals but also have by definition third-country workers. Therefore, while the individual differences are exacerbated in this international setting, the complexity of legal provision also requires that the management approach is indeed more proactive and overarching so that it can accommodate current law as well as foreseeable changes.

Diversity management discourse with its promise to recognize and value individual difference came at the right time in North America and Western Europe when these legal changes were taking place. Japanese global firms present a different picture altogether. The reasons for this are manifold. Whilst Japan hosts the headquarters of a large proportion of the world's global firms, Japanese labour law has remained largely unaffected by the expansion of anti-discrimination legislation in the last three decades. Whilst an Equal Employment Opportunity Law was introduced in Japan in 1986, this came too little and too late, and with limited impact and scope. The law only tackles sex equality, and had provision for only direct forms of sex discrimination, where indirect forms of sex discrimination are not considered unlawful. This point was raised by Rengo in their efforts to lobby the government for a change of law to incorporate indirect discrimination. Whilst direct discrimination may tackle overt forms of discrimination, it fails with regard to subtle forms of discrimination, where a single rule has a disproportionate impact only on one gender. For example, the long hours of work culture in Japan effectively keeps career opportunities away from women who are expected to carry out a disproportionate share of domestic duties in corporations that value face time and presentation culture. Among other factors, the weakness of the law meant that the Japanese labour market has retained a strongly sexsegregated profile in comparison to other industrialized countries. Furthermore, Japanese global firms have retained a homogeneous workforce in their headquarters in Japan. The core workers were predominantly male and overwhelmingly Japanese nationals. This model presents a contrast to increased heterogeneity in other global organizations in Europe and North America. Japanese business and management schools have not broken the mould to offer courses in equality and diversity management, as such skills were not required explicitly by the recruiting companies.

Whilst the globalization of Japanese firms have not engendered diversification of their managerial workforces, Japanese society, customs and labour market dynamics have altered to entertain greater levels of diversity. For example, the proportions of women who enter the labour market, and women who wish to have careers, have increased (JILPT 2005). Family sizes have decreased, and Japan has started receiving migrant labour, particularly from South American countries (descendents of earlier Japanese migrants there) and other foreign nationals that have arrived for work. Increased concerns over management of

Box 3.1   The settlement of lawsuits against the Mitsubishi Motor Company

The US Equal Employment Opportunity Commission, June 11, 1998:

MITSUBISHI MOTOR MANUFACTURING AND EEOC REACH VOLUNTARY AGREEMENT TO SETTLE HARASSMENT SUIT

NORMAL AND CHICAGO, ILL. Mitsubishi Motor Manufacturing of America, Inc. (MMMA) and the US Equal Employment Opportunity Commission (EEOC) announced today that they have reached a $34 million settlement, subject to court approval, that resolves all claims in the lawsuit filed on April 9, 1996, by the EEOC on behalf of a class of current and former MMMA employees who were subjected to an alleged pattern and practice of sexual harassment at MMMA's Normal, Illinois, manufacturing plant since 1990.

Source: http://www.eeoc.gov/press/6-11-98.html

diversity and some high profile cases abroad, such as the discrimination law suits against the Mitsubishi Motor Corporation (see **Box 3.1**), as well as the changes in the internal labour market, has encouraged global firms in Japan to consider diversity issues with some degree of resolve.

Other institutional actors that may have an impact on diversity management approaches of global organizations in Japan, such as the Ministry of Health, Labour and Welfare in Japan, Rengo, and Nikkeiren, have international links. For example, Rengo has strong links with the International Confederation of Free Trade Unions (ICFTU), the Asia Pacific trade union organization, as well as strong ties with labour unions in Europe, particularly in the UK and the US. The Rengo interview revealed that there is much sharing of policy, expertise and knowledge at the international level. Indeed, Japanese Rengo has adopted elements of equality policy by the ICFTU. The official from Rengo termed some of the work–life balance policies that emanate from abroad as 'inspirational'. Furthermore, the diversity management report of Nikkeiren is well informed by the literature on diversity management arguments in North America. These three institutions, as well as the changes in social mores in Japan, may serve as levers to consider diversity and equality as pertinent issues for Japanese global firms.

Providing a historical review of the opening up and incorporation of Japanese labour into the 'free world', Nakakita (2005) identifies a shift from 'political' to 'economic' organization of work in the post Second-World-War era in Japan, attributing this shift to the international diplomacy coming from Europe and the US. Nakakita explains that the British interest in trade unionism and democratic reform in Japan's labour policy was not only a philanthropic desire to promote Japanese democracy. Indeed, development of a strong trade union tradition in Japan was seen as a way to curb Japanese competitiveness in labour costs. Despite this critical perspective, international pressures and collaboration has also had a positive impact on the standards of labour in Japan.

In addition, Aguilera and Jackson (2003, 462) argue that diffusion and adoption of American institutional forms in Germany and Japan did not result in convergence in these countries during the post-war reformation. The process was one of hybridization. The authors also suggest that there is a second phase of reformation in both countries:

> Today, Germany and Japan are attempting to introduce 'shareholder value' management style to their past institutions of strong labor participation. It remains to be seen whether a stable and distinct corporate governance hybrid will emerge, or whether institutional tensions will cause institutional erosion.

The way that the diversity management approaches originating from North America will be appropriated by Japanese companies will serve as a litmus test for the convergence and divergence debate. Although global organizations, by definition, should be able to transcend cross-national differences and offer policy and practices that do not simply reflect their countries of origin but their compound knowledge of global trends and patterns, the case of Japanese firms in the automotive industry suggests that global diversity management has not yet developed as a functional area of work, and indeed domestic diversity management has only been discussed in the last five years.

Overall, the global effects on the take-up of global diversity management approaches are not likely to diminish. Despite efforts to hold on to traditional ways of work and organization, reforms in diversity management approaches, as well as identification of tensions and stumbling blocks, are well underway.

National and discourse effects: much ado about nothing

There are a number of institutional actors that have an impact on the national policy on equality and diversity in Japan. The Ministry of Health, Labour and Welfare has a study group which examines issues of gender equality. They publish reports and disseminate their findings widely, even if the resulting publications are merely informative and do not even constitute policy guidelines. Rengo and Nikkeiren are also active in the debates over equality and diversity. A common goal that both Rengo and Nikkeiren subscribe to is a commitment to workers' welfare. However, there is a schism between approaches that Rengo and Nikkeiren take, regarding how worker welfare may be achieved, and whether diversity management is an effective means to achieving it. Nikkeiren has a study group, made up of 15–18 members drawn from Nikkeiren staff and employees from member institutions. The study group conducted a survey across a good cross-section of members on diversity management and published a report in 2002. The summary of the report provides a definition of diversity strategy:

> Avoiding the hitherto established standards within firms and society and taking into consideration the values and concepts of various attributes (gender, age, nationalities, etc.) this is a strategy which responds to the changes in business environment in a rapid and smooth manner to achieve firm growth and individual happiness.

The definition by Nikkeiren suggests that the diversity management approach seeks to address two significant concerns: organizational performance and individual well-being. The report also lists four principles of diversity which is informed by the literature in North America and Western Europe on the subject. These four principles are:

1   diversity is a strategy that utilizes diverse human resources;
2   diversity brings organizational growth and individual happiness;
3   diversity considerations are underpinned by personnel management principles of recognizing different attitudes and values;
4   top management should change its consciousness and implement an 'offensive strategy' using the concept of diversity.
(Nikkeiren 2002. (In 2002, the Japan Federation of Employers' Associations (Nikkeiren) merged with the Japan Federation of Economic Organizations (Keidanren)))

Rengo, on the other hand, identifies recruitment of women members, and the closing of the gap between terms and conditions of work for part-time and temporary workers and those for the full-time core workforce, as their main issue for diversity. Rengo officials explain that indeed women and foreign national workers are disadvantaged due to this gap. It is not surprising to see that employers' unions pursue a business case argument, whereas the workers' unions point of departure is the elimination of inequality and disadvantage. Trade union organizations in Japan might have shied away from and kept quite about the concept of diversity due to an earlier introduction of the concept by the employers' unions, suggesting that diversity is about making best use of workers, emphasizing the utility aspect of the concept, and failing to acknowledge its moral imperative that diversity is a necessary but not a sufficient condition for equality of opportunity.

Although Rengo does not have an official objection to the diversity management approaches advocated by Nikkeiren, Nikkeiren has an objection to Rengo's agenda for equalizing standards for peripheral and core workers: the employers' association argues that as core and peripheral workers are conducting different tasks and have different contractual agreements, it is fair to offer them different terms and conditions. The Nikkeiren officials have also highlighted that their approach is consistent with the philosophy of 'recognizing and valuing difference' as espoused in their diversity management philosophy. This is an interesting point in that diversity management literature can be used to advocate different ideologies and prescribe different solutions. It very much depends on which factors are considered as markers of difference and which forms of difference should be valued and recognized. The value laden nature of diversity management discourse has caused it to be attributed different meanings in different institutional settings and in representing different political and economic interests.

Although it is possible to note that there is a schism between Rengo and Nikkeiren in terms of their interpretations of diversity management, it is not possible to talk of these two institutions as counterparts in a fair game of industrial relations. Indeed, the trade union movement is relatively weak in Japan, as it is characterized with 'enterprise unionism': the main union activities are carried out at the enterprise union level. This involves discussions with management on terms and conditions of work, as well as negotiation and reconciliation activities. Neither the sectoral unions, that is the Japanese Automotive Workers Union (JAW), nor Rengo, are actively involved in negotiations with employers. Furthermore, none of the documents produced by Rengo or Nikkeiren has any power of enforcement. These documents are neither policy guidelines nor recommendations for members. They contain mostly informational material that may, at best, serve only to raise awareness.

Beyond the classical interplay between the industrial relations actors in Japan, two significant cultural norms underpin the weakness of equality and diversity debate in the country. Although it would have been highly presumptuous of us to claim even a surface level understanding of Japanese culture, the following two highly observable attributes were evident during our interviews. First, the conventions of social interaction in Japan do not allow much scope for confrontational political debate. Interviewees often referred to a lack of political and ideological support for equality in Japan. Transformation towards equality and acceptance of diversity does not take place on its own. It requires political will as well as structural changes that will make workplaces more welcoming for people with different backgrounds. One scholar explained that the gradual nature of social reforms in Japan, and an explicit focus on economic rather than political reformation, has meant that patriarchal relations were not challenged and remained out of the social reform agenda. The second social phenomenon, that complemented the overall apolitical outlook of Japanese diversity and equality debate, was the absence of an individual or collective complaints culture. Another scholar has identified that the case law was available in Japan but the number of legal complaints were far and few between. This was also reflected in the number of complaints that unions have received. In 2004/05 Rengo statistics suggest that sex discrimination complaints to Rengo by individuals totalled 259: 96 of these were raised by men and 163 by women. These complaints were predominantly for harassment issues, with only seven complaints for outright sex discrimination in the period. These figures are very low in comparison to levels of individual complaints received by trade unions and industrial tribunals in Western countries. Although this may be due to multiple reasons, a Rengo official suggested that discrimination and harassment cases are often settled at the organizational level and that there are indeed very few, if any, examples of such cases being taken to the courts of law. Absence of an industrial tribunal system also makes litigation against sex discrimination in Japan more difficult than other industrialized countries.

Although it is theorized that global organizations have policies which transcend their national origins, the Japanese case illustrates that this may not be so as the Japanese global firms retain a largely national and male-dominated workforce (Arimaru 2004). Much of the academic knowledge on diversity management is of North American origin. Hence it is highly context specific, suited to the institutional and legal framework of its context. In the case of Japan, the influence of institutional actors is very weak, and national mechanisms to enforce diversity management approaches are absent. Nevertheless, the growing diversity in the Japanese population and labour force may serve as a lever of pressure for change.

Organizational and sectoral effects

A diversity trainer from New York explains that 'a stumbling block for any diversity manager is showing trainees the link between diversity management and business performance' (De Valk 1993: 11). This epitomizes the problems that the diversity officer has cited as relevant in the case of Japan, alongside an emergent backlash against equality and diversity in the case-study organization. Many global companies in the automotive manufacturing sector in North America, Europe and Japan now have diversity management efforts, initiatives and offices. The unique attribute of diversity initiatives globally is that such initiatives express the necessity of moving diversity efforts from the diversity office to the line management level so that diversity principles can be operationalized at the level of practice.

Whilst employers across Japan are concentrating on 'hard' measures of bene-fiting from labour flexibility, by decreasing the size of core workers and increasing the flexible workforce through outsourcing of temporary workers, 'diversity management' appears to many managers as 'propaganda', a 'fashion' or a 'fad' that will take its place next to other inflated management ideals of the past. This belief was dominant across some of the interviews with scholars, and also was implicit in the absence of response by Rengo to the diversity management report of Nikkeiren.

The studies that explore diversity management in Japanese companies are few and far between: Arimura (2001) has conducted a study to investigate the extent of localization of workforce and diversity, in regard to race/ethnicity and sex in Japanese companies conducting business in the US (where society itself is rapidly diversifying), as well as considering its necessity. The ques-tionnaire survey involved 1,168 enterprises with 50 or more employees (of which 109 replied), and was conducted in 1999/2000. The study reveals that, compared to the US average, the proportion of white and African workers are low, whereas the proportion of Asian and Hispanic workers was higher, in Japanese firms. The Japanese companies employed only a few women. This pattern is exacerbated at senior posts, where Japanese workers dominate the workforce. Japanese companies tend to emphasize corporate social respon-sibility (CSR) as justification for supporting diversity, while the US companies cite competitiveness as a key reason. The paper concludes that the Japanese companies need to reconsider justification of localization and diversification of their workforces, in order to respond to rapid social changes in the US labour market. It is also necessary that localization and diversification efforts also target top officer levels. Although localization is evident, it should also be noted that the majority of the 'local' employees are actually white workers, and women are relatively few in the workforce. In order to facilitate change, awareness-raising activities should be provided. It is also important to note that these changes are necessary as the localization and diversification strat-egies outlined in Arimura's work are essential for compliance with the Equal Employment Opportunity Act in the US.

Arimura (2004) also considers whether 'diversity management' is penetrable and effective in Japanese society, and, if not, what factors hinder its devel-opment. Arimura used a questionnaire survey of 30 (out of 282) US-based companies, which conduct business in Japan (that have headquarters advanced in diversity management and that employ 50 or more regular employees). This paper reveals that diversity is proceeding more in US companies in Japan than in Japanese-owned companies: except for the employment of older workers, they especially show improvement in diversity in sex, by promoting female employees to managerial jobs. Most of them pronounce their will towards diversity, and a main purpose is to gain competitiveness. Furthermore Arimura examines the measures taken, revealing that communication and work–life balance perspectives are utilized by almost half of them, while other measures, that is documentation of diversity, diversity training, disposition towards having a managerial post responsible for diversity matters, accountability and mentoring, are utilized only by 20 to 30 per cent. There are a certain number of advanced companies which adopt most of these measures.

A review of institutional websites of global car manufacturing companies in Japan reveals that only very few of the organizations have recently set up offices to tackle diversity issues, and even those which have are more concerned about domestic rather than global diversity concerns. The case-study company that participated in this project also has a diversity management office which was established in 2004 with the initiative of the Chief Executive Officer. The diversity office has five members of staff. It reports to both the executive committee and to the head of human resources.

The take-up of diversity management initiatives in the automotive sector is not unique to the Japanese car manufacturing companies: William Brooks, vice president of corporate relations for General Motors, explained at a conference in Britain that:

> The people joining the workforce are not like us, do not want to be like us, and will not work in places where people demand they be like us . . . They are going to celebrate their differences and we have got to learn how to manage them. There were business benefits to having a diverse workplace . . . GM's utility truck business, where 55 per cent of purchases and 85 per cent of decisions to purchase are made by women, having a male-dominated workforce would clearly be disadvantageous here . . . GM still had a long way to go in accepting global diversity. How can we talk about being a global organization when the whole of the board is American? (*People Management* 1995: 16)

The case of the automotive sector in Japan is very different from the case of automotive sectors in the US and the UK: although the Japanese automotive firms have been setting up diversity management offices, these offices are domestic in nature. They tackle domestic diversity management concerns. In terms of coordination of global diversity management efforts, the executive directors of human resource management are identified as possible overseers of such coordination activities. Although now most organizations have domestic diversity management offices, none of the automotive sector companies have specific 'global' diversity management offices. This role appears to have been assumed by an executive human resource management function. Although global diversity management offices are not available, the national networks have diversity management offices locally in each country, with localized practices reflecting the requirements of the local branch. The global diversity management model that is observed in Japanese companies is more akin to a multinational management model, which is characterized by localizing its practices according to the requirements of the national network.

The automobile companies are internationally hard pushed to increase their productivity and performance measures. The case of the diversity initiatives in the US is interesting. The diversity management approaches are very diffuse. There are many small, medium and large scale initiatives that are branded as diversity management initiatives. These range from community-related activities to integration of diversity principles in performance evaluation schemes. Some of these were highlighted in Chapter 2.

The location of the diversity office generally indicates the content of the diversity management initiatives. In the case of the Japanese firm, the diversity management initiative was part of the human resource management function. Furthermore diversity management offices are relatively small in size, with smaller budgets and resources than their European and American counterparts.

Individual effects

It is possible to identify an individual behind every successful diversity management initiative. This study also uncovered that individual commitment to diversity by the executive director of the case-study company, as well as by consecutive directors of Nikkeiren, has fostered diversity management initiatives. The campaign in Rengo had a more diffuse ownership. Interviews suggested that powerful individuals with clout in organizations can elevate the status of diversity management and support programmes and initiatives. The individual support afforded by senior executives is essential in the recognition of diversity as a key institutional prerogative and a strategic concern for the organization.

3.4   Conclusion

In this chapter, we have explained the main diversity management theories and offered a theoretical framework for studying global diversity management practices. Diversity initiatives can be listed as a large number of demographic categories which are accepted as proxies for workforce diversity. However, at the level of practice, pragmatism prevails and organizations restrict themselves to a select number of categories such as gender, ethnicity and disability, often defined by law and customs of the local industry.

It is important to differentiate between antecedents, perceptions, reality, consequences, moderators, outcomes, perspectives, policies and consequences of diversity and management of diversity. Whilst some organizations may consider their policies and organizational statements on global diversity management as proxies of their commitment and effective management of diversity, a similar approach to equal opportunities in employment has proven instrumental merely in encouraging many companies in the 1980s to issue statements that they are equal opportunities employers (Cockburn 1989). However, issuing policies have proven poor replacement for real change in practice.

Overcoming the policy and practice gap is one of the challenges that face the diversity management officers. The diversity management discourse continues to draw on dominant discourses of power, such as organizational and individual performance and social and legal compliance, in order to legitimize its proposed practices. Conversely, this way of legitimating does little to transform power relations that threaten to eradicate the existence of the differences that diversity management discourse espouses to value. There is need for more sophisticated approaches which offer a range of cases for diversity management.

Box 3.2   Main drivers for setting up a global diversity management initiative – the case of global diversity management in Japanese car manufacturing firms

Global effects

- global demographic trends;
- global competition and competitive behaviour;
- global agreements such as Labour Standards.

Regional and national effects

- legal considerations;
- economic considerations;
- social and cultural considerations;
- institutional actors such as trade and employers' unions, associations and equality pressure groups.

Organizational effects

- structure of the global operations (centralized vs decentralized);
- position of the diversity management office;
- power of the diversity management office;
- integration of the diversity management office to other units and functions;
- strength of the business case arguments;
- strength of the moral and ethical case arguments.

▶

▶

Diversity office effects

- status of the diversity office in the organization;
- power and prestige of the diversity office in organizational change;
- resources of the diversity office;
- vision of the diversity office;
- quality of the design in diversity management;
- quality of conformance to the diversity management design.

Individual effects

- status of the diversity manager in the organizational structure;
- power and drive of the diversity manager;
- resources of the diversity manager;
- availability of diversity champions;
- drive, power, prestige and resources of diversity champions.

Global diversity approach

- multidomestic – each country has its own diversity approach;
- multinational – the practice is highly localized with little transfer across national borders;
- global – a global and centralized perspective that transcends national differences with diffusion of knowledge on diversity management;
- regional – regional rather than national frameworks are in operation such as European, Asian, etc.

Appendix A: Speeches by senior officers of Nikkeiren about their commitment to diversity

Exercise: Reflecting on the speeches below, identify the key drivers for diversity management for the Nikkeiren (Japan Business Federation) and contrast this with the drivers for diversity management espoused by the trade unions in Japan.

The 39th Japan–US Business Conference Speech by Chairman Hiroshi Okuda, Japan Business Federation. 'The Political and Economic Situation in Japan', 21 October 2002.

Because of that, by March of next year Japan Business Federation intends to issue a vision for the renaissance of Japan, and it will include a concrete outlook for the future shape of the country and recommendations pertaining to the institutional reforms necessary to translate that vision into reality. The philosophy that underlies that vision can be succinctly defined this way: 'Attaining dynamism through diversity. The effort will entail altering our uniform lifestyle and the consensus approach exemplified by the collective orientation that has underpinned the pursuit of material affluence in the postwar era; instead, we must create a society that attaches paramount importance to the diverse values and individuality of each and every person, a society in which individual differences are mutually respected. If individuals and companies set diversified goals and then create the energy needed to engage freely in the activities required to achieve those goals, I feel certain we will be able to structure a new economy and society in Japan. A long-standing aim of Japan Business Federation has been the achievement of 'small government' through regulatory reform, and this too is an attempt to build a vibrant society that will enable full play to be given to the creativity and ingenuity of both private individuals and companies. It is incumbent upon us to pursue that agenda ever more vigorously. To that end, we need to make greater use of the very best in human resources, technologies, and know-how from overseas.

The 22nd World Gas Conference in Tokyo, Speech by Chairman Hiroshi Okuda. 'Challenges and Perspectives of the Japanese Economy and Industry', 2 June 2003.

Last year when I assumed the post of Chairman of Nippon Keidanren, I proposed two basic principles. The first principle is 'attaining dynamism and creation through diversity'. The second principle, which is needed to support the first, is 'empathy and trust'. In other words, corporations and individuals must identify their own specific goals and must endeavor to achieve these goals on their own responsibility. Even when these goals differ, corporations and individuals must be bound strongly together through mutual empathy and trust, so that the dynamism found in individual diversity can lead to overall economic and social development.

Draft Notes for the Address by Nippon Keidanren Chairman Hiroshi Okuda to the Inaugural Meeting of the STS forum, 14 November 2004

To facilitate the sustained prosperity of the human race, it is essential that scientists, politicians, corporate executives, and professionals representing a broad diversity of backgrounds continue to gather together under one roof and engage in a dialogue committed to the solution of the problems we share.

The 41st Japan–US Business Conference, Speech by Chairman Hiroshi Okuda, Nippon Keidanren. 'The Political and Economic Situation in Japan', 15 November 2004.

For the past several years, Nippon Keidanren has worked actively with related governmental agencies, universities and research institutions through such means as holding Academic–Business–Government Coalition Promotion Conference that promote interaction among industry, academia and government. In a world of increasingly diversified and advanced research and development, it is important for each side to recognize the role played by the others and to take responsibility for promoting stronger ties, with universities and research institutes conducting basic research and basic technological development from a mid-term, governmental perspective, and industry pursuing process innovation and product innovation that anticipates consumer needs. I feel confident that if each sector undertakes reforms while giving free rein to their ideas, we can generate dynamic diversity and boost Japan's overall R&D strength.

'Why Decentralize?' Mita Katsushige, Vice Chairman, Keidanren, February 1995.

The second reason for decentralization is that Japan finds itself in the midst of vast changes both domestically and internationally. At home, we are making the transition from the 'how to' age to the 'what to' age. Companies are being asked to show more self-dependence; instead of 'me-too' strategies that seek conformity, they must be able to say 'this is what we make and you'll find it nowhere else'. Internationally, the situation has best been summed up by Yasushi Akashi, Special Representative of the Secretary-General for the former Yugoslavia, who said, 'The postwar world must respect differences. We are no longer divided into the two camps of communism and liberalism. The world is a more varied and colorful place than that.' This 'respect for differences' involves both a 'recognition of differences' and an 'acceptance of differences'. This is just as true for individuals and nationalities as it is for states, and within any one country it also holds true for different regions. As is the case with corporate autonomy, decentralization is crucial because it enhances the potential for more richly varied regions. That is why I think Mr Akashi's comment captures the essence of the changes that are taking place. Decentralization in Japan is a recognition of 'internal diversity' and it is reaching a stage that should put it on par with the recognition of 'external diversity' that comes with internationalization.

'The Importance of the United States–Japan Relationship', Toyoda Shoichiro, Chairman Keidanren, October 1995.

Japan will need a healthy dose of entrepreneurship to break out of the stagnation in which our economy is mired. We need to propagate the kind of entrepreneurial vitality displayed by US venture businesses, including the way they celebrate diversity and honor individuality. Bringing that kind of vitality to bear in blazing new industrial sectors could contribute immensely to reinvigorating the Japanese economy.

'Culture and Diversity', Masaharu Shibata, Vice Chairman, Nippon Keidanren, June 2003.

Even after the year 2004 when the EU expands to include 25 countries and national borders are removed in the economic area, such cultural diversities of European countries will remain as a source of dynamism and progress. Diversity was one of the keywords in the Position Paper of the Committee on Management and Labor Policy in last December. The discussion seemed to have centered on such issues as 'no pay increase' and 'reviewing regular pay increases'. However, the main issue of Management and Labor is how to materialize the diversification of employment formats. Therefore, I made my recommendation that the negotiation style should shift from the 'struggle' of the traditional shunto to more discussion-centered meetings, hoping this year will be a turning point. I aspire for a society full of dynamism in which workers can apply their personal characteristics and diverse individuals take active parts.

Messages from *Economic Trend*, 'La Dolce Vita', Hiroshi Okuda Chairman, Nippon Keidanren, June 2004.

Italians honor freedom and diversity. They are respectful of each other's work and livelihoods. They share a love for their towns and cities, and that common devotion engenders a spirit of trust. When I became chairman of Nippon Keidanren, I declared a commitment to the dynamism of diversity, to sympathy and trust, and to spiritual fulfillment. I now find myself serving a very unexpected second term as chairman. Witnessing 'la dolce vita' in person has inspired in me a redoubled commitment to those principles.

Messages from *Economic Trend*, 'Japan's Falling Birthrate: Let's not Be Complacent', Takahide Sakurai, Vice Chairman of the Board of Councillors, Nippon Keidanren, August 2005.

Population policy is always in need of timely adjustment, whether major or minor. And now we need a major change of policy direction, particularly with respect to the family. For many decades we have taken the 'modern family', consisting of a married couple and their children, as the only proper form of family unit. We have averted our gaze from unmarried couples, and continued to look at divorce as an aberration, even though it has become quite common. Despite this conservatism the diversification of people's family arrangements shows no sign of abating. Professor Shigeru Maruyama of Kanagawa University has come out with an interesting book about changes in the family system (*Kazoku no metaphor*, Waseda University Press). In it he suggests that, as democratic thinking filters into the Japanese psyche, carrying with it the ideas of personal liberty and equality, it may only be natural that people run away from the so-called modern family, with its patriarchic nature. After all, this particular paradigm of family was dominant in Japanese society for no more than fifty years or so, from around 1920 through the 1970s. The government should give up on the idea of creating a picture of the 'ideal' family and trying to get everybody to conform to it. Professor Maruyama convincingly argues that the authorities should shift to a stance of accepting the diversity of people's lifestyle choices and adjusting its policy mix accordingly. I strongly hope that the blue-ribbon panels like the Council for Gender Equality and the Council on Measures for Society with Decreasing Birthrate will come up with strategic concepts for flexible measures to respond to the actual transformation of the Japanese family – the home base of childbearing.

Appendix B: Interview schedule for the global diversity management case study

Exercise: Using the interview questions below, replicate the above case study in a global organization and organize in-class discussions. If these will be used for in-class discussion purposes, it is advisable that students conduct one or more of a number of expert interviews, the transcripts of which can be discussed in the classroom.

You and your organization:

1. What is your responsibility or job role in relation to diversity and management in this organization?
2. How do you fit in the organizational structure?

Diversity and Equality in Your Organization:

3. How did your company reach to its current position in diversity and equality?
4. Could you describe your company's current diversity structure to me?
5. Do you offer specific facilities for certain group of employees?
6. What are the activities/initiatives/programs that are implemented in order to reach diversity goals?
7. Which initiatives do you consider more successful?
8. In promoting diversity do you use different messages to different groups of employees?
9. How would you describe the impact of diversity management policies and practices on organizational culture?

Mainstreaming and involvement:

10. How do diversity management policies or initiatives relate to the overall corporate objectives and strategies?
11. Literature suggests that it is difficult to involve line managers in diversity efforts. How do you get them to actively contribute to and take responsibility about the diversity efforts?
12. How do you get senior managers to actively contribute to and take responsibility about the diversity efforts?
13. How are the employees involved in the design and implementation of diversity policies and practices?
14. Could you please explain the employee resource groups dealing with diversity issues?
15. Are the trade unions involved in the diversity efforts in your organization? Please explain.
16. What would you say on the different groups of employees' reactions to diversity programs?

Monitoring:

17. How are diversity initiatives evaluated/monitored?
18. Do you have employee attitude surveys to monitor the impact of diversity efforts?
19. Up to now, what benefits are derived from the diversity program?
20. Up to now, what are the costs associated with diversity management?
21. What is the customer base of the organization (diversity of customer base?)
22. How common are the incidents of sexual and ethnic harassment in your organization?

Appraisal, recruitment and training:

23. Do you keep records of demographic profiles of the workforce?
24. Are there targeted recruitment efforts?
25. Are hiring, promotion and compensation practices monitored with respect to their conformity with equal opportunities principles?
26. How are performance appraisals related to diversity efforts in your organization?
27. Does your organization offer diversity awareness training?

Future:

28. In summary, how would you define the current state of your organization with regard to embracing diversity and supporting equality? `
29. How do you plan to modify the diversity program in the future?

Personal Details:

We are trying to build a profile. May I lastly ask you some personal details?

30. What are your educational qualifications?
31. What is your functional background/training?
32. Gender?
33. Age?
34. Ethnicity?
35. Nationality?
36. Do you practise a religion?
37. Do you have a disability?
38. Could you please tell me any additional comments you feel are relevant to our understanding of diversity management strategy of your organization?
39. May I have your contact details?
40. Who else I can talk to about diversity management in your company?

Further reading

Adams, S.M. (1998) 'Models of Conflict Resolution in Japanese, German and American Cultures', *Journal of Applied Psychology*, vol. 83, pp. 316–23.

Banerji, K. and Sambharya, R.B. (2004) 'Cracks in the Vertical Keiretsu: Switching the Behaviour of Suppliers in the Japanese Automobile Industry', *Academy of Management Best Conference Paper*, IM: G1–G6.

Kodama, M. (2000) 'Business Innovation through Customer-value Creation: Case Study of a Virtual Education Business in Japan', *Journal of Management Development*, vol. 19, pp. 49–70.

Kodama, M. (2003) 'Strategic Innovation in Traditional Big Business: Case Study of Two Japanese Companies', *Organization Studies*, vol. 24, no. 2, pp. 235–68.

Kranias, D.S. (2000) 'Cultural Control: The Case of Japanese Multinational Companies and their Subsidiaries in the UK', *Management Decision*, vol. 38, no. 9, pp. 638–48.

Levy, B. (2002) 'The Competitiveness of MNCs in a Globalized and Regionalized Economy: The War for Talent and the Role of Women Executives', *Management International*, vol. 7, pp. 103–11.

Satow, S. and Wang, Z. (1994) 'Cultural and Organizational Factors in Human Resources Management in China and Japan: A Cross-cultural Socio-economic Perspective', *Journal of Managerial Psychology*, vol. 9, pp. 3–11.

Siemon, R. (2001) 'Top Team Characteristics and the Business Strategies of Japanese Organizations', *Corporate Governance*, vol. 1, pp. 4–12.

Styhre, A. (2002) 'Constructing the Image of the Other: A Post-colonial Image of the Adaptation of Japanese Human Resources Management Practices', *Management Decision*, vol. 40, pp. 257–65.

National and Discourse Effects

Diversity Management at the National Level

4.1 Introduction

This chapter looks at national effects of global diversity management. Much of what we know of diversity management comes in the form of nationally based studies from the US and other industrialized countries of the world. The domestic knowledge of diversity is often focused at the level of the organizations in which diversity management initiatives are conducted. This chapter presents another national study, but at multiple levels of analysis, looking at issues of national, organizational and individual concern in management of diversity.

Reflecting on the findings of a national questionnaire survey with 285 diversity officers in the UK, we examine the diversity management practices in organizations and do this in terms of the role of diversity managers as professionals. The findings of the survey suggest that diversity management in the

UK has made some advances in terms of growing out of the human resource management field in which it is traditionally located. Despite its short history, diversity management has gained considerable currency. However, there is still room for improvement in bringing diversity management efforts in-line with best practices. The study reported here reveals that the diversity office and officers do not enjoy favourable status or positions in their organizations. We provide tabular displays of survey findings which indicate the current state of practice and the take-up of diversity management discourses. Finally, we set a number of questions for future research agendas.

4.2   State of the Nation: diversity management

Diversity management is often considered a calling for organizations and diversity managers, who see that there is a business case for diversity in order to pursue strategies for organizational change. At least this is often the case in the academic and practitioner press, which attributes characteristics such as champions, tempered radical and change agents to describe equality and diversity officers. The purpose of this chapter is to explore the validity of this assumption and map out the state of diversity management in the UK through the findings of a field research on diversity management, which is based on a survey of 285 diversity and equality officers.

The field survey that is described here was funded by the Chartered Institute of Personnel and Development, and it is the final stage of a larger action research study on diversity management that has taken place over five years. The research is unique in the sense that it is the first comprehensive diversity management survey administered nationally in the UK. Despite the popularity of the issue in both academic and practitioner circles alike, nation-based empirical research, which explores the general practice of managing diversity, is lacking. Accordingly, this survey is designed to provide evidence on a wide set of diversity management issues in the UK.

The questionnaire survey was designed as a multilevel tool incorporating broad macro-environmental issues such as external drivers for diversity for organizations, meso-level organizational attitudes to processes, mechanisms and systems for managing diversity, as well as micro-level dynamics involving the role of the diversity, and equality officers in managing change. The design of the study is based on a survey of current diversity measurement instruments and reflects the multifaceted nature of the diversity work that takes place in the UK organizations.

The survey was carried out through a self-completion online questionnaire, which was piloted for clarity and accessibility. The survey was then presented on the Chartered Institute of Personnel and Development (CIPD) website and promoted over a period of six weeks during February and March 2006. A newsletter was sent to the members of the CIPD, who have affinity to the subject of diversity and equality. These members were selected from the CIPD database which listed membership interests. Furthermore, other bodies, such as the Equal Opportunities Commission and the Commission for Racial Equality, have displayed links to the questionnaire on their websites.

The research generated 285 completed questionnaires by equal opportunities and diversity officers in the UK. The overall response rate was very favourable, as the survey specifically targeted equality and diversity professionals. The replies were received from 224 female and 61 male respondents from a broad age range. The overall spread of respondents was very representative in terms of organizational size, location, industry, and sector (see Appendix A for further details of the distributive attributes of the survey participants).

The literature suggests that diversity management is a calling. However, the findings of the survey are counter-intuitive in this regard. We have identified that the current status of diversity management at macro-, meso- and micro-levels is far removed from being a calling. Below we will systematically describe why our study reveals that diversity management does not enjoy the industrial status which is ascribed to it in the literature.

4.3   Drivers for diversity management: macro-level

In the literature it is argued that diversity management represents a shift from the focus of the equal opportunities approach on representation and legislation to that of inclusion and a voluntary and proactive stance regarding the organizational change. In other words, it is frequently stated that diversity management is marked by a voluntary approach on the side of employers that come forth due to the business realities of the age, rather than due to a legal enforcement by the state that is associated with equal opportunities practices (Thomas 1990; McDougall 1996).

One of the sections of the survey aimed to explore the key drivers for diversity management for the organizations. We asked respondents to rank 18 statements from one to five according to their importance in terms of being key drivers for diversity management in their organizations. The respondents were allowed to rank different statements at the same rank. Interestingly, although the literature suggests that diversity management thrives on a business-case argument, our study suggests that diversity management is indeed predominantly driven by legal compliance concerns. The survey results showed that the most important motivation for managing diversity is 'legal pressures' with 68 per cent of the respondents ranking it as among the top five drivers. Other key reasons that were seen as among the top five drivers by the respondents

Table 4.1 What are the key drivers for diversity in your organization? Please select all that apply. Rank the top 5 from 1 to 5, with 1 being the most important

	Percentage of respondents					
Drivers are	1 most important	2nd	3rd	4th	5th	Total
Legal pressures	32.3	12.6	6.0	4.9	11.9	**67.7**
To recruit and retain best talent	13.3	16.5	18.6	8.1	7.4	**63.9**
Corporate social responsibility	12.6	16.8	15.1	11.2	6.7	**62.4**
To be an employer of choice	15.4	14.7	14.4	10.2	7.0	**61.7**
Because it makes business sense	16.8	14.0	13.7	7.4	8.1	**60.0**
Because it is morally right	13.3	10.5	15.1	9.5	10.5	**58.9**
To improve business performance	6.0	10.2	15.1	9.8	7.0	**48.1**
To address recruitment problems	8.4	11.2	12.3	8.4	7.0	**47.3**
Belief in social justice	8.8	11.2	11.9	8.8	5.3	**46.0**
Desire to improve customer relations	5.3	8.1	14.7	7.7	7.4	**43.2**
To improve products and services	9.5	8.8	13.0	4.6	6.7	**42.6**
To improve creativity and innovation	5.6	8.1	14.0	8.1	6.7	**42.5**
Desire to reach diverse markets	6.0	6.7	11.2	7.4	8.4	**39.7**
To improve corporate branding	5.3	7.0	13.0	6.7	5.3	**37.3**
To enhance decision-making	2.8	8.4	14.7	4.9	4.2	**35.0**
Trade union activities	2.8	4.2	7.7	6.3	11.2	**32.2**
To respond to the competition in the market	5.6	6.0	9.5	6.7	3.9	**31.7**
To respond to the global market	5.6	2.5	8.4	5.6	7.4	**29.5**

were 'to recruit and retain best talent' (64 per cent), 'corporate social responsibility' (62 per cent), 'to be an employer of choice' (62 per cent) and 'because it makes business sense' (60 per cent). **Table 4.1** outlines the key drivers for diversity management in the organizations of the participants. The scale for

Table 4.2 Top ranking drivers for managing diversity

Drivers	The most important driver Percentage of respondents
Legal pressures	32.3
Because it makes business sense	16.8
To be an employer of choice	15.4
To recruit and retain best talent	13.3
Because it is morally right	13.3
Corporate social responsibility	12.6
To improve products and services	9.5
Belief in social justice	8.8
To address recruitment problems	8.4
Desire to reach diverse markets	6.0
To improve business performance	6.0
To respond to the global market	5.6
To respond to the competition in the market	5.6
To improve creativity and innovation	5.6
Desire to improve customer relations	5.3
To improve corporate branding	5.3
To enhance decision-making	2.8
Trade union activities	2.8

this question required respondents to list five key drivers for diversity management in their organizations.

The research findings are even more striking when we look at key drivers that are ranked first in terms of its importance. Again, legal compliance was the most popular answer, but this time it is differentiated from other categories in a more clear way. Thirty-two per cent of the respondents ranked 'legal pressures' as the most important driver for diversity management in their organizations. The second most popular driver of diversity was 'because it makes business sense'. However, only 17 per cent of the respondents reported the business case as being the most important driver for their organizations (See **Table 4.2**).

In addition to the general statement of 'because it makes business sense', the survey question specified different dimensions of business benefits of diversity management in line with the propositions put forward in the diversity literature. It is suggested by several authors that workforce diversity contributes to the bottom line through:

- helping to meet the demands of diverse customers, hence increasing market share (Fernandez 1991; Cox and Blake 1991; Morrison 1992; Cox 1993; Thomas 2004);
- giving competitive edge to the organizations in our times of globalization (Adler 1986; Adler and Ghadar 1990; Marable 2000; Chevrier 2003);

- enhancing labour relations and reducing the labour turnover, absenteeism and recruitment costs (Fernandez 1991; Morrison 1992; Cox 1993; McEnrue 1993; Woods and Sciarini 1995);
- improving the quality and performance of the internal workforce in terms of skills, creativity, problem solving and flexibility (Nemeth 1986; Bantel and Jackson 1989; Fernandez 1991; Kirchmeyer and McLellan 1991; Morrison 1992; McEnrue 1993; Smith *et al.* 1994; Hambrick *et al.* 1996; Bhadury *et al.* 2000).

The survey findings reveal that much more understanding is needed about the implications of managing diversity if it is to add value to business and deliver its full potential. **Table 4.3** demonstrates that most respondents fail to consider the elements of diversity that can add value to business, even though 60 per cent recognize that diversity makes business sense. They simply focus on the contribution of diversity to the bottom line predominantly in terms of 'recruiting and retaining best talent', which is ranked among the top five drivers by amongst two thirds of respondents.

Our research findings indicate that organizations do not consider most of the above specific benefits of workforce diversity as being key drivers for them. Overall, 'to improve business performance' was among the most important five drivers for managing diversity for only 48 per cent of the research participants. It seems that organizations that participated in the survey understand the contribution of diversity to the bottom line predominantly in terms of

Table 4.3   Key drivers for diversity in terms of business benefits (ranking of top 5 from 1 to 5, with 1 being the most important)

| Drivers | Percentage of respondents | | | | | |
	1	2	3	4	5	Total
To recruit and retain best talent	13.3	16.5	18.6	8.1	7.4	**63.9**
Because it makes business sense	16.8	14.0	13.7	7.4	8.1	**60.0**
To improve business performance	6.0	10.2	15.1	9.8	7.0	**48.1**
To address recruitment problems	8.4	11.2	12.3	8.4	7.0	**47.3**
Desire to improve customer relations	5.3	8.1	14.7	7.7	7.4	**43.2**
To improve products and services	9.5	8.8	13.0	4.6	6.7	**42.6**
To improve creativity and innovation	5.6	8.1	14.0	8.1	6.7	**42.5**
Desire to reach diverse markets	6.0	6.7	11.2	7.4	8.4	**39.7**
To improve corporate branding	5.3	7.0	13.0	6.7	5.3	**37.3**
To enhance decision-making	2.8	8.4	14.7	4.9	4.2	**35.0**
To respond to the competition in the market	5.6	6.0	9.5	6.7	3.9	**31.7**
To respond to the global market	5.6	2.5	8.4	5.6	7.4	**29.5**

'recruiting and retaining best talent', which is ranked among the top five drivers by 64 per cent of the respondents.

On the other hand, improving customer relations and market share does not seem to be strongly related to managing diversity by the employers. Only 43 per cent of the respondents ranked 'desire to improve customer relations' in the top five, and 'desire to reach diverse markets' was among the top five drivers of diversity only for 39 per cent of the respondents. Similarly, responding to globalization and competition as drivers of diversity scored poorly with only 29 per cent of the respondents reporting 'to respond to the global markets' in their top five, and 32 per cent indicating that 'to respond to the competition in the market' is among the top five drivers of managing diversity for them.

The statements that relate diversity management to improving the quality and performance of internal workforce were also proved to be unpopular among the survey respondents as key drivers for managing diversity. Only 42 per cent of the respondents reported 'to improve creativity and innovation' to be among the top five drivers for diversity. This figure was 42 per cent and 35 per cent for 'to improve products and services' and 'to enhance decision making', respectively.

When we turn to the rates at which each of these specific potentials of diversity were ranked as the most important drivers for managing diversity, the findings demonstrate an even more limited understanding of the business case for diversity management. Only 6 per cent of the respondents reported that to improve business performance is the most important driver for diversity in their organization. More specifically, 'desire to improve customer relations' was ranked top by 5.3 per cent of the respondents; 'desire to reach diverse markets' by 6 per cent; 'to respond to global markets' by 5.6 per cent; and 'to respond to the competition in the market' by 5.6 per cent. Similarly the rates of being ranked top for the statements regarding workforce productivity and efficiency were low, with 'to improve creativity and innovation' being ranked first by 5.6 per cent of the organizations; 'to improve products and services' by 9.5 per cent; and 'to enhance decision-making' by only 2.8 per cent. Again, the highest scoring driver as the top rank was related to recruitment. Of the respondents, 13.3 per cent ranked 'to recruit and retain best talent' as the most important key driver for diversity management in their organizations.

Overall, the findings from this section of the survey demonstrate that drivers for diversity management are to a large extend limited to legal compliance for these organizations in the UK. This results clearly in a conflict with the argument that diversity management policies are internally driven, since it makes business sense, unlike the equal opportunities policies which are externally driven by anti-discrimination legislation. As revealed by the survey results, the most important business motive for the organizations to adopt diversity management policies and practices continues to be the consideration of legislative pressures. Furthermore, the business benefits of diversity management are mostly linked to the area of human resources, more specifically to the issue of recruitment. These findings uncover that the business case for diversity is not fully developed and understood by the organizations in the UK, and that diversity management is not integrated into the logic of other business functions in the organizations, such as marketing, product development, customer relations. This means that the organizations relate the forces of demographic demand to their recruitment and selection processes. However, they do not capture diversity issues as relevant to the changes of the market in terms of products and marketability. Therefore, in a sense, diversity is only welcome as an employment logic rather than as a broader guiding business principle.

4.4   Diversity management policy and practice in UK organizations: meso-level

In addition to the emphasis of business case, another characteristic of diversity management, which differentiates it from the equal opportunities perspective, is frequently stated in the academic and practitioner literature as its inclusive nature. It is argued that the equal opportunities framework proved to be insufficient in dealing with workplace discrimination by limiting its scope to gender and ethnicity, which in turn led to a backlash by the majority group members in the organizations and to stereotyping of individuals as members of some demographic groups (Thomas 1990). Accordingly, it is put forward that the diversity management approach has an advantage over the equal opportunities perspective due to its emphasis on difference as opposed to the focus of the equal opportunities' approach on sameness.

Kandola and Fullerton (1998: 7), who produced the most influential definition of diversity management in the UK, include a wide range of differences in their definition of diversity, as can be seen in their definition of diversity management:

> The basic concept of managing diversity accepts that the workforce consists of a diverse population of people. The diversity consists of visible and non-visible differences which will include factors such as sex, age, background, race, disability, personality and work style. It is founded on the premise that harnessing these differences will create a productive environment in which everyone feels valued, where their talents are being fully utilized and in which organizational goals are met.

However, the results of the survey demonstrate that the understanding of diversity in the UK organizations is not based on such an inclusive approach.

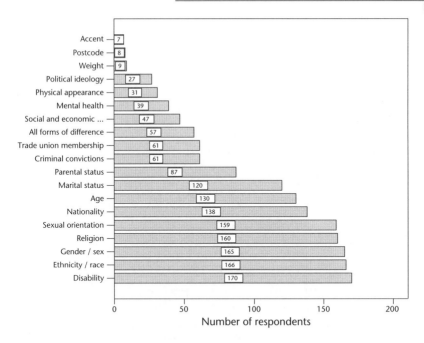

Figure 4.1   Which of the following categories does your diversity policy cover?

We asked respondents which categories of diversity are covered by their organization's diversity policy. The answers show that the categories of diversity that are most frequently reported to be covered are the ones protected by the anti-discrimination legislation in the UK (see **Figure 4.1**).

According to the survey results, 59.6 per cent of the organizations participated in the survey covered disability in their diversity policies; 58.2 per cent race and ethnicity; 57.9 per cent gender; 56.1 per cent religion; 55.8 per cent sexual orientation; 48.4 per cent nationality; 45.6 per cent age. Only 20 per cent of the respondents stated that their organizations' diversity policy covers 'all forms of difference'.

Furthermore, inclusion rates of diversity categories which are not covered by the employment legislation were very low among the participating organizations. For instance, only 16.5 per cent of the organizations included social and economic background in their diversity policy; 10.9 per cent physical appearance; 3.2 per cent weight; 2.8 per cent postcode; 2.5 per cent accent; 13.7 per cent mental health; 9.5 per cent political ideology. Diversity management literature in the main advocates a greater range of social divisions to be included in diversity policies. Indeed, discussions which set diversity management and equal opportunities refer to the multiplicity of heterogeneity factors, including gender, ethnicity, disability, age, sexual orientation, social background, physical attributes, etc., in the diversity literature. Our findings

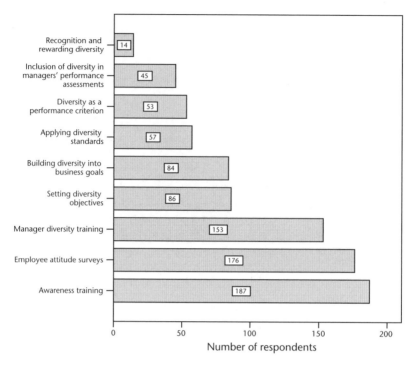

Figure 4.2 Which of the following diversity activities does your organization have?

above suggest that, indeed, the progress towards more inclusive approaches to diversity management strands has remained stunted. A relatively small number of categories are being included in diversity management policies in the majority of the organizations, and in a small number of organizations a broader range of diversity strands are covered by organizational policy.

Respondents were asked to indicate the type of diversity activities their organizations use, as shown in **Figure 4.2**. While many organizations have taken positive steps by providing awareness training and carrying out employee attitude surveys, the activities that would help ensure diversity management is practised across the whole organization are less common. For example, diversity is a performance criterion in only 19 per cent of the organizations, and diversity-related goals are included in managers' performance assessments by only 16 per cent of organizations. It is only in a number of progressive organizations that achievement in diversity management has been recognized in the performance management system and considered an integral part of the line managers' role.

Furthermore, in 95.1 per cent of the organizations diversity achievements were not rewarded and recognized, and 70.5 per cent did not build diversity into their business goals. Similarly, just 20 per cent of the respondents reported that their organization applies diversity standards. Curiously, 69.8 per cent of the respondents reported that they do not set diversity objectives. These findings demonstrate that diversity management activities in the UK organizations remain at a very superficial level, largely limited to training activities. In the absence of objective setting, reward and recognition, and applying diversity standards and measurements, it is hard to see how the diversity management process could possibly have the necessary clout to initiate a cultural change in the organizations in the UK.

4.5   Diversity and equality officers as agents of change: micro-level

Another characteristic that is attributed to diversity management in the literature, which may potentially make it a progressive approach, is its ability to initiate organizational change. Indeed, the most important area that diversity management promises an improvement on the equal opportunities framework is the emphasis on cultural change in the organizations (Cox and Blake 1991; Mighty 1991; Dobbs 1996; Liff 1996; Gilbert and Ivancevich 2000). In the previous section, we outlined the limited nature of systems, policies and activities to engender a change process in the organizations who participated in the research. In addition to these structural elements, the resources under the disposition of the diversity and equality officers are crucial since they will be the agents or facilitators throughout the organizational change process. In the survey, we asked the diversity and equality officers several questions to explore their resources and power as individuals.

Key factors that impact upon the levels of power, prestige and resources available to diversity and equality officers in their organizations are:

- organizational commitment and buy in;
- status of the diversity function and diversity practitioner; and
- mainstreaming of diversity management throughout different functions.

To start with, senior management support and ownership, as well as involvement of different organizational actors at different levels and functions, are important determinants of the status and authority of the diversity managers and equality officers (Parker 1999; Meyerson 2001a; Meyerson 2001b). Only 41.9 per cent of the respondents agreed with the statement that in his/her organization 'senior management encourages diversity', with only 15.8 per cent of the respondents choosing the 'strongly agree' option. We also asked about the levels of personal ownership assumed by different organizational actors in diversity-related activities and issues. The survey findings demonstrate that level of ownership decreases by level of authority in the organizations which

Table 4.4 How much personal ownership do people at the following levels assume in diversity-related activities and issues?

	Percentage of respondents				
Organizational level	No ownership 1	2	3	4	Total ownership 5
Board members	10.4	15.5	30.7	27.5	15.9
Senior management	5.1	12.8	32.7	36.2	13.2
Middle management	6.0	19.8	43.3	22.6	8.3
Junior management	8.3	27.0	42.9	17.5	4.4
Non-managerial workers	15.0	30.4	41.9	10.7	2.0
Trade union representatives	8.0	10.9	44.0	28.0	9.1

participated in that research. Highest level of ownership was reported to be assumed by board members and senior management who display some level of or total ownership regarding diversity issues in 43.4 per cent and 44.5 per cent of the organizations. This figure decreases by job level to 27.4 per cent for middle management, 19.3 per cent for junior management, and 11.3 per cent for non-managerial workers. However, these results may not be very surprising considering the fact that 35.4 per cent of the organizations do not involve their employees in the design and implementation of diversity policies and practices. Survey findings demonstrate that level of ownership for diversity decreases by level of authority in the organizations, with the highest level reported to be assumed by board members and senior management, as shown in **Table 4.4**.

Respondents believe that more ownership is needed at senior level. Furthermore, senior-level management was documented in our study. However, only less than half of the participants agreed that senior management encourages diversity (see **Table 4.5**).

Furthermore, formal structures of diversity management are as important as the commitment and ownership by the organizational actors, for diversity managers to gain the necessary status and authority to realize their roles. These formal structures include the status of diversity office and individual diversity and equality officer, and integration of diversity management objectives in the different functions and levels of the organization, which in turn establish the legitimacy of diversity managers' actions in intervening and controlling the processes in other functions to meet the goals of diversity management policy (Jones et al. 1989; Parker 1999; Acker 2000; Meyerson 2001a; Meyerson 2001b).

Firstly, as Parker argues, one of the ways through which diversity and equality officers may gain 'clout' in two ways is holding a senior position. The position of the diversity manager within the organizational hierarchy and the level of authority allocated to him/her also illustrates the extent of centrality of the

Table 4.5 Please rate your level of agreement with the following statements

Statement	Percentage of respondents				
	Strongly disagree 1	2	3	4	Strongly agree 5
In my organization senior management encourage diversity	4.3	16.5	35.6	27.3	16.2
It is very important for my diversity role to know the names and faces of senior staff and be able to approach them easily	0.0	1.8	9.2	41.5	47.4
My organization aims to make sure that diversity and equality are at the heart of everything it does	4.0	25.3	32.5	27.1	11.2

diversity management in the mainstream organizational policies and strategies. According to the survey results, the majority of the respondents (41.1 per cent) are at middle management level, and the majority of these (66.3 per cent) earns between £21,000 and £40,000 annually. Furthermore, although 86.7 per cent of the respondents is employed full-time, only 15.5 per cent of them is contracted to work full-time on diversity management (see **Figures 4.3 and 4.4**). These results uncover the fact that managing diversity is not prioritized in the organizations in the UK, and being a diversity and equality officer is not among the most prestigious and resourceful roles in the organizations. Although our respondents reported relatively high levels of senior management ownership of the diversity issues, lack of seniority of the diversity practitioners can be interpreted by other organizational actors as a reflection of a lack of commitment by the senior management (Lawrence 2000).

In addition to the individual position of the diversity or equality officer within the organizational hierarchy, the position and status of the diversity office within the organizational structure establishes a crucial source of legitimacy and power for the actions and decisions of diversity managers (Jones *et al.* 1989). The survey results show that in 61.8 per cent of the organizations there is not a specialized diversity or equal opportunities function, and 66.3 per cent of the organizations do not have a budget for diversity. On the other hand 61.4 per cent of the respondents stated that the tasks they have undertaken in relation to managing diversity have increased in the last few years.

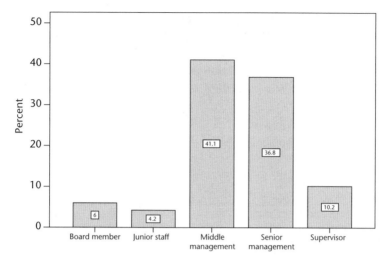

Figure 4.3 At what level is our current role in the organization?

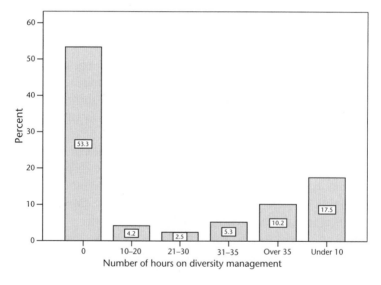

Figure 4.4 How many hours a week are you contracted to work on diversity management?

Conversely, only 13.7 per cent of them reported that the number of people under their supervision has increased in parallel with the increase in their tasks. These findings clearly demonstrate that diversity and equality officers are overstretched in terms of their job role and try to function with very limited financial and human resources. In addition to the lack of resources, diversity office and officers seem to be short of the necessary level of power and influence to initiate an organizational change as a part of their diversity management role. Only 45.8 per cent of the respondents believed that the most senior person of the diversity function has some level of authority over others in the organization. Similarly, only 38.6 per cent of the respondents thought that the diversity office is influential within the organization.

These results reveal that the diversity office and the diversity and equality officers, most of the time, lack the authority to influence different functions of the organization, despite the fact that implementation of diversity management and programmes is associated with an organizational change process. This dilemma faced by the equality and diversity officers, due to their position in the organizational hierarchy, might be overcome if the diversity management objectives are integrated into the different functions or business areas of the organization. However, the survey results are not very encouraging in that respect either. Only 37.2 per cent of the respondents reported that their organizations 'aim to make sure that diversity and equality are at the heart of everything it does'. One of the sections of the survey aimed to understand in more detail the level of integration in the mainstream business. We asked respondents whether diversity is central to the different departments in their organizations. According to the answers, diversity was central to the human resources function in most of the organizations (81.2 per cent), as might be expected. This is followed by diversity being central in communication and advertising in 53.6 per cent of the organizations; in strategic management in 53.5 per cent of the organizations; and corporate social responsibility in 49 per cent of them. However, these figures dropped when it came to the 'core' business functions, with only 11.4 per cent of the organizations reporting that diversity is central in their finance and accounting function; 18.5 per cent in manufacturing and production; and 34.8 per cent in marketing and sales. Clearly, these findings reveal that diversity management is not mainstreamed in the organizations in the UK and still enjoys a marginal status.

4.6   Political and multistakeholder context of diversity management

What is really curious and paradoxical in the light of the above evidence then is the dominance and perseverance of the discourse that diversity management is the way forward for equity in the workplace. Further research should explore why diversity management discourse, despite its apparent ineffectiveness, is warmly embraced by the corporate circles in the UK. Maybe the answer lies in the political nature of the diversity debate in the UK. There is a diversity industry in the UK, made up of diversity officers in public, private and voluntary sectors, diversity consultants, specialists, champions, legislators

(Equal Opportunities Commission, Commission for Racial Equality, Disability Rights Commission, etc.), professional bodies (including the Chartered Institute of Personnel and Development), employers unions (Confederation of British Industry) and trade unions (the Trades Union Congress). These actors in the diversity industry have different stakes and interests in diversity management. Whilst some actors in the industry, for example the employers, focus on the economic contribution of diversity, other segments focus on elimination of inequalities (e.g. trade unions) or welcoming of diversity (diversity practitioners).

The dialogue between these groups contributes to the development of sophisticated diversity management discourses, which combine a diverse range of arguments in support of diversity management. However, it is important to note that these stakeholder groups do not have equal power and influence in regulating work, employment and organization in the UK. In the case of Britain, employers have a stronger voice in regulating the labour market, whilst the voice and influence of trade unions and the state agencies have been curbed through decades of deregulation. In this context, it is not surprising to see that diversity management, with its emphasis on individual difference, has been embraced fully in the corporate circles, whilst equal opportunities which emphasizes collective rights and group-based equality issues has fallen out of grace.

Whilst the corporate stake in the adoption of diversity management discourse is well documented, little attention is paid to the co-optation of different interest groups, such as workers, trade unions and the social community, in adopting diversity management discourses. This co-optation promises a take up of a discourse which refers to 'valuing of difference' with little real impact, and instead a preference for hard equality concerns, such as eliminating pay inequalities, sexism, racism and other exclusionary and discriminatory practices. There has also been a general flight from moral arguments and discourses of discrimination, exclusion and inequality.

It is interesting that diversity management discourse flourish in national contexts where the welfare state has been weakened through deregulation and privatization. In North America and the UK, the decline of the welfare state has given a push to workfare practices where the responsibility for delivering social and economic integration and equality are delegated to organizations. Withdrawal of the state from regulation of social and economic relations, and the forward march of the corporate control in these vacated domains, prepares a fertile ground for diversity management discourse.

We do not wish to suggest that the low take-up of diversity management issues in Continental Europe are unproblematic, as there is better provision of welfare state in this region. It is indeed important for context-specific discourses and practices to be developed, which are sensitive to the configurations of significant actors with regulatory influence on labour market processes. One of the key contributions that diversity management discourses can make to the formulation of strategies to manage equality and diversity in any context is its emphasis on difference. We contend that in any labour market, it is important to recognize how difference is coded, what forms of difference are rewarded and which forms are excluded, marginalized and overlooked.

4.7   Conclusion

The national effects of global diversity management, which we examined in this chapter, require special attention with regard to macro-, meso- and micro-level dynamics. At the macro-level, particular attention should be devoted to social, economic structures and key actors and stakeholders who have a role in regulating employment and social relations. The historical trajectory of these social and economic relations is also key to our understanding. The perspective that these actors take in managing diversity management would set a broad framework in which meso-level industrial and organizational approaches can be shaped. At the organizational level, there are different sets of competing stakes, goals and influences which need to be considered. At the micro-level are the enactments of relations whose logics are informed by meso- and macro-level discursive configurations.

Most research on diversity management takes a single-level approach. We would argue that a realistic assessment of diversity management requires a multilevel analysis which explores complex and rich sets of interlocking relations across levels. For future research, we would argue that political, social and economic forces for diversity should be explored in order to understand organizational level practices. Justification for organizational level processes and practices may lie at the intersection of macro- and micro-levels of relations.

Diversity management theory is saturated with claims of improved business performance through diversity. However, the evidence for this remains relatively patchy. Furthermore, the causal relationship between high levels of heterogeneity across all strands of diversity and improved business performance is demonstrably tenuous. The study that we present here also identifies that the practice and theory of diversity management has a wide gap. The future theoretical development in the field requires a more realist approach, drawing on empirical as well as discursive evidence in reformulating what comes next.

Chapter 5 reviews the theory and policy of tackling the gender pay gap as part of a diversity management initiative. It brings together organizational, national and international insights.

Appendix A: **Profile of the respondents**

Sex	Percentage of the respondents
Male	21.4
Female	78.6
Age group	
16–25	3.2
26–30	10.9
31–40	30.2
41–50	41.8
51–60	13.3
61–65	0.7
Managerial level	
Board member	6.0
Senior management	36.8
Middle management	41.1
Supervisor	10.2
Junior staff	4.2
Diversity role	
International/global-level responsibility	1.4
European-level responsibility	2.8
National-level responsibility	13.0
Organizational responsibility	40.7
Unit-level responsibility	35.1
Sector	
Chemicals, oils and pharmaceuticals	2.8
Construction	0.4
Electricity, gas and water	0.7
Engineering, electronics and metals	2.8
Food, drink and tobacco	2.1
General manufacturing	1.4
Mining and quarrying	0.4
Paper and printing	0.4
Textiles	0.7
Other manufacturing/production	3.9
Professional services	10.5
Finance, insurance and real estate	5.3
Hotels, catering and leisure	2.1
IT services	2.1
Call centres	0.4

(Continued)

Sector (Continued)	Percentage of the respondents
Media	1.1
Retail and wholesale	3.5
Transport, distribution and storage	2.8
Communications	1.4
Other private services	4.2
Private sector services – voluntary, community and not-for-profit	3.2
Private sector services – care services	1.4
Private sector services – charity services	1.8
Private sector services – housing association	0.4
Private sector services – other voluntary	1.1
Central government	0.6
Education	12.6
Health	5.6
Local government	11.6
Other public services	7.4
Voluntary, community and not-for-profit – care services	3.9
Voluntary, community and not-for-profit – charity services	3.9
Voluntary, community and not-for-profit – housing association	4.2
Voluntary, community and not-for-profit – other voluntary	3.2

Organization size	
250 or less	35.4
251–500	9.5
501–1,000	13.7
1,001–5,000	20.7
5,001–10,000	6.7
10,001 or more	10.5

Region	
North-east England	3.9
North-west England	7.7
Scotland	11.6
London	18.2
Yorkshire/Humberside	7.0
Midlands	15.8
Wales	2.8
South-east England	17.9
South-west England	12.3
East of England	5.3
Northern Ireland	1.8

Appendix B: Questionnaire for the State of the Nation study

Exercise: The questionnaire below may be used in replicating the study reported in this chapter. Once similar data is collected the results may be compared with the reported study and similar, different and emergent patterns that the data presents may be discussed in class.

A. Diversity and Equality in Your Organization

Does your organization have a diversity management programme or initiative?

Yes   ☐   No   ☐

Does your organization predominantly use the term a) equality b) diversity c) both interchangeably?

What level was the person who first proposed the idea of equal opportunities and diversity management in your organization?

a) Board of Directors
b) Senior Management
c) Middle Management
d) Junior Management
e) Non-managerial level

Do you have a written diversity management or equal opportunities statement?

a) Yes   If yes, does it specify the consequences of violating the policy?
            Yes/No . . . .
b) No

B. Diversity Unit/Office in Your Organization

Is there a specialised diversity office in your organization?

a) Yes   If yes,   Since which year? . . . .
            How many full-time equivalent persons work in it? . . . .
b) No   If no, is there a plan to open an office in the future? Yes/No . . . .
c) No longer. It was mainstreamed in year . . . . .

Does your organization have someone whose main responsibility is managing diversity/equal employee opportunities?

a) Yes   If yes, to what extent does this person have power and prestige within the organization on a scale of 1 to 9? (1 = with no power or prestige, 9 = with extreme power and prestige)
Scale: . . . .

b) No

Does your organization have someone whose main responsibility is managing work-life balance?

a) Yes   If yes, to what extent does this person have power and prestige within the organization on a scale of 1 to 9? (1 = with no power or prestige, 9 = with extreme power and prestige)
Scale: . . . .

b) No

C. Diversity Strategy in Your Organization

Does your organization have a diversity strategy?

a) Yes, since year . . . . . .   If yes, go to the next question
b) No   If no, go to the next section

What proportion of your staff are involved in drawing up the diversity management strategy in your organization?

		Proportion of staff involved
1	Board members	
2	Senior management	
3	Middle management	
4	Junior management	
5	Non-managerial workers	
6	Trade unionists	

What measures were included in your organization's overall diversity strategy? Please tick all that apply.

Diversity Measures	Initially	Now
Diversity awareness training		
Diversity monitoring system		
Diversity management training		
Diversity as performance criteria		
Rewarding diversity achievements		
Setting diversity targets		
Setting diversity quotas		
Integrating diversity in business strategy		
Monitoring customer diversity		
Employee attitude surveys		
Other: please write . . .		

Has the scope of the diversity strategy changed over time?

a) It has *not* changed
b) It has expanded
c) It has narrowed

What are the drivers behind the introduction and current state of your diversity strategy? Please tick all that apply.

Drivers of Diversity	Initially	Now
Legal pressures		
Social changes		
Changes in the labour market		
Economic and financial considerations		
Shortage of labour supply		
Growth in demand for labour		

Drivers of Diversity	Initially	Now
Desire to increase organizational performance		
Desire to enhance customer relations		
Desire to expand to diverse markets		
Globalisation of business		
Recruiting and retaining best talent		
Belief in social justice		
Desire to do the right thing		
Other: please write . . .		

D. Diversity Policy in Your Organization

Do you have a diversity policy in your organization?

a) Yes, since year . . . . . .
b) No please go to Section E

What are the targeted issues in your diversity policy and activities?

a) gender/sex
b) ethnicity/race
c) sexual orientation
d) age
e) disability
f) nationality
g) religion
h) physical appearance
i) social and economic background
j) spent criminal conviction
k) marital/parental status
l) other: please write . . .

How are employees involved in the design and implementation of diversity policies and practices?

a) employee responses were *not* considered
b) employee consultation via surveys and meetings

c) employee representation on boards
d) feedback from employee groups
e) trade union consultation
f) work-council consultation
g) human resource feedback system
h) other: please write . . .

What actions are taken in order to maximize employee 'buy-in' of diversity policies?

a) employee participation in diversity initiatives
b) communicating diversity message and policy across the organization
c) training and education activities in diversity management
d) diversity policy integrated in performance and strategic management systems
e) employee 'buy-in' is assumed and it was *not* pursued
f) other: please specify

How do diversity management policies or initiatives relate to the overall corporate objectives and strategies?

a) Corporate objectives and strategies are *not* linked with diversity management policies and initiatives
b) Diversity management policies and initiatives are an integral part of the overall corporate objectives
c) Diversity management policies and initiatives are tenuously linked with the corporate objectives

E. Diversity Activities and Monitoring in Your Organization

How do you rate the availability of the below diversity related facilities and activities in your organization?

		Not available					Fully available	
1	Grievance system for harassment and bullying for all	1	2	3	4	5	6	7
2	Disability access	1	2	3	4	5	6	7
3	Child care facilities for all	1	2	3	4	5	6	7
4	Fast-tracking promotion system for diversity	1	2	3	4	5	6	7
5	Career development programme for all	1	2	3	4	5	6	7
6	Flexible hours for all	1	2	3	4	5	6	7
7	Job sharing for all	1	2	3	4	5	6	7
8	Equality and diversity training for all	1	2	3	4	5	6	7
9	Maternity provision	1	2	3	4	5	6	7
10	Paternity provision	1	2	3	4	5	6	7
11	Transparent and formalised system of performance evaluation for all	1	2	3	4	5	6	7
12	Targeted recruitment and retention efforts for diversity	1	2	3	4	5	6	7
13	Community involvement activities	1	2	3	4	5	6	7
14	Work–life balance programme for all	1	2	3	4	5	6	7
15	Mentoring programme for all	1	2	3	4	5	6	7
16	Others: please write . . .	1	2	3	4	5	6	7

To what extent does your organization:

		Not at all					Always	
1	emphasize diversity as part of the organization's mission	1	2	3	4	5	6	7
2	include diversity-related goals in managers' performance assessments	1	2	3	4	5	6	7
3	engage in targeted recruitment of underrepresented groups	1	2	3	4	5	6	7
4	monitor selection rates of underrepresented groups	1	2	3	4	5	6	7
5	make specific efforts to retain members of underrepresented groups	1	2	3	4	5	6	7
6	provide diversity training	1	2	3	4	5	6	7
7	provide mentoring programs for members of underrepresented groups	1	2	3	4	5	6	7
8	provide formal developmental feedback	1	2	3	4	5	6	7
9	assess employee beliefs about the fairness of organizational policies	1	2	3	4	5	6	7
10	monitor pay decisions to ensure fairness to underrepresented groups	1	2	3	4	5	6	7
11	monitor promotions to ensure fairness to underrepresented groups	1	2	3	4	5	6	7
12	monitor incidents of sexual and ethnic harassment	1	2	3	4	5	6	7
13	offer grievance procedures	1	2	3	4	5	6	7
14	others: please write …	1	2	3	4	5	6	7

How are diversity initiatives and profiles evaluated/monitored?

a) diversity is *not* monitored
b) staff profiles are monitored
c) customer profiles are monitored
d) the impact of diversity initiatives is monitored
e) the impact of diversity training is monitored
f) performance outcomes by diversity are monitored
g) other: please specify. . .

If diversity is monitored, who is responsible for monitoring activities?

a) the designated diversity management unit
b) a designated diversity officer
c) human resource manager
d) line management
e) trade union

Are there regular reports regarding the position of diversity?

No   ☐   Yes   ☐

If yes, how regular? Every . . . . . . days/weeks/months/years

Which of employee statistics do you desegregate by the following categories? Please tick all that apply

	Sex	Race/Ethnicity	Age	Sexual orientation	Disability	Nationality	Religion	Others: Please indicate
Recruitment								
Turnover rates								
Performance								
Promotion								
Training								
Pay								
Contract type								
Organizational level								
Grievance								
Harassment and bullying								
Others: please write								

Is data collected on harassment and/or bullying reported in your organization based on the below categories? How frequent are the incidents?

	Harassment and bullying by	Is data collected? (Y or N)	Never				Very frequent		
1	Sex	Yes / No	1	2	3	4	5	6	7
2	Race	Yes / No	1	2	3	4	5	6	7
3	Age	Yes / No	1	2	3	4	5	6	7
4	Sexual orientation	Yes / No	1	2	3	4	5	6	7
5	Disability	Yes / No	1	2	3	4	5	6	7
6	Nationality	Yes / No	1	2	3	4	5	6	7
7	Religion	Yes / No	1	2	3	4	5	6	7
8	Physical appearance	Yes / No	1	2	3	4	5	6	7
9	Social and economic background	Yes / No	1	2	3	4	5	6	7
10	Spent criminal conviction	Yes / No	1	2	3	4	5	6	7
11	Marital status	Yes / No	1	2	3	4	5	6	7
12	Other: please write. . .	Yes / No	1	2	3	4	5	6	7

Are there any follow up mechanisms for assessing the impact of diversity management initiatives?

Yes ☐   No ☐

If yes, which of the below are measured?

a) employees' level of commitment
b) employees' performance
c) employee satisfaction
d) employees' perception of fairness
e) level of organizational performance
f) improvements to creativity, innovation, problem solving and decision making
g) diversification of customer base
h) level of customer satisfaction
i) cost of labour turnover, absenteeism
j) quality of recruitment
k) discrimination lawsuits

F. Diversity of Your Employees and Customer Base

How diverse is your customer base in terms of the below categories? Do you collect data on these categories? Indicate by 'Y' for yes and 'N' for No across from each category.

	Diversity by	Is data collected? (Y or N)	Not diverse						Very diverse
1	Sex		1	2	3	4	5	6	7
2	Race		1	2	3	4	5	6	7
3	Age		1	2	3	4	5	6	7
4	Sexual orientation		1	2	3	4	5	6	7
5	Disability		1	2	3	4	5	6	7
6	Nationality		1	2	3	4	5	6	7
7	Religion		1	2	3	4	5	6	7
8	Physical appearance		1	2	3	4	5	6	7
9	Social and economic background		1	2	3	4	5	6	7
10	Spent criminal conviction		1	2	3	4	5	6	7
11	Marital status		1	2	3	4	5	6	7
12	Other: please write. . .		1	2	3	4	5	6	7

How diverse is your staff profile in terms of the below categories? Do you collect data on these categories? Indicate by 'Y' for yes and 'N' for No across from each category.

	Diversity by	Is data collected? (Y or N)	Not diverse						Very diverse
1	Sex		1	2	3	4	5	6	7
2	Race		1	2	3	4	5	6	7
3	Age		1	2	3	4	5	6	7
4	Sexual orientation		1	2	3	4	5	6	7
5	Disability		1	2	3	4	5	6	7
6	Nationality		1	2	3	4	5	6	7
7	Religion		1	2	3	4	5	6	7
8	Physical appearance		1	2	3	4	5	6	7
9	Social and economic background		1	2	3	4	5	6	7
10	Spent criminal conviction		1	2	3	4	5	6	7
11	Marital status		1	2	3	4	5	6	7
12	Other: please write. . .		1	2	3	4	5	6	7

What proportion of your workers are female, male, white, non-white or with disabilities?

	In your organization	In managerial grades	On your board of directors
Male workers			
Female workers			
White workers			
Non-white workers			
Workers with disabilities			

G. Your Evaluation of Diversity Management in Your Organization

How is the availability and overall success of the diversity related activities in your organization?

		Available? Circle your choice	Very unsuccessful						Very successful
1	. . .diversity management strategy?	Yes / No	1	2	3	4	5	6	7
2	. . .diversity management policies?	Yes / No	1	2	3	4	5	6	7
3	. . .diversity management initiatives?	Yes / No	1	2	3	4	5	6	7
4	. . .diversity management training?	Yes / No	1	2	3	4	5	6	7
5	. . .diversity awareness training?	Yes / No	1	2	3	4	5	6	7
6	. . .diversity monitoring activity?	Yes / No	1	2	3	4	5	6	7
7	. . .employee 'buy-in' for diversity issues?	Yes / No	1	2	3	4	5	6	7
8	. . .management 'buy-in' for diversity issues?	Yes / No	1	2	3	4	5	6	7

Are some groups of employees strong supporters or opponents of diversity efforts than others?

		Strong Opponent				Strong Supporter		
1	Male employees	1	2	3	4	5	6	7
2	Female employees	1	2	3	4	5	6	7
3	Minority ethnic employees	1	2	3	4	5	6	7
4	Majority ethnic employees (White British)	1	2	3	4	5	6	7
5	Workers with disabilities	1	2	3	4	5	6	7
6	Workers *without* disabilities	1	2	3	4	5	6	7
7	Heterosexual workers	1	2	3	4	5	6	7
8	Workers with other sexual orientations	1	2	3	4	5	6	7
9	Older workers	1	2	3	4	5	6	7
10	Younger workers	1	2	3	4	5	6	7

What was the degree of overall organizational resistance and support to the below diversity activities?

		Strong Resistance				Strong Support		
1	diversity management strategy	1	2	3	4	5	6	7
2	diversity management policies	1	2	3	4	5	6	7
3	diversity management initiatives	1	2	3	4	5	6	7
4	diversity management training	1	2	3	4	5	6	7
5	diversity awareness training	1	2	3	4	5	6	7
6	diversity monitoring activity	1	2	3	4	5	6	7

How are the attitudes and behaviours at different levels to diversity issues in the workplace?

		Oppositional				Supportive		
1	The organization	1	2	3	4	5	6	7
2	Board members	1	2	3	4	5	6	7
3	Senior management	1	2	3	4	5	6	7
4	Middle management	1	2	3	4	5	6	7
5	Junior management	1	2	3	4	5	6	7
6	Non-managerial workers	1	2	3	4	5	6	7

How well informed and conscious are the below categories of employees about diversity management issues?

		Uninformed				Well informed		
1	Board members	1	2	3	4	5	6	7
2	Senior management	1	2	3	4	5	6	7
3	Middle management	1	2	3	4	5	6	7
4	Junior management	1	2	3	4	5	6	7
5	Non-managerial workers	1	2	3	4	5	6	7

How much responsibility do the below categories of employees assume in diversity related activities and issues?

		No responsibility				Much responsibility		
1	Board members	1	2	3	4	5	6	7
2	Senior management	1	2	3	4	5	6	7
3	Middle management	1	2	3	4	5	6	7
4	Junior management	1	2	3	4	5	6	7
5	Non-managerial workers	1	2	3	4	5	6	7

What was the level of support and opposition from the below departments and groups to the diversity initiatives?

		Strong opposition					Strong support	
1	Marketing and sales	1	2	3	4	5	6	7
2	Finance and accounting	1	2	3	4	5	6	7
3	Communication and advertising	1	2	3	4	5	6	7
4	Strategic management/corporate strategy	1	2	3	4	5	6	7
5	Human resources	1	2	3	4	5	6	7
6	Manufacturing and production	1	2	3	4	5	6	7
7	Equality and diversity	1	2	3	4	5	6	7
8	Advertising	1	2	3	4	5	6	7
9	Branch network	1	2	3	4	5	6	7
10	Suppliers	1	2	3	4	5	6	7
11	Customers and consumers	1	2	3	4	5	6	7
12	Community	1	2	3	4	5	6	7
13	Shareholders	1	2	3	4	5	6	7

How would you evaluate the impact of diversity management policies and initiatives on the following?

		Negative impact					Positive impact	
1	Employees' attitudes and behaviours in terms of equality and diversity	1	2	3	4	5	6	7
2	Representation of diverse groups at different levels of organization	1	2	3	4	5	6	7
3	Employees' level of commitment	1	2	3	4	5	6	7
4	Perceptions of fairness and justice	1	2	3	4	5	6	7
5	Employee performance	1	2	3	4	5	6	7
6	Employees' job satisfaction	1	2	3	4	5	6	7
7	Cost of labour turnover	1	2	3	4	5	6	7
8	Level of absenteeism	1	2	3	4	5	6	7
9	Quality of recruitment	1	2	3	4	5	6	7
10	Discrimination lawsuits	1	2	3	4	5	6	7
11	Interaction between employees from diverse backgrounds	1	2	3	4	5	6	7
12	Organizational performance	1	2	3	4	5	6	7
13	Creativity and innovation in the organization	1	2	3	4	5	6	7
14	Problem solving and decision making	1	2	3	4	5	6	7
15	Business success with regard to market penetration	1	2	3	4	5	6	7
16	Diversification of customer base	1	2	3	4	5	6	7
17	Level of customer satisfaction	1	2	3	4	5	6	7

How do you rate the competence of workers to deal with diversity issues and manage a diverse workforce effectively?

		Not competent				Fully competent		
1	Board members	1	2	3	4	5	6	7
2	Senior management	1	2	3	4	5	6	7
3	Middle management	1	2	3	4	5	6	7
4	Junior management	1	2	3	4	5	6	7
5	Non-managerial workers	1	2	3	4	5	6	7

H. Career Development in Your Organization

Please rate your level of agreement with each of the following statements: (Please X one ☐ for each)

	Strongly Disagree			Strongly Agree
Training and career development programmes in this organization include a full range of management skills	☐	☐	☐	☐
Information on career development is offered to all employees	☐	☐	☐	☐
All vacant posts within the organization are advertised	☐	☐	☐	☐
Jobs tend to be given to people 'in the know' in this organization	☐	☐	☐	☐
There are opportunities for progression within the organization	☐	☐	☐	☐
Staff receive sufficient information about career opportunities within the organization	☐	☐	☐	☐
The organization supports individual career planning and career development	☐	☐	☐	☐
The organization considers the individual's needs . . .	☐	☐	☐	☐
Flexible working practices (flexi-time, job-share, working from home) are the norm	☐	☐	☐	☐
Secondment opportunities are widely available	☐	☐	☐	☐
The organization is an open environment where all employees have the opportunity to reach their full potential	☐	☐	☐	☐

I. Childcare Facilities in Your Organization

Please rate your level of agreement with each of the following statements: **(Please X one ☐ for each)**

	Strongly Disagree		Strongly Agree	
There is after school or holiday childcare facilities . . .	☐	☐	☐	☐
The organization has good childcare arrangements . .	☐	☐	☐	☐
After school provision is available for all employees . .	☐	☐	☐	☐
All employees can take advantage of these arrangements	☐	☐	☐	☐

J. Work Relationships in Your Organization

Please rate your level of agreement with each of the following statements: **(Please X one ☐ for each)**

	Strongly Disagree		Strongly Agree	
Managers are equipped with adequate skills for dealing with diversity and equality issues	☐	☐	☐	☐
Good time management is encouraged in this organization	☐	☐	☐	☐
Management behaviour reflects organizational values and priorities	☐	☐	☐	☐
Managers listen and motivate employees	☐	☐	☐	☐
Employees who had not had linear career paths are recognised	☐	☐	☐	☐
I feel under pressure to get my work done	☐	☐	☐	☐
Managers are equipped with good skills for recruitment and promotion	☐	☐	☐	☐
Networking opportunities in this organization break down traditional hierarchical barriers	☐	☐	☐	☐
I make use of networks for personal purposes	☐	☐	☐	☐
This organization consults our customers	☐	☐	☐	☐
Our customers treat our employees with respect	☐	☐	☐	☐
I feel there is opportunity for networking with different groups of people within the organization	☐	☐	☐	☐
Networking opportunities in this organization perpetuate traditional hierarchical barriers	☐	☐	☐	☐

K. Equality and Diversity for All in Your Organization

Please rate your level of agreement with each of the following statements:
(Please X one ☐ for each)

	Strongly Disagree		Strongly Agree	
Employment practice in this organization is informed by a commitment to equality for all	☐	☐	☐	☐
This organization ensures all types of employees gain access to training and career development opportunities	☐	☐	☐	☐
The organization encourages equal numbers of men and women in management positions	☐	☐	☐	☐
The management of this organization encourages diversity	☐	☐	☐	☐
My colleagues think favourably about career progression regardless of gender	☐	☐	☐	☐
Equality and diversity are the aims of all the activities within the organization	☐	☐	☐	☐
My colleagues think favourably about the career progression of lesbians and gay men	☐	☐	☐	☐
The population of the area is well represented in the workforce of this organization	☐	☐	☐	☐
Gays and lesbians feel safe to be open about their sexuality in this organization	☐	☐	☐	☐
My colleagues think favourably about the career progression of people from black and minority ethnic groups	☐	☐	☐	☐
The organization values diversity as a way to deliver better services	☐	☐	☐	☐
My colleagues think favourably about career progression regardless of age	☐	☐	☐	☐
The organization supports its suppliers, subsidiaries and affiliates in achieving equality and diversity at work	☐	☐	☐	☐
My colleagues think favourably about the career progression of people with disabilities	☐	☐	☐	☐
The organization responds to a diversity of need	☐	☐	☐	☐
My colleagues think favourably about the career progression of people from different religions	☐	☐	☐	☐
The organization encourages the career progression of people from both genders	☐	☐	☐	☐

	Strongly Disagree		Strongly Agree	
This organization listens to its costumers and involves them in the development of services that recognise and value diversity	☐	☐	☐	☐
The organization encourages the career progression of lesbians and gay men	☐	☐	☐	☐
The organization encourages the career progression of people of all ages	☐	☐	☐	☐
The organization encourages the career progression of people with disabilities	☐	☐	☐	☐
The organization encourages the career progression of people from different religions	☐	☐	☐	☐
The organization encourages the career progression of people from black and minority ethnic groups	☐	☐	☐	☐

L. You and the organization

How satisfied are you with the following? (**Please X one ☐ for each**)

	Extremely Dissatisfied		Extremely Satisfied
Your colleagues	☐	☐	☐
The amount of responsibility you are given	☐	☐	☐
Your line manager	☐	☐	☐
The recognition you get for your work	☐	☐	☐
Your chance of promotion	☐	☐	☐
Your rate of pay	☐	☐	☐
The current appraisal system	☐	☐	☐

Please indicate how important each of the following factors is to you. (**Please X one ☐ for each**)

	Not Important			Very Important	
Reward – pay, conditions and benefits	☐	☐	☐	☐	☐
Recognition – e.g. things that make you feel valued (non-financial)	☐	☐	☐	☐	☐
Fairness – feeling that organizational decisions are made fairly and consistently	☐	☐	☐	☐	☐

	Not Important				Very Important
Training – feeling sufficiently trained for your job	☐	☐	☐	☐	☐
Flexibility – feeling that you have sufficient opportunity to try for other jobs	☐	☐	☐	☐	☐
Worker/Management relations – feeling that you know the names and faces of senior staff and could approach them easily	☐	☐	☐	☐	☐
Support – feeling that management are aware and supportive of any difficulties you encounter in performing your job	☐	☐	☐	☐	☐
Communication – feeling fully informed of what is going on within the organization	☐	☐	☐	☐	☐
Autonomy – feeling trusted to perform your job and use your expertise	☐	☐	☐	☐	☐
Equality – feeling that you have experienced equality of opportunity during your employment with the organization	☐	☐	☐	☐	☐
Diversity – feeling that you work in a multi-cultural environment	☐	☐	☐	☐	☐

M. Your Personal Attitudes

Please rate your level of agreement with each of the following statements:
(Please mark one box for each)

	Strongly Disagree			Strongly Agree
I do this job for the money	☐	☐	☐	☐
I prefer to work to a strictly defined set of working hours	☐	☐	☐	☐
I do not identify with the organization's goals	☐	☐	☐	☐
I expect to be paid for any overtime I do	☐	☐	☐	☐
Having a career means personal development	☐	☐	☐	☐
My long term future does not lie with this organization	☐	☐	☐	☐
Having a career is important to me	☐	☐	☐	☐
Having a career means going up the ladder	☐	☐	☐	☐
I come to work purely to get the job done	☐	☐	☐	☐
I believe in equality and diversity	☐	☐	☐	☐

N. Your Current Role

In which category would you situate yourself?

Executive	☐	Supervisor ☐	Front Line	☐
Senior Management	☐	Officer ☐	Administrative	☐
Middle Management	☐	Junior staff ☐	Trainer	☐

What is the nature of your employment contract? (Please X all the ☐ that apply)

Duration: Permanent ☐   Fixed-Term ☐   Temporary ☐

Hours:

Part-Time (less than 20 hrs/wk)	☐
Jobshare	☐
Contracted hours (between full and part-time)	☐
Full-Time (35 hrs or above)	☐
Condensed hour (full-time weekly hours in fewer than 5 days)	☐
Annualised hours (a certain number of hours in one year)	☐

How many hours are you contracted to work?

Under 10 ☐   10–20 ☐   21–30 ☐   31–35 ☐   Over 35 ☐

How many hours a week are you contracted to work on diversity management?

. . . . hours

Within which salary (yearly) band would you situate yourself?

£0–£10000	☐	£41000–£50000	☐	£81000–£90000	☐
£11000–£20000	☐	£51000–£60000	☐	£91000–£100000	☐
£21000–£30000	☐	£61000–£70000	☐	+ £100000	☐
£31000–£40000	☐	£71000–£80000	☐		

Do you report to the CEO of your company on diversity?

Yes ☐   No ☐

Do you sit in on the corporate strategy meetings?

Yes ☐   No ☐

On a scale of 1 to 9, 1 being the lowest hierarchical rank and 9 being the highest rank within your organization, roughly at what level would your job/position be characterized? Circle your choice.

Yours rank :   1   2   3   4   5   6   7   8   9

On a scale of 1 to 9, 1 being the lowest band of pay and 9 being the highest, of the salaries in your company, within which band does your salary fall?

Your salary band: 1   2   3   4   5   6   7   8   9

How many years (approximately) have you worked for this organization?

Less than a year ☐   1–2 yrs ☐   3–5 yrs ☐   6–10 yrs ☐   +10 yrs ☐

Were you recruited from within the organization?   Yes ☐   No ☐

What is your functional background/training?

a) specific training on equal opportunities and diversity management
b) general management training
c) human resource management training
d) financial management training
e) marketing management training
f) engineering and production management training
g) other professional training: please specify

If you have left a previous job to join this organization, why did you leave?

Restricted career progression	☐	Inadequate salary	☐
Personal reasons	☐	Lack of care/valuing staff	☐
Lack of flexibility within the job	☐	Question not applicable	☐

How many years (approximately) have you been in your current role?

Up to a year ☐   1–2 yrs ☐   3–5 yrs ☐   6–10 yrs ☐   +10 yrs ☐

Have you been promoted since joining this organization?

a) Yes   If yes, how many times have you been promoted?
              1 ☐   2 ☐   3 ☐   +3 ☐
b) No

Have your job responsibilities changed during your current role? (indicate *one* category only)

a) Yes, increased in scope of tasks undertaken ☐
b) Yes, increased number of people I supervise ☐
c) Yes, increased in scope of tasks *and* number of people I supervise ☐
d) Yes, decreased in scope of tasks undertaken ☐
e) Yes, decreased in number of people I supervise ☐
f) Yes, decreased in scope of tasks *and* number of people I supervise ☐
g) No change ☐

If there have been changes in your current responsibilities, what has been the *main* cause of this change? (indicate all that apply)

a) Decision by immediate supervisor ☐
b) Staff leaving the department ☐
c) Staff joining the department ☐
d) Change in organizational structure ☐
e) Self-sought change ☐
f) Change in my personal circumstances ☐
g) Customer/market needs ☐
h) Introduction of new technology ☐
i) No change ☐

Do people report directly to you? If yes, how many people?

0 ☐   1–3 ☐   4–8 ☐   9–15 ☐   16–20 ☐   +21 ☐

How many people are in your team/section/department (including yourself)?

1–10 ☐   11–20 ☐   21–30 ☐   31–40 ☐   41–50 ☐   +50 ☐

How many people are in your organization?

1–20 ☐   21–200 ☐   201–1,000 ☐   1,001–5,000 ☐
5,001–10,000 ☐   +10,000 ☐

O. Your Details

Gender: Male ☐   Female ☐

Age: 16–25 ☐   26–30 ☐   31–40 ☐   41–50 ☐
       51–60 ☐   61–65 ☐   65+ ☐

Ethnicity: Please indicate the box which you feel most nearly describes your ethnic group.
(classification extracted from Census 2001)

White   **Mixed**

British   ☐   White and Black Caribbean   ☐
Other Mixed   ☐
Irish   ☐   White and Black African   ☐
Other White   ☐   White and Asian   ☐

Asian or Asian British   **Black or Black British**

Indian   ☐   Caribbean   ☐
Pakistani   ☐   African   ☐
Bangladeshi   ☐   Other Black   ☐
Other Asian   ☐

Other ethnic groups

Chinese   ☐   Other ethnic group   ☐

Qualifications: Please indicate *all* the qualifications (or their equivalents) that you currently hold.

CSEs/School Certificate   ☐   Masters Degree   ☐
GCE 'A' Levels/BTEC/'Highers'   ☐   Doctorate (PhD, D Phil)   ☐
GCSE/GCE 'O' Levels   ☐   Professional Qualifications ☐
Bachelor Degree (BA/BSc)   ☐   None   ☐

What is your responsibility/job role in relation to diversity and management in this organization?

a) Unit level responsibility   ☐
b) Organizational responsibility   ☐
c) National level responsibility   ☐
d) European level responsibility   ☐
e) International/global level responsibility   ☐

How did you gain the expertise required for your current role in diversity management? **(Please 'X' all choices that apply)**

a) Formal education   ☐   Please specify: . . . . . .
b) In house training   ☐   Please specify: . . . . . .
c) External training   ☐   Please specify: . . . . . .
d) Work experience   ☐   Please specify: . . . . . .

e) Diversity networks   ☐   Please specify: . . . . . .
f) Other   ☐   Please specify: . . . . . .

Are you personally involved in politics?

Yes   ☐   Please specify: . . . . . .
No   ☐

Are you a member of any networks or groups on diversity/equality?

Yes   ☐   Please specify: . . . . . .
No   ☐

Do you have regular contact with the other institutions/companies who are implementing diversity policies and programmes?

Yes   ☐   Please specify: . . . . . .
No   ☐

Do you have other dependants?   Yes ☐   No ☐

Do you have a disability?   Yes ☐   No ☐

If not, go to the next question.

If yes, how would you describe it? (Please 'X' all choices that apply)

I have a specific learning disability (for example, dyslexia)   ☐
I am blind or partially sighted   ☐
I am profoundly or partially deaf   ☐
I am a wheelchair user   ☐
I have Autistic Spectrum Disorder or Asperger's Syndrome   ☐
I have mental health difficulties   ☐
I have an invisible disability, for example, diabetes, epilepsy or
  a heart condition   ☐
I have a disability, special need or medical condition that is
  not listed above   ☐

Do you practise a religion?   Yes ☐   No ☐

If not, go to the next question.

If yes, which one do you practise?

Buddhism   ☐   Judaism   ☐   Other ☐
Christianity ☐   Islam   ☐
Hinduism   ☐   Sikhism   ☐

Please provide us with any additional comments or information that you feel are important to note about management of diversity in your organization:

Thank you very much for your cooperation

Further reading

Harvey, C. and Allard, M.J. (eds) (2002) *Understanding and Managing Diversity*. New Jersey: Prentice Hall.

Kirton, G. and Greene, A. (2000) *The Dynamics of Managing Diversity: A Critical Approach*. Oxford: Butterworth-Heinemann.

Kurowski, L.L. (2002) 'Cloaked Culture and Veiled Diversity: Why Theorists Ignored Early US Workforce Diversity', *Journal of Academic History*, vol. 40, pp. 183–91.

Loirbecki, A. and Gavin, J. (2002) 'Critical Turns in the Evolution of the Diversity Management', *British Journal of Management*, vol. 11, pp. 17–31.

McDougall, M. (1996) 'Equal Opportunities versus Managing Diversity: Another Challenge for Public Sector Management?', *International Journal of Public Sector Management*, vol. 9, no. 5/6, pp. 62–72.

Nyambegera, S.M. (2002) 'Ethnicity and Human Resources Management Practice in Sub-Saharan Africa: The Relevance of the Managing Diversity Discourse', *International Journal of Human Resources Management*, vol. 13, no. 7, pp. 1077–90.

Ratman, C.S.V. and Chandra, V. (1996) 'Sources of Diversity and Challenges before Human Resources Management in India', *International Journal of Manpower*, vol. 17, pp. 76–108.

Sanches, J.I. and Brock, P. (1996) 'Outcomes of Perceived Discrimination among Hispanic Employees: Is Diversity Management a Luxury or Necessity?', *Academy of Management Journal*, vol. 39, pp. 704–19.

▶

Soni, V. (2000) 'A Twenty-first-century Reception for Diversity in the Public Sector: A Case Study', *Public Administration Review*, vol. 60, pp. 395–408.

Stedham, Y.E. and Yamamura, J.H. (2004) 'Measuring National Culture: Does Gender Matter?', *Women in Management Review*, vol. 19, pp. 233–43.

Strydom, J.B and Erwee, R. (1998) 'Diversity Management in a Sample of African Companies', *South African Journal of Business Management*, vol. 29, pp. 1–14.

Tatlı, A., Özbilgin, M., Mulholland, G. and Worman, D. (2006) *Managing Diversity Measuring Success*. London: Chartered Institute of Personnel and Development.

Teicher, J. and Speairtt, K. (1996) 'From Equal Employment Opportunity to Managing Diversity: The Australian Experience', *International Journal of Manpower*, vol. 17, pp. 109–33.

Policy and Practice of Diversity Management at the National Level: Tackling the Gender Pay Gap

5.1 Introduction

Labour market demographics as well as working patterns are ever changing. In our times of economic growth, one of the key changes in the distributive profile of labour markets has been the increased access of previously under-represented groups to work. Although the reasons for this change in labour market composition are multifaceted, skills deficiencies in the labour markets, employers' desire to recruit and retain the best talent, as well as social and legal changes towards greater levels of equality of opportunity, have contributed to an increase in the proportion of female workers in the labour market. Despite legal reforms and social changes, the gender pay gap continues to persist; and the potential and skills of women still remain underutilized due to rigidities in the labour market stemming from occupational segregation, pay discrimination and the traditional organization of work. For instance women working full-time earned 17 per cent less than the men working full-time, based on mean hourly pay, while the gender pay gap between female part-time workers and male full-time workers was 38 per cent in the UK in 2005 (Annual Survey of Hours and Earnings 2005).

The causes of the gender pay gap are varied and complex. Thus, the actions to be taken to reduce it should not be limited to pay discrimination, and they should also tackle its multiple causes, including direct pay discrimination, occupational segregation and the impact of family responsibilities. This chapter provides an exploration of policy and practice of global diversity management at the national level, taking gender pay gap diagnostic checks as an example. The chapter starts with a focus on the UK case, with a summary of the findings of the Equal Pay Review surveys, and then looks at the reasons for the gender pay gap and the business case for a diagnostic check, taken from comparative and international perspectives. We also outline different models and approaches to a possible equality check that have been developed internationally.

In the appendices we provide summaries of diagnostic check tools, and two sets of interview schedules, one developed for providers and another for the users of diagnostic checks, in order to elicit their requirements. The appendices may be used both for further research and in order to facilitate in-class discussions.

5.2   Monitoring and tackling the gender pay gap

In their submission to the Women and Work Commission, the Equal Opportunities Commission (EOC) in the UK pointed out that they remain convinced that employers have some responsibility for closing the pay gap in Britain and that employer action is needed to tackle all three causes of the gap within their control, and not just pay discrimination. Subsequent to the EOC's recommendations, early 2006 was marked with the publication of the long-awaited report of the Women and Work Commission, which was headed up by Baroness Prosser. The report, which was critical of the fact that the gender pay gap has remained wide in the UK, has far reaching implications for the future of the debate in the country, which suffers from one of the widest gender pay gaps amongst all European Union member countries. In the light of these findings, one of the recommendations of Women and Work Commission (2006: 71) is 'the development of a new tool, an equality check, to help employers understand where their contribution might best lie'.

Tackling the gender pay gap is one of the key priorities of the EOC. Within this framework, it launched the 'Valuing Women' campaign and established the Equal Pay Task Force in 1999; it published the *Just Pay* report of the Task Force in 2001; and it launched the Equal Pay Review (EPR) Kit in 2002. In

2001, the EOC set targets that 50 per cent of large organizations should have completed an EPR by the end of 2003 and that 25 per cent of other organizations should have conducted an EPR by the end of 2005. Similarly, the Government has set a target that 45 per cent of large employers should have carried out an EPR by the end of 2008. However, previous EOC research shows that in addition to pay discrimination, there are two other major reasons for the gender pay gap: occupational segregation and the impact of family responsibilities (Olsen and Walby 2004). This section outlines the Equal Pay Reviews and the gender pay gap debate in the UK.

Equal pay reviews

The EOC launched the EPR Kit in 2002 as a tool to tackle the gender pay gap in the UK. Subsequently, it commissioned annual EPR surveys (Neathey *et al.* 2003; Brett and Milsome 2004; Schäfer *et al.* 2005; Neathey *et al.* 2005; Adams *et al.* 2006), the first of which was conducted in 2002, to monitor the rates of progress regarding EPR completion in the organizations in Great Britain. According to these survey results:

- In 2002, 54 per cent of organizations had no plans to carry out an EPR. This figure rose to 68 per cent in 2003 and 2004 surveys, and to 82 per cent in 2005. This reduction in EPR activity can be explained by the introduction of small- and medium-sized organizations in the 2003, 2004 and 2005 samples, and the declining interest in EPRs amongst small employers.
- In 2003, 49 per cent of large employers and 62 per cent of small and medium enterprises (SMEs) had no EPR activity. This compared with 71 per cent of small, 65 per cent of medium and 46 per cent of large employers with no EPR activity in 2004.
- Large organizations were more likely to have an EPR activity than the small (21 per cent in 2004) and medium sized organizations (35 per cent in 2004). However, the EPR activity among the large employers have also stagnated between 2004 and 2005, with only 34 per cent of them stating in 2005 that they had completed an EPR.
- Public sector employers were more likely to have conducted, or be in the process of conducting, an EPR, or to have planned to start one (68 per cent in 2003) compared with employers of the private services sector (37 per cent in 2003) and the manufacturing sector (33 per cent in 2003). In 2005, 28 per cent of public sector employers had their first EPR in progress compared to only 5 per cent of private sector employers.
- Proportions of large organizations with an EPR activity (either having conducted an EPR, or were in the process of conducting one, or planned to do so)

rose from 36 per cent in 2002, to 45 per cent in 2003 and to 54 per cent in 2004.

- The proportion of large organizations that had completed an EPR rose from 15 per cent in 2003 to 33 per cent in 2004 and 34 per cent in 2005.

The evidence from these surveys shows that although considerable progress has been made, particularly in public sector and large organizations following the introduction of the EPR Kit in 2001, EPR activity may now be in decline amongst private sector employers. This calls for the establishing of a stronger business case argument for conducting an EPR as well as raising the awareness among employers regarding the gender pay gap and EOC guidance and recommendations about carrying out an EPR.

Searching for the main drivers of EPR, several studies conducted in recent years have showed that employers who have conducted an EPR were driven by a desire to become employers of choice and that an EPR was seen to make good business sense (Brett and Milsome 2004; Schäfer *et al.* 2005; Neathey *et al.* 2005). Conversely, all of the EOC commissioned EPR surveys suggested that employers with no EPR activity believed that they had already provided equal pay for women and men (Morrell *et al.* 2001; Neathey *et al.* 2003; Brett and Milsome 2004; Schäfer *et al.* 2005; Neathey *et al.* 2005).

In 2002, 60 per cent of the organizations were not aware of the EOC's Equal Pay Review Kit (Neathey *et al.* 2003). Moreover, in 2003 and 2004 surveys the majority of organizations that have conducted an EPR reported designing their own review process, but claimed to follow the EPR process set out in the Equal Pay Review Kit (Brett and Milsome 2004; Schäfer *et al.* 2005). However, case study research conducted by Neathey *et al.* (2005) revealed that the proportion of employers who followed the model strictly was considerably smaller. For instance, only a small minority of organizations that are involved in the case study research checked whether their job evaluation systems (JES) were non-discriminatory or introduced a new JES as a basis for equal work comparisons. This situation led to serious inadequacies in the EPR process (Neathey *et al.* 2005).

Most of the organizations limited their EPR to gender pay differences and did not review the pay differences stemming from other factors such as ethnic origin, age and disability (Neathey *et al.* 2003; 2005). The narrow scope of EPRs which solely rest on gender renders it impossible to monitor and tackle the impact of multiple forms of discrimination on gender pay gap as experienced by female workers from disadvantaged backgrounds. Furthermore, Neathey *et al.* (2005) found that there was a considerable variation among the organizations regarding the coverage of EPRs. Only a few organizations had conducted an EPR with comprehensive coverage whereas the majority of organizations displayed a very limited approach to EPR process. For instance, it is found that coverage of different aspects of remuneration was considerably varied between case study organizations as some organizations limited their EPR only to basic pay. Ironically, unequal access to all aspects of a remuneration package was found to be one of the crucial factors contributing to gender pay gap (Neathey *et al.* 2003; 2005). These findings suggest the necessity of a more standardized and informed approach to EPR in Britain in order to reveal the real extent of the gender pay gap.

Causes of the gender pay gap

Previous EOC research shows that in addition to pay discrimination, there are two other major reasons for the gender pay gap: occupational segregation and impact of family responsibilities. Olsen and Walby (2004) found that the jobs that women work in accounts for 5 per cent of the gender pay gap, with women's employment being concentrated into occupations with high proportions of female workers (10 per cent) and in small- and medium-sized organizations (5 per cent). The majority of female employment (60 per cent) in the UK is concentrated in 10 out of 77 occupations which are mostly low-paid private services occupations (Grimshaw and Rubery 2001). Thus, occupational segregation continues to persist in the UK, with women dominating administrative and secretarial (80 per cent) and personal service jobs (84 per cent) and remaining a minority in professional work. In contrast, men continue to hold the most skilled trades (92 per cent) and process, plant and machine operative jobs (85 per cent) (EOC 2004; Miller and Neathey 2004).

A further 36 per cent of the gender pay gap is associated with lifetime working patterns, including women's shorter full-time employment experience (19 per cent) and longer part-time employment (3 per cent), and more interruptions to their employment for children and family care, in comparison to men's (14 per cent) (Olsen and Walby 2004). Grimshaw and Rubery (2001) observed that nearly 44% of women in the UK work part-time and this largely contributes to the gender pay gap: unlike full-time work which is associated with wage increase in line with the length of service, part-time work is associated with a slight wage reduction in real terms (Olsen and Walby 2004). In 2004, 74 per cent of the women who work part-time stated children and domestic family responsibilities as the main reasons for working part-time (Labour Force Survey 2005). Limited availability of flexible working arrangements and work-life policies in better paid jobs, as well as insufficient maternity and paternal leave entitlement, and limited childcare provisions, disadvantages women due to their disproportionately larger share in caring responsibilities. As a result , women are often locked in temporary or part-time jobs with limited job security and where they are paid 38 per cent less per hour than men in full-time work (Olsen and Walby 2004; EOC 2005a). Furthermore, 45 per cent of part-time female workers are employed in jobs that under-utilize their skills (Green 2005). In order to address these and other realities of segregation and inequality, the Labour Government published the *Fairness at Work* White Paper in 1997 that led to the 1999 Employment Act which includes sections on 'family friendly' practices and labour market flexibility. Similarly, in the spirit of the Lisbon Strategy of 2000, the European Union has recently launched Guidelines for Employment Policies (2005–2008), offering policy guidelines which seek to foster full employment by promoting a new life-cycle approach to work, including better reconciliation of work and private life and support for working conditions that are conducive to active ageing, a term that denotes policies of age and employment through which older citizens are encouraged to remain active participants in the labour market (COM 2005: 141).

Labour market rigidities in terms of occupational segregation (both horizontal and vertical) and organization of work contribute to the gender pay gap, not only through the gender inequality in basic pay rates, but also through reduced access to remuneration, promotion, training and career advancement opportunities. Due to the unequal distribution of family and caring responsibilities between men and women, female workers are more likely to have part-time working contracts compared to male workers. Part-time working in the UK is not only associated with relatively lower-status jobs in comparison to full-time working, but also part-time workers are marginalized and disadvantaged in their organizations in terms of having reduced entitlement to a range of benefits such as unsocial hours premia, pension contributions, performance-related pay and bonuses, having fewer prospects for career advancement and limited access to training and career advancement opportunities (Grimshaw and Rubery 2001; Neathey *et al.* 2003). Furthermore, payment of bonuses and performance-related pay, as well as training opportunities, tend to be uncommon in occupations where women's employment is concentrated. Similarly, the 'glass ceiling' continues to persist as an invisible barrier to the progress of women into senior posts in their organizations. According to the findings of the *Annual Survey of Hours and Earnings* (2005) only a third of managers and senior officials are female and, even then, women are often employed in lower paid branches of management, such as personnel and marketing management, compared to their male counterparts who tend to be employed as senior managers and senior officials in the same professions and branches. This situation supports Olsen and Walby's (2004) refutation of the simplistic assumption that relates the gender pay gap to lower levels of human capital (experience, skills and qualifications) held by women. However, as explained above, female workers are disadvantaged in the processes by which human capital is acquired due to occupational segregation and the impact of family responsibilities (Olsen and Walby 2004).

As these research findings suggest, the causes of the gender pay gap are multidimensional. Thus, the actions to be taken to reduce the gender pay gap should not be limited to pay discrimination and should also tackle the other two causes of the pay gap: occupational segregation and the impact of family responsibilities. However, gender pay discrimination may not be studied in isolation from other forms of discrimination.

The EOC's submission to the Women and Work Commission argued that action across all these causes was stalling (EOC 2005b):

- Equal pay reviews are being carried out by leading-edge employers and are on the business agenda, but the voluntary approach to pay reviews has stalled. Two-thirds of employers have no plans to carry out equal pay reviews; and the proportion was the same in 2004 as in 2002 and 2003.
- Other discrimination remains unacceptably high – for example, 30,000 working pregnant women are losing their jobs each year because of discrimination, and 45 per cent of pregnant women at work experience some form of discrimination.
- There has been little or no change over the last ten years in the proportion of women in areas like construction and engineering.
- Despite the growth in part-time working, part-time working is still overwhelmingly concentrated in low paid occupations and the part-time pay gap remains the same as it was 30 years ago.

The EOC's proposal was for a new duty on private sector employers to eliminate discrimination and promote equality. In practice this obligation to take action to close the pay gap would require employers to carry out a simple, speedy check to enable them, in consultation with the workforce, to establish whether they have a gender pay gap and where they should target action. This 'equality check' would need to identify the scale of the gap and consider vertical and horizontal segregation, like work and work of equal value and any other causes, in order to have evidence of what action employers need to take and the ability to target action appropriately.

The Women and Work Commission considered the case for making pay reviews mandatory, but commissioners were divided on the issue and so unable to make a recommendation. The Commission did, however, identify a number of practical proposals that might make a difference in the workplace, including the EOC's proposal for an equality check. They identified the potential advantages of such an approach are that it would enable employers to focus quickly on areas that call for action whilst giving them flexibility in terms of what action to take.

5.3 The business case for a diagnostic equality check

The Women and Work Commission failed to reach a consensus on whether to recommend making EPRs mandatory through legislation. In developing a case for mandatory EPRs, it stated that 'many stakeholders reported managerial ambivalence and even hostility towards EPRs . . . Some managers simply feel that EPRs are a diversion from business aims with no significant contribution to increasing profits and competitiveness' (Women and Work Commission 2006: 80). On the other hand research from the countries with mandatory EPRs in place show that conducting an EPR does not always lead to necessary adjustments to pay systems by the employers, and neither does it lead to an automatic reduction in the gender pay gap (Human Resources Centre of Canada 2001; Pay Equity Task Force Final Report 2004). Furthermore, one of the key stakeholders in the UK, the CBI, displays disapproval of an idea of compulsory EPRs, claiming that 'the nature of pay gap is such that it would not be sensible for all employers to undertake a pay review and could well distract employer and government focus and resources away from tackling the causes of the gender pay gap' (cited in Women and Work Commission 2006: 82). Within that framework, some of the commissioners of the Women and Work Commission argue against compulsory EPRs and support 'a voluntary risk-based approach, where employers only undertake EPRs if they perceive a risk of unlawful discrimination' (Women and Work Commission 2006: 81). In this climate, it seems crucial to develop a diagnostic equality check which may pave the way for convincing the employers to proactively undertake EPRs as well as to make other adjustments to tackle all three causes of the gender pay gap. Accordingly, it is important to develop a convincing business case for a diagnostic equality check.

In the current social and economic context of the UK, effective management of equality and diversity is not a choice but a requisite for any workforce strategy. The reality which faces the business corporations of all sizes and types is the diversity of their customers and human resources. The image of an employee pool composed of white, able bodied, heterosexual males does not hold true anymore. Rather, the figures show that the workforce of the 21st century is becoming more and more diverse with respect to racial or ethnic origin, gender, age, sexual orientation and political and religious belief. Indeed this bare reality of the diversification of the labour market is one of the main mottos that underlies the need for proactive and progressive equality and diversity programmes and policies, which draw on business case as well as ethical or justice case arguments.

5.4 Existing models of and approaches to an equality check

There is a wide range of tools that are developed to audit equality and diversity. The nature of these tools varies extensively by organizational size, sector and industry, and by national considerations, including the legislation and the dynamics of industrial relations. Diagnostic checks are not always termed as such. Tools, instruments, models, monitoring activities, assessment, as well as interventions, are some alternative terms that share common characteristics with diagnostic checks. There are also successful examples of diagnostic methods developed in other aspects of work as well as equality and diversity.

In this chapter 'diagnostic check' is used as a term to refer to ways in which a social–organizational issue is monitored; and based on this monitoring a number of strengths and weaknesses are identified and prescriptions are offered to attend to the weaknesses. This section provides an assessment of these diagnostic checks in equality and diversity as well as in other areas of work. Appendix A provides a summary of each diagnostic check that we have considered in this project.

Information on diagnostic checks in the field of equality and diversity is very fragmented and often partial. It was not possible, for example, to identify with precision who the tool is aimed at, the resources needed to do it, how interactive it is, the take-up, the cost, how long it takes, the existence of a support network of advisers, whether it provides a score and action plan, and if it offers accreditation or an award. The key reason for the fragmented nature of the data on these diagnostic checks was the competitive and crowded nature of the diagnostic checks in the field of diversity and equality. Indeed, all of our respondents have noted that the market is saturated with diagnostic check systems which are in direct competition with one another for potential users. This competition causes the providers to protect information such as the fee, potential market for the tool, current number and profile of the users, the length, content and scope of some of the tools. All of this information was considered sensitive by the providers. Nevertheless, we were able to identify three key attributes – coverage, format and sector – for each diagnostic check that we have studied. **Tables 5.1 and 5.2** outline the tools that we have reviewed across these three attributes.

The tables provide this information for 22 tools for diagnostic checking, benchmarking and auditing in the field of equality and diversity, and nine tools for guidance and information on the field. We have clustered the information on diagnostic checks, benchmarking and auditing tools in the same category, as these terms are often used interchangeably in practice. Our assessment of the first category of tools identifies much variance by coverage across these tools. Whilst 12 of the tools provided coverage on all strands of equality and diversity, the other tools focused either on individual aspects or a limited range of multiple strands of diversity. Coverage in terms of focus on business processes was highly variable. Three quarters of the tools focus on processes of human resource management, whilst there are tools which stretch the diversity focus to fields such as service delivery, strategy formulation, change management and trade union organization issues.

Table 5.1 Tools for audit, diagnostic and benchmarking

Tool	Coverage	Format	Sector
1 Balanced Score Card	Business processes, outcomes and activities	Self-assessment, voluntary	All sectors
2 Breakthrough	Gender, HRM	External audit, voluntary	SMEs
3 The Diversity Driver	Diversity management: customer base, internal workforce	Self-assessment, voluntary	All sectors
4 Developing Services for Minority Ethnic Older People: Audit Tool by the Department of Health	Minority ethnic, older workers: workforce and service delivery	Diagnostic questionnaire and action template: self-assessment	Health services sector
5 DiverCity Audit (Recruitment and Employment Confederation, REC)	Generic	Self-assessment and external audit	Recruitment sector
6 Diversity Diagnostic (Recruitment and Employment Confederation, REC)	Generic	Self-assessment, online	Recruitment sector
7 Diversity @ Work Toolkit	Diversity management disadvantage in labour market HRM issues	Self-assessment	Ireland, Greece, Netherlands and Poland; all sectors
8 Diversity Excellence Model (DEM)	Diversity management: link diversity to bottom line	Self-assessment	All sectors
9 EFQM Business Excellence Model	Quality benchmark	Self-assessment	All sectors
10 Equality standard for local government	Race, sex, disability	Self-assessment and external audit	Local government

No.	Tool	Focus	Method	Sector
11	Everyone is Welcome at Tesco Audit Tool	All strands of equality: Balanced Score Card approach	Self-assessment	Retail sector
12	Health and Safety Diagnostic Check	Health and Safety	Point checks and self-assessment	All sectors
13	International Personnel Association Diagnostic Check	Diversity management best practice benchmarking	Self-assessment	Public service sector
14	Investors in Diversity	Diversity: HRM and culture	External audit	All sectors
15	Investors in People	Training and development	External audit	All sectors
16	NHS Wales (2003) Equality Audit Tool	All strands, HRM	External audit and self-assessment	Health services sector
17	Opportunity Now Benchmarking Tool	Gender	External audit	All sectors
18	Race for Opportunity Benchmarking Tool	Race	External audit	All sectors
19	Racial Equality Means Business – a standard for racial equality for employers	Race	Self-assessment	All sectors
20	Stand up for us: challenging homophobia in schools – NHS Schools Homophobia Self-Review Tool	Sexual orientation	Self-assessment checklist	Education sector
21	The Grimsby Institute of Further and Higher Education Tool	Diversity management; change management	Online audit	Education sector
22	Trades Union Congress Collective Bargaining and Equality Audit Tool	All strands of equality; all union activities	External audit	Trade unions

Table 5.2 Summary of diversity and equality tools

1 Directing Equal pay in ICT (DEPICT)	Equal pay	Information	ICT
2 Diversity Benchmarking Group	Diversity	Information, guidance	All sectors
3 The CIPD Change Agenda	Diversity management: all strands, all processes	Information and Guidance	All sectors
4 Diversity Dividend	Diversity management	Online development system of guidance	All sectors
5 Equality and diversity in adult and community learning: a guide for managers	Inclusive learning, equality and diversity	Information	Local authority
6 Equal Opportunities Guidance from Government Office for London	Legislation	Information	Government office
7 National Council for Voluntary Organizations Equal Opportunities Checklist	Generic equal opportunities	Web-based check-list	Voluntary service sector
8 The Athena Swan Charter	Gender, HRM	Guidance and information	Higher education
9 The Jive Development Partnership	Sex segregation	Cooperative learning activities	Male-dominated sectors

Half of the tools in the study use self-assessment as the format of diagnostic check. The rest of the tools are driven by external audit. Nevertheless, all the tools that are designed around external audit allow for a measure of self-assessment for their users. Ten out of 22 tools are offered to organizations in all sectors. Twelve of the tools are specifically offered to one sector or a cluster of sectors. Diagnostic checks in equality and diversity are not unique to the UK alone. Indeed, there are successful examples of diagnostic checks in other countries.

Sweden

One of the central considerations for the effectiveness of the diagnostic check tools is the role of the State and the law. The success of the Swedish law in engendering real changes towards gender parity in pay deserves particular attention:

> Section 10 of the Equal Opportunities Act concerns wage surveys and analysis, and states that the purpose is to identify, rectify and prevent unwarranted differentials in pay and other terms of employment between women and men. Swedish legislation distinguishes itself in a number of ways in an international comparison. For example, pay differentials that are identifiable but cannot be explained, either on an individual level or a group level, shall be calculated and rectified as soon as possible but at the latest within three years (Section 11). In this connection, it is interesting to note that pressure can be used by ordering fines if gender equality plans or wage surveys do not comply with the law (Sections 34 and 35). Since wage surveys must be carried out every year, JamO has made it practice to no longer grant an extension of more than six months. Since 2001, the trade union organizations on central or branch level may apply to order fines. This change in the law was seen as an opportunity to vitalize the participation of local trade unions in wage survey work. (JamO 2005: 3)

As the Swedish experience reveals, the legal and national context in which the pay gap is combated would have a significant impact on the effectiveness of any tools that are designed for this purpose. Our study reveals that the UK lacks strong legal support and powers that the Swedish legal system affords to its national agency of equality and diversity.

Australia

Examples of relevant guidelines produced by the Human Rights and Equal Opportunity Commission is the The Equal Pay Handbook which provides guidance to employers on their obligations under the equal remuneration provisions of the Workplace Relations Act 1996 (ILO 2006). The Equal Pay

Handbook is designed to assist employers to meet their obligations under federal industrial and anti-discrimination legislation. It is also relevant to employees, equity practitioners and unions. It contains essential equal remuneration principles, explanatory material, case law, case studies and an equal remuneration audit methodology. The Handbook is intended to contribute to an understanding of pay equity and the implementation of equal remuneration in the workplace.

Section 1 explains the concept of equal remuneration and discusses the relevant legislation. Section 2 examines equal remuneration in practice by looking at a number of equal remuneration problem areas: lack of transparency in pay systems, discretionary payments, allowances, performance payments, superannuation, and the impact of hours of work and market value. The section begins with a discussion of the pay-setting context and the equal pay situation in Australia. Throughout, sets of principles are included which, if adhered to, will help ensure that men and women doing work of equal value receive the same remuneration. Section 3 discusses the objective appraisal of jobs and highlights areas of potential sex discrimination in job evaluation systems. Section 4 is an equal remuneration audit methodology, designed to enable employers to carry out in-house assessments of their compliance with the requirements of the equal remuneration legislation.

The Pay Equity Tool of the Australian Government's Equal Opportunities for Women in the Workplace Agency (EOWA) is an analysis tool to assist individuals identify pay inequities in their organization. The tool provides information and guidance on pay equity and the business case for pay equity. The tool also allows individuals to run a diagnostic check of their organization in terms of pay equity and a payroll analysis. There are also case studies and detailed information to guide the users. The tool benefits from a step-by-step guide to implementation. It contains a set of simple and straightforward questions. It offers specific guidelines based on answers. However, the tool also suffers from some weaknesses. It focuses on gender pay equity. However, other strands of diversity are not paid due attention. Therefore, the tool is rather specialized and focused on gender.

Canada

In 1991, the former Department of Human Resources Development Canada launched the Equal Pay Program, a major review of pay equity compliance by federally regulated employers. The Equal Pay Program applies to employers covered by the Canada Labour Code, that is, all federally regulated companies, regardless of size. The wider jurisdiction of the Canadian Human Rights Act includes all companies covered by the Canada Labour Code plus all federal Crown corporations and the federal public service (ILO 2006).

This programme is a proactive approach which gives employers an opportunity to understand and implement pay equity. A three-step process is used in order to determine employer compliance and respond to non-compliance:

- Education – an educational visit from regional Labour Affairs Officers to inform employers of their obligations and the means by which to fulfil these obligations.
- Monitoring – visits to the same employers to verify progress, obtain general information and answer any questions.
- Audit/inspection (on-site inspection) – if the Equal Pay Inspector identifies reasonable grounds for believing that gender-based wage discrimination exists, then the case is referred to the Canadian Human Rights Commission (see the chapter on Legislative and Administrative Institutions) for investigation and resolution. Audits verify that the actions taken by employers to implement pay equity have placed them in compliance with the law.

The Canadian model offers a comprehensive and sophisticated model of diagnostic checks, as it is backed up by a strong legal provision and provides much support to the organizations in the process of diagnostic checks.

The Netherlands

The Dutch model is policy driven. Equal Pay Action Plan 2000 sets out policies which are administered by the Ministry of Social Affairs and Employment. These policies are underpinned by these research findings (ILO 2006):

- Equal pay is strongly correlated to the general process of women's emancipation.
- Development of an instrument with which job evaluation schemes can be tested for sex-neutrality.
- Research on whether/how equal pay can be guaranteed when new, more individual and flexible pay schemes are introduced.
- Publicity for equal treatment and equal pay legislation. This campaign will be partly based on the European equal pay code of practice.
- Works councils, which have the legal duty to monitor the equality of men and women in their companies, will be targeted by a campaign especially directed at members.
- Social partners will be stimulated to take up the issue of equal pay by being provided with extensive information on the topic being included in the agenda of the regular meetings between the social partners and the Cabinet. In addition, the Government will ask the Labour Foundation and its equivalent in the public sector, the ROP, for advice on the problem.

- The Government will offer to pay social partners for voluntary audits of their job evaluation systems.
- The Labour Inspectorate will continue to research this issue on a regular basis.

  If there is not enough progress, the Plan proposes measures such as formal standards and investigations under the Equal Treatment Act.

The Ministry of Social Affairs and Employment has the aim of ensuring that the works council:

- puts the subject of equal pay on its own agenda and draws it to the attention of employers and employees alike;
- examines whether there is unequal pay (contrary to the law) in its own organization and, if so, informs the employer of the unequal pay; and,
- in the event of unequal pay, takes concerted action with the employer to introduce equal pay in accordance with the law.

The US

Pay equality efforts in the US seek to raise the awareness of the organization as well as individual women about the gender pay gap and how this may be addressed. The Women's Bureau of the Department of Labor in the US has issued a number of publications to guide employers and female workers in implementing equal pay, including for instance:

- Ten Steps to an Equal Pay Self-Audit for Employers – a guide for employers in laying down equal pay policies; and,
- Working Women's Equal Pay Checklist – offered to educate women about the steps they can take to achieve equal pay.

Comparative insights

After studying a range of eight measures for equality and diversity from Ireland, the Netherlands, France, Sweden and the UK, Berge et al. (2004) draw some interesting conclusions:

1 instruments which have an influence on the processes of decision-making are more effective than instruments that only apply external constraints to this process;
2 instruments which involve cooperation between stakeholders are more successful than others which do not, because the stakeholder involvement enhances the impact of initiatives;

3   successful instruments recognize and capture variation across size and scope of organizations;

4   instruments of change which provide route maps with tool-kits, diagnostic checks and models can help enhance employers' understandings of processes and issues of equality and diversity;

5   a single body may provide a stronger force for change towards equality, uniting all strands of equality and diversity;

6   pay equality instruments should be designed in a way which captures the reality of reporting systems in organizations.

Our findings in this study also concur with some of those above. However, we have shown that the currently available tools do not provide an adequate response to the recommendations of either the above report or our conclusions. As **Tables 5.1 and 5.2** suggest, the available diagnostic check, benchmarking, information and guidance tools only present a partial coverage in terms of their reach across the UK industry, the strands of equality and diversity that they cover and their format, that is self-assessment versus externally audited and sectoral coverage. Indeed, absence of a generic national diagnostic tool which has been widely adopted has been a key reason why this research has been commissioned by the EOC.

5.5   Conclusion

In this chapter, we have demonstrated that diagnostic checks are replacing equal pay reviews in recognition of the fact that gender pay gaps have multiple causes. Currently, the diagnostic checks in equality and diversity are adopted by organizations voluntarily without the force of law. The main drivers for voluntary take-up of diagnostic check initiatives have been varied. These included the business case, the moral case and legal compliance arguments. There are several commercially available tools which are based on the business case. The successful diagnostic check models in this category are integrated and mainstreamed into all business processes and activities, including organizational strategy and performance management and reward systems. However, the main weakness of diagnostic checks that depend on voluntaristic business case arguments is that they may be abandoned once the business case reasons that have brought them to the business context are no longer available. For example, whilst labour and skills shortages deem diversity and equality significant business concerns, if there is no shortage in the labour market, organizations may not choose to take up diagnostic checks that rest on business case arguments. Furthermore, the business case arguments may be in conflict with the minimum requirements of law.

Relying on a single argument, that is business, social or compliance arguments, often deems the success of diagnostic checks partial. Successful models of diagnostic checks are sensitive to the varied arguments of support. The trend in the industry is to use tools of diagnostic check that explore issues of gender, ethnicity and disability. Diagnostic checks are rare in other strands of equality due to the fact that the other strands have entered the legal framework in the UK relatively more recently when compared to the classical strands. It is nevertheless important to offer a tool which encompasses all the strands. Examples of this are the tools that are developed under the banner of 'diversity diagnostic'. It is, however, important to note that even in more sophisticated tools, gender and ethnicity often serve as cross-cutting themes around which other strands of equality and diversity are explored. This trend gives a feeling of hierarchy across categories of diversity. This is not a very positive development as each strand of equality brings with itself a unique set of issues and only very cross-cutting concerns. Therefore, hierarchical organization of diagnostic checks may indeed marginalize the concerns of strands that are subsumed under the main strands.

Diagnostic tools are available in different formats including paper-based, web–based, as well as electronic-media, formats. Whilst some of the formats are based on a set of questions, examples of good practice or criteria for performance and others involve auditors to request evidence and documentation. There are also tools which are provided in a wider range of formats and offer all of the above aspects. Availability of different formats improves the accessibility of the tools, deeming their delivery sensitive to sectoral, occupational and other contextual variations.

Diagnostic tools are provided by a diverse range of organizations including learned membership organizations, government agencies, universities, funding bodies, large employers, public, private and voluntary sector networks, university research centres and consultancies. Some of these organizations provide diagnostic tools that specifically focus on one or several strands of diversity or equality, whilst others provide generic tools. They demonstrate variable degrees of success in terms of their reach to organizations. Due to the commercial value of the tools, access to certain tools is limited to payment of membership fees. However, other organizations choose to make their tools available free of charge. Furthermore, some other tools are offered as part of a badge or pledge, and compliance is measured through a system of audits, for which a charge is levied.

Some diagnostic checks aim to simply document equality, diversity or discrimination in work settings. There are also other checks which transcend data collection efforts and also provide measures and criteria for change, based on a survey of responses. Yet other tools also incorporate ways of assessing the impact of the implementation of plans of change and offer methods of feedback loops to change strategic plans of change.

The diversity of drivers, processes, formats, outcomes and audits of diagnostic check systems requires us to inspect closely which diagnostic checks are more effective means of organizational diagnostic and change. The review of diagnostic check tools suggests that sophisticated and successful diagnostic checks have some common characteristics:

1   they draw on multiple drivers for adoption, including legal compliance, business case and moral arguments;
2   they incorporate a survey instrument, provide examples of and criteria for good or best practice, as well as an audit system which may lead to a badge or a pledge;
3   they are made available through a wide range of media; and
4   they incorporate a survey instrument which informs action plans and offers mechanisms of organizational action, feedback, and monitoring and impact assessment activities.

In the next chapter, we will present the views and expectations of different stakeholders in terms of an equality diagnostic check.

Appendix A: Summary of currently available tools

Exercise: Compare and contrast the strands of diversity and equality that the below tools involve. Critically examine inclusion and exclusion of each strand.

It is possible to categorize the currently available tools on equality and diversity across their uses as (I) tools for audit, diagnostic and benchmarking; and (II) tools for guidance and information tools.

I   Tools for audit, diagnostic and benchmarking

1   Balanced Score Card

Balanced Score Card (BSC), as proposed by Kaplan and Norton (1996), is an internal benchmarking tool which serves for the purpose of focusing attention on business processes, outcomes and activities that are of import for the organization as well as its external constituents. The BSC integrates both qualitative and quantitative measures of equality and diversity, linking them firmly to the strategic objectives of the organization. The tool suggests that each aspect of the organizational process should be integrated with the others in order to create a sense of joined-up thinking across organizational processes, aims and objectives. Equality and diversity dimensions have been linked to the BSC in many large private sector organizations in the UK. In practice, this manifested itself as a set of objective measures. Organizations which use the BSC as their orientating tool for integrating their equality and diversity strategies are able to demonstrate unambiguously how and to what extent their equality objectives have been achieved. One concern over the implementation of the BSC in terms of diagnosing equality and diversity has been the variable nature of the significance that is attributed to equality and diversity issues in the UK. Should equality be perceived as less relevant to business success, it runs the risk of being excluded from the BSC practice. Thus the concern is that of sustainability of equal opportunities initiatives as part of the BSC process.

2 Breakthrough

Manchester Metropolitan University Business School (MMUBS) has developed an interactive software-based diagnostic tool (Breakthrough) that seeks to measure gender-based EO practice in SMEs. It was funded by the European Social Fund and aimed to promote the business case for gender-based and other forms of equality, and to aid SME development and education by diagnosing organizations' individual strengths and weaknesses in their gender equality practices. Eighty eligible organizations (with fewer than 250 employees each) took part. The diagnostic check has highlighted deeply rooted problems of gender equality in the SME sector and generated an individually tailored report to each organization that benchmarked them against minimum legal requirements, the Equal Opportunity Commission's best-practice guidelines and the average performance of other organizations of similar size. The Breakthrough tool offers a method by which SMEs can be assessed in terms of their legal compliance. However, the tool focuses solely on gender based equality and it has not been widely adopted.

3 The Diversity Driver

The Diversity Driver is a structured self-assessment tool for organizations to benchmark where they are in terms of diversity management. It has been developed by The Back to Work Company, BQC Performance Management Ltd and the Fair Play Partnership, with support from Yorkshire Forward. Like the Diversity Excellence Model (DEM), it is also based upon the European Foundation for Quality Management (EFQM) Excellence Model and provides a baseline upon which to build plans and check progress regarding diversity management. It focuses on the customer base of the organization as well as the internal workforce. The driver enables organizations to identify their strengths and weaknesses in the field of diversity so as to prioritize areas for action. The Diversity Driver targets all sorts of organizations by type and size, including small and large organizations, public, private and voluntary sector organizations.

4   Developing Services for Minority Ethnic Older People: Audit Tool by the Department of Health

Designed in a way which reflects the National Service Framework for Older People (Department of Health 2001) and the Race Relations (Amendment) Act 2000, this audit tool has been prepared by the Department of Health to act as practice guidance for all councils with social services responsibilities, and other local stakeholders aiming to improve services for minority ethnic older people. It includes a diagnostic questionnaire and an action plan template, both of which improve services for minority ethnic older people. The audit tool is intended for use by lead council officers for social care for older people, and a number of key stakeholders that the Department of Health strongly suggests be involved in the overall process. The key stakeholders include: councils with housing responsibilities, the local NHS, local voluntary organizations with interests in minority ethnic older people, individual users and representatives of minority ethnic older people, and local providers of social care services. The diagnostic questionnaire allows councils, along with key stakeholders, to examine and review their current service arrangements for these people. It is not a pass/fail checklist; rather, it is a simple but effective way of assessing the adequacy of the help offered to minority ethnic older people, and to initiate thinking about areas where further progress is needed. The diagnostic questionnaire is structured around four major sections that cover fundamental issues associated with improving services. The sections are: (1) understanding minority ethnic older people's issues; (2) minority older people and access; (3) services; and (4) providing a suitable workforce.

5   DiverCity Audit (Recruitment and Employment Confederation, REC)

The REC is planning to start auditing their members in the area of diversity and equality by 2007. At the time of research, they were in the process of finalizing the draft audit scheme and piloting it. The DiverCity Audit will require agencies to demonstrate their compliance with equality legislation. The DiverCity diagnostic is tailored in-line with the size of the agency. The levels of the diagnostic become more demanding depending on the size of the company. Different sets of questions are asked depending on whether the organization has up to 49 staff or more than 50. The tool has fewer questions for small organizations and more sophisticated expectations are placed on larger organizations. Hence the agencies with less than 50 employees need to demonstrate that they meet minimum requirements (Level 1), whereas agencies with 50 or more employees are required to meet more comprehensive criteria (Level 2). At both levels the DiverCity diagnostic covers religion and belief, gender, sexuality, disability, ethnicity, age and ex-offenders, and it investigates integration of diversity and equality issues throughout various processes and policies of the agencies. The areas that are assessed by the audit include: equal opportunities policy; recruitment, selection, training, promotion, discipline and dismissal; anti-harassment policy; adjustment and accommodation for the candidates with disabilities; equality training for managers and any staff responsible for recruitment and selection; vacancy advertisements; communicating the equal opportunities policy; monitoring; record keeping during the recruitment and selection process. Additionally, there is a third level for the 'diversity champions', that is for the companies of all sizes who wish to mainstream DiverCity within their overall corporate strategy. At this level, the audit aims to identify the business case for diversity for the individual agency in question and to provide the agency with practical recommendations and an action plan tailored to its needs and circumstances. The third level of the DiverCity audit covers: management and leadership; resourcing the commitment; policy, planning and strategy; recruitment, retention and work life balance; training and development; internal communications; marketing and community engagement; procurement and supplier diversity; and monitoring and evaluating the impact. However, one of the weaknesses of this tool remains its partial attention to the issue of flexible working and work–life balance issues.

6 Diversity Diagnostic (Recruitment and Employment Confederation, REC)

The REC also offers a diversity diagnostic check, which is a voluntary measure that is available via the REC website. The diagnostic check is open to all organizations and accessible to agencies of all sizes including small-sized organizations. Organizations can freely turn to this page to assess their current practices in terms of diversity. The diagnostic aims to help the recruitment agencies 'to become more inclusive organizations' and investigates the levels in which equality and diversity issues are addressed throughout the different operations of an agency. The areas covered in the diagnostic are advertising, selection, monitoring and training. Upon the completion of the diagnostic, a score-based assessment is offered and a corresponding action plan is provided for the organization.

The Diversity Diagnostic also includes a business case for equality and diversity. The business benefits of diversity as given by the diagnostic are:

- increased customer satisfaction;
- more effective marketing strategies;
- increased market share;
- being an employer of choice;

- lower staff turnover;
- enhanced PR;
- increased productivity;
- increased creativity and innovation;
- enhanced ability of problem solving;
- being a best practice organization; and
- operating within the law.

The diagnostic also points out the changing demographics in the labour market in terms of ageing population, increasing number of women, migrant workers and people from diverse cultural backgrounds in the labour market. It concludes that in our times of skill shortages in many sectors and regions in the UK, the recruitment agencies should look at diverse sources of labour which will also help them to meet the needs of their clients whose workforces are becoming more diverse as well. The REC tool is a very effective self-assessment tool that helps organizations to put their current efforts in diversity into a critical perspective. However, the voluntary nature of the tool means that organizations should already value diversity in order to engage with this tool.

7   Diversity @ Work Toolkit

DiManT is a 24-month pilot project being undertaken by partners from Ireland, Greece, the Netherlands and Poland. It targets the development of practices to facilitate access to employment for people most disadvantaged in the labour market. The project aims to identify existing tools for the development and implementation of diversity policy in the workplace, generate requirements on the needs for enhanced tools in the area, field test the diversity management toolkit, disseminate the toolkit widely to policy-makers, trainers and practitioners and develop an online version of the training course and toolkit and a European Website for diversity management.

The toolkit will address the needs of minorities in gaining access to employment by training people who either directly or indirectly facilitate access to employment. The project will train significant stakeholders who are responsible for the integration of marginalized groups. These stakeholders include: human resource managers, trade unions and policy-makers in the workplace. The toolkit has two main parts. It offers descriptions of a five-stage process for implementing diversity management which includes getting started; identifying problems and opportunities; organizing solutions; implementation; and evaluation and consolidation. These stages are made up of a number of activities, each of which is described in detail. A set of tools which supports each of these phases of activities is provided. Getting started is concerned with setting up the diversity management project in an efficient way. It deals with issues such as marketing the programme, developing support for the programme, setting up a project team, scoping the project and developing reporting relationships. Identifying problems and opportunities is concerned with assessing the needs and opportunities for diversity management in the organization, assessing exciting activities in the area of diversity management and identifying new issues for incorporation into the developing diversity management programme. Organizing solutions is aimed at the problems and opportunities which have been identified previously. The activities of this phase enable the organization to develop and plan the diversity management programme which has been tailored to the needs of the workplace. The implementation phase describes the activities that the organization will need to undertake in order to implement their diversity management programme. It deals with such issues as the creation of workplace policy in the area, the development and implementation of training and the raising of awareness amongst employees of diversity management. The evaluation and consolidation phase aims to integrate the diversity management programme into general HRM policy and practice. It does so through establishing monitoring and evaluation mechanisms for each stage of the process of implementation. This enables the programme to be improved and for its integration into general organizational practice.

The toolkit also provides a set of tools which support the activities of each of the phases. These tools are of two types. First, tools have been developed specifically for DiManT. Second, DiManT has undertaken a survey of tools which are generally available in the area. There is a two-level description provided for each tool which has been included in the toolkit. The first level is a standardized, general level description of the tool. The second-level description consists of the tool itself, where these are available. Where it has not been possible to obtain the source tool, a reference to where it may be obtained is provided.

8   Diversity Excellence Model (DEM)

DEM has been developed by the National School of Government. It is based on the European Foundation for Quality Management (EFQM) Excellence Model and links diversity to it. The EFQM Excellence Model is used as the standard to address and measure diversity and to link diversity to the bottom line. DEM aims to provide organizations with a robust tool to self-assess their diversity and measure their progress in diversity management by charting progress over the years. The Model takes a stakeholder approach to diversity management with its focus on expectations and perceptions of a wide range of constituent groups. Thus, it provides a framework to assess in detail the integration of diversity through all functional areas. Currently DEM is used predominantly by public sector organizations including City of London Police; Civilian Equality Unit, NI; Crown Prosecution Service; Defence Procurement Agency; Department for Health, Social Services and Public

Safety, NI; Home Office; Inland, Revenue – Cumbernauld; Lancashire Police; Merseyside Police; Metropolitan Police; Northumbria Probation Service; and Wiltshire Constabulary.

The DEM has a guide and an assessment tool. The guide describes the EFQM criteria which are translated into a set of diversity-excellence indicators. The assessment tool is a sophisticated questionnaire which enables assessors to identify how their organization is fairing in terms of equality and diversity. The assessors are then able to identify in which of the three stages that their organization can be located in terms of their equality and diversity practice: getting started, best practice or excellence. The main strength of the model is the dual structure that it offers. It identifies a set of criteria and a method to assess organizational performance against those criteria.

Although the model allows for an internal focus on equality and diversity concerns at the level of the organization, it suffers the same setbacks as the EFQM model as outlined below: a lack of contextual understanding and over-simplistic attribution of causal relationship between enablers of diversity and positive organizational outcomes.

There is also intersectoral variation in measurement of equality and diversity. In the UK, private, public and voluntary sectors have taken different routes to measuring and diagnosing equality and diversity: the Balanced Score Card approach has been widely adopted across the large private sector firms, the Diversity Excellence Model of the Cabinet Office has been adopted by the public sector organizations, and more recently the voluntary service sector has been reviewing the developments within the public and private sectors, borrowing instruments from both. The reasons for the divergence in the development of equality measures across sectors are manifold. However, the main reason has been the fundamental differences behind sectoral motives in taking up equality initiatives. Whilst the business value considerations have been predominant in the private sector for the take-up of diversity initiatives, the desire to be a good practice employer and to meet the needs of a diverse population has been driving the public sector agenda. The voluntary sector has been particularly driven by a concern over widening their volunteer base and aligning their volunteer profiles with those of the communities that they serve. Therefore, the differences between measurement tools that have been developed to capture equality concerns in these three dominant industries should be understood in this context.

9 EFQM Business Excellence Model

The EFQM Business Excellence Model (2005), which was introduced in 1993 in order to serve as a benchmark for quality awards in Europe, is one of the most established models of business excellence. It is overviewed as 'a non-prescriptive framework based on nine criteria. Five of these are "Enablers" and four are

"Results". The "Enabler" criteria cover what an organization does. The "Results" criteria cover what an organization achieves. "Results" are caused by "Enablers" and feedback from "Results" help to improve "Enablers"'. The EFQM model, similar to all other business models, suffers from two problems. First the model does not directly engage with the issue of equality and diversity and hence fails to relate business excellence to one of its key indicators. Second, the model suggests a simplistic causal link between 'enablers' and 'results'. This approach fails to recognize the existence of structural constraints and contextual variables that impinge upon the results that organizations achieve.

10   Equality standard for local government

Having been modelled on previous CRE standards for racial equality in local government, Racial Equality Means Quality, Equality Standard aims to help local authorities to monitor and assess all their equality work using a single standard for race, sex and disability. The standard was produced in partnership with the Commission for Racial Equality, Equal Opportunities Commission, the Disability Rights Commission and the Employers' Organization for Local Government. Like the Racial Equality Means Business standard, it is also based on a measurement framework across five levels, and demonstrates Racial Equality Means Business standard's adaptability and flexibility to be adjusted to cover different strands of workforce diversity.

11   Everyone is Welcome at Tesco Audit Tool

The audit tool that is offered by Tesco is a self-assessment tool which contains a matrix of two dimensions, organizational processes (six items) and organizational outcomes (eight items), against which organizational practices of diversity can be measured and assessed. The tool includes the organizational processes of work environment, recruitment and selection, rewards and recognition, career development, customer focus, and product and services development. The organizational outcomes include commitment, policy, strategy and planning, communication, implementation, accountability, measurement and review and realignment. In this two dimensional matrix, organizational practice is assessed at five levels, level one being little evidence of diversity practice and level five indicating a sophisticated approach. Each level is defined in terms of expected practices.

The Tesco tool is inspired by the Balanced Score Card approach. Its main focus on diversity management is the business case for diversity. Therefore the key strength of the tool is that it seeks to locate organizational performance in diversity, linking it with other organizational processes and outcomes and at varied levels of engagement. However, the tool is a voluntary measure which requires executive-level support in order for it to serve as an effective tool for measurement and organizational change.

12 Health and Safety Diagnostic Check

A single legal framework regulates the risks to health and safety associated with work activity in Britain. The Health and Safety Commission (HSC) and the Health and Safety Executive are non-departmental bodies which have overall statutory responsibility for health and safety at work. The statutory responsibility of the HSC includes reflecting on research by the HSE and other constituent organizations and groups (including employers, managers, trade unions, scientific and technological experts) in order to propose health and safety law and standards to Ministers. The Health and Safety at Work (HSW) Act was introduced in 1974, around the time of the introduction of equality laws. The main principle of the British system is that responsibility for health and safety lies with those who own, manage and work in industrial and commercial undertakings. They should conduct their own risk assessments and take their own measures. Workplace representatives have played significant roles in addressing health and safety needs. The law considers reasonably practicable action as a measure.

The Health and Safety Executive offer a stepwise risk assessment tool which helps organizations to self-assess their health and safety risks. This tool is supplemented with information on requirements for reducing risk and promoting good practice (HSE 2006). As the tool is backed by strong legislation, its take-up is nationwide. Health and safety inspectors have important statutory powers, including entering workplaces without warning. If they are not satisfied by health and safety standards they can issue improvement or prohibition notices and can prosecute for the most serious failings. Some inspectors have generic training on systems and principles whilst others are specialized in a single industry or sector.

The health and safety system offers a truly excellent model which has been hailed as an ideal system in progressive circles of equality and diversity debate. The reason for this has been the comparably stronger impact of the health and safety diagnostic and legal system when compared to the impact of the equal opportunities system, which was established around the same time as the health and safety system in the UK. The health and safety diagnostic system benefits from stronger institutional support, where the HSC and HSE assume significant political and practical power in regulating industrial practices.

13 International Personnel Association Diagnostic Check

Neil E. Reichenberg, the Executive Director of the International Personnel Management Association, reported that they have developed and tested a best-practice benchmarking tool for managing diversity in the public service sector. Their study has examined a wide range of initiatives on the basis of six criteria: the success of the initiative over time, evidence of qualitative and quantitative business results, availability of recognizable positive business outcomes such as customer satisfaction improvements, innovation, transferability of the initiative to other organizations, and purposefulness and meaningfulness of the initiative for the benchmarking purposes. Subsequently, a range of best practices are identified and presented through the United Nations reports to an international audience. Benchmarking for best practices in equality and diversity is useful for identification of different approaches to equality and diversity checks, not only at the inter-organizational level, but also for the development of intra-organizational capacity, through identification of best practices in decentralized organizations where coordination of equality and diversity efforts may pose a managerial challenge.

14   Investors in Diversity

The Investors in Diversity is a new standard which aims to support and enable organizations to adopt, develop and benchmark behaviours and practices which promote inclusion, equality, diversity and achievement. It also seeks to enable organizations to measure their progress as well and be recognized for achievements. The main objectives of the Investors in Diversity standard are to support candidate organizations that are committed to inclusion, assist candidate organizations to learn about their stakeholders, support candidate organizations to develop and sustain an inclusive and adaptive organizational culture and environment, help candidate organizations to measure their success, and provide accreditation to achieving candidate organizations.

IiD offers a route map, to any organization, based on a diagnostic of current achievement level. It supports organizations towards inclusion of all stakeholders via an informed and self-determined organizational culture shift. It measures distance travelled against a cross-sectoral national standard and it offers recognition for success, through its membership system.

15   Investors in People

Investors in People (IiP) is a national initiative which links training and development to business strategies with a view to improving organizational performance. IiP is a widely used national standard by which subscribing organizations develop their business strategy and align all business activity to support their organizational aims. Nearly 36 per cent of the UK employees subscribe to the IiP standards. The standard also encourages equality and diversity in workplaces, work–life balance practices, and linking of these to main activities and processes of the organizations. However, the IiP standard, at the same time, does not offer a single standard for all institutions to adopt. Indeed, it allows for individuals to consider their own unique circumstances due to their size, industry, competition, etc., and to specifically tailor the aims and objectives of their IiP standards.

16   NHS Wales (2003) Equality Audit Tool

NHS Wales Equality Audit is a self-assessment tool which is based on a questionnaire of structured and open-ended questions. The data is collected centrally in order to identify examples of good practice. Organizations are asked to complete two sections in the Equality Audit. A section of information is provided in order to increase the understanding of equality inside the workplace. However, this is an optional exercise. The tool focuses on action taken by the organization to promote equality. In section one, organizations are required to respond to a series of statements by indicating whether this accurately reflects action taken by the organization to promote equality. Section two focuses upon the collection of workplace data to provide an equality profile of the organization. Additionally organizations are asked to give details of progress since the last audit; to provide evidence of good practice innovation; to record any additional comments and identify further action required. The main advantage of this tool is that it includes all strands of equality in all processes of work.

17   Opportunity Now Benchmarking Tool

Opportunity Now is a business-led campaign that claims to work with employers to realize the full potential of women at all levels and in all sectors of their workforce. There are over 360 employers signed up to the Opportunity Now Benchmark from all sectors. Organizations have to pay a membership in order to benefit from a survey on gender equality and diversity in the workplace. This allows them to chart their progress on mainstreaming diversity and to compare their progress with other employers. The survey focuses on the motivation for the organization to take action on gender equality/diversity, the action that the organization is taking, their policies and procedures in place, and their effectiveness. The benchmarking tool also explores the impact of the individual and organizational action. Employers receive an analysis of their performance and score, and are given one-to-one advice and guidance on how to improve.

18   Race for Opportunity Benchmarking Tool

Race for Opportunity (RfO) is a network of private and public sector organizations working across the UK to promote the business case for race and diversity. Race for Opportunity requires organizations to underpin strategies with actions, in order to generate a positive impact on business performance. RfO works with affiliated organizations across four key areas of business activity which demonstrate the business case for race equality: employment, including recruitment, selection, progression and retention; marketing to ethnic minorities as profitable consumers; engaging ethnic minority businesses in their supplier chain and as business partners; community involvement activities and initiatives to ensure inclusion of ethnic minority individuals and communities.

The campaign draws on national and regional demographic information about the current and emerging workforce in order to encourage employers to take part. Organizations that work with RfO are working on race to support their business objectives in terms of their bottom line, becoming an 'employer of choice', enhancing their corporate reputation and profile amongst ethnic minority stakeholders and other groups in the wider community. RfO supports organizations via its benchmarking programme (also available online) which provides a clear evaluation of each organization in relation to the network, relevant sector trends and top ten performing member organizations. RfO supports the results with feedback in debrief sessions. These include a report on strengths and weaknesses and support in attaining a diverse competitive workplace and environment. It also offers consultation on a one-to-one basis and advice and support tailored to each member organization's needs; brings organizations together via a programme of events to discuss topical development and share good practice; and provides publications, research, legal updates and briefing papers to keep organizations informed and engaged on race diversity issues.

19   Racial Equality Means Business – A standard for racial equality for employers

Racial Equality Means Business is a benchmarking standard for employers launched by the Commission for Racial Equality (CRE). It aims to help employers to move beyond mere compliance with legislation to design and adopt practical policies on racial equality to boost staff performance and customer loyalty. The standard is based on the methodology of total quality management and complementary to those initiatives that encourage a people-centred approach to management. Although the standard has been drawn up with larger employers in mind, it provides a model flexible and adaptable enough to meet the needs of different types of organizations. Therefore, the standard can be utilized in a wide range of situations as a flexible managerial tool. Based on the business case for equality, Racial Equality Means Business is designed as a self-assessment measure to help indicate the future areas of action and measure the past achievement.

The standard provides the employers with a checklist of the range of actions that may be involved in designing, planning and implementing racial equality programmes. More importantly, the standard includes a framework for measuring achievement across six broad areas at five levels. These areas are: policy and planning; selecting, developing and retaining staff; communication and corporate image; corporate citizenship; and auditing for racial equality. The measurement at each area starts with a first level which covers the very basic foundational requirements for an effective programme and through the subsequent levels progresses towards actions that focus on change and positive outcomes.

Although Racial Equality Means Business standard is designed particularly to assess racial equality programmes, it can be used in conjunction with standards designed for other particular groups such as women, people with disabilities and older employees, or it can be adjusted to include different forms of diversity.

In addition to Racial Equality Means Business, which is a general standard for employers, the CRE also designed other standards targeting specific audiences, examples including Learning for All, for education institutions, and Bridging the Gap and Measuring the Gap, for acute, community, and ambulance services, NHS trusts, and social care providers such as social services departments and residential and nursing homes.

20   Stand up for us: NHS Schools Homophobia Self-Review Tool

This checklist is offered as a self-review tool to audit a school's current position in relation to challenging and responding to homophobia. It is categorized according to the ten aspects of the NHS's whole-school approach and includes space to record a school's progress against the criteria. The tool offers main criteria for challenging homophobia, and examples of evidence across these ten aspects from the school is required in a blank box. The ten aspects that are covered in this tool are: leadership; management and managing change; policy development; curriculum planning and resourcing including working with external agencies; teaching and learning; school culture and environment; giving pupils a voice; provision of pupils' support services; staff development support needs, health and welfare; and partnership with parents/carers.

21   The Grimsby Institute of Further and Higher Education Tool

The Grimsby Institute of Further and Higher Education and Focus Consultancy Ltd has formed a partnership to develop a number of diversity products. These products have been developed with an emphasis on Further Education but can arguably be adapted to provide diversity solutions for other organizations or sectors. Focus Consultancy Ltd is a multi-ethnic and interdisciplinary consultant in Europe. Established in 1986, it specializes in the area of change management within multicultural settings and market places, and focuses on cultural diversity when it presents a special challenge. There are a number of products the partnership has developed under the name 'Inspire Publishing Ltd'. The online diversity audit tool aims to assess how effectively diversity is being managed within an organization. This tool is written specifically for the Further Education sector. It can be adapted to other sectors. This online diversity diagnostic tool is designed for implementation alongside the online audit in order to enhance the audit process and attempt to assess the culture of the organization.

Age discrimination in employment became unlawful in 2006. The legislation has caused the implementation of major changes in retirement practices, statutory redundancy and unfair dismissal laws. It has also impacted on occupational pensions, service related benefits, recruitment, promotion and training policies. An online audit tool has been developed in order to address issues of age discrimination.

A full diversity audit is offered to identify areas of existing or potential discrimination and make recommendations for change. The audit will provide valuable information for action and the promotion of equality of opportunity, now and in the future, preparing a college to meet its moral and legal obligation. The objectives of the audit are therefore to assess the management systems in-line with the requirements of legislation. The full diversity audit will include a range of the above tools accompanied by a full desk audit of documentation and a site visit. Included in the process is a three-month and a six-month review stage where progression in the management of diversity is expected.

Although the Grimsby Institute tools have 'diversity' as one of the issues they cover, their main focus is on legal compliance and discrimination rather than positive aspects and the business benefits of diversity.

22   Trades Union Congress Collective Bargaining and Equality Audit Tool

The 2003 audit provided a benchmark of the equality dimension of all union activities. It covered union priorities for equality, rules, structure, membership, collective bargaining, services to members, publicity, campaigns and unions as employers. It considered equality in relation to gender, race, disability, sexual orientation and age. Reflecting on the 2003 audit has led to some improvements in the 2005 audit, particularly in response to the national union survey element of the 2005 Equality Audit. In total 46 of the TUC's 67 affiliated unions replied – around two-thirds of the total; and although larger unions were again more likely to respond than smaller ones, the proportion of the TUC's membership covered by the survey was much higher at 97.4 per cent. This audit report serves as a benchmark against which unions can assess their performance in terms of collective bargaining and equality.

II   Tools for guidance and information

1   Directing Equal Pay in ICT (DEPICT)

The Directing Equal Pay in ICT (DEPICT) is a project funded by the European Social Fund (ESF) and the University of Salford. The project took place between January 2005 and December 2006. The study examined the gender pay gap within the ICT industry. It aims to expose the barriers to women's pay and progression, and concludes that these barriers are embedded within organizational pay structures and reward systems. It examines the interplay between the gender pay gap and the under-representation of women in the ICT labour market. One of the expected outcomes of the project was to provide a basis for presenting solutions to the problem of the gender pay gap. The DEPICT project currently offers a web-based survey, which allows women in the sector to provide information about their pay, progression and working conditions. This study is currently ongoing.

2   Diversity Benchmarking Group

The Diversity Benchmarking Group has been launched by a specialist consultancy, Proactive Reputation Management (PRM), in association with Complinet, a supplier of business information and software solutions. The group seeks to enable organizations active in diversity to achieve their objectives. It is currently focused on the research of diversity objectives and strategies, diversity implementation and embedding, experience of group members – effectiveness, enablers and barriers, international perspectives – and employee demographics. Facilitated by PRM and Complinet, the members compare and contrast approaches, share experiences and identify good, best and future practice. Both UK and international practices and experience are explored. Members include Aviva, the British Army, BT, Co-operative Insurance Society, Co-operative Bank, HM Prison Service, Metropolitan Police Service, Procter & Gamble, Prudential, the Royal Navy, SEEBOARD Energy and UBS Warburg. The main strength of the group is the exchange of good practice between members. However, the group does not currently offer its own generic tool for diversity management.

3   The CIPD Change Agenda

The CIPD Change Agenda on Measuring Diversity (Tatlı *et al.* 2006: 17) provides a checklist of areas that need to be regularly measured and monitored in terms of equality and diversity:

- employees' equal opportunities and diversity attitudes and behaviours;
- representation of diverse groups at different levels of organization;

- figures of recruitment, performance appraisal, promotion and compensation with respect to different categories of employees;
- employees' level of commitment and belongingness;
- employees' performance and satisfaction;
- cost of labour turnover, absenteeism, recruitment and discrimination lawsuits;
- communication and interaction between employees from diverse backgrounds;
- organizational performance, creativity, problem solving and decision–making;
- business success with regard to market penetration, diversification of customer base and level of customer satisfaction.

The change agenda is currently supplemented with a survey which was conducted by the CIPD: Diversity Management – State of the Nation. The survey questionnaire adopts a three-dimensional approach in assessing the current level of diversity awareness and practice in the UK organizations. It examines individual, organizational and group and national activities across the fields of equality, diversity and inclusion. The report findings suggest that the current practice of diversity and equality in the sample organizations remain unsophisticated. Despite evidence of greater interest in policy-making, the empirical evidence on diversity practice and benefits of diversity concerns remain very stunted. The study suggests that organizations that adopt sophisticated diversity measures are few and far between.

The strength of the change agenda and the related survey tool is its sophisticated and inclusive approach to equality, diversity and inclusion. The survey tool does not only consider shallow-level diversity, but includes all diversity and equality strands, as well as business activities that are associated with diversity. However, the main weakness of the questionnaire is that it currently does not allow for organizations to measure themselves against others.

4   Diversity Dividend

The Diversity Dividend is an online development system, sponsored by the London Development Agency, and is designed to assist businesses in devising successful diversity strategies. The Diversity Dividend aims to be an open platform assisting organizations to track progress on how well they are integrating good employment practices into their business. This means that where companies have already made strides in adopting good practice, and have been recognized within an existing standard or by a credible agency, this will have currency within the Diversity Dividend. Therefore the Diversity Dividend does not offer a competition to the other tool, but supplements it with an umbrella system of business development. The Diversity Dividend provides case studies of good practice across thematic areas of systems, resources, stakeholders, society, results and leadership, and across a diversity of strands of gender, age, disability, race, religion and sexuality.

The Diversity Dividend professes commitment to working with owners and promoters of diversity-related standards in order to ensure that their initiatives are given the appropriate level of weighting within the Diversity Dividend. The Diversity Dialogue has established a dialogue with the British Quality Foundation, EFQM, The London Stock Exchange's Corporate Social Responsibility initiative and the Chartered Institute for Personnel and Development, and is seeking collaboration with Investors in People and others. The main strength of the Diversity Dividend approach is its connectedness with other providers of diagnostic tools.

5 Equality and diversity in adult and community learning: a guide for managers

Building on the concepts of inclusive learning and widening participation, this guide sets these equality and diversity issues in the context of the Learning and Skills Council remit and the Common Inspection Framework. It outlines new legislative and reporting requirements for local authority adult education. It concludes by pulling the strands together in a self-assessment tool that can be used by both managers and coordinators as a starting point for evaluating and improving provision. This self-assessment tool reviews ten aspects of diversity practice, including strategy, policy and procedures, identifying needs, action planning, access and resources, support, curriculum development, teaching and learning, staffing and development, and monitoring and review. These aspects of practice are queried at three levels of sophistication, ranging from novice to confident expertise.

6 Equal Opportunities Guidance from Government Office for London

This guidance has been developed and written in consultation with a large number of stakeholder groups and in response to the increasing demand for accessible information concerning equality of opportunity in programme delivery across London, with particular reference to the European structural funds administered by the Government Office for London. The guidance is targeted at a wide audience, including project applicants, existing projects and co-financing organizations, and outlines best practice for small organizations. In order to meet the demands of the target audience the guidance offers a range of information from European and the United Kingdom legislation, equal opportunities in employment, as well as other useful contacts. Most of the chapters are stand alone, allowing specific issues to be looked up. The guidance is intended to be a 'living document' which will be updated and developed as new legislation comes into effect.

7   National Council for Voluntary Organizations Equal Opportunities Checklist

The National Council for Voluntary Organizations offers a web-based checklist of seven items for equal opportunities. The list suggests that organizations produce an equal opportunities policy; eliminate direct and indirect gender, marital status, age, religion, colour, race, nationality, ethnicity and disability discrimination from their human resource management systems; combat the gender pay gap; and establish grievance procedures for complaints of discrimination and investigate such complaints fully. The NCVO checklist concentrates mostly on issues of legal compliance but fails to highlight issues at the intersection of business benefits and equality and diversity.

8   The Athena Swan Charter

The Athena Swan Charter, offered by the Royal Society, is a scheme for recognizing excellence in science, engineering and technology (SET) employment in higher education (HE). Membership of the Charter is open to all UK universities who are committed to working towards the achievement of the aims of the Athena Project. The Charter principles reflect learning from the first five years work by the Athena Project and its partner universities. The principles which Charter members are asked to accept are (1) to address gender inequalities requires commitment and action from everyone, at all levels of the organization; (2) to tackle the unequal representation of women in science requires changing cultures and attitudes across the organization; (3) the high loss rate of women in science is an urgent concern which the organization will address; (4) the system of short-term contracts has particularly negative consequences for the retention and progression of women in science, which the organization recognizes; (5) there are both personal and structural obstacles to women making the transition from PhD into a sustainable academic career in science, which requires the active consideration of the organization; and (6) the absence of diversity at management and policy-making levels has broad implications which the organization will examine. Charter members are expected to demonstrate their commitment to the Charter principles by developing an action programme for their implementation and by reporting their progress on an annual basis. How members approach this will depend on the stage they are at, what they have identified as their key priorities and their staff and organizational profiles.

9   The Jive Development Partnership

The Jive Development Partnership is aiming to address one of the causes of the gender pay gap and horizontal sex segregation, by establishing a network of desegregation hubs which seek to eliminate barriers that are in the way of women who seek inclusion in male-dominated fields of employment across the UK. Led by the Let's Twist Initiative, JIVE brings together women's training centres, employers' organizations from the most segregated sectors of the labour market, mainstream training and educational institutions, careers services and the National Equal Opportunities Commission. All of these partners cooperate actively in the Development Partnership's activities at both regional and national levels. Each regional hub offers a package of interrelated measures, which consists of the following elements. Gender equality courses are offered for managers, lecturers, trainers and support staff of further and higher educational institutions and work-based training providers, enabling them to meet the learning needs of women who are training for employment in male-dominated sectors. Modular training is tailored for careers guidance professionals and careers teachers and aims to assist them to become 'change agents' who can overcome stereotyping and encourage girls and women to consider work in the engineering, construction or technology sectors as a potential career path. Support is given to companies in the use of a gender audit tool developed by JIVE, to help analyse any recruitment and retention issues that companies may be experiencing. Encouragement is offered to women and girls who are working and/or training in male-dominated sectors within the four regions. This mentoring programme offers professional and personal support during the early stages of training and career development. The key strength of this initiative and its diagnostic approach is that it is embedded in a stakeholder approach and covers a wide range of integrated activities for constituent groups.

Appendix B: Interview schedule for potential users

Exercise: The below questions may be used to assess how a gender pay gap diagnostic check may be received by the organizations that may take up such a tool. In class, discussions may focus on the transcripts of one or more interviews that are conducted by representatives of an organization in order to assess their reactions to and expectations for a diagnostic equality check.

Explanation:

This interview is conducted as a part of a research project funded by the Equal Opportunities Commission. The aim of this research is to scope the need for and requirements of a diagnostic equality check for the UK employers. No individual names will be revealed and they will be kept strictly confidential.

1. **The sector and the size of the company?**
   PROBE: What is the proportion of male/female staff?

2. **What is your position in the organization?**

3. **Do you know what the gender pay gap is in your organization?**
   PROBE: if yes how did you diagnose it and if not what would you do about it?
   PROBE: what would motivate you to want to find out?

4. **Did you undertake an EPR?**
   PROBE: Why (not)?
   PROBE: What would encourage you to undertake this?
   PROBE: If yes, what was the result and which actions did you take?

5. **Do you use any monitoring and diagnostic tools to ensure a nondis-criminatory payment structure?**
   PROBE: Why (not)?
   PROBE: If yes, which tools do you use?
   PROBE: If yes, what are the merits and disadvantages of these tools?
   PROBE: Do you use any anecdotes/stories to ensure senior and middle management engagement in undertaking diagnostic checks?

6. **Do you have an equal opportunities/diversity initiative, programme, plan or activity? What is it?**
   PROBE: Up to now, what action has your organization taken to progress in the field of diversity and equality?
   PROBE: What actions are planned for the future?

7. **What kind of monitoring and diagnostic tools do you use in order to measure progress towards diversity and equality in your organization?**
   PROBE: Could you tell me which areas of employment and HR issues and which strands of diversity are covered by these tools?
   PROBE: What are the merits and disadvantages of these tools?
   PROBE: Who has overall responsibility for monitoring progress? e.g. HR/Diversity Officer

8. **What areas do you currently monitor in terms of potential sources of a gender pay gap?**
   PROBE: pay systems and structures, job evaluation schemes; horizontal and vertical sex segregation; diversity and equality awareness training; recruitment and selection; performance appraisal and promotion; training and career development, mentoring and coaching; communication; work–life balance and flexible working policies and programmes; anti-harassment and bullying policy, and grievance procedure; maternity/paternal leaves and childcare facilities – and people with caring responsibilities.
   PROBE: Do you conduct any needs analysis for your female and male employees? If yes, do you take any actions on the basis of that? – explain.

9. **The EOC is planning to develop a diagnostic equality check which will cover different areas of HR and which will be adaptable to different strands of diversity. Do you believe that there is a need for such a diagnostic equality check in the current business environment? Why?**

10. Could you be persuaded to engage with a diagnostic equality check? How?

11. Is a diagnostic tool compatible with your needs and priorities? Why? How?

12. What would be the possible cost considerations that may be associated with such a diagnostic check?

13. Would such a tool enable you to focus on areas that call for action and give you the freedom to decide what actions to take? How?

14. Which format for such a tool would work for you?

15. Could a diagnostic check be developed to include all three causes of gender pay gap (pay discrimination, occupational segregation and work–life balance)? How do you think it would look like?

16. Could such a diagnostic check fit with the requirements of your reporting mechanisms (for example, Operating Financial Reviews/ Human capital reporting)? How?

17. Would a diagnostic equality check help you develop a more generic approach to cover other equality strands? How? Why?

18. What other business/diagnostic tools do you use in your organization? (IiP, Health and Safety, etc.)
    PROBE: What are the merits and disadvantages of these tools?
    PROBE: What are the weaknesses of these tools?

19. What do you think are the factors which make other diagnostic tools successful?

20. What are your general recommendations for a feasible and efficient diagnostic check?

21. Could you please tell me any additional comments you feel are relevant to our understanding of your views and needs regarding a diagnostic equality check?

Thank you very much for your time and support.

Appendix C: Interview schedule for providers

Exercise: The below questions may be used to assess the kind of gender pay gap diagnostic checks that are offered by providers of diagnostic check tools, including universities, consultancies, government agencies, trade unions and professional bodies. In class, discussions may focus on the transcripts of one or more interviews that are conducted by providers of diagnostic tools in order to assess the characteristics of their tool and their views on the competitive tools in the market.

Explanation:

This interview is conducted as a part of a research project funded by the Equal Opportunities Commission. The aim of this research is to scope the need for and requirements of a diagnostic equality check for UK employers. No individual names will be revealed and they will be kept strictly confidential.

1. **The sector and the size of your organization?**

2. **What is your membership/client profile?**
    PROBE:Which sectors, what sizes?

3. **Your position in the organization?**

4. **Do you know the current state of gender pay gap in your sector and between your members/clients?**
    PROBE: If yes how did you/they diagnose it?
    PROBE: If not how would you do it – what would motivate you/them to want to find out?

5. **Do you have an action plan on gender pay gap for your members/clients?**
    PROBE: What is it?
    PROBE: Are you aware of any programmes and initiatives that your individual members/clients have set up?
    PROBE: Are you aware of any examples of good practice?

6. **Did your members/clients undertake an EPR?**
    PROBE: Why (not)?
    PROBE: What would encourage them to undertake this?
    PROBE: If yes, what was the result and which actions do they take?

7. **Do your members/clients use any monitoring and diagnostic tools to ensure a nondiscriminatory payment structure?**
    PROBE: Why (not)?
    PROBE: If yes, which tools do they use? (merits and disadvantages of these tools?)
    PROBE: Do you recommend your members/clients any such tools to ensure a nondiscriminatory payment structure? What are they?
    PROBE: If yes, what are the merits and disadvantages of these tools?

8. **Do you conduct any equality needs analysis based on gender for your member/client organizations?**
    PROBE: If you do, do you take any actions on the basis of that? Explain.

9. **How do your members/clients measure progress towards equality? Do you offer/advise a tool for your members/clients? What is it?**
    PROBE: Do you know who has overall responsibility for monitoring progress in your member/client organizations? e.g. HR/Diversity Officer

10. **Which areas do you currently monitor in terms of potential sources of a gender pay gap between your members/clients?**
PROBE: pay systems and structures, job evaluation schemes; horizontal and vertical sex segregation; diversity and equality awareness training; recruitment and selection; performance appraisal and promotion; training and career development, mentoring and coaching; communication; work–life balance and flexible working policies and programmes; anti-harassment and bullying policy, and grievance procedure; maternity/ paternal leaves and childcare facilities – people with caring responsibilities.
PROBE: Which of these areas do your members/clients monitor?

11. **Do you believe that there is a need for a diagnostic equality check in the current business environment? Why?**

12. **Could you be persuaded to engage with a diagnostic equality check and encourage your members/clients to undertake it? How?**

13. **Is a diagnostic tool compatible with your and your members'/clients' needs and priorities? Why? How?**

14. **What would persuade your members/clients to use such a tool?**

15. **What would be the possible cost considerations that may be associated with such a diagnostic check?**
PROBE: How would the cost consideration differ in-line with the size of organizations?

16. **How would such a tool enable your members/clients to focus on areas that call for action and give you the freedom to decide what actions to take?**

17. **Which format for such a tool would work for your clients/members? Could you explain?**

18. **Could a diagnostic check be developed to include all three causes of gender pay gap (explain this in the interview)? How do you think it would look like?**

19. **Could such a diagnostic check fit with the requirements of your members'/clients' overall reporting mechanisms?**

20. **Would a diagnostic equality check help your members/clients develop a more generic approach to cover other equality strands? How? Why?**

21. **What do you think are the factors which make other diagnostic tools successful?**

22. **What business/diagnostic tools do you provide for members/clients? Could you explain these tools?**
PROBE: Are they diagnostic?
PROBE: How do they work?

PROBE: What areas do they cover?
PROBE: Which ones work better? Why?

23. **How did you design and advertise these tools?**

PROBE: How did you develop them?
PROBE: How would you evaluate the take-up?
PROBE: How did you market and advertise these tools?
PROBE: How did you persuade the organizations to use your tools? (business case?)
PROBE: Do you use any anecdotes/stories in support for convincing your clients/members to use diagnostic checks?

24. **What are your general recommendations for a feasible and efficient diagnostic check?**

25. **Could you please tell me any additional comments you feel are relevant to our understanding of your views and needs regarding a diagnostic equality check?**

26. **Do you know any other institutions or any of your members/clients that may be interested in participating in our research?**
PROBE: May I have their contact details?
PROBE: Could you introduce me to them?

Thank you very much for your time and support.

Further reading

Acker, J. (2000) 'Gendered Contradictions in Organizational Equity Projects', *Organization* vol. 7, no. 4, pp. 625–32.

Adams, L., Carter, K. and Schäfer, S. (2006) *Equal Pay Reviews Survey 2005*. EOC Working Paper Series no. 42, Equal Opportunities Commission.

Brett, S. and Milsome, S. (2004) *Monitoring Progress on Equal Pay Reviews*. EOC Research Discussion Series, Equal Opportunities Commission.

Itzin, C. and Newman, J. (eds) (1995) *Gender Culture and Organizational Change: Putting Theory into Practice*. London and New York: Routledge, pp. 273–86.

Ledwith, S., and Colgan, F. (eds) (1996) *Women and Organizations: Challenging Gender Politics*. London: Macmillan.

Miller, L. and Neathey, F. (2004) *Advancing Women in the Workplace: Case Studies*. Equal Opportunities Commission Working Paper Series no. 13, Manchester: EOC.

Morrell, J., Boyland, M., Munns, G. and Astbury, L. (2001) *Gender Equality in Pay Practices*. EOC Research Discussion Series, Equal Opportunities Commission.

Olsen, W. and Walby, S. (2004) *Modelling Gender Pay Gaps*. EOC Working Paper Series no.17, Equal Opportunities Commission.

Witz, A. (1992) *Professions and Patriarchy*. London and New York: Routledge.

Diagnostic Equality and Diversity Checks   **6**

6.1   Introduction

Diagnostic equality checks are important mechanisms for fostering equality and diversity in national and organizational settings. This chapter presents a research project which sheds light on our understanding of national-level policy as relevant to global diversity management. Presented are the findings of a study with interviews with the representatives of public, private and voluntary sector employers, their membership organizations and providers of diagnostic checks and benchmarks, as well as a review of academic and practitioner literature on the different models of diagnostic checks and on the business case for equality and diversity. First, we map out the views and recommendations of the respondents for a successful and well-received diagnostic equality check. Then we examine the views of the research participants on diagnostic equality checking in terms of coverage and format. Finally, we present the conclusions arising from the research findings and provide recommendations on the design, development and promotion of the diagnostic equality check.

In Appendix B, we provide a diagnostic equality check tool which can be used in order to monitor diversity and equality at the organizational level. This tool can also serve as a learning resource for in-class discussions.

6.2 Identifying and surveying the stakeholders of diagnostic equality checks

The study, which informs this chapter, drew upon a review of academic and practitioner literature as well as in-depth interviews with representatives of providers of diagnostic or monitoring tools, potential users and their membership organizations. The work was conducted in three phases. The work in the first stage aimed:

- to review the specialist publications in human resource management and equal opportunities fields;
- to review the existing models and approaches for monitoring equality in the UK, e.g. Racial Equality Means Business, Equality Standard, Learning for All, Bridging the Gap and Measuring the Gap, Diversity Excellence Model, Investors in People Standard and The Diversity Driver;
- to review the approaches or models that have been developed in other countries with a specific focus on the models put forward by the European Union.

The second stage of the project aimed:

- to carry out a consultation exercise on the development of an equality check with providers of diagnostic or monitoring tools and membership organizations;
- to carry out a survey of potential users in differently sized public, voluntary and private services and manufacturing sectors to investigate their views on the best approach to achieving the EOC's aims of a diagnostic equality check.

In the consultation exercise, we conducted 34 interviews with the representatives of provider institutions and membership organizations. In the survey, in order to increase the number of respondents who were able to comment on the possible approaches for a diagnostic check to cover all three causes of gender pay gap, a booster sample was drawn from an EOC list of employers which had expressed a commitment to reducing the gender pay gap. In the selected organizations, we conducted 28 in-depth interviews with the human resource managers or equal opportunities specialists or other organizational actors who might take the lead in the process of conducting a diagnostic equality check.

Drawing on the findings from the review of the literature and of the existing models and approaches, we devised two separate semi-structured interview schedules that we used in our interviews with the providers and membership institutions and with the potential users. This interview schedule aimed to investigate:

- the nature of the participating organization's membership or clients;
- the range of services/support they offer to their clients/members;
- the tools/diagnostic checks, if any, they offer, and how they developed and promoted these tools;
- the need for a diagnostic equality check in the current business environment;
- what would persuade them to advocate a diagnostic equality check;
- how the organizations would be encouraged to engage with a diagnostic equality check and what would be the possible areas of difficulty in engaging them;
- what kind of organization would be harder to engage to take a proactive approach, why and what can be done;
- what would be the possible cost considerations for different organizations;
- to what extent it would enable employers to focus quickly on areas that call for action and give them the freedom to decide what actions to take;
- which formats would work best for the employers;
- the coverage of such a diagnostic check to include all three causes of the gender pay gap;
- the possibility of designing a diagnostic check in the absence of workforce monitoring;
- where such a diagnostic check would fit with the requirements of Operating Financial Reviews/Human capital reporting;
- how it would fit the Better Regulations Task Force;
- how it would be compatible with the needs and structures of organizations from different sectors and of organizations of different sizes;
- how a diagnostic equality check would be capable of a more generic approach to cover other equality strands;
- what could be adopted from the existing HR/diagnostic models and what are the merits and disadvantages of the existing models;
- the factors which make other diagnostic tools successful;
- the general recommendations of other diagnostic tools as to what makes a feasible and efficient diagnostic check.

We devised a separate interview schedule for the potential users with a view to investigating their views on the best approach to achieving the EOC's aims of a diagnostic equality check and to carry out a needs analysis for such a diagnostic check. During the interviews with the potential users we aimed to address the following issues:

- which areas the participating organizations currently monitor as potential sources of the gender pay gap (i.e. pay systems and structures; horizontal and vertical sex segregation; training and development; recruitment and selection; promotion; career development, mentoring and coaching; communication; work–life balance and flexible working policies and programmes; maternity/paternal leaves and childcare facilities);
- whether they conduct any needs analysis for their female and male employees and what kind of actions do they take on the basis of that;
- what kind of monitoring/diagnostic tools they use to ensure a non-discriminatory payment structure and what the merits and disadvantages of these tools are;
- whether they believe that there is a need for a diagnostic equality check in the current business environment;
- whether and how they could be persuaded to engage with a diagnostic equality check;
- whether this would be compatible with their needs and priorities;
- what would be the possible cost considerations that may be associated with such a diagnostic check;
- whether it would enable them to focus on areas that call for action and give them the freedom to decide what actions to take;
- which formats would work best for them;
- how a diagnostic check could be developed to include all three causes of the gender pay gap;
- how such a diagnostic check would fit with the requirements of Operating Financial Reviews/Human capital reporting;
- how a diagnostic equality check would help them develop a more generic approach to cover other equality strands;
- what they consider to be the factors which make other diagnostic tools successful;
- what their general recommendations are for a feasible and efficient diagnostic check.

In total, we conducted 62 semi-structured in-depth interviews which lasted around 45 minutes to an hour with the providers, potential users and membership organizations. All interviews were conducted via telephone with the exception of two face-to-face interviews. With the permission of the participants all interviews were tape-recorded and fully transcribed for the purposes of qualitative analysis. In addition we sent the survey form to ten provider and employer organizations for whom a telephone interview was not permissible and who preferred to fill in the survey form. Two provider organizations and two employers completed the survey form and returned it back to us. Hence, the analysis in this chapter is based on the responses from 66 research participants (see Appendix A for a table of research participants). As mentioned previously, the research participants were from three main groups of organizations: employers, employer membership organizations and providers of diagnostic checks or benchmarks. In terms of their focus and specialism, membership and provider organizations which participated in the research covered a wide range of sectors (public and private), industries (recruitment, local government, science, higher education, health, fire rescue services, police services), organizational sizes (large organizations and SMEs), and equality, diversity and employment issues (HR, CSR, employment relations, reputation management, gender, race, disability, sexual orientation, general diversity). The potential users included in the sample were from public and private services sectors and there was one respondent from a voluntary sector organization. In terms of industry the employers in our sample showed a rich variation which includes recruitment, local government, higher education, fire rescue services, police services, defence, civil service, ministerial departments, banking and finance, retail, energy and communication. Lastly, 28 of the potential users participated in the research were large organizations.

Finally, in the third stage, all data gathered was analysed. This chapter provides possible options for a diagnostic equality check to enable employers to assess the likelihood of discrimination across all three causes of the gender pay gap, as well as a convincing business case to encourage the employers to adopt a proactive approach to engaging in a diagnostic check. A full account and discussion of the findings are also provided. Also included is an indication of the possible problem areas and recommendations for developing a diagnostic equality check.

6.3   What makes a diagnostic check successful?

Reflecting on our study findings, in this section we explore the factors which make a diagnostic check successful. We first question whether there is a need for strong legislation in order to support a diagnostic check, then we outline the role of business case arguments in promoting the diagnostic check among employers. Recognition of the tool by key stakeholders and users, as well as its benchmarking potential, are explored as key strategies for increasing the take-up of the tool. Lastly, we will focus on the effective promotion strategies for a diagnostic equality check, including partnerships and consultation with key stakeholders, setting up an advisory committee, and creating a network of equality champions.

During the interviews we asked the research participants what they thought made a diagnostic check successful and what their general recommendations to the EOC would be to increase the take-up of the new tool among the employers in the UK. Fifty-two out of 66 respondents believe that the tool is likely to be more successful if it helps employers to manage their people strategically as in the case of IiP, the success of which is attributed to its ability to support organizations to meet their targets and to share best practice.

However, apart from the tool's ability to strategically support the operations of the organizations, interviews revealed that there are some other key factors that lie behind the success of a diagnostic or benchmarking tool. These are strong legislation, a convincing business case, recognition and benchmarking, and effective promotion. This section outlines the opinions of the research participants regarding each of these factors.

Is there a need for strong legislation and government support?

It has become evident from the research that strong legislative backing is one of the major factors that contribute to the success of a diagnostic tool. This is congruent with the Swedish experience as explained earlier. Particularly respondents from provider organizations thought that any diagnostic tool would be more successful and efficient, if it is built into business and investment planning through legal enforcements, and have less chance of being marginalized.

All of the respondents agreed that the Health and Safety Executive's suite of tools and guidance is one of better-known institutional provisions, partly because it is strongly supported by legislation. For instance, a respondent from a large provider organization in the area of gender equality said that health and safety requirements are built into the mindset of businesses of all sizes since there are tangible risks such as being closed down and fear of prosecution.

However, all respondents were aware that the issue of equality and diversity does not have strong legislative clout despite the fact that legislation could be the most effective medium to drive equality and diversity. So at present there is not a legislative backing that is strong enough to encourage employers to undertake a diagnostic equality check. One of the strategies suggested by nine respondents was integrating the diagnostic equality check into the health and safety requirements to engage the SMEs and other employers which are not traditionally proactive in the field of equality and diversity.

Twenty-six respondents argued that the success of Investors in People is also to a certain extent related to strong government support. They argued that the EOC should lobby the Government to back the diagnostic equality check. One of the respondents suggested that there should be an element of compulsion, either in legal terms or in contractual terms, if the tool wishes to achieve high levels of reception among organizations of all sizes and in different sectors.

Three-quarters of respondents from provider organizations pointed out that it is particularly hard to engage SMEs due to their limited resources, as well as their relatively low awareness levels regarding equality and diversity. Accordingly, either legal enforcement or making the diagnostic check part of procurement is essential to ensure high levels of take-up among the SMEs. On the other hand, the respondent from a local authority argued that the tool needs to get acknowledgement from the National Government Framework to engage the highest number of local government organizations. Similarly, the Cabinet Office commitment is cited as crucial for encouraging the civil service departments.

It became clear through the interviews that legislation and government support are important motivators for employers. This was particularly evident in the interviews with the respondents from the public sector who displayed a more positive attitude towards progressive legislation in the field of diversity and equality. All of the public sector employers pointed out that the Gender Equality Duty could be an efficient motivator for the public sector organizations. Similarly, they argued that if it is to be a generic tool, combining it with the Single Equalities Scheme and Commission for Equality and Human Rights (CEHR) may be a good strategy to increase the take-up. For instance, the respondent from a provider organization in the health sector stated that a generic diagnostic equality check would be very useful for the NHS employers in the context of the new discrimination legislation, the Single Equality Act and the Gender Equality Duty. Similarly, the respondent from a provider organization in the higher education sector said that she believes the higher education institutions will welcome a new diagnostic equality check due to the new legislation and because they do not want to lag behind local government in the diversity and equality field.

In summary, strong legislation and government support are crucial for the success of a new tool, and if the tool were offered on a voluntary basis, without legal enforcement, this would be its weak spot.

Ideally to ensure maximum effect the diagnostic check should be a legal requirement for employers, however many employers and their representative bodies are unsupportive of legal compulsion. Nevertheless, 60 respondents suggested that in the absence of strong legislation, legislative focus to convince the employers might not be a very wise strategy since it may drive away the organizations from engaging with a diagnostic equality check. Therefore, the legal case for a diagnostic equality check should also be informed by a firm understanding of business case arguments.

Is the business case an important driver for employers?

Both providers and potential users and their membership organizations, except for one, emphasized the importance of including a strong and convincing business case in the diagnostic check to persuade employers to engage with the tool. However, these respondents argued that the EOC should take into account that drivers for undertaking the diagnostic check may vary according to the size and sector of the organizations. Within that context, 37 respondents claimed that public sector organizations could be engaged relatively easily compared to the private sector companies through a legal case around Gender Equality Duty. Making a strong business case argument is crucial in involving private sector employers. However, 'value for money' is becoming increasingly prominent for the public sector as well. For instance, the respondent from a provider organization in the health sector said that there are competing priorities for NHS Trusts and attention is mostly around finances at present. Hence, she reasoned that a strong business case argument is essential to persuade the NHS employers to use the new tool. Hence, both legal and business case logics are currently in evidence across public, private and voluntary sectors. So the new tool needs to capture both the legal and business case arguments.

Two-thirds of the potential users from both public and private sectors also told us that they are concerned with the cost implications of undertaking such a diagnostic check. They thought that budget considerations would be a barrier for many organizations in conducting the diagnostic equality check.

Hence, it is argued by 31 respondents that the tool should include a proper cost benefit analysis. These respondents also suggested that the costs associated with different sizes of organizations should be taken into account. The research identified two dimensions of the potential cost that may be associated with a diagnostic check. The first is related to the actual cost of conducting the diagnostic, such as running and set-up costs, which will vary with the size of the organizations. The second is the cost related to the results of the diagnostic, since organizations will need to put systems in place in order to improve in the areas that display gaps. Accordingly, the cost–benefit analysis that may be included in the tool needs to cover both dimensions of cost incurred by the diagnostic check.

Sixty-two out of 66 respondents pointed out that undertaking such a diagnostic check is a serious resource issue, and that the tool should present a clear business case in such a way as to encourage the highest possible level of involvement and commitment by different organizational actors throughout the process.

Generally diversity and equality activities in the organizations are seen as the responsibility of only one person: the equality and diversity officer. Conducting a diagnostic check can be a very laborious process, and equality officers are generally left alone to promote diversity and equality in their organizations. Accordingly, 54 respondents in our sample argued that conducting a diagnostic check is a labour intensive process, which requires commitment from top management and staff, as well as allocation of resources to the departments in the organizations responsible for undertaking the check. One of the respondents commented on the importance of organizational buy-in as follows:

> Commitment from the top to actually do it, if it's labour-intensive to get the staff to do it, collect the data. You need commitment from the department to say 'yes, I will give you two hours of my time to actually go through', preparing to put together evidence to support their statements. First you need commitment from the top to do this, then you need buy-in from the people who are actually going to provide you with information. Because we're all very busy people and we need top management to do this because they believe that this will help our business. Top management also needs to give resources to these departments.

Presentation of a well-founded business case argument for the new diagnostic equality check is crucial for gaining commitment of the senior management team. Through demonstrating the bottom-line benefits of equality and diversity, a strong business case argument will promote a genuine understanding of the necessity of undertaking the diagnostic check and prevent the use of cost and budget considerations as excuses for not conducting it.

Accordingly, all respondents but one argued that a strong and convincing business case argument should be integrated into the diagnostic equality check not only to persuade the employers to undertake one but also to ensure the effectiveness and efficiency of the process through engaging people at different levels across different functions of the organization. In the words of one of our respondents:

> You know, businesses still need to function, still need to deliver on their commitments. So the tool needs to actually show that there are benefits. I appreciate that not all the benefits are tangible, but it needs to highlight, you know, what are the long-term intangible benefits. Why should organizations take up this journey, if you like?

Furthermore, it is stated that the tool should include a detailed business case to engage the HR and equality officers with expert knowledge, a business case which is less complicated and a more straightforward version that can be used by HR and equality and diversity specialists when pitching the tool to their managers or directors. For instance the respondent from a large retail company told us that she would like the EOC to provide her with a separate business case document which highlights the costs of undertaking the diagnostic versus not undertaking it, so that she would be able to convince the senior management of the company to invest in conducting the diagnostic.

One of the most frequently made points was regarding the necessity of structuring the tool in a way to give the users a good feeling. It is argued by 53 respondents that the new diagnostic check should be a positive tool focusing on positive aspects of equality and diversity rather than a negative judgemental tool pointing to non-compliance. One respondent explained this as follows:

> Like a positive tone rather than just sort of coming in and saying, well, you know, we are going to issue you with this order of non-compliance and all that. That doesn't really bode well as an organization. I think powers of persuasion are much more useful than the power of authoritarian language.

Hence, the starting point of the tool should be positive in that sense of making clear that the diagnostic check process aims to support the users in capitalizing the benefits of equality and diversity. In the words of another respondent:

> I think, organizations need to realise that they would benefit from such a diagnostic tool, that they don't feel like there's another diagnostic tool coming our way and is it going to be used to see how bad we are. Organizations don't respond very well to that. It would be useful if the starting point were that this is just a tool for you to see for yourself where you are. We are out here to support you.

Two-thirds of the respondents argued that such a positive tool would make it easier for the HR managers or equality and diversity officers to convince their senior management teams. The tool should help HR managers or diversity and equality officers to identify the current position of the organization in terms of its key strengths and help them to plan strategies for future development in the field of equality and diversity.

In terms of making a case for equality and diversity, a strong business case argument is necessary but not sufficient. Three-quarters of the respondents underlined that a business case argument should not preclude inclusion of ethical and legal cases as well. The ethical case in terms of 'doing the right thing' and 'being a best practice employer' is an important driver for employers in the UK since it also indirectly contributes to the bottom line through good publicity, which in turn provides the employers with an access to a more diverse range of customers. For instance a respondent from a provider organization in the higher education sector argued that being committed to diversity and equality would give the universities a competitive advantage in terms of recruiting more and diverse students. Another respondent highlighted the importance of reflecting the diversity of customers and society. Yet another respondent mentioned that the EOC could capitalize on the risk of public blame and ridicule that organizations may have to face if they do not take action.

As argued by 12 respondents from provider organizations, legal compliance is the key driver for the SMEs. Indeed, being compliant with the legislation is an important issue for organizations in all sizes and sectors. The legal case for equality and diversity can be associated with risk minimization. The EOC should highlight that undertaking the diagnostic equality check will help organizations to reduce any risks in relation to breaching the discrimination law, thus to avoid tribunals. In that context a quarter of respondents thought that the EOC should emphasize the potential penalties of not undertaking the diagnostic check, for example possible employment tribunals to encourage their engagement. On the other hand, slightly more than half of the respondents believed that a milder strategy should be followed when capitalizing on legislation so that employers will not feel like they are being 'hit with a stick'.

As reported in the field research, there are two dimensions of business case for a diagnostic equality check: (i) costs associated with not undertaking the diagnostic check; and (ii) tangible and intangible benefits of conducting the diagnostic.

Firstly, costs and risks of not undertaking the diagnostic equality check may potentially make a strong business case. The respondent from a large private sector employer said: 'I think it would be good to highlight the cost as in "This is how much it will cost to do it, and if you don't do one, this is the potential cost"'.

The main costs of not undertaking the diagnostic, as they were highlighted in the interviews, ranged from high labour turnover, to losing talented employees due to discrimination and work–life balance issues, to tribunals and the associated bad publicity. Therefore, the tool should include a well-founded risk analysis to demonstrate the potential costs of not taking action in the short and long term.

Secondly, among the potential benefits of undertaking the diagnostic as pointed out by the research participants are:

- being an employer of choice which will give the advantage of having access to a wider talent pool, reducing recruitment and labour turnover costs, recruiting and retaining the best talent;
- improved organizational performance and efficiency due to less sickness leave, higher levels of employee satisfaction and commitment, increased productivity and creativity;
- enhanced trust relationship and communication with employees;
- savings and increased retention rates related to flexible working;
- a happier and healthier workforce;
- improved customer relations and service delivery; and
- a positive corporate image and reputation.

Accordingly, all respondents except one underlined that the tool needs to highlight the long-term and short-term, tangible and intangible, benefits of conducting a diagnostic equality check. To do that, the diagnostic tool should include robust data in terms of facts and figures, such as statistical evidence regarding business benefits, for example estimated demographic composition of the UK labour force by 2020, demographic composition of customers and consumers by 2020, etc. For instance, the respondent from a large private sector finance organization explained that the tool should be forward looking in terms of its business case through projecting the future demographic trends and helping employers to put mechanisms in place to effectively respond to those trends. Similarly, a respondent from a higher education institution pointed out the issue of an ageing workforce, stating that 50 per cent of their staff is over 55. So, she argued that there is a strong business imperative for them based on demographics.

One of the possible methods of presenting a business case argument, as put forward by more than half of the respondents, was through inclusion of case studies which demonstrate how organizations that undertook the equality check benefited from the process and improved their business performance. Nevertheless, it was stated by all respondents but three that it would be most convincing if the business case is tailored according to the size and sector of the organizations, since drivers and priorities may vary with sector and size. Thus, rather than presenting a single general standard business case for all types of organizations, the tool should offer a set of business case arguments which will more directly relate to organizational size and sector in a less complicated way. Significantly a respondent from one of the provider organizations which works with SMEs told us that lack of understanding regarding issues of diversity and equality is widespread, and practice is poor, among SMEs, and that they do not prioritize equality and diversity. She told us that to engage with SMEs her organization started with the business case but ended up with the legal case. However, she still believed that there is a business case for the SMEs around the diverse set of skills and flexibility that may be brought into an organization through equality and diversity.

The difficulties of engaging SMEs and making a business case that will convince them were emphasized by all respondents from provider organizations. For instance, another respondent pointed out that SMEs believe that their agenda is overcrowded and they will act only on priorities. For that reason, he argued that it is important to include a clear and straightforward business case in the tool to display the tangible benefits of undertaking the diagnostic check: using examples. The evidence suggests that the best strategy to engage SMEs is to include some form of legislative enforcement or to ensure that the diagnostic check is part of procurement.

Similarly, the respondent from a provider organization whose clients are SMEs in Wales told us that while working with the individual organizations, where diversity and equality are not at the forefront, their business consultants talk instead about contracts with public sector and procurement. Thus, he suggested that in order to engage the SMEs the new tool should talk their language, which is mostly based on 'money, contract and procurement'. Moreover, contract requirements may act as a key driver for not only SMEs but also for large organization as well. Two-thirds of the respondents thought that one of the factors behind the IiP's success is related to the fact that organizations with Investors recognition benefit from a wider pool of contracting organizations.

Are recognition and benchmarking key selling points?

Another strategy for a successful diagnostic check is highlighting the reputation of management in order to motivate the employers to undertake the diagnostic. In the cases where there is strong legislation, employers can be encouraged to undertake a diagnostic check by pointing out the risks of not doing so, that is tribunals. As for the cases where legislation is weak, a more positive encouragement strategy is necessary. Within that context, all but one of the respondents suggested that, in addition to a strong business case, employers are more likely to be convinced to use the new tool if it has a national recognition, which is crucial for credited benchmarking. Accordingly it is pointed out by these respondents that having been benchmarked, and subsequently having an accredited badge, does indeed make strong business sense for organizations, due to the financial benefits of accreditation.

All respondents agreed that success and proactivity of the organizations should be recognized and awarded if they are expected to commit resources to undertaking the diagnostic and taking action in-line with its results. For instance two-thirds of the respondents believed that the Investors in People standard is well received by the employers in different sectors and of different sizes, because it is a benchmarking process and the organizations are awarded with a badge which has a nationwide recognition.

Another respondent from a large retail company said that her organization would be interested in an industry-based comparative diversity and an equality tool with benchmarking. Similarly, the respondent from a large private financial institution stated that the new tool should be based on benchmarking and not on compliance, if the EOC wishes to increase the take-up. The respondent from another large financial institution said that the benchmarking process should be a rigorous and credible one where organizations have to prove themselves, as in the case of the IiP standard, so that it will have real value.

However, 39 respondents argued that the demands of employers, in terms of the level of rigour of the tool, might vary from organization to organization. It is even argued that a too rigorous and demanding tool may drive away the organizations which have limited resources or the ones which are not proactive enough to commit sufficient resources. For instance, 13 respondents stated that

SMEs are very much interested in seeing where their competitors are, hence they would be interested in being benchmarked against other similar organizations, but many do not have the resources or are not proactive enough to go through a very rigorous, laborious, costly and long diagnostic check process. Thus, it is suggested that SMEs would be most interested in a tool which will benchmark them against legal compliance and against their competitors.

However, whatever the level of demands put on the organizations by the tool, respondents unanimously agreed that the diagnostic check should be evidence based rather than just being a tick-box exercise and should require organizations to provide evidential data, at least in the priority areas. Being evidence based will contribute to the accountability of the tool. In this regard, two-thirds of the respondents also pointed out that the credibility of the provider is crucial in maximizing take-up. There are currently too many tools, which significantly diminishes their individual credibility.

The interviews highlighted the desire that employers have for good publicity: that of being identified as leaders in any field and being commended. Thus, all but one of the respondents agreed that giving credit to the users of the diagnostic equality check is one of the key strategies to engage employers. However, there were different views on how this can be done. The first view was that the diagnostic check could result in a badge or a sort of award to the organizations which undertake it. A respondent from a higher education institution suggested that the EOC should give awards to the good practice employers. On the other hand, the second view was that giving a badge is not a good idea in the equality field due to the risk of organizations just going for the badge. Yet, the organizations should be provided with some kind of feedback. Lastly, publishing a list of best practice organizations or launching a pledge to engage the organizations with the diagnostic equality check were among the suggestions.

In summary, all of our respondents believed that benchmarking and recognition are among the key selling points for the new diagnostic equality check because they will provide them with enhanced reputation and recognition as well as an understanding of their situation in terms of diversity and equality. Additionally, it is argued that the tool should benchmark the employers:

1   against what constitutes minimum practice;
2   against other similar organizations (competitors or industry);
3   against the local population and against the national standard.

How can the diagnostic check be promoted effectively?

It was suggested throughout the interviews that the EOC needs to adopt a clever promotion strategy since the market is crowded with many diagnostic checks and benchmarks. All respondents thought that the EOC should utilize traditional promotion methods, such as press advertising and communicating the tool through launch events and workshops. It was also pointed out that specialist press, such as Personnel Today and IDS, could be utilized. Rather than plain advertising, the EOC should use several promotion strategies simultaneously to reach as many organizations as possible at both regional and national levels, and to convince them to undertake the diagnostic check.

However, the promotion strategy should be sensitive to the size differences between the organizations. For instance it was argued by the respondents from SME provider organizations that flyers and direct telephone sales would prove to be the most effective advertising strategies in the case of SMEs. Furthermore, different communication channels should be exploited to reach organizations in different sectors. Four main strategies were put forward during the interviews: establishing partnerships with key stakeholders, consultation with key stakeholders, setting up an advisory committee, and creating a network of equality champions.

All respondents emphasized the importance of partnership with key stakeholders for any good promotion strategy. The new diagnostic tool needs a very good communication strategy to ensure that organizations will not feel like the new tool is being imposed on them. Sixty-one respondents argued that diagnostic tools or benchmarks are successful because of their strong linkages to business. It was also pointed out that it may be more effective and efficient to target business support networks rather than individual businesses. The importance of lobbying the Government to support the tool was discussed.

Lastly, the respondent from a trade union claimed that class action is the best way to push employers to undertake a diagnostic check and take subsequent action in-line with the results. In addition, one of our respondents from a large private financial services organization told us that they undertook an EPR upon the request of the trade union. Thus, engaging the trade unions came out in the interviews as another effective way of promoting the tool. Accordingly, the key organizations that the EOC needs to partner at national level, according to the respondents, were the CBI, Chamber of Commerce, Cabinet Office, Department of Trade and Industry (DTI), TUC, Chartered Institute of Personnel and Development (CIPD), Learning and Skills Council, and the Sectors Skills Council. However, 46 respondents also highlighted the importance of establishing partnerships with the organizations or institutions which exert influence on specific sectors or different sizes of organizations.

Regarding organizational size, it is hardest to reach and engage SMEs. There are disparities between organizations of different sizes regarding awareness of diversity and equality. Hence the promotion strategy should take into account this variation in the levels of awareness. Within that framework, the Advisory, Conciliation and Arbitration Service (ACAS), Business Links, HM Revenue and Customs, the Federation of Small Businesses (FSB), and other business support channels were mentioned as potentially the most effective organizations to communicate and promote the tool among SMEs. It is further argued that the diagnostic equality check can be linked to the mainstream advice from these organizations. Moreover, the dynamics of getting information to SMEs are very different from that of large organizations. For instance, it is stated by a provider who works with SMEs that main information channels for SMEs are accountants and local people. So he argued that the EOC might also consider partnering with the Accountants Association to promote the tool.

In terms of taking into account the sector and industry differences throughout the promotion of the tool, partnership with sector or industry-specific umbrella organizations will encourage the potential users to undertake to use the tool. More than three-quarters of the respondents told us at some point in the interviews that information and experience sharing and partnerships are very widespread in their sectors. These partnerships will provide the EOC with an insider's knowledge, which will help it to better understand the specific dynamics of each sector, as well as an opportunity to take a more active role in different sectors. The organizations named in the interviews as potential partners were the Audit Commission and the Society of Chief Personnel Officers (SOCPO) for local government; the National Council for Voluntary Organizations for the voluntary sector; the Health Care Commission for the health sector; the University Colleges Association and the Equality Challenge Unit for the higher education sector; and the Practitioners Forum and the Chief Fire Officers Association for Fire Rescue Services.

In addition, more than half of the respondents from provider organizations and membership institutions displayed a willingness to partner with the EOC for promoting the tool, as well as for capacity building for the diagnostic. They stated that they could act as promoter, communicator and liaison in their sector or area of specialism.

In addition to partnerships with key stakeholders, an inclusive consultation process with key stakeholders when developing the tool is critical. The promotion process indeed starts as early as the consultation, during the development of the tool. Fifty-six respondents claimed that consultation is a very effective strategy to get by with, even before drafting the tool.

Thus, it is suggested that there should be a robust consultation process in which representatives from trade unions, the Government, employer representative bodies and potential users from public, private and voluntary sectors would be involved. Through this early engagement with the stakeholders, it would be possible both to develop a tool that would meet the needs of and prioritize the potential users, and to establish a network of volunteers at the outset. Additionally, the EOC may organize focus groups and regional workshops for consultation. If the new tool is a generic one, consultation with other equality and benchmarking bodies, and employer forums such as the Commission for Racial Equality (CRE), the Disability Rights Commission (DRC), Stonewall, Opportunity Now, Age Positive, Race for Opportunity, is critical for sharing experience and expertise. This will eliminate possible overlaps and conflicts with the tools that are currently available in this field.

There was unanimous support for the idea that, as a part of the consultation process, there should be a separate advisory committee which will be more directly involved with and committed to the new diagnostic equality check. Alternatively, it is possible to establish a list of volunteering organizations to give opinions and make suggestions throughout the process of developing the diagnostic equality check. The advisory committee should be made up of key employers in their respective sectors as well as academics and providers. One of the respondents further suggested that the EOC should initially focus on the good practice organizations and the organizations which want to be good practice employers but who are not because of unconscious ignorance. Moreover, more than half of the respondents said that the EOC should show early models of the tool to the members of the advisory committee to engage them from the beginning. Lastly, the EOC may use the committee members to pilot the tool and may later include the positive results from that pilot in the actual tool.

Three-quarters of the respondents argued that having a network of champions who will promote the diagnostic equality check within their organizations and sectors is critical for increasing the take-up of the tool. Equality champions may work at four different levels: organizational, sectoral, regional and national.

Firstly, undertaking a comprehensive diagnostic equality check requires genuine commitment from the top management and involvement of middle management. Progressive action in the field of diversity and equality is about 'winning the hearts and minds of people' in the organization, and it requires involvement of organizational actors at different levels and functions.

Equality and diversity officers may not be powerful enough in their organization in terms of their decision-making power as well as the resources available to them. Thus, in order to encourage engagement with the diagnostic equality check, it is important to identify the key people in the organizations who have formal or informal power to make change. High profile people should champion the tool in different sectors and regions. For instance, the respondent from a provider organization in the higher education sector argued that the tool should be championed by the chancellors in the universities.

Twenty-eight respondents added that not only high profile individuals but also respected organizations should champion the diagnostic check. By respected organizations, these respondents referred to organizations which are well known and have a good reputation, as well as being financially successful. Initial buy-in from such credited organizations is argued to be one of the most effective marketing and advertising strategies. An electronic network, as well as regional and sectoral subnetworks, can be established to promote experience and information sharing between the equality champions.

This section has explored the factors that make a diagnostic check successful. Our findings are presented in **Boxes 6.1–4** below.

Box 6.1   Is there a need for strong legislation and government support?

- strong legislative backing is one of the major factors that contribute to the success of a diagnostic tool;
- issue of equality and diversity does not have a strong legislative clout despite the fact that legislation could be the most effective medium to drive equality and diversity;
- either legal enforcement or making the diagnostic check part of procurement is essential to ensure high levels of take up among the SMEs;
- legislation and government support can be important motivators for the employers;
- the legal case for a diagnostic equality check should also be informed by a firm understanding of business case arguments.

Box 6.2   Responses to the question whether the business case is an important driver for employers to undertake the diagnostic check

- Legislative focus on diagnostic checks may drive away proactive approach: the emphasis should be on the business benefits of undertaking the diagnostic.
- The benefits of undertaking the tool against the costs of it should be very clearly stated within the tool. The tool should be explicit in terms of how the tool will contribute to the bottom line.
- That the EOC should take into account that drivers for undertaking the diagnostic check may display variation in-line with the size and sector of the organizations.
- Budget considerations can be a barrier for many organizations in conducting the diagnostic equality check.
- The tool should include a proper cost–benefit analysis.

▶

- Undertaking such a diagnostic check is a serious resource issue and the tool should present a clear business case in such a way as to encourage the highest possible level of involvement and commitment by different organizational actors throughout the process.
- Conducting a diagnostic check is a labour-intensive process which requires commitment from top management and staff.
- A strong business case argument will promote a genuine understanding of the necessity of undertaking the diagnostic check and prevent the use of cost and budget considerations as excuses for not conducting a diagnostic equality check.
- The tool should include a detailed business case to engage the HR and equality officers with expert knowledge and a less complicated and more straightforward version of this business case, which can then be used by the HR and equality and diversity specialists in pitching the tool to their managers or directors.
- The necessity of structuring the tool in a way to give the users a good feeling.
- The starting point of the tool should be positive in the sense of making clear that the diagnostic check process aims to support the users in capitalizing on the benefits of equality and diversity.
- A positive tool will make it easier for the HR managers or equality and diversity officers to convince their senior management teams.
- The ethical case in terms of 'doing the right thing' and 'being a best practice employer' is an important driver for the employers in the UK, since it also indirectly contributes to the bottom line through good publicity, which in turn provides the employers with access to a more diverse range of customers.
- The tool should include a well-founded risk analysis to demonstrate the potential costs of not taking action in the short and long term.
- The tool needs to highlight the long-term and short term, tangible and intangible, benefits of conducting a diagnostic equality check.
- It would be most convincing if the business case is tailored according to the size and sector of the organizations, since drivers and priorities may vary with sector and size.
- The best strategy for engaging the SMEs is to include some form of legislative enforcement or to ensure that the diagnostic check is part of procurement.
- The new tool should talk the language of the SMEs, which is mostly based on 'money, contract and procurement'.

Box 6.3   Responses to the question whether recognition and benchmarking are key selling points for a diagnostic check

- Another strategy for a successful diagnostic check is highlighting the reputation of management to motivate the employers to undertake the diagnostic.
- Success and proactivity of the organizations should be recognized and awarded if they are expected to commit resources to undertaking the diagnostic and taking action in-line with its results.
- Demands of employers in terms of level of rigour of the tool may vary from organization to organization.
- SMEs would be most interested in a tool which will benchmark them against legal compliance and against their competitors.
- A diagnostic check should be evidence based rather than just being a tick-box exercise, and should require organizations to provide evidential data at least in the priority areas. Being evidence based will contribute to the accountability of the tool.
- Credibility of the provider is crucial to increase the take-up.
- An equality check should be an accountable and credible tool, with a level of authority, so that employers will be convinced that there is a financial incentive for using it.
- Employers will always appreciate good publicity, being identified as leaders in any field and being commended.
- Benchmarking and recognition are among the key selling points for the new diagnostic equality check because they will provide them with good reputation and recognition as well as an understanding of their situation in terms of diversity and equality.
- Additionally, the tool should benchmark the employers: (a) against what constitutes minimum practice; (b) against other similar organizations (competitors or industry); (c) against the local population and the national standard.

Box 6.4   Responses to the question: how can the diagnostic check can be promoted?

- The EOC needs to adapt a clever promotion strategy, since the market is crowded with many diagnostic checks and benchmarks.
- Four main strategies were put forward during the interviews: establishing partnerships with key stakeholders, consultation with key stakeholders, setting up an advisory committee, and creating a network of equality champions.
- All respondents emphasized the importance of partnership with key stakeholders for any good promotion strategy.
- Diagnostic tools or benchmarks are successful because of their strong linkages to business.
- Importance of lobbying the Government to support the tool should be acknowledged.
- There are disparities between organizations of different sizes regarding the awareness of diversity and equality. Hence the promotion strategy should take into account this variation in the levels of awareness.
- Partnership with sector or industry-specific umbrella organizations will encourage the potential users to undertake to use the tool.
- An inclusive consultation process with key stakeholders when developing the tool is critical.
- There should be a robust consultation process with the key stakeholders. Through this early engagement, it would be possible both to develop a tool that would meet the needs of and prioritize potential users, and to establish a network of volunteers at the outset.
- There should be a separate advisory committee which will be more directly involved with and committed to the new diagnostic equality check.
- Having a network of champions, which will promote the diagnostic equality check within their organizations and sectors, is critical for increasing the take-up of the tool.
- Not only high profile individuals but also respected organizations should champion the diagnostic check.

6.4   Views on a diagnostic equality check

This section outlines the respondents' views on the coverage and format of a diagnostic equality check. Firstly, the respondents' views on the coverage of the tool are identified. The discussion starts from with whether there is a necessity for a diagnostic equality check and our study provides an affirmative response for a generic one. Then we explain the needs and priorities of the potential users and providers in terms of coverage of the tool. Coverage across human resource management, organizational culture, customers and service users are explored. Then we investigate how employers can be encouraged to adopt a proactive approach before and after undertaking the diagnostic check. We explore common reasons for resistance to a proactive stance and factors that contribute to a wider use of a diagnostic check as a progressive tool. Further, we question differences between ready-made action plans and flexible approaches in encouraging the employers to take proactive action. Lastly, we identify the key points made by the research participants on the format of the diagnostic check. Various attributes of an ideal format for a diagnostic check are explored. The options of self-assessment and external audit, as part of a new diagnostic check, are investigated. We have analysed whether a single tool or a family of tools were deemed as more appropriate for a generic diagnostic equality check.

Views on the coverage of the tool

This section maps out the opinions of the research participants in terms of coverage of a diagnostic equality check under three headings: diversity strands, organizational areas and action plans.

When we asked the respondents whether they believe in the necessity of a diagnostic equality check, all of them pointed out that there is an inflation of diagnostic or benchmarking equality tools in the UK. Nevertheless, three-quarters of the participants were receptive to the idea of a new diagnostic check which can reconcile these different tools. Although there is a widespread scepticism regarding diagnostic checks, the study identified that there is a need for a generic check that can help organizations identify and prioritize a wide range of equality and diversity needs and activities.

There is a benchmarking fatigue in the business community as a direct consequence of the complexity and multiplicity of the diagnostic tools that are available on diversity and equality, as well a great deal of confusion about equality and diversity monitoring. All respondents from potential users made reference to their experience of labouring over extensive red tape and paperwork stemming from the inflation of benchmarks, each of which appeared to ask for variations of the same information.

The strongest unanimous point made by the public and private sector employers and providers was that a new tool which will solely focus on gender would not be successful. Twenty-one of the respondents also pointed out the weaknesses of the existing benchmarks and argued that the diagnostic checks that focus on a single dimension of diversity are problematic due to their inability to address multiple discrimination issues. For instance, a respondent from a local government organization argued that this is a weakness of the existing benchmarks, such as Opportunity Now, Race for Opportunity and Stonewall, and it makes it difficult for them to carry out a comprehensive equality impact assessment in an efficient way.

On balance, three-quarters of the respondents asserted that there is a market for a generic equality and diversity tool. All of the potential users pointed out that they would welcome a new diagnostic tool if it covered all six strands of diversity included in the legislation. Similarly, more than half of the providers and all membership organizations pointed out that a comprehensive and holistic tool, which would cover all diversity strands, would be well-received since it would be more practical, productive and cost and time efficient for employers to have a single diagnostic check. In other words, most of the research participants including providers, potential users and their representative bodies, such as membership organizations, believe that a generic diagnostic equality check is a necessity in the current business environment, which is crowded with far too many such diagnostic and benchmarking tools.

The generic tool should be particularly useful for reaching SMEs, as it is impossible for them to undertake a separate check for each dimension of diversity, due to their limited resources. In order for a diagnostic check to be useful for the SMEs, the new check should include all strands of diversity.

Forty-three of the respondents argued that it would be very timely to develop a generic equality check which would be consistent with the Single Equality Act and the Commission for Equality and Human Rights (CEHR). However, 12 respondents claimed that the new tool should go beyond not only legislation but also concepts of equality and diversity, and that it needs to be based on an inclusion model which will go beyond the standard six strands and also cover diversity characteristics such as personality traits. In fact three respondents strongly argued that there is only a space for an inclusion tool and that it will have value only if it is capable of replacing the existing tools that focus on a single dimension of diversity.

Nevertheless, two-thirds of the participants argued that if the new tool has the ability to replace the existing benchmarks, it will make business sense for the organizations, since it will free them from the burden and cost of frequently repeating similar checks, as they currently do. One of the respondents explained this as follows:

A lot of institutions are grappling at the moment with impact assessments in terms of some of the equality legislation, and if you assess your practices in terms of race, then six months later you go back to the same managers and services and say, well, can you assess your practices in terms of disability and then can you do it in terms of gender, it becomes almost like a legislative burden, and I think if there was a general equality check that allowed us or guided us in terms of checking our practices right across the equality and diversity themes, I think that might be more practical in terms of institutions checking their procedures.

However, whilst being general and generic, half of the participants argued that the tool should be balanced in terms of its accommodation of different strands of diversity, and that it should cover areas where there is less legislative focus, such as sexual orientation and religion, in a robust way as well. In the words of one respondent from a higher education institution:

> I think it should cover all the diversity scene. So, we know that the legislation is sometimes more involved in some areas such as race and disability than others, but I think it should cover right across the areas such as sexuality and faith.

In addition, 20 respondents pointed out that a diagnostic equality check needs to acknowledge that each strand of diversity has its own peculiar characteristics, that is, the tool should include some strand-specific questions as well as general questions. Another idea was to make some sections of the diagnostic check optional to give employer the flexibility to choose which areas to focus on.

Forty-four of the respondents argued that the new tool should not be only generic but also general and comprehensive in its scope. It is pointed out by these participants that the tool should not be limited to pay discrimination but should address all three causes of the gender pay gap. Two respondents stated that the EPR process requires a lot of work but only focuses on pay. These respondents argued that the new equality diagnostic check should have a broader focus so that organizations will be able to learn more about themselves at the end of the process. The study revealed four aspects of coverage of the tool: (i) human resource management; (ii) cultural issues; (iii) customer and service users; and (iv) prioritizing topics and areas.

All respondents asserted that the tool should cover all areas of human resources which directly or indirectly contribute to the gender pay gap, such as recruitment and selection, training and development, work–life balance programmes, leadership, mentoring, coaching and career development, and occupational segregation, as well as pay structures and practices. Half of the respondents also argued that focusing explicitly on the gender pay gap may scare the employers and drive them away from engaging with the diagnostic equality check. Additionally, three-quarters of the respondents emphasized the need for a generic diagnostic equality check which will cover all areas of employment, and function as a comprehensive equality and diversity impact assessment. Furthermore, the importance of including monitoring activities in the tool is mentioned throughout the interviews, since this is crucial in shifting attitude and creating a culture change.

Eleven respondents argued that the tool should include not only the formal procedures and practices but also informal aspects of organizational life. For instance, organizational culture and behavioural aspects, such as harassment and bullying, were among the areas that were mentioned in the interviews as the possible areas to be covered by a new diagnostic equality check. One of the respondents argued:

> I think it should also cover behavioural aspects such as mutual respect, bullying and harassment. Those types of issues, because that's all about having a good and positive community. I think also about how the organization itself engages with the community, so it's not simply about having a nice internal community within the organization, but it's about how the organization interacts with any partners, in terms of contractors, how it sells itself to other institutions. So, in other words, it will encourage us to look outside and encourages us to be ambassadors of good behaviour, and it encourages us to do that with the institutions that we work with. So I think that it should be as holistic as possible.

As apparent in the above words, a new diagnostic check should encourage the employers to look outside of their organizations, to their local community, contractors and customers.

The tool should appeal to the needs of the customers and service users as well as assessing the internal processes. The tool may cover external relations such as service delivery, customer relations and community involvement. All research participants from public sector organizations, but one, reported that service delivery is one of the hottest priority areas for them. Hence, they argued, it would be very useful and productive for them if the tool has a service delivery dimension as well. On the other hand our respondent from the large voluntary sector organization argued that for them the issue of recruiting and managing volunteers is as important as employment relations and service delivery. He explained that although they have a very different make-up compared to public sector organizations, voluntary sector organizations are generally categorized under the public sector when a new diagnostic check or benchmark is being designed. He said that issue around working with volunteers is one of the challenges peculiar to the voluntary sector. Hence he argued that the new tool should recognize the peculiarities of the voluntary sector and should cover the priority areas for these organizations as well.

Thirty-nine of the respondents pointed out that the tool should have clarity in terms of the areas and topics included. Splitting the tool into clear categories in terms of different areas was one of the suggestions raised during the interviews. Such clear sectionalization may also give the employers the flexibility to follow a step-by-step diagnostic in which they can choose which areas to focus on according to the basis of their priorities. A piecemeal approach would make the diagnostic check process more manageable and less confusing for the users. For instance, a respondent from a large private sector retail company suggested that the diagnostic check should have clearly described and defined sections. However, she argued that in the first instance there should be a summary page with boxes for each section/area, as in the case of EPR Toolkit, and that employers should be able choose their preferred areas of focus:

> You could maybe follow it and there was a more detailed section that came as a flow chart on a summary page, if you follow steps, say, you could either go one way or the other, so it would start thinning it down. Like drop-down boxes for you to follow off, so it wouldn't be so daunting. You could look at certain things. You know what I mean? For example in Equal Pay Review, it's starting with this overall data, and then breaking it down isn't it, into smaller and smaller parts? So this could be the same with the flow chart, you could break it down.

How can the employers be encouraged to adopt a proactive approach?

One of the biggest problems with most of the existing diagnostic checks and benchmarking exercises is that each becomes an end in itself and evolves into a 'tick-box' approach. It is emphasized by three-quarters of the respondents that the new tool should not only diagnose problems and gaps regarding equality and diversity, but should also indicate possible actions that can be taken to improve the state of organizations in terms of diversity and equality.

Both employers and their membership institutions explained that upon collecting evidence and data within the scope of a benchmarking exercise, employers, most of the time, do not know how to interpret that data and what actions to take. One of the respondents from a provider organization explained:

> I think one of the reasons why employers don't take action now, or as much action as we would like to see on equalities, is that they don't know what to address. So I think developing a good diagnostics toolkit, enables them to break down the task that they face. I think it has to be clear that if employers are going to undertake such an exercise and going through all this a toolkit or checklist assessment, if they're not going to act on it there's no point in it. I think that's another one of the things with Equal Pay Review, organizations felt they had to undertake them, and the Equal Pay Review became the end in itself and they didn't know what to do once

they'd done it, they just threw lots of resources into doing that but didn't know what to do next.

This situation clearly limits the possibility of proactive action which should follow the diagnostic. This is an important issue particularly for the organizations which do not have internal expertise to make sense of the diagnostic or benchmark results and to translate the assessment into action planning. Research participants noted that if a benchmarking tool is not capable of delivering an explicit agenda for proactive action, there is the risk of inaction or reactive approach both by small- and medium-sized organizations, which do not have the resources to employ diversity and equality experts, and by large organizations without sophisticated diversity and equality programmes and systems already in place.

It is generally argued by the research participants from both employer and provider organizations that if the EOC wishes the diagnostic equality check to promote proactive and progressive action, the focus of the tool should be on how the diagnostic is going to help the users and guide users to translate the results of the check into action and objectives rather than solely identifying the problems. It is argued that the tool should provide the users at least with a methodology to use the results of the assessment for action planning. Hence, the new tool should help users to:

1 diagnose the problems;
2 interpret the results;
3 take actions.

Offering an example, a respondent from a higher education institution used the analogy of a health check to illustrate his point. He said that the diagnostic check should take the temperature of the organization at a particular point in time, and that acknowledging the diagnostic will not cure the illness by itself but it should lead to a treatment process which will include formulating and delivering action plans. He also pointed out that this process has to be repeated regularly to ensure a healthy organization in a cycle of assessment, mobilization and implementation. He claimed that most of the existing benchmarks and diagnostic checks fall short of such a continuum, which could be detrimental to realizing a transformation in the organizations in terms of diversity and equality. He said that the new tool should be based on a very robust methodology to promote equality and diversity in the UK, particularly since most of the organizations tend to sideline equality and diversity issues and merely pay lip-service to it.

In summary, a new diagnostic equality check should include action plans or indications of possible action points. However, there were different views on how a diagnostic equality check can result in proactive action by the users.

Twenty-three respondents argued that action plans can be presented through case studies. Nineteen others thought that including checklists within the tool would be an effective way of indicating the key areas for action. Still, 15 others believed that the tool should provide more structured and ready-made action plans. At the most general level, there were two different opinions among the respondents about the level of flexibility of the action plans: providing ready-made action plans and assuming a flexible approach. Twenty-three participants argued that a loose and flexible approach to action planning may not be successful for all organizations, due to the variation between them in terms of diversity and equality expertise, as well as other resources committed for developing action plans. Nevertheless, independent of their views on the nature and methods of indicating action plans or points, all respondents agreed that in order to avoid a 'tick-box' approach, the new tool should make it very explicit that the outcomes of the diagnostic check are crucial, and that the tool is a medium or facilitator for realizing the aim of enhancing equality and diversity in the user organizations.

Two-thirds of the participants argued for the necessity of tailoring the action plans according to the size, culture and priorities of the organizations, since the levels of cultural readiness and resources of the users vary extensively. Indeed, respondents who argued for a flexible approach, or those who believed in the efficiency of a more structured approach alike, underlined that a diagnostic equality check needs to take into consideration the organization's size in terms of areas covered in the diagnostic, and that the action plans and guidance should be at some level tailored according to the size of the organization. Moreover, six respondents argued that it is not only an issue of size but also one of organizational culture and approach, in terms of diversity and equality. One respondent said:

> Culture, I would stress, yet again . . . It's all very well having the technical content in these tools, to tick the boxes, but unless people address culture and how to change culture within an organization.

Thus, these respondents strongly emphasized that the level of understanding of and commitment towards diversity and equality may be even more decisive in terms of differentiating organizations, since there may be very progressive SMEs on the one hand but large organizations with little or no understanding of equality and diversity on the other. Hence they argued that the separating line should be the organizational culture, not the size of the organization. In the words of one of the respondents:

> I don't think size is as important as the culture, where the organization is at. Some organizations will be more comfortable talking about stuff like equal pay, and other organizations won't be.

This is an interesting argument in terms of suggesting that an organization's size alone may not be an indication of its needs and priorities about a diagnostic equality check or that it may not predict its potential for engagement with such a check. Thus, when developing the diagnostic equality check, the differences in terms of organizational culture as well as size should be addressed.

Fifteen respondents thought that it would be most effective, useful and practical if the tool provides the users with ready-made action plans at the end of the diagnostic check. There were various views among the respondents who found ready made action plans useful, in terms of the coverage of the action plans. Eleven respondents argued that the action plans should be comprehensive, because the employers need holistic equality and diversity action plans, which should also help to put balanced and consistent equality policies and systems in place across their organizations.

On the other hand, four argued that the action plans should be focused on high impact areas and should set clear targets. It is stated by these respondents that, particularly for the SMEs which have limited resources, it would be most useful and practical if there is a prioritization between necessary action areas rather than providing them with a long list of actions which may confuse and paralyse them. Furthermore, a respondent from a membership organization argued that local government organizations have an agenda which is extremely crowded with numerous action plans, and for that reason the new diagnostic check should provide them with a focus on the critical action areas.

A third view was that the action plans provided by the tool should be comprehensive but that the actions have to be broken down into clearly defined sections. It is suggested that there can then be a checklist for each action type under these sections. Another suggestion was that, so as to give flexibility to the users, the tool may provide action plans at different levels, starting from the actions to be taken for minimum compliance and progressing into more sophisticated and proactive levels of action. Integrating hierarchical levels within the tool also addresses resources and capacities of organizations of different sizes. For instance, the representative bodies and providers for SMEs pointed out the difficulty of engaging them in diversity and equality issues. They argued that the most effective way to increase take-up among SMEs is to start with basic compliance and awareness raising, then gradually engage them to be more progressive and proactive.

On the other hand, 32 respondents argued that the tool should assume a more flexible approach and should be indicative of possible action areas rather than directly and explicitly providing an action plan. They claimed that because one size does not fit all, action plans should be tailored according to the state, nature and characteristics of each individual organization.

The most common view among this group was to provide the users with 'risk areas' or 'areas for action/improvement', in-line with the results of their diagnostic, so as to give them the flexibility to decide which actions to take. The respondent from a large civil service organization stated that providing the organizations with ready-made action plans may be dangerous in terms of reducing the level of commitment. He believed that organizations themselves should develop their actual action plans, which is a crucial learning process in itself. Furthermore, he felt that the organizations are more likely to commit to improvements, where they are accountable for preparing their own improvement plan. He said that the tool's role should be providing the organizations with the depth of knowledge and information that is required for equality and diversity action planning. Hence, he concluded that the tool should provide guidance and emphasize the key themes for improvement, but it should stop short of making specific recommendations. A more flexible and less prescriptive approach and case studies can be used to demonstrate possible action plans and scenarios which will also help organizations to better visualize themselves as assuming a proactive approach.

Similarly, it is stated by 17 respondents that the results of diagnostic check should be capable of pinpointing the hot areas which require action in an organization. Several methods are suggested for highlighting the problem areas and gaps by establishing a traffic lights system to display the state of the organization in specific areas, or by flagging where there is a breach of legislation. These respondents also argued that at the end of the diagnostic check organizations should be provided with a conclusion about their strengths and weaknesses in terms of equality and diversity, and the tool should map out in an encouraging, proactive and practical way the possible actions that can be taken. However, the tool should not include ready-made action plans, but guidance and insights to help the organizations to decide on their priorities and actions.

One-third of the respondents argued that after completing the diagnostic check, and when organizations are developing their action plans, there could then be consultancy support, with organizations being informed about where they could go for further help. In the cases where the organizations cannot afford to get consultancy help, it is suggested, there should be one-to-one advice and guidance provided by the EOC.

Three-quarters of the respondents emphasized that the diagnostic check should focus on change and function as an organizational change tool. Within that framework, one of the interesting suggestions was to organize the tool around three temporal dimensions: past, present and future: so that users would be able to monitor the change in their organization by undertaking the diagnostic. In that sense, the tool should not be only forward looking in terms of offering future action plans or points, but should have a retrospective element through which the users will be able to assess the effectiveness and usefulness of their diversity and equality initiatives in the past and present.

Twenty-seven respondents pointed out that an efficient diagnostic check should be also capable of raising awareness through the questions and areas included, which would demonstrate the important issues and dimensions of diversity and equality. The process of undertaking the diagnostic check should open up a dialogue in the organization in terms of workforce diversity and equality issues, and should focus attention on the problematic areas. So, even the diagnostic check exercise itself may have the potential to promote a cultural change through raising awareness, which is the key to any change process.

Two-thirds of the respondents pointed out that whether the diagnostic check itself includes action plans or not, it might be a good strategy to encourage the users to pledge themselves to take action in-line with the results of the diagnostic check. It is further argued that the tool should include a convincing business case for proactive and progressive action on the side of the employers and should demonstrate the business benefits of not only conducting the diagnostic check, but also taking action as a result of it.

If the diagnostic check maps out the problem areas and explains the risks of not taking action such as tribunals, the employers will be more proactively willing to take action. However, the action plans or action points or areas should be represented in a positive and suggestive way to avoid the tool becoming scary for the employers and to persuade the users that the diagnostic check aims to help them rather than to control or force them.

Views on possible formats for the tool

In this section of our study we investigated the different views amongst the research participants in terms of possible formats for the diagnostic equality check. The discussion on the format of presentation, and of undertaking the diagnostic, is followed by an outline of possible options for the tool.

Our study has revealed a wide range of format considerations for effective design and implementation of a diagnostic check. The interviews revealed that accessibility is one of the key features that make a diagnostic check successful. All respondents argued that the check should be user friendly so that it would be accessible to the widest range of audiences and encourage involvement across businesses. The tool should be presented in a way that is easy to understand and that may include checklists and charts that can be circulated across the organization. It was also pointed out by 42 respondents that if the tool is accessible for the senior managers, there will be a higher level of organizational buy-in and commitment. In summary, the research findings revealed that the more accessible the tool, the higher will be the level of commitment and ownership throughout the organization, which is very important in terms of reliability of the diagnostic check and the effectiveness of the tool to encourage progressive and proactive action upon the diagnostic.

Three-quarters of the respondents stated that the tool should be presented in such a way that it should look simple, since a complicated-looking tool may discourage many employees at the first instance. However, they pointed out that simplicity should not bring superficiality and less rigour. It was stated that the diagnostic check should not be a thick and lengthy document which will look time consuming, but at the same time it should be capable of creating an understanding and awareness. The general view was that the presentation of the tool should be very well thought out, systematic and straightforward, and that it should be economical about use of space.

All participants argued that the tool should be in plain English, without any jargon or 'blinding with science', so that it would be accessible to all sizes of organizations and to everybody in an organization, and that organizations would not need to buy consultancy. One respondent explained:

It needs to be user friendly and more like plain English and not full of jargon. Because some of the diagnostic tools I can see the phrasing as, blinding with science comes to mind, you know, using big words and they sound more kind of impressive. That doesn't help. You need to understand. People really do need to understand what kind of question, what's behind this, and it needs to be in very plain English.

The language used in the tool should be tailored according to sector and should be sensitive to the terminology of each sector. For instance, the respondent from a provider organization for higher education institutions (HEIs) stated that the questions in the tool should be interesting and not too simplistic: that the tool should be pitched to the intelligence of the audience.

Sixty-one respondents believed that understanding and undertaking the diagnostic check should not require expert knowledge. Accessibility and usability of the tool by different organizational actors is crucial since the process of undertaking the diagnostic will be most time and cost effective if it can be reached by persons at different levels and functions of the organizations, instead of being accessible only to the HR professionals or diversity and equality officers. Such accessibility will also contribute to the take-up of the diagnostic check among the SMEs which do not have in-house expertise most of the time. Furthermore, in the case of large organizations, it is important that the tool is understandable by the middle managers, who will use the tool at team level.

In addition to simplicity and accessibility, clarity was put forward as another necessary feature of a diagnostic equality check. All respondents emphasized the necessity of developing a tool which is clear and transparent in terms of its purpose and outcomes. In order to ensure clarity, a diagnostic check should include the following features:

- clear and measurable definition of the terms and categories to avoid misinterpretations;
- a good index and easily understandable and clear questions;
- clear and explicit indication of the evidence or key data required to carry out the diagnostic check;
- clearly set benchmarking deadlines;
- a transparent and straightforward method of scoring; and
- be practical and designed in a way to make the diagnostic check less time consuming.

All of the respondents except four argued that the tool should be available in as many different formats as possible, including online, CD-ROM and hard copies, to increase the accessibility by different types and sizes of organizations. Their more detailed expectations were:

- an online diagnostic tool which is easily downloadable for internal use;
- an interactive online tool combined with online expert advice and guidance to prevent potential misunderstandings;
- an electronic data submission system for benchmarking;
- an electronic automated system for analysis of the current state of the user in terms of equality and diversity upon the completion of the diagnostic.

However, the variation in the level of technology use among the organizations should be taken into account, and the diagnostic check should be available in multiple formats for the highest possible accessibility. For instance, it is argued by eight respondents that technology literacy is relatively lower among the SMEs, and that some do not have the Internet, and for those reasons hard copies will work best for many of them. Similarly, the research participant from a large voluntary sector organization stated that technology use is weaker in that sector.

In addition, 12 other respondents argued that using the tool should require the lowest possible level of technology for the employers. On the other hand, eight respondents argued that the tool should be user friendly, but that a sophisticated use of technology and programming should be utilized to make the diagnostic check more practical and less labour intensive for the users. Nevertheless, all respondents agreed that the tool should not look complicated in order not to scare the employers.

A quarter of the potential users also argued that it would be most effective and practical for them if the tool could be designed in a way to be adaptable to the existing HR software packages, such as PeopleSoft and LinkHR. They argued that, because employers already have such software systems in place, it will be very convenient if the new tool could be integrated to these systems, which will in turn increase the take-up of the tool. However, this is not easily achievable due to the variety of reporting systems used by the organizations in the UK.

Nevertheless, three-quarters of the potential users argued that even if the tool does not have a hundred per cent fit to the specific reporting systems, it should be capable of being embedded in the existing reporting mechanisms. For instance, it will be very beneficial if the information gathered for the diagnostic check, as well as the findings, can be integrated into the annual human capital and CSR reports, or be useful for business planning. Furthermore, the tool should be designed in a way of being capable of the mainstream reporting mechanisms in an organization, instead of being marginalized as one of the activities of the human resources department or diversity and equality office. It was emphasized that the new tool should sit well with the philosophical approaches of performance management and peer review in order not to be sidelined. For example, the respondent from a fire rescue services organization emphasized the danger of marginalization, and she argued that the diagnostic check should be built into corporate planning. Similarly, the respondent from a local government organization pointed out the importance of making the diagnostic check a part of the mainstream where it is linked to the business and financial strategy of the organization.

As well as capability of integration into the mainstream reporting mechanisms of the organizations, the tool should be adaptable to their current equality and diversity monitoring systems. Particularly the respondents from local government organizations and their membership/provider institutions argued that local government is different from other sectors in the sense that there is already a well-established and well-received standard tool. Hence they were concerned about how the new diagnostic check will work alongside the Equality Standard. One of the respondents from a local government organization said that there is already enough confusion among the local authorities, and he asked how the new tool will complement the Equality Standard and whether they will be more confused. The respondent from a provider organization argued that the take-up would be higher among local government if the new tool supported the Equality Standard and the data collected for it could be used for the new diagnostic equality check. Similarly, a respondent from a health sector provider organization stated that it would be useful if the new tool was adaptable to the Positively Diverse programme, which is a change management programme signed up to by 50 per cent of NHS employers.

All respondents argued that ability to exploit the existing feedback and monitoring mechanisms will give the tool a competitive advantage since it will reduce the costs of undertaking the diagnostic. Hence it is suggested by the respondents from different sectors that in order to increase the level of efficiency and productivity, and to decrease the cost, the EOC should ensure that commonly used equality and diversity tools feed into the development of the new tool.

When asked about the possible formats for a diagnostic equality check, another discussion centred around the method of carrying out the check. The interviews revealed three different views regarding whether the diagnostic check should be undertaken internally or externally.

Half of the respondents argued that the new diagnostic equality check should be a self-assessment tool that is combined with training and guidance. Among these respondents, the general consideration was about the tendency of external audits making the organizations defensive and reactive. For example, the respondent from a large civil service organization argued that a self-assessment process rather than an external audit would work best for them due to security reasons. Similarly, the research participant from a provider organization in the higher education sector said that self-assessment would be preferred by universities since they are resistant to external audits and that they have enough expertise to undertake a diversity and equality self-check.

Twenty-seven respondents urged the EOC that an external audit process may scare away the potential users from undertaking the diagnostic check at all. Another advantage of opting for self–assessment, as discussed by the respondents, was that this has the potential for opening up a dialogue in the organization and raising awareness, hence bringing about cultural change, since it will require organizational members to be actively involved and to assume direct responsibility throughout the process, unlike an external audit, which is dominantly carried out by the external actors.

One of the respondents argued that the choice between an internal and external audit process depends on the nature and structure of the organization. Yet he reported that self-assessment will be more effective for his organization because it will give them more opportunity to involve the trade unions. From a different angle, a respondent from a large provider organization in Wales claimed that a diagnostic check should be a self-assessment tool due to the very practical reason that external audit is impossible since there are between 50,000 and 70,000 SMEs alone in Wales, and that the EOC does not have the resources to meet the demand.

However, organizations can be provided with training about undertaking the diagnostic, as well as with efficient and practical support through a free helpline. Provision of external support is crucial throughout the self-assessment process. Organizations would be more likely to welcome such a tool because they would feel more comfortable with an internal process, though they would need well-informed advisors to be able to carry out the assessment process with accuracy. Thus, it is argued by half of the research participants, the EOC should not only provide the users with advice and guidance but should also partner with other organizations such as ACAS, Business Links, Learning and Skills Council, CIPD and other provider and membership institutions, in order to enhance the level of accessibility, reach and effectiveness of external support available for the employers.

However, the respondents who preferred self-assessment were also aware of the risk of self-diluting, hiding problems and the subjectivity that may be brought in by such a form of assessment. Several solutions were offered to avoid that risk. For instance, the respondent from a provider institution which serves the science and education sector argued that it should be clearly underlined that organizations cannot get away with untrue results: 'I would go for self-assessment, but with an underpinning that they can't get away with anything that isn't true!'.

To ensure the highest possible level of objectivity, she suggested that organizations be required to submit their results which will then be published by an independent panel. Another respondent from a large civil service organization suggested that there could be an informal external audit, in the form of training the assessors and raising awareness, particularly of the senior and middle management teams. Still another respondent argued that the tool should have the capacity to encourage organizations to be honest, self-aware and ethical through integrated positive and practical support, particularly at the early stages of the diagnostic check.

Around two-thirds of the respondents also discussed the issue from a resources perspective. However, there were conflicting views in terms of suitability of a self-assessment process for the large organizations and SMES. In terms of human resources and level of expertise, 26 respondents argued that a self-assessment tool is ideal for large organizations if they have trained internal auditors, but not for SMEs which do not have either in-house expertise or sufficient human resources to carry out a self-assessment. On the other hand, 18 respondents discussed the issue in terms of economic resources and the cost of hiring external auditors, and they believed that self-assessment would suit SMEs best, who may not be able to afford to pay for an external audit.

Thirteen respondents suggested that an external audit is necessary for objective evaluation since organizations may tend to be economical about the truth in a self-assessment. These respondents also argued that external audits are more likely to encourage organizations to take a proactive approach. Moreover, it is pointed out that an external audit tool would be more efficient and the take-up would be higher than with a self-assessment tool, since benchmarking would be possible only through an external audit. Accordingly, an external audit should be accompanied by some form of accreditation, such as an award or a badge, so that organizations would be willing to commit resources to it.

Regarding the option of an external audit, one of the main considerations was who would carry out the process. Most of the time it is stated that the audit body should not be the EOC itself but independent third-party organizations which could be academic or consultancy. Franchising the audit was suggested as an option. There could be a tendering process to select the organizations which would conduct the external audit. However, it is important that audit bodies should be independent of the EOC to secure confidentiality and trust. Furthermore, three-quarters of the respondents who argued for an external audit said that the EOC should partner with the organizations representing different industries and sectors, both to increase the legitimacy of the benchmark and to structure the actual audit process.

On the other hand, one-third of the respondents proposed a middle-way, which would give organizations a flexibility to choose between a self-assessment and an external audit. One common suggestion was that the diagnostic check should be a self-assessment at the first stage, and that then this should be followed by an external audit and benchmarking exercise. Our respondents from local government organizations proposed that the Equality Standard model could be adopted. The Equality Standard includes five levels, three of which are self-assessment. On the other hand, assessment at level three, where there is a transition from planning to development, and at level five, where the whole process is revised, requires external validation, carried out by external auditors. As in the case of the IiP, organizations pay for the external assessment, which lasts between three to five days, depending on the size of the organization, and which is valid for three years. The EOC could use a similar model in terms of combining a self-assessment and an external audit. One of the respondents from a provider organization made a different suggestion in terms of introducing an external control or audit element to the diagnostic check. He argued that the diagnostic could be carried out through self-assessment. However, there could be some spot checks under Section 75 Obligations to ensure that the process works effectively.

All of the research participants believed that designing a stand-alone tool applicable to all kinds of organizations is a major challenge. They discussed how the diagnostic equality check needs to take into account the differences between the organizations in terms of size, sector and industry, since those differences have a large impact upon the needs, priorities and resources of the organizations. Hence, when developing the tool, the EOC should identify the needs and priorities of different types of organizations, rather than designing a tool which is based on a blanket approach.

Generally, interviews revealed two different approaches. Eleven respondents argued that there should be a single, standard tool which will offer advice and guidance tailored according to size and sector. On the other hand remaining respondents believed in the necessity of a family of tools rather than a single tool for all types and sizes of organizations, in order to address differences between organizations. Among the most frequently referred differences that the EOC should take into account when designing the tool were the differences in terms of size and sector.

Half of the respondents argued that public and private sector distinction is crucial since both the drivers for, and the needs and priorities about, a diagnostic equality check would significantly vary with sector. Accordingly, there should be two separate parallel benchmarks for these sectors. Furthermore, the new tool should also take into account the differences between the public and voluntary sector. For instance, a respondent said that even when a benchmark or diagnostic is tailored according to the sectoral differences, the voluntary sector is included under public sector and it is not acknowledged that it has a very different make-up and priorities than the public sector. Thus, he said that he would like to see the new tool addressing the specific needs and priorities of the voluntary sector organizations as well.

On the other hand two-thirds of the respondents underlined the importance of organizational size difference in terms of determining capabilities, drivers and needs of organizations to undertake a diagnostic equality check. Within that framework, the new tool can follow the approach of EPR in terms of taking into account organizational size. For instance, a respondent from a large provider organization argued that there should be at least two different versions of the diagnostic check, one tailored to needs and resources of the micro and small organizations, which do not have a separate human resources function, and another one which will be offered to the other organizations, which are larger and with specialized human resources functions. The respondent from an SME membership organization urged the EOC to acknowledge the variety between the SMEs as well. She suggested that the needs and resources of businesses which do not employ any staff are very different from those which have say 250 employees.

Nevertheless all of these respondents agreed that conducting the diagnostic check would bring in different challenges for employers in different sizes. SMEs tend not to have in-house expertise and systems in place, and they may need external support for undertaking the diagnostic. Moreover, SMEs have very limited resources in terms of time and financial and human resources. As pointed out by 45 respondents, most of the existing benchmarks suit only the larger organizations with their bigger resources.

However, all respondents but one believed that the diagnostic check should target SMEs as well as large organizations, but urged the EOC to address the differences between potential users in terms of size. In addition to the variation in terms of levels of resources and expertise stemming from the organizational size, seven respondents pointed to the issue of relevance. Detailed and specific questions in some areas may be irrelevant to the SMEs. One-sixth of respondents suggested that the tool could include standard sections, targeting organizations of all sizes, and specific sections that would consist of different questions for different sizes of organizations.

However, 26 respondents also stated that small size is not always associated with disadvantage. It is pointed out that small organizations tend not to have complex governance structures and that their management teams are often closer to ground than in the case of large organizations. Hence, smallness of their size may provide the organizations with an advantage, since carrying out the diagnostic check might be less complicated, faster and more straightforward for them, as well as being less costly. One of the respondents claimed that undertaking the diagnostic would be easiest for the small organizations because it would not require committing too many resources. He then suggested that it would be hardest and relatively costly for the medium-sized organizations because they are not small enough to make the process simple and straightforward and are not big enough to take advantage of the economies of scale.

From a slightly different angle, it was argued by 14 respondents that initiating change and making progress following the diagnostic might be relatively easier and faster for the SMEs compared with large and complicated organizations. On the other hand, 23 respondents from provider organizations and large employers claimed that a new diagnostic equality check may be overburdening for the large organizations, which already have several benchmarks in place. The respondent from a large local authority said that the council is already drowned by the process of gathering evidence for various benchmarks and impact assessment exercises. For that reason, he told us that he was concerned about how complex the new tool would be and how much expertise would be required to undertake the diagnostic. One respondent implied that to overcome this challenge, the tool should be flexible enough to be customized to the needs and resources of individual organizations. Thus, the individual organizations should be able to relate themselves to the tool, and for that the diagnostic equality check should be closely based on the business activity, mission and vision of each organization.

Two-thirds of respondents said there should be not only different tools to address the needs and priorities of organizations in different sizes and sectors, but also a family of tools or a multidimensional flexible tool to cover the different reasons of the gender pay gap in order to give employers the flexibility to choose which areas to focus on.

Still others pointed out that, in addition to differences in terms of size and sector, the tool should take into account the cultural differences between organizations. The needs and priorities, and the levels of engagement and expectations of the potential users, would vary in-line with their level of sophistication in terms of equality and diversity. Accordingly, it is suggested by 18 respondents that a staged tool would be most effective in terms of addressing cultural differences between employers.

One-third of the respondents believed that a step-by-step piecemeal format would be more encouraging, particularly in the case of the organizations which are not very much committed to equality and diversity, and which do not have a proactive approach in order to gradually engage them in the process. Alternatively, a range of tools could be designed, each corresponding to different levels of benchmark, such as a micro-benchmark, which would put minimum demand on the organization in terms of evidence required, and a macro–benchmark, which would be more sophisticated and detailed. Such a model may increase the take-up of the tool among the employers, since it would provide them with the flexibility to make an informed choice on the basis of their resource and budget constraints.

This section has explored the respondents' views on the coverage and format of a diagnostic equality check. **Boxes 6.5–6.7** summarize the scope of these views:

Box 6.5   Views on the coverage and format of a diagnostic equality check

- there is an inflation of diagnostic or benchmarking equality tools in the UK;
- there is a benchmarking fatigue in the business community as a direct consequence of complexity and multiplicity of the diagnostic tools that are available on diversity and equality;
- a new tool which will solely focus on gender would not be successful;
- there is a market for a generic equality and diversity tool;
- it would be very timely to develop a generic equality check;
- if the new tool has the ability to replace the existing benchmarks, it will make business sense for the organizations, since it will free them from the burden and cost of frequently repeating similar checks;
- the generic tool should be particularly useful for reaching SMEs, as it is impossible for them to undertake a separate check for each dimension of diversity due to their limited resources;
- the tool should be balanced in terms of its accommodation of different strands of diversity, since each strand of diversity has its own peculiar characteristics;
- the new tool should be not only generic but also general and comprehensive in its scope;
- the tool should not be limited to pay discrimination but should address all three causes of the gender pay gap;

▶

- the tool should cover all areas of human resources which directly or indirectly contribute to the gender pay gap;
- the tool should include not only the formal procedures and practices but also informal aspects of organizational life;
- the tool should appeal to the needs of the customers and service users as well as assessing the internal processes.

Box 6.6   Responses to the question: how can employers be encouraged to adopt a proactive approach?

- A new tool should not only diagnose problems and gaps regarding equality and diversity, but also indicate possible actions that can be taken to improve the state of organizations in terms of diversity and equality.
- If a benchmarking tool is not capable of delivering an explicit agenda for proactive action, there is the risk of inaction or reactive approach by small- and medium-sized organizations, which do not have resources to employ diversity and equality experts, and large organizations without sophisticated diversity and equality programmes and systems already in place.
- The focus of the tool should be on how the diagnostic is going to help the users and guide them to translate the results of the diagnostic check into action and objectives rather than solely identifying the problems.
- A new diagnostic equality check should include action plans or indications of possible action points.
- In order to avoid a 'tick-box' approach, the new tool should make it very explicit that the outcomes of the diagnostic check are crucial, and that the tool is a medium or facilitator for realizing the aim of enhancing equality and diversity in the user organizations.
- A loose and flexible approach to action planning may not be successful for all organizations, due to the variation by diversity and equality expertise, as well as other resources committed to developing action plans.
- Organizational size alone may not be an indication of an organization's needs and priorities about a diagnostic equality check or may not predict an organization's potential for engagement with the diagnostic check.
- When developing the diagnostic equality check, the differences in terms of organizational culture as well as size should be addressed.
- There were two different views among the respondents on how the tool could encourage the employers to take proactive action: providing ready-made action plans and following a more flexible approach.

- There were various views among the respondents who found ready-made action plans useful, in terms of the coverage of the action plans:
  - action plans should be comprehensive;
  - action plans should be focused on high impact areas and should set clear targets;
  - action plans provided by the tool should be comprehensive but the actions have to be broken down into clearly defined sections.
- The respondents who thought that the tool should assume a more flexible approach also suggested that:
  - the tool should be indicative of possible action areas rather than directly and explicitly providing an action plan;
  - case studies can be used to demonstrate possible action plans and scenarios which will also help organizations to better visualize themselves as assuming a proactive approach;
  - results of a diagnostic check should be capable of pinpointing the hot areas which require action in the case of each organization;
  - when organizations are developing their action plans there can be consultancy support and organizations may be informed about where they can go for further help.
- The tool should be not only forward looking in terms of offering future action plans or points, but should have a retrospective element through which the users will be able to assess the effectiveness and usefulness of their diversity and equality initiatives in the past and present.
- The process of undertaking the diagnostic check should open up a dialogue in the organization in terms of workforce diversity and equality issues and should focus attention on the problematic areas.
- The tool should include a convincing business case for proactive and progressive action on the side of the employers and should demonstrate the business benefits of not only conducting the diagnostic check, but also of taking action as a result of it.

Box 6.7   Possible formats of the diagnostic tool

- Accessibility is one of the key features that make a diagnostic check successful.
- The more accessible the tool, the higher will be the level of commitment and ownership throughout the organization.

- The tool should look simple since a complicated-looking one may discourage many employees at the first instance.
- The tool should be in plain English without any jargon.
- Understanding and undertaking the diagnostic check should not require expert knowledge.
- The tool should be clear and transparent in terms of its purpose and outcomes.
- The variation in the level of technology use among the organizations should be taken into account and the diagnostic check should be available in multiple formats for the highest possible accessibility.
- The tool can be designed in a way to be adaptable to the existing HR software packages.
- The tool should be capable of being embedded in the existing reporting mechanisms.
- The tool should be adaptable to the existing equality and diversity monitoring systems.
- The interviews revealed different views regarding whether the diagnostic check should be undertaken internally or externally:
  - the new diagnostic equality check should be a self-assessment tool that is combined with training and guidance;
  - risk of self-diluting, hiding the problems and subjectivity may be brought in by self assessment;
  - an external audit is necessary for objective evaluation since organizations may tend to be economical about the truth in a self–assessment;
  - benchmarking would be possible only through an external audit;
  - a middle way would give the organizations a flexibility to choose between a self-assessment and an external audit.
- A diagnostic equality check needs to take into account the differences between the organizations in terms of size, sector and industry.
- Public and private sector distinction is crucial.
- Organizational size differences are important in terms of determining capabilities, drivers and needs of organizations to undertake a diagnostic equality check.
- The diagnostic check should target SMEs as well as large organizations.
- Change and making progress following the diagnostic might be relatively easier and faster for the SMEs.
- A family of tools or a multidimensional flexible tool is necessary to cover the different reasons for the gender pay gap.

6.5 Conclusion

In this chapter, we have outlined the requirements for a diagnostic check tool, the process of developing it and its promotion and action plan. Availability of national policy on diversity and equality tools, as well as the nature and scope of such tools, have a significant impact on global diversity management practice, as these tools reflect the overall conception of the organizational level initiatives. Our findings indicate that the market requirements for a diagnostic tool are that it should be stepwise, multidimensional, sophisticated, and yet easy to follow. Based on these fundamental principles, we outline a tool below and define its main premises and key attributes. The tool that emanates from the requirements of the providers and users of a diagnostic tool should have the following attributes.

The tool should be stepwise. This means that it should have a number of components that, when completed, reveal the current status of the organization, hence facilitate the drawing up of action plans. Also, in between these two processes, the tool should be supplemented with awareness-raising information, which can be in the form of examples of good practice, case studies or directions for use.

The tool should be multidimensional. Multidimensionality takes a number of forms:

- The diagnostic check should involve all strands of equality and diversity.
- It should engage with individual, organizational and societal concerns and adopt a multilevel approach which seeks to reveal the source of the pay gap in a wider range of constituent fields.
- The diagnostic check should involve all stakeholders of equality and diversity in organizations. Although the tool may be used by a diversity officer, it should have wider potential impacts for all workers.
- The tool should allow for internal and external networking and information sharing and benchmarking activities that will strengthen the position of the progressive organizations in the industry.
- The diagnostic check should have a widespread voluntary component through which organizations can establish their current status and an audit component which may be through a system which offers pledges or badges or compulsory audits which currently requires legal changes.
- The tool should not only offer a way to diagnose, it should also highlight areas of weakness, strength and how these issues can be addressed.
- The tool should be both evidence based in terms of retrospective, current and future policies and practices.

The tool should be sophisticated yet accessible. The above requirements mean that the proposed diagnostic check should be a sophisticated yet non-technical tool that is highly accessible. This will involve offering both standard and specifically tailored aspects to the tool to make it sensitive and more relevant to the context and priorities of individual organizations.

In Appendix B, we are offer a draft tool. The draft tool provides a set of questions against which evidence may be presented. The first part involves a set of questions that are about the nature of the organization, the sector and the industry in which the organization operates. These questions will then help the diagnostic check to be specifically tailored to suit the size, sector and industry considerations.

The second part of the tool involves four components, which correspond to the four columns of the questionnaire. The first asks questions on multiple constituents of diversity and equality, ranging from work cultures to the pay gap. The second component allows for the respondents' answers. The third allows for examples of evidence in three layers: (a) minimum requirements; (b) good practice; and (c) best practice. The fourth component urges the organization to provide their specific evidence at one of these three levels. It is this second part of the tool that will map out organizational practice.

The third part of the tool then offers specifically tailored guidelines for organizations to move from the minimum legal requirement to good practice to best practice. The ultimate aim of the tool will be to bring the organization to a standard where all minimum legal requirements are satisfied and progressive approaches are implemented. This part essentially involves setting up action plans for the organizations.

The fourth part of the tool should then involve independent auditors to examine and authorize evidence that is provided by the organizations. In this stage, a badge can be offered to certify that the organization has provided sufficient evidence of good practice. The system may also bring forth some standards of progress for retaining the badge.

The draft tool which we provide should be further developed. The process in which the diagnostic check can be developed is as important as the final outcome. Organizations are more likely to adopt a new tool if they participate in its development. With this in mind three specific activities should be implemented:

1 *Consultation.* The tool should be prepared in consultation with key stakeholders and constituent organizations. The process of consultation was partly conducted through the survey which we described above. However, the draft tool we outline is not yet shared with the key stakeholders. It would benefit from developing further particularly in specific strands of

equality and with sensitivity to size and sector. The consultation exercise may be supplemented with a pilot study in several organizations across a range of sectors to erase any future difficulties with implementation. It is also important to recognize that there are ongoing changes in the field of equality and the pay gap. Therefore, in order to make the diagnostic check sensitive to these changes, an advisory committee should be established with a select number of representatives from key stakeholder organizations.

2   *Creating a network of equality and diversity champions*. This group will serve to implement best practice as well as promoting the tool at different forums. The group may serve to promote the tool both at organizational, regional, national and sectoral levels.

3   *Partnerships with key stakeholders*. Our study has highlighted that partnerships are essential if the diagnostic check is aiming to reach a national base of organizations. Partnerships should be established with learned organizations which have wide professional and other forms of membership. Providers of current diagnostic check tools should also be invited to engage in partnership activities. These partnerships will serve to promote the tool as well as establish information, advice and training activities.

Appendix A: Table of research participants

	Sector	Industry	Size	Position	Gender
1	Provider	General/race		Senior Policy Officer	Female
2	Private services	Recruitment	Large/international	HR Manager	Female
3	Private services	Recruitment	Large/international	Corporate Account Manager	Male
4	Provider/consultancy	General/diversity		Head of Operations	Male
5	Public Sector	Local government	Large	Diversity Manager	Female
6	Trade union	Communication		Assistant Secretary	Female
7	Provider	General/HR		Development Manager	Female
8	Provider/membership institution	Recruitment sector		Member of Research Team	Female
9	Private services	Retail	Large	Diversity Manager	Female
10	Provider/consultancy	General/diversity		Director for Business Operations	Female
11	Provider	Wales/gender		Employment Director	Male
12	Provider/consultancy	General/diversity		Director	Male
13	Public sector	Education	Large	Equality and Diversity Manager	Male
14	Public sector	Planning	Large	Human Resources	Female
15	Public sector	Planning	Large	Recruitment, Policy and Strategy	Male
16	Provider	Science and HEI		Programme Manager	Female
17	Provider	General/sexual orientation	developing	Researcher	Male
18	Private services	Banking and finance	Large/international	Diversity Manager	Female
19	Public sector	National Assembly/Wales	Large	Senior Equality and Diversity Adviser	Female
20	Public sector	Wales/Business Development	Large	Equality and Diversity Manager	Female
21	Private services	Banking and finance	Large/international	Head of Diversity	Female
22	Private services	Banking and finance	Large	Senior manager CSR	Male

(*Continued*)

Appendix A: (Continued)

	Sector	Industry	Size	Position	Gender
23	Provider/membership institution	Personnel and development	Large	Diversity Manager	Female
24	Provider	SMEs/equality		Researcher	Female
25	Provider/consultancy	General/diversity		Director	Male
26	Provider/consultancy	General/diversity		Director	Female
27	Provider	Local government		Head of Diversity	Female
28	Provider	Employment issues		Deputy Editor	Female
29	Provider	Employment issues		Head of Diversity and Discrimination Law	Male
30	Public sector	Local government	Large	Head of HR	Male
31	Provider/membership institution	Local government, fire and police services		Member	Male
32	Provider/membership institution	Fire services		Lead for equalities and diversity	Male
33	Provider/inspector	Police services	Large	Personnel, training and diversity	Male
34	Public sector	Fire services	Large	Director of People and Performance	Female
35	Private services	Communication	Large	Diversity Officer	Female
36	Provider/consultancy	General/equality and diversity		Consultant	Female
37	Provider	General/employment relations		Senior advisor, equality and diversity	Female
38	Provider/consultancy	Reputation management	Medium	Principal	Male
39	Private services	Retail	Large	HR Officer	Female
40	Public sector	Science and research	Large	HR Officer	Female
41	Provider	General/gender		Steering Group Member	Female
42	Private services	Finance	Large	HR Officer	Female

	Sector	Area	Size	Role	Gender
43	Public sector	Defence	Large	Deputy Director, Service Personnel Policy	Male
44	Private services	Energy	Large	HR Officer	Male
45	Provider	General/race		Senior Private Sector Policy Officer	Female
46	Public sector	Police services	Large	Acting Chief Inspector	Male
47	Voluntary sector	Poverty	Large	ODM	Male
48	Provider/membership institution	SMEs		Campaigns Manager	Female
49	Provider	HEIs/diversity		Policy Officer	Female
50	Provider/consultancy	General/diversity		Principal Senior Consultant	Female
51	Public sector	Education	Large	Equality and Diversity Manager	Male
52	Provider	General/race		Steering Group Member	Male
53	Provider/consultancy	General/diversity		Consultant	Female
54	Provider	CSR		Researcher	Female
55	Provider	Health sector	Large	Information and Intelligence Manager	Male
56	Public sector	Education	Large	Equal Opportunities Officer	Female
57	Public sector	Education	Large	Director of HR	Male
58	Provider	General/employment relations		Head of EO Diversity	Male
59	Provider	General/HR		Director of Development	Female
60	Private services	Finance	Large	Executive Director, Head of Diversity	Male
61	Provider	SMEs/equality		SME Equality Project	Male
62	Public sector	Ministerial department/internal affairs	Large	Equality & Diversity Team	Female
63	Provider	General/disability		Head of Information and Research	Female
64	Private services	Retail	Large	Head of HR	Male
65	Private services	Entertainment	Small	Director	Male
66	Private services	Translation	Small	Director	Male

Appendix B: Draft Diagnostic Equality Check

Exercise: The below diagnostic may be used in order to assess equality and diversity in an organization. Students should identify an organization, for example the university in which they are studying. Then, they may collect data in order to fill the boxes below and discuss their findings in class.

Section 1: Your organization

Which sector does your organization primarily operate in? Please tick ☑one box only.

1. Manufacturing and production

a. Agriculture and forestry ☐
b. Chemicals, oils and pharmaceuticals ☐
c. Construction ☐
d. Electricity, gas and water ☐
e. Engineering, electronics and metals ☐
f. Food, drink and tobacco ☐
g. General manufacturing ☐
h. Mining and quarrying ☐
i. Paper and printing ☐
j. Textiles ☐
k. Other manufacturing/production ☐

2. Private sector services

a. Professional services (accountancy, advertising, consultancy, legal etc) ☐
b. Finance, insurance and real estate ☐
c. Hotels, catering and leisure ☐
d. IT services ☐
e. Call centres ☐
f. Media (broadcasting and publishing etc) ☐
g. Retail and wholesale ☐
h. Transport, distribution and storage ☐
i. Communications ☐
j. Other private services ☐
k. Voluntary, community and not-for-profit ☐
l. Care services ☐
m. Charity services ☐
n. Housing association ☐
o. Other voluntary ☐

3. Public services

a. Central government ☐
b. Education ☐
c. Health ☐
d. Local government ☐
e. Other public services ☐

4. Voluntary, community and not-for-profit

a. Care services ☐
b. Charity services ☐
c. Housing association ☐
d. Other voluntary ☐

5. How many people are employed by your organization in the UK?

a. 250 or less ☐
b. 251–500 ☐
c. 501–1000 ☐
d. 1,001–5,000 ☐
e. 5,001–10,000 ☐
f. 10,001 or more ☐

6. Where are the staff in your organization located? Please select all locations that apply:

a. Whole UK ☐
b. North-east England ☐
c. North-west England ☐
d. Scotland ☐
e. London ☐
f. Yorkshire/Humberside ☐
g. Midlands ☐
h. Wales ☐
i. South-east England ☐
j. South-west England ☐
k. East of England ☐
l. Northern Ireland ☐

Questions	Answers	Examples of evidence	Your evidence
Equality, Diversity and Culture			
To what extent do you agree with each of the following statements?	Strongly disagree Strongly agree 1 2 3 4 5		
Managers are equipped with adequate skills for dealing with diversity and equality issues			
Flexible working is encouraged in this organization			
Management behaviour always reflects organizational values and priorities			
Colleagues listen to and respect each other			
Colleagues feel under pressure to get my work done			
Formal and informal networks in my organization enable diverse people to talk to each other			
We always consult our customers			
Our customers always treat our employees with respect			
Colleagues always feel comfortable about networking with different groups of people in this organization			

My organization is always prepared to make adjustments to people's different work–life balance needs							
In my organization all employees are prepared to ask for different work–life arrangements that they need							
In my organization there are many opportunities to develop new skills at all levels							
Information on career development is offered to all employees							
In my organization people are encouraged to develop their skills							
All vacant posts within my organization are advertised internally							
All vacant posts within my organization are advertised externally							
Jobs tend to be given to people 'in the know'							
There are plenty of opportunities for progression within my organization							
There is good communication about internal job opportunities in my organization							

(Continued)

Questions	Answers	Examples of evidence	Your evidence
Equality, Diversity and Culture (Continued)			
My organization sets out to encourage all employees to reach their full potential			
Please rate your level of agreement with each of the following statements. My colleagues think that:	Strongly disagree Strongly agree 1 2 3 4 5		
. . . an employee's religion shouldn't stop them from being promoted			
. . . employees should be promoted fairly			
. . . employees' sexuality shouldn't stop them from being promoted			
. . . employees' ethnicity shouldn't stop them from being promoted			
. . . an employee's age shouldn't stop them from being promoted			
. . . an employee's disability shouldn't stop them from being promoted			
. . . an employee's weight shouldn't stop them from being promoted			

Please rate your level of agreement with each of the following statements. In my current organization:	Strongly disagree 1 2 3	Strongly agree 4 5			
. . . employment practice is informed by a commitment to equality for all					
. . . the workforce reflects the diversity of the local population					
. . . senior management encourage diversity					
. . . people are not afraid to be open about their sexuality					
Please rate your level of agreement with each of the following statements. My current organization:	Strongly disagree 1 2 3	Strongly agree 4 5			
. . . encourages equal numbers of men and women in all management positions					
. . . aims to make sure that diversity and equality are at the heart of everything it does					
. . . values equality and diversity as a way to deliver better services					
. . . actively supports its suppliers, subsidiaries and affiliates regarding equality and diversity					
. . . recognises that it's important to respond to individual needs					

(Continued)

Questions	Answers	Examples of evidence	Your evidence
Equality, Diversity and Culture (Continued)			
. . . consults with its customers and clients to identify diverse needs about goods and services			
. . . encourages the career progression of both men and women			
. . . encourages the career progression of lesbians and gay men			
. . . encourages the career progression of people of all ages			
. . . encourages the career progression of people with disabilities			
. . . encourages the career progression of people of different religions			
Equality and diversity function			
Is there a specialised diversity/equal opportunities function in your organization? When was the specialist function created?			
Has your organization mainstreamed its diversity/equality opportunities function? When was the function mainstreamed?			

Does your organization plan to open a specialised diversity/equal opportunities function in the future?		
Does your organization have a budget for diversity?		
How many people work on diversity and equality in your organization?		
Which of the following areas of expertise do the members of the equality and diversity team have? Specific training on equal opportunities General management training Human resources management training Financial management training Marketing management training Engineering and production management training Employment/discrimination law training Specific training on equality and diversity management Other professional training: please specify		
How much influence does the equality and diversity function have within your organization?		
Does your organization have a written diversity management or equal opportunities policy statement?		

(*Continued*)

Questions	Answers	Examples of evidence	Your evidence
Equality and diversity function (Continued)			
Does the statement spell out the consequences of breaching the policy?	Yes No Not applicable		
Does your organization have an international equality and diversity policy?			
Does your international equality and diversity policy differ in content and approach from your domestic policy?			
Which of the following applies when considering the term used predominantly in your organization?	We generally use the term 'equality' We generally use the term 'diversity' We generally use 'equality' and 'diversity' interchangeably		
Does your organization have someone whose main responsibility is managing diversity/equal employee opportunities?			
How much authority does the most senior person in the equality and diversity function have over others in the organization?	No power Extreme Power 1 2 3 4 5		
Are work–life balance issues part of the work in your equality and diversity function?			

Does someone in your equality and diversity team report regularly to the board of your company on diversity?					
Diversity and equality strategy in your current organization					
Does your organization have an equality and diversity strategy?					
When was the equality and diversity strategy first implemented?					
Is your equality and diversity strategy integrated with the business strategy?					
Which of the following equality and diversity activities does your organization have?	Awareness training Reward and recognition for equality and diversity achievements Monitoring customer profile Workforce monitoring and targeting system setting equality and diversity quotas Employee attitude surveys Setting equality and diversity objectives Work–life balance system Equality and diversity as performance criteria building equality and diversity into business goals Other – please specify:				

(Continued)

Questions	Answers	Examples of evidence	Your evidence
Diversity and equality strategy in your current organization (Continued)			
Which of the following are the most influential ways of communicating equality and diversity in your organization?	Company newsletters Internal company TV channel Internet/intranet Events Internal company communications Speeches by top management Posters and leaflets Focus groups Employee surveys Personnel and team brief meetings Informal conversations Training Other – please specify:		
How has the scope of the equality and diversity strategy changed over time?	It has not changed It has expanded It has narrowed Not applicable		
What are the key drivers for equality and diversity in your organization? Rank the top 5 from 1 to 5, with 1 being the most important.	Legal pressures Corporate social responsibility To address recruitment problems Because it makes business sense To be an employer of choice		

Belief in social justice Desire to improve customer relations Desire to reach diverse markets To improve business performance To respond to the global market To recruit and retain best talent To respond to the competition in the market Because it is morally right To improve creativity and innovation To improve products and services To enhance decision-making To improve corporate branding Trade union activities				
Diversity and equality policy in your current organization				
Do you have an equality and diversity policy in your organization?				
When was the policy first implemented?				
When was the policy last reviewed?				

(Continued)

Questions	Answers	Examples of evidence	Your evidence
Diversity and equality policy in your current organization (Continued)			
Which of the following categories does your equality and diversity policy cover? Please select all that apply. If not applicable, please proceed to the next question.	Criminal convictions Postcode Marital status Accent Parental status Mental health Disability Stress Nationality Work–life balance Religion Age Gender/sex Social and economic background Weight Harassment and bullying Physical appearance Political ideology Ethnicity/race Trade union membership Sexual orientation All forms of difference Other: please specify		
Do you involve employees in the design and implementation of equality and diversity policies and practices?			

In what ways do you involve them?	Meetings Focus groups Trade union consultation Feedback from employees Networking/affinity groups Employee representation on boards Work-council consultation Employees are not directly involved Other: please specify	
What actions are taken in order to maximise employee engagement in equality and diversity policies?	Please select all that apply: Communicating equality and diversity message and policy across the organization Training and education activities in equality and diversity management Equality and diversity objectives integrated in performance and strategic management systems Employee involvement in community action programmes No action taken Other: please specify	
How often are equality and diversity management policies or initiatives related to overall corporate objectives and strategies?	Always Sometimes Never	

(Continued)

Questions	Answers	Examples of evidence	Your evidence
Diversity and equality activities in your current organization			
Have provisions been made for the following?	Please select all that apply: Harassment and bullying policy Disability access Childcare Equal pay audit Career development programme Flexible hours Job-sharing Practical equality and equality and diversity training Maternity provisions Paternity provisions Fair performance management system Targeted recruitment and retention to create a balanced workforce Corporate social responsibility Work-life balance programme Mentoring programmes Equality and diversity as part of the organization's mission Inclusion of diversity-related goals in managers' performance assessments Objective-setting		

Equality and diversity monitoring in your current organization

Monitoring information is important to track equality and diversity progress. This section aims to help us understand how equality and diversity is monitored in your organization.

	Balanced scorecard Applying equality and diversity standards Other: please specify
Does your organization collect monitoring information?	
Which of the following are monitored?	Staff profiles ☐ Customer profiles ☐ Other: please specify
For which of the following categories do you monitor the diversity of your customer profile and staff profile?	Please select all that apply: Customer profile Staff profile Sex ☐ Ethnicity/race ☐ Age ☐ Sexual ☐ Disability ☐ orientation Religion ☐ Nationality ☐ Physical appearance ☐

(Continued)

Questions	Answers	Examples of evidence	Your evidence
Diversity and equality activities in your current organization (Continued)			
	Social and economic background ☐ Criminal convictions ☐ Marital status ☐ Postcode ☐ Parental status ☐ Mental health ☐ Political ideology ☐ Weight ☐		
Does your organization monitor the following?	Selection rates of under-represented groups Employee beliefs about the fairness of organizational policies Pay decisions to ensure fairness for all Promotions to ensure fairness for all Incidents of harassment and bullying		
Does your organization use monitoring information in connection with the following?	Recruitment Turnover rates Performance Promotion		

	Training Pay Type of contract Organizational level Grievance Harassment and bullying Please note here any other monitoring information that your organization uses
Approximately, what percentage of workers in the following categories are represented in your organization?	Organization as a whole Managerial grades Board of directors Don't know Female workers Non-white workers Workers with disabilities
Is your organization age-diverse?	Yes ☐ No ☐ Don't know ☐
What is the majority age profile that your organization employs?	Young ☐ Middle-aged ☐ Old ☐ Balanced ☐ Don't know ☐
Does your organization attempt to measure the impact of equality and diversity management initiatives?	Yes No We are investigating the option
Which of the following measures do (or would) you use to monitor equality and diversity in your organization?	Impact assessment Employee performance appraisals

(Continued)

Questions	Answers	Examples of evidence	Your evidence
Diversity and equality activities in your current organization (Continued)			
	Balanced scorecards Diversification of customer base Employee attitude surveys Psychological contract issues Level of employee commitment Absenteeism Number of tribunal cases Level of customer satisfaction Number of complaints and grievances Business performance Labour turnover Ability to recruit Improvements to problem-solving and decision-making Other: please specify		
How would you rate your organization's performance in comparison with your competitors on each of the following?	Lower than average Average Top 25% Top 10% Don't know		

Not applicable
Service quality
Level of productivity
Profitability
Rate of innovation
Revenue growth
Customer satisfaction
Employee satisfaction
Stock market performance

Your evaluation of diversity and equality in your current organization

What was the degree of overall organizational resistance and support to the below equality and diversity activities?

Strong resistance				Strong support
1	2	3	4	5

Equality and diversity management strategy
Equality and diversity management policies
Equality and diversity management initiatives
Equality and diversity management training
Equality and diversity awareness training
Equality and diversity monitoring activity

(Continued)

Questions	Answers	Examples of evidence	Your evidence
Your evaluation of diversity and equality in your current organization (Continued)			
On balance, what are the general attitudes and behaviours about equality and diversity at different levels within your workplace? Oppositional Supportive 1 2 3 4 5 Organization as a whole	Board members Senior management Middle management Junior management Non-managerial workers Trade union representatives		
How much personal ownership do people at the following levels assume in diversity-related activities and issues?	No ownership Total ownership 1 2 3 4 5 Board members Senior management Middle management Junior management Non-managerial workers Trade union representatives		
To what extent is equality and diversity central to activities in the following departments in your organization?	Not central Very central 1 2 3 4 5 Don't know/not applicable Marketing and sales Finance and accounting Communication and advertising Strategic management/ corporate strategy		

	Human resources Manufacturing and production Equality and diversity Advertising National/regional/local – branches/chains Suppliers Customers and consumers CSR Shareholders
How effective is equality and diversity management in improving the following in your organization?	Not effective Very effective 1 2 3 4 5 Don't know/not applicable Employees' attitudes and behaviours in terms of equality and diversity Representation of diverse groups at different levels of the organization Employees' levels of commitment Personal perceptions of fairness and justice Employee performance Employees' job satisfaction Cost of labour turnover Level of absenteeism Quality of recruitment Number of discrimination claims

(Continued)

Questions	Answers	Examples of evidence	Your evidence
Your evaluation of diversity and equality in your current organization (Continued)			
	Interaction between employees from diverse backgrounds Business performance Creativity and innovation in the organization Problem solving and decision making Business successful with regard to market penetration Diversification of customer base Level of customer satisfaction		
Pay Gap			
Do you have a job evaluation scheme?			
Has your scheme been designed with equal work in mind?			
Do you monitor equal pay for equal work across all strands of equality? a) like work b) work rated as equivalent and c) work of equal value			

Do you collect and compare and collect pay data to identify any significant equal pay gaps? a) Do you calculate average pay and compare average basic pay and total earnings? b) Do you compare access to and amounts received of each element of pay for all categories of equality?				
Do you establish the causes of any significant pay gap and assess the justification for them?				
Do you have an equal pay action plan?				
Do you have an equal pay policy?				
Do you assess the impact of your equal pay action plan and policy?				
Do you regularly review and monitor your equal pay?				

Further reading

Carroll, G.R. and Hannan, M.T. (2000) 'Why Corporate Demography Matters: Policy Implications of Organizational Diversity', *California Management Review*, vol. 42, pp. 148–63.

Liff, S. (1996) 'Two Routes to Managing Diversity: Individual Differences or Social Group Characteristics', *Employee Relations*, vol. 19, no. 1, pp. 11–26.

Neathey, F., Dench, S. and Thomson, L. (2003) *Monitoring Progress towards Pay Equality*. EOC Research Discussion Series, Equal Opportunities Commission.

Neathey, F., Willison, R., Akroyd, K., Regan, J. and Hill, D. (2005) *Equal Pay Reviews in Practice*. EOC Working Paper Series no. 33, Equal Opportunities Commission.

Neck C.P., Smith W.J. and Godwin J.L. (1997) 'Thought Self-leadership: A Self-regulatory Approach to Diversity Management', *Journal of Managerial Psychology*, vol. 12, pp. 190–203.

Schäfer, S., Winterbotham, M. and McAndrew, F. (2005) *Equal Pay Reviews Survey 2004*. EOC Working Paper Series no. 32, Equal Opportunities Commission.

Thomas, R.R. (1990) 'From Affirmative Action to Affirming Diversity', *Harvard Business Review*, vol. 68, no. 2, pp. 107–17.

Women and Work Commission (2006) *Shaping a Fairer Future*. London: Women and Work Commission, DTI.

Discourses of Diversity Management: Telling the Story of Diversity Management

7.1 Introduction

In the previous chapter, we focused on the interplay between national-level policy and global diversity management, arguing that the latter activities take place at the national level. In this chapter, we explore national-level discourse of diversity management as a key rationale for cross-national divergences in practices of global diversity management approaches. We will identify the discourse effects of diversity management, using a storytelling approach. We particularly focus on the two dominant discourses of the legal and the business case for diversity and equality at work. What is commonly termed as 'the business case for equality and diversity' among professionals of diversity management is a set of stories of variable sophistication that are constructed in order to engender and negotiate organizational change. The research project that we report here draws on three independent studies, which generated over 90 interviews and 285 completed questionnaires with members from a wide range of organizations: diversity professionals from public, private and voluntary sector organizations and trade unions, and from providers of diversity management tools, as well as public servants from government agencies with a specific remit for diversity and equality.

In this chapter, we will explore the story of the business case for diversity and how this is used to negotiate organizational change initiatives and achieve support and recognition from within and without the organizations. We argue that the sophistication of the story of the diversity case is correlated with the success of the diversity management initiative in the organization. Our study reveals the significance of tacit learning through networks and communities of practice for the development of sophisticated business case stories. However, this is set against a context of porous professional boundaries for diversity and equality officers. We argue that the absence of formal means of professionalization increases the reliance on networks for the development of business case arguments. However, the evidence suggests that the networks for diversity professionals are rare and under-resourced. We also elaborate on the current status of equality and diversity officers in their organizations, since their relative power is not only associated with the content of the stories that they tell but also with the terminology that they use and the prestige and authority of their respective positions. Through these studies, we explore the linkages between organizational status of the diversity professionals with the stories that they develop.

7.2　Storytelling

Storytelling is increasingly used in organizational settings to exchange information, to make sense of the past and the present, to evaluate resources, to predict future trends and to carve out plans and strategies. Individuals use stories in order to stake their claim in limited organizational resources, to legitimize their past and present actions as well as future plans. The same is also true in the broad field of diversity management, in which the policy-makers, professionals, trade union representatives, consultants and providers of tools and systems draw on competing stories in order to legitimize, promote and realize their strategies. In order to capture the nuances across a wide range of stories which coexist in the field of diversity management, we adopt Boje's (1991a: 8) broad definition of story: 'an exchange between two persons during which a past or an anticipated experience was being referenced, recounted, interpreted or challenged'. This definition allows us to draw on a greater range of interviews in which we have accumulated stories of diversity management.

Boje's (1991a: 9) notion of 'storytelling organization' suggests that 'people participate in a wide variety of stakeholder groups to process information and manage the collective memory of the organization through storytelling'. There are clear organizational benefits to this conception of storytelling organization. Kahan (2006: 25) argues that 'high quality collaboration relies on multiple, conflicting points of view coming together in a collective intelligence that honours the contribution of each perspective'. Our aim in this chapter is not to provide an analysis of storytelling around diversity management alone. Instead, we look at storytelling in the field of diversity management, exploring the stories in a range of subfields across the public, private and voluntary sectors in the UK, with a view to investigating strategies and political intentions for sharing and acquiring organizational power through storytelling.

Most of the research in the field of storytelling remains at the intra-organizational level. However, extra-organizational stakeholder research is not uncommon. Durgee (1988), for example, explores storytelling between a group of consumers whose connectedness in storytelling is not mostly about one another but about a product that they all use. Similarly, in our study the limited interaction between our participants is compensated by their interconnectedness to the broad field of diversity management in the industry. Extra-organizational connectedness through storytelling has also been studied. Heugens (2002) describes how storytelling is used as a way to influence public policy by stakeholder groups in the global foods industry, subsequent to the introduction of genetically modified food items. Heugens's study illustrates that the stakeholders adopted competing stories, and suggests that further research is required to understand how, contrary to expectations, competing stories endure and coexist in the same field, each one failing to establish a firm hegemony.

Several researchers have attempted to explore multiple stories in single fields of analysis. For example, Auyero (2002) examined the accounts of protesters in the Santiagazo Riot in Argentina in 1993. His ethnographic interviews with the protesters reveals that their memories and presentations of the events in the riot were not independent of, but in dialogue with, the official and mainstream discourses surrounding the riots. The author explains that the protesters constructed their individual stories of the event. However, their stories were constructions of individual experiences, hopes and frustrations intertwined with the political discourses of the time. Therefore, the individual variations of their stories were moderated by the collective and official stories of the event. Lerner (1992) explains that stories are not simple narratives that are transferred from the storyteller to the listener. The stories are shaped by both parties as well as other stakeholders in a co-generative process.

Bringing the stakeholder perspectives and multiple voices to the organizational level, Boje (1991b) argues that stakeholders listen to, construct, challenge, adopt and promote stories in order to facilitate change in organizational settings. We demonstrate that this is also the case in the wider field of diversity management at the level of industry, where stakeholders promote stories which support their situated political perspectives. However, the stories that the stake-holders choose are moderated by the stories of the other stakeholders, as they engage with dialogue in different forums. Analysing the local and central gov-ernment initiatives of modernization as reflected in accounts of storytelling, Llewellyn (2001) demonstrates that institutional stories are not fully adopted by individuals, and that there is not a direct relationship between organiza-tional power and the impact of individual stories: individuals with organiza-tional influence do not necessarily have more influential stories.

Transcending the issue of multiple stories, several authors have explored the possible uses of storytelling and the competition between stories. Arguably, storytelling has a capacity to facilitate transfer of explicit and tacit knowledge (Hannabus 2000; Swap *et al.* 2001). However, two-way interaction is a crude reduction of the potential of storytelling in organizational settings. In reveal-ing the multiple stories of Disney, Boje (1995) uses the frame of the play *Tamara*, a play which takes place concurrently across a number of rooms in a venue, and due to its design generates partial stories for the audience, which can only be in one room at one time with only a few actors to watch. Boje demonstrates that this set-up is akin to the reality of storytelling organizations in which stakeholders have partial accounts which lead to the construction of divergent stories. The fragmented stories that stakeholders generate are con-tested, adopted and refuted by diverse audiences. However, the situation is slightly different in the case of dialogue between stakeholders, which has a moderating impact on the style and content of stories.

However, multiple voices and multiple stories are not infinitely independ-ent, but linked through co-generative processes of interdependence. The example of the field of the media illustrates the significance of interconnect-edness in storytelling. Shumate *et al.* (2005) explain that interconnectedness in the field of the media means that the stories of stakeholders are not local-ized or fragmented but globalized and reified. On the other hand, studies of storytelling in organizational settings mainly focus on discursive practices as well as bodily performances. Indeed there are technological advances, such as training videos and self-study audio and visual packs, which help profession-als construct their stories. Gershon and Page (2002) alert scholars to the per-mutations of storytelling relevant to technologies that can facilitate improved communication of stories and the diffusion of information. Glassner (1999: 1) also heralds the coming of an age of technological advances in storytelling systems: 'These technologies will not eliminate other, more traditional media, just as television did not eliminate film, and film did not eliminate novels. But they will open the door to new kinds of stories that can be told in new ways'.

In summary, our interest in storytelling in diversity management is not only to reveal haphazard stories on diversity management but to reveal intentional-ity of storymaking and storytelling practices. There is an explosion of studies which suggest that storytelling is a new form of capital that organizations and individuals can deploy in order to achieve their objectives. McLellan (2006) notes that stories can be collected, created and told in order to generate corporate benefits. Morgan and Dennehy (1997) and Parkin (2004) note that storytelling is an important managerial skill which can be developed through training activities. Vance (1991) even argues that formalizing storytelling in organizations is a means of organizational development. Arguably, storytelling can be used to develop organizations, as well as individuals (Ready 2002; Grisham 2006), or to reveal individual identity in the context of organizational structures (Ward and Winstanley 2004). Boyce (1995: 134) explains that there are wider intentional uses of storytelling in organizations: '(a) confirming the shared experiences and shared meanings of organizational members; (b) expressing the organizational experience of members or clients; (c) amending and altering the organizational reality; (d) developing, sharpening and renewing the sense of purpose held by organizational members; and (e) preparing a group for planning, implementing plans, and decision making in line with shared purposes'.

Our brief review points to a growth in utilitarian and instrumental perspectives on storytelling, which is now seen as an individual and organizational resource to be explored and exploited. Our main research question then becomes: What are the underlying logics and mechanisms for the heterogeneity in diversity management stories across subfields of the diversity management field in the UK?

7.3 Methods

Our approach to storytelling is one of critical storytelling (Barone 1992) through which we investigate the real stories of a spectrum of constituent representatives in subfields of diversity management, not as indifferent bystanders but with keen attention to the ways stories are used to share political and others forms of power in work settings. Our approach is similar to the conception of critical storytelling offered by Boyce (1996: 9): through a study 'which addresses structures and expressions of oppression at both macro and micro levels'.

Storytelling literature is saturated with qualitative studies that explore storytelling from highly contextualized perspectives. Quantitative insights, however, are rare in storytelling research. However, as Skranefjell and Tonnessen (2003) explain, it is also possible to tell stories of statistical data. In this paper, we are drawing on both qualitative-interview and quantitative-survey data.

The findings that we report here draw on four field studies which generated over 90 interviews with diversity officers from a wide range of organizations: voluntary, public and private sector organizations, providers of diversity management tools, and public sector regulators of diversity and equality.

We explore storytelling across four constituent subfields of diversity management knowledge and practice: the academic subfield, the cultural subfield, the institutional subfield and the business subfield. We define subfields as sites in which there is a shared meaning, an underlying and common institutional logic and a process of diversity management. In order to collate the stories of diversity management in these subfields, we have reviewed the academic literature, drawn on two field studies – an interview and a questionnaire survey with diversity management professionals from industry – funded by the Chartered Institute of Personnel and Development (CIPD) and two studies funded by the Equal Opportunities Commission (EOC).

7.4 The academic subfield of diversity management

The academic subfield of diversity management is characterized with a conception of diversity which links labour heterogeneity with organizational performance. Diversity management emerged in the 1990s in the US as a management discourse and practice which was underpinned by a belief that there is a business case for increased heterogeneity at work. It was initially offered as an alternative to equal opportunities (Kandola and Fullerton 1994), which was branded as being limited to legal compliance and the moral case for equality. However, it was considered as a complementary approach (Kirton and Greene 2000) to equal opportunities. Scholars have grappled with alternative definitions of diversity management. Although it can be simply defined as 'a management philosophy of recognizing and valuing heterogeneity in organizations with a view to improve organizational performance', the key difficulty in defining it has been the multiplicity of vested interests by multiple stakeholder groups and constituent subfields as outlined above. These multiple vested interests in these subfields often translate into divergent expectations about the aims, processes and proposed outcomes of recognizing difference as well as its assumed and real difference to concepts of equality and equity (Agocs and Burr 1996).

Poor scholarship on diversity management has been prolific and has often failed to provide evidence for the causal relationship between increased diversity and its professed organizational benefits. The research in the mainstream of diversity management has been *a priori* (see for example Gatley and Lessem 1995), with discourses which claimed but failed to demonstrate causal linkages between workforce or cultural diversity and effective management or business performance. Absence of empirical support for the business case arguments, as well as the inattention of the early diversity management literature to power disparities at work, was largely responsible for the poor reputation of the subject in critical management scholarship. Furthermore, Cheng (1997) argued that the reduction of diversity to single-level issues, such as micro-level analysis of discrimination when discrimination resides at the level of institutional history, and single category studies, such as work solely on women as a unified category when women's heterogeneity is evident, have been effective strategies to retain the status quo of white, male, patriarchal domination and supremacy through academic research.

It is important to note both discourses and absences in the story of diversity management in the academic subfield, because the particular perspectives that the scholars subscribe to, as well as the nature of the platforms on which these stories are told, affect the nature and tone of the diversity management stories and practice in other subfields. Despite the expansion of the business and moral case arguments for diversity management in recent years, diversity management remains a largely contested discourse among critical management circles. The spectrum of studies that academics tell of diversity management is wide, ranging from classical interpretation of the business case stories of labour diversity to critical stories which seek to reveal the intricate relationship between diversity and conflict. However, in the main, the academic story of diversity management is characterized with a discourse driven by business and moral case arguments, rather than legalistic arguments such as compliance with the law or aversion to sanctions. Therefore, in the absence of sanctions, the processes of diversity management are governed through highly voluntaristic 'softly-softly' approaches, rather than regulatory frameworks. The stories of the academic subfield are locked into a future-facing, yet merely discursive, domain, with little attention given to what really happens in practice when professionals of diversity management seek to negotiate their plans and strategies in this voluntaristic framework.

7.5   The cultural subfield: social culture and diversity management

The cultural subfield of diversity management includes the objective historical structures of discrimination, inequality in society and change in the labour market. The historical dynamics of these structures frame the diversity problem in a society through the construction of the 'majority' and 'minority' categories and the corresponding 'advantage' and 'disadvantage' in employment (Cavanaugh 1997; Prasad and Mills 1997). The significance of the historically constructed categories of 'difference', in relation to the design and implementation of the diversity policies and activities, was evident throughout the interviews. For instance, the issue of religion in terms of the Catholic/Protestant split has dominated the narration of organizational diversity policy by the diversity manager who works for a public institution in Northern Ireland, whereas it was not mentioned at all by any of the other diversity managers who are based in England. It was apparent that, due to the unique historical and political trajectory of the region where the Protestant population has been socially constructed as the 'majority' and the Catholic population has been made the 'minority', religion has come forth as one of the focal points of intervention in the diversity management process. On the other hand, the diversity manager of a large financial sector company argued that they set diversity targets for their branches in-line with the local make-up of the labour market:

> In some parts of the country, the geographical make-up and the internal reality within the business unit enables us to put a focus on a particular issue that wouldn't be relevant to all parts of the business. So clearly we couldn't set a strategy saying that everybody must recruit 40 per cent ethnic minority employees.

He then gave their diversity activities in Leicester as an example to qualify his point. He said that in Leicester the company runs various diversity programmes and activities which target Indian customers and employees, since the city has a large Indian population. The diversity manager of a large supermarket chain made the same point in relation to prioritizing between different possible diversity targets and activities:

> We manage diversity on a case by case basis. For example our stores in central London where they might have more of an issue of ethnic diversity, they have to manage that on an ongoing basis.

The importance of the demographic composition of the labour market for managing diversity is cited in the literature as a proof of the pressing need for diversity management (Ivancevich and Gilbert 2000). However, the demographic composition of the labour pool may also hinder the efforts towards an inclusive workplace. For example, in some cases, certain demographic groups may be interpreted as 'negligible' regarding the priorities of diversity management programmes, due to their low numerical presence, although the experience of inequality and discrimination by the members of these groups may be even more remarkable. The interview with the diversity manager in a local government organization was very informative in terms of pointing out that pitfall. When asked about the selection and recruitment of diverse groups of employees and their respective representations in the internal workforce, he argued that the Council is very successful regarding the gender dimension of diversity, with high levels of female representation at all levels of their workforce, including the top management level. When prompted about workforce figures on ethnicity, he reluctantly accepted that the number of employees from black and ethnic minority (BME) backgrounds is low, because the town is a 'predominantly white town'. He said that the demographic make-up of the town leads to difficulties in engaging with people from BME communities, as well as to managers' being inexperienced in managing an ethnically diverse workforce. The diversity manager from another local government institution made the same point in a much more explicit manner, and problematized the issue as follows:

> The challenge for us always is our community. Our community in terms of traditional diversity around BME residences is quite low, it's about 4 per cent. In our current organization it's about 2 per cent. So in the grand scheme of things, in terms of numbers and in terms of our population, trad-itionally diversity wasn't seen as a major issue. Now it's understood over the last 4–5 years that it's much more of an issue in terms of working with inclusive communities and looking to work with hard to reach groups and all the issues around social inclusion.

He then put forward the undeniable influence of the cultural field on the field of diversity management, when he argued that managing diversity requires a change in the culture of the organization:

> It's slow and obviously we have to change the culture. But it will not hap-pen overnight. It's not only the organization, the society. As employers sometimes we are coping with society at work and it's difficult to make decisions about the society. It's very difficult.

Clearly, these words show the impact of the culture of discrimination and inequality in the society on individual organizational fields and on the field of diversity management at a more general and overarching level. In constructing the stories of the cultural field, the participants have often reflected on the links between the history and current make-up of their internal and external communities. The cultural field shapes the stories of diversity managers, situ-ating these stories in the specific social and cultural circumstances of the organ-ization. The stories that reflect on the cultural field also give the impression that there is little that an organization can do to challenge inequalities which reside in the wider society. Therefore, the extent of the organizational respon-sibility in the stories of the cultural subfield is often restricted to replicating the social order of diversity in institutional settings. Stories of the cultural subfield are often told by diversity professionals in their interactions with insiders, with whom they negotiate their requirements, and with externals, to whom they represent the organization's diversity management approaches. Stories of the cultural subfield are highly discursive, rather than critical.

7.6 The institutional subfield of diversity management

The institutional field refers to the institutionalized structures regarding diversity and equality. Institutional structures and actors that reproduce or combat inequality in the area of employment have an influence on the handling of the issue of workforce diversity by organizations. As Kirton and Greene (2000) suggest, organizational diversity management policies need to be situated within the context of employment and anti-discrimination legislation on the one hand, and institutional actors in the field of employment, such as professional and legal bodies and trade unions, on the other hand.

Despite the differences in each organization's definition of diversity, which varied from the group-based differences to the individual-based differences, it was clear from the interviews that the categories which are included in the UK anti-discrimination legislation, that is gender, race and ethnicity, sexual orientation, religious belief, age, and disability, set the content and targets of most of the diversity management policies and programmes of the organizations which participated in this research. For instance, the diversity manager of the large supermarket chain argued that including religious belief in their diversity framework is the biggest present challenge for them:

> Religious belief legislation was a big change for us in terms of how we can be more accommodating to different types of religions and beliefs. I think as far as other changes, we'd always been pretty well attuned to sexual orientation, age discrimination. Our oldest employee is 79. So there's never been an issue that people staying on working in the company beyond the retirement age. We've always welcomed that. So I think probably the biggest change was the religious beliefs one. That did change a little bit about how we approached certain requests for time off to celebrate different festivals and so on. That made us re-examine our policies in that respect and we are continuing to look at how we can improve that as time goes on.

The company's other diversity manager mentioned the 'religious factbook' they have published and distributed within the company as an example of an initiative within that context. She said:

> It has a calendar with different festivals, all helping to make our managers feel better equipped to know, to understand a bit more about what each event will mean to each religion.

On the other hand, the diversity manager of a city borough council saw the recent age legislation as the biggest challenge at the time the interview was conducted:

> The other major challenge I think as an employer is the impact of age legislation, the cultural impact of age in the way that we all through our own prejudices think of age. Not so young or old . . . And as a council, the issue of demographics of age in terms of demands for services around older people is a huge challenge for most local authorities about the elder care, about the need for the linkages between social care and health.

The issue of age was also the most pressing one for the British diversity manager of the global energy and petrochemicals company. When prompted about her future agenda, her short but strong answer was: 'Age, age, age and age'. She said that the company has a global diversity and inclusiveness policy and that 'The UK policy will incorporate both these global standards, but we would also make sure that we're compatible with the UK legislation'. Thus, she pointed out that one of her major responsibilities is to implement the new diversity legislation and to look at the 'legislative aspect of the diversity and our reputation in the UK'.

The impact of legislation on diversity policies was also evident in the interview with one respondent from the other local government institution. He argued that they amend their diversity and equality policy in-line with UK legislation and that currently categories of disability, gender, race, age, sexual orientation and religion are included in it. Both of his examples of successful diversity and equality initiatives were related to the relatively recent anti-discrimination legislation:

> Older workers policy has been introduced 12 months ago in partnership with the unions. We ended the retirement age at 65 and people can apply to work longer. We have another initiative at the moment which is called supporting people in employment to provide more opportunities for disabled people. We introduced it February this year.

As it becomes clear from all these examples and stories from the diversity managers of the organizations, from both the private and public sector, legislative structure and changes, to a large extent, govern the diversity policy and programmes of these organizations, and catching up with the new anti-discrimination legislation is high on their agenda. This is an interesting finding because it conflicts with one of the main pillars of diversity management approach which is frequently emphasized in the literature. In mainstream diversity management, scholars argue that diversity management policies and programmes are proactive and internally driven by bottom-line consider-ations, as opposed to the equal opportunities policies that are externally dri-ven by anti-discrimination legislation (Thomas 1990; McDougall 1996). However, the interviews we have conducted show that legislative factors con-tinue to be one of the most influential motivations behind diversity policies and programmes in both public and private sector organizations which are reactively responding to the new anti-discrimination legislation.

In addition to legislative structure, the institutional field also impacts upon the field of diversity management through the medium of institutional actors. Interviews with diversity professionals from large private and public sector organizations reveal that governmental institutions exert influence on their diversity management approach and programmes. Such organizations include professional institutions such as CIPD and The Society of Personnel Officers in Local Services; employer initiatives and networks such as Opportunity Now, Race For Opportunity, Employers' Forum On Disability, and the Employers' Forum On Age; and the trade unions.

To start with most respondents pointed out their work with the CIPD. Unsurprisingly, all of the respondents from public sector organizations men-tioned their collaborative work with CRE. The words of the diversity manager of a local government organization exemplify this:

> We have an equality standard. That's got five levels in it. It was originally around race and we worked it up with CRE. A lot of councils have actually signed up to move forward in terms of their levels. When you get to level five, it basically means that your organization has diversity and equality fully integrated with all of your business processes as an organization and would have demonstrable evidence.

In addition, the respondents who are diversity managers in different local gov-ernment organizations singled out the 'best value performance indicators', which are the national targets put forward by government and on which the councils have to report monthly. They also mentioned the 'corporate performance assess-ment', which is an external 'inspection' of the performance of the councils by government, of which one of the key elements is to review 'the extent to which diversity is embedded within the organization's day to day practice'.

Among the diversity managers of private companies, only two of them, who work in the same large supermarket chain, mentioned that they work with CRE when exemplifying the importance of collaboration with external networks and institutions to develop the best practice. One of them said:

> You know that we took part in the CIPD. Also obviously we belong to the employers' forum on disability, the employers' forum on age. And we network

through these organizations quite extensively really to make sure that what we do is to develop best practice. So, for example, where we've done some ethnicity awareness training we worked with the CRE to get their input as well to make sure that what we're doing is along the right line.

Although CRE was not named by the other diversity managers of private sector companies, all of them suggested that their organization is a member of several external diversity networks and forums, including Race for Opportunity, the Employers' Forum on Disability, the Employers' Forum on Age, Opportunity Now, CPI's Equal Opportunity Panel and RRC Vanguard Network. The respondent from the global energy and petrochemicals company said that these networks are crucial, not only because they keep them up to date with the developments in the field, but also because they are important for benchmarking. Another respondent, a diversity manager of a large financial sector company, was very proud when he said: 'We've recently been named as top performer in the Race for Opportunity's annual benchmarking survey'. Thus, diversity and equality networks are influential in setting the content and scope of the diversity management policies and activities in individual organizations. Both public and private sector organizations need to observe and be aware of the standards set by these external networks in order to be benchmarked and, in turn, to have a good external reputation regarding diversity and equality.

Interestingly, the issue of partnership with the trade unions was not as forthcoming in any of the interviews as the collaboration with CRE, CIPD or membership in diversity networks were. The respondents mentioned the trade unions only when asked, and the responses were generally very short and abrupt, simply stating that the trade unions are supportive of their organizations' diversity policy. Diversity managers of only two private sector companies gave a more extended picture of their work with the trade unions. One of these was the large supermarket chain both of whose diversity managers emphasized the importance of partnership with the trade unions. One of them argued: 'The initiatives that we have we can do hand in hand really with the unions. It's a way of sharing initiatives, sharing learning really'. The other exemplified the relationship between the company and the trade unions in the field of diversity management as follows:

They were supportive in the discussions we had with them. I mean they're doing a lot of work themselves in terms of diversity awareness training for their field officers. And then we've kept in touch with them in terms of how they're approaching it. Recently, they carried with us a carer survey, within our stores and with our people to see what sorts of problems people were experiencing in terms of caring. So we're quite cooperative with them in a number of different areas related to diversity. We're trying to work together.

The other organization which gave a relatively extensive account of their involvement with the trade unions was the large financial sector organization. On their relationship with the trade unions, the company's diversity manager said:

> We talk to them regularly and provide them with a formal update twice a year, what we've achieved in the preceding six months and what our plans are for the following six months. But I think in truth we do extensive research directly with our employees and customers. The actual priorities that we tackle on an annual basis, we address consultation of our employees directly rather than needing various trade unions. I think it would be fair to say we are really at the leading edge of equality and diversity. Unions are very interested in hearing what we have to say. They don't come to us and tell us what we need to be doing because I think they are quite impressed that we have such a robust strategic work in the case.

What is striking in the above quotation is the emphasis that the company does the employee consultation by directly approaching the employees rather than 'needing trade unions' in the process. The idea of 'direct consultation' in that case, and the apparently minor mention of the trade unions in the narrations of the other diversity managers from both public and private sector organizations, reveal that the diversity management approach is associated with the diminished role of the trade unions. That characteristic of the diversity management approach is also cited in the literature. For instance, Liff (1996) pointed out that, different from the equal opportunities approach which is associated with traditional industrial relations framework, the diversity management approach adopts the human resource management perspective to labour relations. In other words, the industrial relations perspective of managing labour is based on the conception of workforce as a collective and stresses the role of trade unions for representing workers' interests. Conversely, the human resource management perspective treats employees as individuals rather than part of collectives and emphasizes involvement, commitment and loyalty (Liff 1996). In turn, the diversity management approach's identification with the human resources management framework leads to a diminished role of trade unions when companies are dealing with diversity and equality issues, and in effect to situating the employees at the receiving end of the diversity management process, which relies primarily on senior management approval.

In construction of the stories of the institutional subfield of diversity management, it is important to note the differences across institutional actors. Commissions of equality, such as the EOC, CRE and DRC, have different approaches to the issue of diversity when compared with organizations in the public, private and voluntary sectors, as well as the Confederation of British Industry, CIPD or other professional bodies or trade unions. These differences are only reconciled in multistakeholder encounters, such as diversity management networks, which facilitate dialogue across divergent institutional stories of diversity management. Such encounters both moderate independent institutional stories and impact on the content and style of diversity management promoted and practised by these institutions.

7.7   The business subfield of diversity management

Diversity management stories are sometimes situated in relation to the business subfield in terms of the dynamics prevailing in the business environment and industrial sector. In the literature it is argued that in order to meet the challenges of the highly competitive business environment, driven by scarce labour resources and flexible consumer orientated production and service delivery, employers need to adopt efficient diversity management strategies and policies (Adler and Ghadar 1990; Loosemore and Al Muslmani 1999; Marable 2000; Soni 2000; Carroll and Hannan 2000; Allard 2002; Ashkanasy *et al.* 2002; Blazevic and Lievens 2002).

All of the respondents mentioned the two-fold focus of diversity management policies in their organizations: the employees and the customers. The diversity manager of the large supermarket chain proposed that it was necessary to 'meet the needs of people of all backgrounds' as follows:

> We are already a number one player in the UK market. To maintain that position and to continue to grow, we do have quite strong growth targets; we needed to reach out to a broader group of customers and broader group of people in the talent pool. So that was almost a business necessity that we understood how people are different either from the customer point of view or staff point of view.

Similarly, another diversity manager said:

> We want to maximise the talents of all our employees irrespective of their personal characteristics and we want all our customers to benefit from high level customer service and feel that the bank values them as customers.

In terms of managing the diversity of their employees, all of the organizations reported that they are monitoring the recruitment and promotion rates of women and ethnic minorities in their workforce, and providing diversity awareness training for their employees and managers. The female diversity manager of the large supermarket chain stated that the company's diversity approach enabled them to recruit people with different talents and skills more easily. She explained this in the following way:

> Now we have more awareness about what different people want out of a job and career and also where we can find these people. For example, different advertising, recruiting people through word of mouth and taking referrals from existing staff is a great way to increase the number of ethnic minority staff in our stores.

The diversity manager of one of the local government organizations mentioned that their staff profile is largely middle-aged and that they wanted to increase the number of young people who are working in the Council, in order to serve the community better. He said that he hopes that their 'corporate parenting' programme, which he sees as one of the most successful diversity management programmes, will help them to recruit more young staff in the future:

> In local government we have a thing called corporate parenting. This relates to the young people who are in the care of the local authority for all sorts of reasons. We call them 'looked after children'. One of the things we've done in the last couple of years as a council is to work with our looked after children to offer them with work placement and shadowing opportunities in order to fill in some of the gaps they may have in their teenage years: very promising in terms of the take-up of the young people.

In the interviews, one of the most frequently mentioned advantages of a diverse workforce was its effect on service delivery. The diversity manager of a large public sector organization in Northern Ireland argued that, in order to connect to the community and provide better service, their workforce has to be representative of the local population. He said that within the scope of its diversity policy, the organization runs positive action programmes to recruit and promote people from different ethnic and religious backgrounds, as well as from different age and gender groups, to reflect the local population. Others also pointed out the relationship between diversity of the workforce and enhanced quality of service delivery or customer satisfaction. For instance, the diversity manager of a large financial organization commented on the issue as follows:

> We have examples of branches where we've now got multicultural teams that better reflect the communities that they serve. If you're a white employee in Leicester, say, where you've got a largely Indian customer base, if you've got Indian colleagues, you can talk to them and you can learn about the Indian culture. And I think a lot of informal education goes on

which helps white employees serve their customers better. They've gained greater insight of different communities, our teams being more diverse.

This example lends support to the argument made by Ashkanasy *et al.* (2002: 328–9) who suggest that in the service-orientated economy employees need to develop the necessary skills and background for communicating with, and for understanding and meeting the demands of, diverse groups of customers. Hence, employers may see recruiting employees from diverse backgrounds as a profitable strategy in order to appeal to different customer groups. The words of the same diversity manager make this connection very clear:

> Diverse teams have definitely made a big impact on the company as an employer and also as a service provider. Because as we get better at serving customers, responding to their differences and they are more likely to come back and buy products and services from us rather than from our competitors which makes us more profitable.

He discussed the impact of the company's flexible work arrangements covered under the diversity policy from a similar perspective:

> Flexible working is another example where perhaps some years ago people who worked part-time or wanted to work differently were frowned upon. But we've got now some really innovative examples of where whole teams of people working different hours and what that's meant is that offices can open earlier and close later because people are doing compressed working or so on. And our customers gained because offices are open from half seven to half seven. And business has benefited because it has not cost us any more money to do that. It's just groups of people who have arranged their working hours differently.

The shift from standardized mass production to flexible production and diversification of goods and services, and its relevance for diversity management, are also cited in the literature (Chevrier 2003). In the interviews flexibility was one of the important themes, particularly for the private sector organizations. For example, the diversity manager of the large supermarket chain stated that the issue providing more flexibility for both the staff and the customers is the focal point of the company's future diversity management agenda. He said:

> In terms of a kind of direction for the coming year, there's much more about how do we get more and more flexibility. How can we operate efficiently while giving our staff and customers the greatest level of flexibility that's in terms of the hours they work and what types of things we've got

on our shelves. It's all about being flexible to meet different people's needs. It's really how we meet our distinct promises in a way that meets the needs of more people.

In the interviews with the diversity managers of the private sector organizations, one of the most important branches of the diversity management activities was related to provision of diversified products and services to attract different segments of the market. Within that framework, the importance of collaboration between the diversity and marketing functions of the companies was emphasized. The diversity manager of one of the financial sector organizations mentioned that they work with the marketing department to do consumer research with their customers from different groups 'about how well they think their banking needs are currently met to understand the gap in our provision of services and the kinds of products we offer', and to develop new services and products on the basis of this research. As an example, he mentioned that the company has recently introduced a range of products and services for the Asian marketplace, including a range of shariah-compliant products for the Muslim customers. Similarly, both of the diversity managers of the large supermarket chain talked extensively about their new product and service ranges which aim to meet the demands of their diverse customer base, such as promotions for religious festivals, and Asian and kosher products. They said that within the scope of its 'customer planned programmes', the company specifically targets the 'ethnic customers and older customers'. During the description of these products and services, the emphasis on profit and sales was striking as the justification for diversity management. One of them argued:

> In terms of where we have had more diverse products ranges that inevitably driven additional sales in certain areas where we have ethnic customer base. For example by having special promotions for festivals, we find out that by tuning into the local customer, we can generate more additional sales in these areas.

Again, another respondent emphasized the profitability of diversity for the company as follows:

> There are probably lots of different things that we can talk about but one thing that had the most impact from the business point of view is actually looking at our enhanced new range of ethnic products, which are obviously much more compatible with the needs of different ethnic minorities in the UK. Obviously you can see the increase in sales and increase in the profit that we get from those customers.

These findings show that attracting and satisfying a wider range of customers are important focus points for the diversity management perspective of the private sector organizations. This emphasis, and particularly the association between diversity programmes regarding service delivery and profitability, was relatively weak in the interviews with the diversity managers from public sector organization. The diversity specialist of a national government organization who supports and helps various public sector organizations in implementing diversity management programmes and policies, explained her concern about the issue as follows:

> The benefit is for the people who work in your organization and the customers of your organization. I mean in terms of the customers, if we talk about the public sector, we are not fit to purpose if we are not managing diversity effectively. Because the tax payers are diverse. And when you are talking about the diversity, you are talking about the majority of the population, not the minority. But I have to say that I do worry about the extent to which I've found people are really doing impact assessment. In terms of policy making and service delivery, people are still taking a reactive rather than proactive approach.

Clearly, for her, the customer side of the diversity management process was as important as the diversity policies and programmes targeting the employees. She thought that public sector organizations need to take a proactive diversity management approach to service delivery to diverse groups in the community, as a part of those organizations' social responsibility, if not for the profit motive. In fact, most of the diversity managers from the public sector organizations talked about their services targeting the disadvantaged groups in society within the framework of their diversity management activities. Examples of these include working with young delinquents from disadvantaged social backgrounds in the case of the organization in Northern Ireland, and programmes for older people and people with disabilities in the case of one of the local government organizations. A diversity manager of the other local government organization strongly pointed out that as a part of their diversity strategy they are monitoring the service take-up by different groups in the town. He said:

> If we got things like education, social services, housing, then all of their mainstream policies would look at the impact of the service delivery or non take-up of services by particular groups. Why BME women for instance in their community seem to get less access to certain types of activities.

Thus, one of the main differences between public and private sector in their diversity management approach regarding the products and services was in terms of the different motives that underlie their understanding. At the beginning of this section we stated that the business field that impacts upon the field of diversity has two components: the business environment and the industrial sector. In other words, in addition to the dynamics prevailing in the business environment, the peculiarities of the industrial sector within which the organization is situated have an impact upon the *field* of diversity management. Specific sectors may offer different patterns of work organization, sector-specific workforce composition and diverse traditions in the field of diversity and equality. Thus, diversity management practices may vary with the sector. The interviews suggest that in terms of sectoral differences, the distinction between public sector and private sector is dominant. The more specific sectoral (or intersectoral) differences do not seem to have a large impact on the diversity management discourse and the policy, although the specific diversity activities and programmes, particularly considering product development, service delivery and marketing, vary within each sector. Nevertheless, in terms of understanding the diversity management approach of the organizations at a more general level, the public sector/private sector distinction is more overwhelming than the differences within each sector. The case of motivations for integrating the diversity dimension to service delivery and product development as explained below serves as a good example of that distinction. In terms of meeting the demands of customers from diverse backgrounds, the dominant motivation behind the diversity management programmes for private sector companies is to increase their sales and profit, whereas public sector organizations are largely motivated by the principle of social responsibility. Quoting again from the interview with the diversity manager of the one of the local government organizations:

> We're working quite actively on that now at the community level. Our community development department works closely with local support groups, with particular local communities some of which have got BME residences who are in social deprivation. We've got education specialists who work with youngsters who need support in the widest sense, not just necessarily about BME residence. In relation to our housing allocation and housing management policy, we've got diversity built into those in terms of social cohesion.

Here, the terminology used throughout the narration is also striking. In terms of service delivery, the stories of public sector diversity managers differ largely from those working in the private sector companies. In the interviews with the private sector diversity managers, for instance, there was no mention of social issues related to poverty, welfare and integration, such as 'social cohesion' or 'social deprivation', nor to their relevance for diversity management.

On the other hand, diversity managers of the public sector organizations did not even once utter the words 'customers', 'profit' or 'growth'. Similarly, for the public sector organizations, social class difference forms an important category of diversity in dealing both with their employees and customers. Two of the diversity managers from the public sector stated that social class is overtly included in their organizations' diversity definition. Conversely, diversity managers from the private sector organizations mentioned social class neither as part of their organizations' diversity definition, nor within the context of their diversity policies and programmes. The business sector in which the organizations and respondents are located have impacted on their stories. The theory of industrial recipes by Spender (1989) suggests that the industrial sector shapes the particular ways that managers apply judgement, and our findings support this. However, we have also found that the other subfields are influential in the construction of diversity stories.

7.8   Popular and unpopular stories of diversity management

We have elaborated on the idea that the choice of stories in subfields are not haphazard. Indeed, the stories are used as frames for allocating resources and for fleshing out certain concerns whilst silencing others. **Table 7.1** illustrates the key stories of diversity management in each subfield and the major omissions in these stories. The academic story of diversity management has been a site for discussion of how diversity management stories are used to stake claims on resources and to raise some concerns and silence others. However, in the subfields of culture, institution and business, the stories are geared towards focusing attention on organizational processes and outcomes. There is a discernible lack of attention given to imbalances of power in stories of these subdomains. Our study of the professional subfield, however, tells a different story of diversity management in the UK. The study suggests that diversity management, despite the stories of the other subfields, is still driven by legal considerations rather than the business case arguments and the diversity professionals, who are expected to deliver organizational change, and who lack the agency and organizational power to affect such change.

There is also the untold story of diversity management (see **Table 7.1**). Although the academic stories, as well as our interview findings, point to the necessity of organizational change in order to realize diversity management plans, our study in Chapter 4 revealed that diversity managers did indeed fail to enjoy such privileges. They had lower levels of pay, job satisfaction and organizational status when compared to their colleagues in human resource departments. It is interesting to note that the qualitative stories of diversity managers

Table 7.1 The subfields, key characteristics of stories, absences in stories

The subfield	Key characteristics	Absences and omissions
Academic subfield	Business case Legal case Moral case Emphasis on organizational benefits rather than sanctions	Agency of the individual diversity officers
Cultural subfield	Links with historical and cultural issues and demography of the situated context	Sanctions for non-compliance with diversity principles The legal case
Institutional subfield	Institutional variations in definitions and key diversity issues due to varied impacts of policy, law, trade unions and other institutional partners and mechanisms	Dialogue among these stakeholders
Business subfield	Dynamics of supply and demand for goods, services and labour impacts on the choice of diversity approaches	Foresight and progressive approaches, transcending demographics

did not give the same picture. Indeed, the interviews with them presented a positive outlook for the profession. We note that stories change when the audience changes. Diversity professionals present different stories when representing their organizations and when explaining their institutional work, and when the survey investigates their own personal lives. Although the received wisdom suggests that interviews would present more deep and critical insights, in our study interviews generated less critical stories on diversity management initiatives and the quantitative survey revealed a very different picture.

Diversity managers feel compelled to represent their organizations in a positive light in the interview situation, and the questionnaire survey presented a better opportunity for them to reveal their real experiences at work.

How, then, can these apparent disparities in stories of diversity management across these subfields, coexist in the broad field of diversity management? Our study reveals that only a very few diversity managers in our studies have professional education or training on diversity management. Most of their knowledge is acquired through professional networks and in-house training opportunities. Absence of formal channels of professional education means that the stories that the diversity managers tell are largely unaffected by academic discourses. Academic–practitioner collaboration in networks, however, provides one partial source for such explicit forms of knowledge transfers. However, networks in the field of diversity management are few and far between. Although connectedness through networks between these subfields moderates stories of diversity management, weakness of network ties across diversity professionals means that divergent stories are retained. It is only healthy that none of the competing stories of diversity management, despite the popularity of some, have absolute hegemony in the field. Although divergence of perspectives may be viewed as a challenge to progress in the field, this sense of plurality is an asset, provided that there are means of negotiating strategies of action across multiple constituencies of diversity management.

Confirming Heugens's (2002) findings, and despite the strength of some stories that have the support of received wisdom behind them, it is surprising to see that multiple stories of a competing nature coexist within the diversity management field. The political and social processes behind this coexistence have been investigated in this chapter. It is not surprising to see that constituent groups such as employers, trade unions and government agencies have different interests and that these are reflected in their stories of diversity management. However, the problem with the divergent stories of diversity management across these subfields is not merely that these stories are inconsistent. It is rather that the stories are not sophisticated enough to capture the reality of diversity management practices, providing only partial accounts.

Therefore, networks and collaborations across these subfields are very important in ensuring that stories of diversity management incorporate consideration of a greater number of stakeholders and constituent groups' stories. The depth of diversity management stories of the academic field owes this to scholarly attention to multiple constituencies in research. Clearly, the success of the diversity management story is predicted by its sophistication to the extent to which the story captures the reality of organizational life. **Table 7.2** outlines the various sources of diversity management knowledge in the UK. Due to the multiplicity of perspectives on diversity management, there is dissent amongst scholars in terms of the authenticity and legitimacy of diversity management and equal opportunities management approaches. Whilst consultants and employers' unions hastily embrace and advocate the concept as a new method for increasing competitiveness and work performance, this has received much scepticism from trade unionists, a cautious reception from government agencies in commissions of equality, and from scholars of critical management and industrial relations disciplines, regarding the adequacy of the concept in addressing their traditional concerns over social and workplace inequalities. Indeed the discussions that ensued suggest that the business case arguments of diversity management have been viewed as a tool of the neo-liberal ideology which has sought to individualize, de-collectivize and de-unionize workforces.

Table 7.2   Sources of diversity management stories

Sources	Key characteristics
Academic writing on diversity management	Not accessible to practitioners
	University courses are being offered
	Legal compliance and discrimination law are better covered
Training courses on equality and diversity	Highly variable and rare in SMEs
Professional networks of diversity management	Rare but most effective means of knowledge transfers
In-house experiential learning	Driven by legal compliance
	Missing link between diversity and performance
Trade unions	Training of trade union representatives
	Disinterest and mistrust
	Driven by legal compliance
Consultancies	Softly-softly approach
	Balanced score card approach
Government agencies	Voluntaristic considerations
	Legal compliance

Bringing the stakeholder groups together can help them moderate their stories of diversity management, reflecting on the accounts of the 'other'. Similar work is common in the field of political science. Drawing on a series of workshops which used mutual storytelling to bring Israeli–Palestinian students together, Bar-On and Kassem (2004) explain that storytelling can be used as a method to address conflict when both parties were allowed to tell their story. In this case, the authors have used the Holocaust and the Al-Naqba Memorial Days as cases for each party to reflect upon. However, storytelling alone is not sufficient for diversity professionals to realize their ambitions of organizational change. Indeed, their relative status as diversity professionals in organizational hierarchies would also shape the stories that they construct of themselves and their plans.

The connections between knowledge and storytelling is important for diversity management professionals whose main resource and power of negotiation is their knowledge of discourses and the supportive evidence which they can use to negotiate their organizational plans for change with a range of stakeholders. However, the conception of storytelling as a tool, lever or resource for organizational change is rather linear. Solorzano and Yosso (2002) argue that the process of storytelling involves at least a two-way interaction. They introduce the concept of counter-storytelling, which provides resources to the storyteller to counteract and refute the stories of the others. As workplace negotiations takes place in multiparty dialogues, it is important not only to present a story which secures the support of the others, but also to develop counter-stories that address the stories of the others.

Counter-intuitively, one of the interesting findings of our study is the relative lack of attention given by academic studies to real difficulties experienced by diversity managers in their efforts to realize their agendas of change. Our study illustrated that diversity managers do not enjoy power and prestige in organizational hierarchies. This is reflected in their relatively low pay and prestige in comparison to human resource professionals in the UK. As these latter are currently struggling to achieve a strategic role in organizations, it is further unrealistic to expect diversity managers to have a leading role in organizational change initiatives, except for a few exceptional cases.

We argue that professions are guardians of stories. Therefore further professionalization of diversity management should provide the means by which more critical discourses can penetrate corporate circles through academic institutions. Indeed, there is evidence to suggest that greater professionalization of diversity management is likely to take place due to the proliferation of bachelors and postgraduate degree courses in the UK in this field. A similar trend was also observable in the legacy of human resource management in the UK. US-based strategic formulations of HRM were moderated with critical considerations of unique traditions of trade unionism and employment law in the UK.

7.9 Conclusion

The majority of the formal and full stories of diversity management come from the private sector. Their machinery of public relations has been churning out stories of success, stories which draw attention to linkages between diversity and business performance. Our study of storytelling in diversity management also reveals a variation across the academic, cultural, institutional, business and professional subfields of diversity management. It suggests that stories of diversity management are relationally constructed. That is, the subfield in which the diversity management story is located, as well as the particular connectedness of the diversity professional to other subfields, help shape the diversity management story that they tell. Interconnectedness (Shumate et al. 2005) has relevance to the story of diversity management, which does not only have a highly contextualized local dimension, but also has national, international and globalized meanings, thanks to the advent of knowledge transfer networks and technologies. Consequently, we argue that the stories reflect the particular position of diversity management and professionals in the subfields of diversity, and their connectedness and interrelatedness to other individuals, sets of stakeholders and circumstances in the broad field of diversity management.

There is also a historical dimension to the construction of diversity management stories, as history frames the legacy of diversity management and informs the scope and content of its stories across all subfields. The legacy of the past is not easily removed. The move from equal opportunities to diversity management in academic and professional circles did not immediately lead to a change from compliance-driven approaches to business-case-driven diversity approaches. Rudiments of old stories of equal opportunities continue to colour and shape the current stories of diversity management.

Further reading

Auyero, J. (2002) 'The Judge, the Cop, and the Queen of Carnival: Ethnography, Storytelling, and the (Contested) Meanings of Protest', *Theory and Society*, vol. 31, pp. 151–87.

Barone, T.E. (1992) 'Beyond Theory and Method: A Case of Critical Storytelling', *Theory into Practice*, vol. 31, no. 2, pp. 142–6.

Boje, D.M. (1991) 'The Storytelling Organization: A Study of Story Performance in an Office-supply Firm', *Administrative Science Quarterly*, vol. 36, pp. 106–26.

Boje, D.M. (1995) 'Stories of the Storytelling Organization: A Postmodern Analysis of Disney as "Tamara-land"', *Academy of Management Journal*, vol. 38, no. 4, pp. 997–1035.

Boyce, M.E. (1995) 'Collective Centring and Collective Sense-making in the Stories and Storytelling of one Organization', *Organization Studies*, vol. 16, no. 1, pp. 107–37.

Boyce, M.E. (1996) 'Organizational Story and Storytelling: A Critical Review', *Journal of Organizational Change Management*, vol. 9, no. 5, pp. 5–26.

Lerner, G.H. (1992) 'Assisted Storytelling: Deploying Shared Knowledge as a Practical Matter', *Qualitative Sociology*, vol. 15, no. 3, pp. 247–71.

McLellan, H. (2006) 'Corporate Storytelling Perspectives', *The Journal for Quality and Participation*, Spring, pp. 17–20.

Morgan, S. and Dennehy, R.F. (1997) 'The Power of Organizational Storytelling: A Management Development Perspective', *Journal of Management Development*, vol. 16, no. 7, pp. 494–501.

Parkin, M. (2004) *Tales for Change: Using Storytelling to Develop People and Organizations*. London: Kogan Page.

Ready, D.A. (2002) 'How Storytelling Builds Next-generation Leaders', *MIT Sloan Management Review*, Summer, pp. 63–9.

Shumate, M., Bryant, J.A. and Monge, P.R. (2005) 'Storytelling and Globalization: The Complex Narratives of Netwar', *Emergence: Complexity and Organization*, vol. 7, nos 3–4, pp. 74–84.

Swap, W., Leonard, D., Shields, M. and Abrams, L. (2001) 'Using Mentoring and Storytelling to Transfer Knowledge in the Workplace', *Journal of Management Information Systems*, vol. 18, no. 1, pp. 95–114.

Vance, C.M. (1991) 'Formalising Storytelling in Organizations: A Key Agenda for the Design of Training', *Journal of Organizational Change Management*, vol. 4, no. 3, pp. 52–8.

Ward, J. and Winstanley, D. (2004) 'Sexuality and the City: Exploring the Experience of Minority Sexual Identity through Storytelling', *Culture and Organization*, vol. 10, no. 3, pp. 219–36.

Sectoral Effects

The Case of Private Sector Recruitment Agencies

8.1 Introduction

Global diversity management is not only affected by the national level of policies and discourses, as discussed in Part II, sectoral conditions and peculiarities also affect the way global diversity management policies gain shape. Despite the growing significance of private employment agencies, there is little research on their actual operations and their impact on the employment prospects of particular groups in society. Even precise numerical figures on the size and activities of these agencies are not available (Wilkinson, 2000). Moreover, the sector has obvious relevance to gender equality at work, although research attention in terms of equal opportunities has been rather limited. Considering their growing role in job placement, it is crucial to understand the attitudes of private agencies towards disadvantaged segments of the labour market and their actions regarding equality of opportunity, alongside those of Government and not-for-profit agencies.

The research project that we present in this chapter was carried out as part of the EOC's formal investigation into 'Transforming Work', which is supported by the European Social Fund (ESF). This investigation aims to promote greater recognition of changing patterns of work and working lives, which have been led by both employers and by employees and jobseekers. This project seeks to identify the state of diversity management in the private sector recruitment agencies and explore their programmes for young people and adults, which affect and inform their routes into work. Particular focus is placed on the agencies' impact upon women's progression into senior-level positions and upon the work–life balance and flexible working patterns. In this chapter, the term 'private recruitment agency' is used to cover the two types of agencies as defined by the DTI (1999): 'employment business', which supplies temporary workers, and 'agency', which supplies recruits to employers. (The terms employment business and employment agency stem from the 1973 Employment Agencies Act, which regulates the sector. However, this definition was later adopted more widely by other organizations.)

We first describe the methodology used in the chapter. Then we map out the state of the private recruitment sector and outline the operations of private sector recruitment agencies. Examining the role of the Recruitment and Employment Confederation (REC), the sector's umbrella organization, we identify how they promote the diversity and equality agenda in the sector. Based on a documentary review and in-depth interviews with representatives of 26 private sector recruitment agencies and recruitment membership organizations, we then offer an analysis of the barriers to equality – that is gender neutrality, gender bias, occupational segregation, the 'passing-the-buck culture' and the lack of equality awareness – and of the drivers for equality – that is organizational size, senior management commitment, external network membership and the business case. Finally, we outline the equality initiatives and trends in the private recruitment sector, focusing specifically on flexible working, staffing and guidance to non-traditional areas of work, and support programmes to help disadvantaged people into work. In the Appendix, we provide an interview schedule which can be used by researchers or students in assessing the state of equality and diversity in the recruitment sector.

8.2   The unique case of the recruitment sector

Labour market demographics, as well as working patterns, are ever changing. In periods of economic growth, one of the key changes in the distributive profile of labour markets has been the increased access of previously underrepresented groups to work. The reasons for this change in the labour market composition are multifaceted. However, skills deficiencies in the labour markets; employers' desire to recruit and retain the best talent; and social and legal changes towards greater levels of equality of opportunity by gender, ethnicity, disability, age, sexual orientation, faith and other social categories, have all contributed to an increase in the proportion of workers with atypical backgrounds.

Despite these developments, the skills of women, black and minority ethnic (BME) groups, individuals with disabilities, gays and lesbians, as well as old and young people, still remain underutilized due to rigidities in the labour market. These stem from occupational segregation, inequality and the traditional organization of work and domestic life. However, there are also signs of positive change. For example, earlier research by the Equal Opportunities Commission (EOC) demonstrated that attitudes of women and men to work and family are changing in Great Britain, as women and men express a greater desire to combine their work and family lives in more productive and balanced ways without having to sacrifice one for the other (Hatter *et al.* 2002; O'Brien and Shemilt 2003).

However, the limited availability of flexible working arrangements and work–life policies in better paid jobs disadvantage women, as they continue to shoulder a disproportionately larger share of caring responsibilities. Consequently, women are often locked in temporary or part-time jobs with limited security, and those working part-time are, on average, paid 40 per cent less per hour than men in full-time work (Olsen and Walby 2004; EOC 2005). Currently 42 per cent of women in the UK work part-time (Hurrell 2006), and this largely contributes to the gender pay gap: unlike full-time work, which is associated with wage increases in-line with the length of service, part-time work is associated with a slight wage reduction in real terms (Olsen and Walby 2004). In 2004, 74 per cent of the women who worked part-time stated children and domestic family responsibilities as the main reasons for doing so (Women and Work Commission 2006: 30). Furthermore, 45 per cent of part-time female workers are employed in the jobs that underutilize their skills (Darton and Hurrell 2005; Green 2005).

Moreover, occupational segregation continues to persist in the UK, with women occupying the majority of administrative and secretarial (81 per cent) and personal service jobs (84 per cent) (Hurrell 2006). They also remain a minority in professional work. The majority of female employment (60 per cent) in the UK is concentrated in ten out of 77 occupations which are mostly in low-paid private services (Grimshaw and Rubery 2001). In contrast, men hold most skilled trades (92 per cent) and process, plant and machine operative jobs (87 per cent) (Hurrell, 2006).

In order to address these and other new economic realities of segregation and inequality, the Labour Government published the Fairness at Work White

Paper in 1997. This led to the 1999 Employment Act, which includes sections on 'family friendly' practices and labour market flexibility. Similarly, in the spirit of the Lisbon Strategy of 2000, the European Union has recently launched Guidelines for Employment Policies (2005–2008). These outline policy guidelines, which seek to foster full employment by promoting a new lifecycle approach to work (better reconciliation of work and private life, and support for working conditions that are conducive to active ageing). They also seek to ensure inclusive labour markets for jobseekers and disadvantaged people, so that race, gender or disability do not limit opportunities for employment (COM 2005: 141). The role of employment services and agencies in the process of improving the matching of labour market supply and demand is spelt out in the Guidelines. These highlight the potential to promote early identification of needs and offer job-search assistance, guidance and training as part of personalized action plans.

Both governmental and non-governmental agencies play a decisive role in job placements as gatekeepers across the UK. At present, the Government is the largest provider of employment advice and guidance services in the UK. However, the role played by the private sector agencies in the field of recruitment and guidance has become more prominent in recent decades. Private sector recruitment agencies make an important contribution to the dynamism and wealth of the UK economy by providing access to employment for 4 per cent of the working population in the UK (Millward *et al.* 2000; Druker and Stanworth 2001; Heery 2004). Therefore, the sector is of key significance in understanding the state of equality and diversity at the point of access to employment.

8.3   Conducting research in the recruitment sector

The chapter draws upon documentary analysis, as well as in-depth interviews with representatives of a range of private sector recruitment agencies and with membership organizations in the private recruitment sector. The work was conducted in two stages. The first stage of the project involved a systematic literature review and a detailed website search. Direct contact was also made with the REC in this phase of the project. First, we reviewed the relevant academic and practitioner literature on the topic in order to place the practice of private agencies in their broad context. We also drew on publications produced by, for example, relevant Government departments (e.g. the DTI) and other institutional bodies (e.g. the REC and the Centre for Guidance Studies at the University of Derby). For this phase, we used the research libraries across the University of London. Second, we simultaneously conducted a website search as an initial exploration of the recruitment and guidance sector in the UK. We reviewed the websites of the private employment and guidance agencies.

Analysis of the REC website was particularly valuable, for two reasons. First, it is an umbrella organization of recruitment agencies. Second, the REC has recently agreed a Diversity Pledge in partnership with Jobcentre Plus and currently encourages its members to commit to the Diversity Pledge. Third, we contacted the REC directly for information on its member agencies and to gain a general picture of equality and diversity approaches in the recruitment sector, particularly around the issues of the advancement opportunities for women and the work–life balance. At the end of this first stage of the project, we produced a list of the general and specialized private sector recruitment and guidance agencies which are considered to be key players in the sector.

The second stage of the project involved a detailed exploration of the private employment and guidance agencies and their programmes. The investigation was informed by two sources: existing documentation (institutional documents and grey literature) on the agencies and programmes, and in-depth interviews. First, documentation collected from private agencies was reviewed with regard to the impact of agency practices on, and support for, the employment of women and minority ethnic groups, as well as other disadvantaged segments of the population, including parents, carers, faith groups, returners and older workers. While doing this, we also paid specific attention to the extent to which these agencies consider the changing needs and priorities of these groups. This study regards gender and ethnicity as cross-cutting themes to explore other aspects of disadvantage and segregation. Second, in March 2006, three interviews were conducted with the representatives of the REC to gather general information on their members, on the equality and diversity approaches in the recruitment sector and on the organization's own equality and diversity perspective. Interviews were also conducted with two representatives of the Interim Management Association (IMA) and one representative of the Association of Executive Recruiters (AER). IMA and AER are the two associations that act under the REC. We have conducted these interviews in order to explore intrasectoral variations in practices of equality and diversity.

Third, in March and April 2006, 9 in-depth, semi-structured interviews were conducted with the representatives of private sector recruitment and guidance agencies and one with an ESF-funded project supporting women's recruitment in IT (the characteristics of all 26 interview participants are summarized in **Table 8.1**). Informed by the interviews with the REC, the IMA and the AER, and drawing on the list of agencies that was compiled in the first stage of the project, we initially selected a total of 28 agencies on the basis of their size, locality and speciality to be interviewed from the list of organizations. Unfortunately, cold calls via telephone and e-mail proved ineffective, with only five organizations granting research access. We therefore elicited the support of the REC, the IMA and the AER, all of which not only advertised the research among their members, but also forwarded the contact details of those

Table 8.1 Summary of interview participants

	Sector	Size
1	Interim executive recruitment	Small
2	Executive recruitment	Small
3	General	Large
4	General/ethnic minority recruitment, Birmingham	Small
5	Office support, secretarial, London	Large
6	General	Large/international
7	Interim executive recruitment/HR and finance	Medium
8	Executive recruitment/HR and finance	Medium
9	Flexible executive recruitment	Medium
10	Office support, secretarial, international	Large/international
11	Office, industrial, catering, driving and construction	Large
12	Interim executive recruitment	Small
13	Interim recruitment/general	Small
14	Interim recruitment/general	Small
15	Executive recruitment/financial services	Small
16	Legal sector	Small
17	General	Small
18	Executive recruitment/financial services, management consultancy, telecoms/media	Small
19	General	Large/international
20	Recruitment and Employment Confederation	Small
21	Recruitment and Employment Confederation	Small
22	Recruitment and Employment Confederation	Small
23	Association of Executive Recruiters	Small
24	Interim Management Association	Small
25	Interim Management Association	Small
26	IT, electronics and communication	Large/international

agencies which showed interest in participating in the study. This proved a more effective approach. Now we were able to ask participant organizations about the agencies which specialize in particular areas, such as business services, legal and advisory services, health, education and hi-tech manufacturing. This snowball sampling technique, which was designed to ensure that various types of agencies were covered, also proved effective.

In order to cover a wide range of organizations, we interviewed representatives of ten small-sized agencies (with ten or less employees); three medium-sized agencies (with between 11 and 499 employees); and six large agencies (with 500 or more employees). The operations of the agencies in our sample range from local to national and international. Furthermore, interviews were conducted with both non-specialized private agencies and with the private agencies that specialize in the recruitment of highly skilled professional workers in specific industries.

Five of the agencies which participated in the research are not specialized in any form of contractual placement and place candidates in all sectors and industries. The sample sought to cover a wide range of sectors and industries where private agencies play a role in recruitment, including the public, private and voluntary sectors. The sector groups/areas served by the participant agencies include human resources; marketing; sales; office support; legal and advisory services; business services, including accounting, information and communication technologies; and engineering and health, among others.

Since it is the progression of women into senior posts, and flexible working issues, that are among the key areas of focus of this research, we conducted ten interviews with executive recruitment agencies, including five which specialize in interim management recruitment, and one which explicitly encourages flexible working. We also sought to access a representative cross-section of agencies that serve women, BME workers and other disadvantaged groups. As well as addressing these issues throughout all interviews, we interviewed an agency that focuses on ethnic and minority recruitment, and an ESF-funded project which aims to promote women's participation in the fields of advanced technology, electronics and communication.

It is important to note that the organizations which participated in the study are the recruitment agencies which either profess a commitment to equality and diversity or have an interest in the subject. The findings of the study should be considered in this light.

Ten interviews were conducted face-to-face and 16 by telephone, with interviews lasting around one hour on average. (All interviews, except one, were tape-recorded and verbatim transcriptions have been made.) The interviews have been fully anonymized and no participant details are disclosed in published materials; the confidentiality of any data supplied for the purposes of this research have also been safeguarded. In order to secure informed consent, the aims, purposes, processes and expected outcomes, as well as the deliverables of the research project, have been communicated to the participants through a cover letter.

We used a semi-structured interview schedule, which was informed by the systematic literature review in the first stage of the project and revised in-line with suggestions from the EOC officials. The main focus of the schedule was to examine the impact of private sector recruitment and guidance agencies on the advancement of women into senior positions. Ethnicity and age were used as cross-cutting categories to explore the agencies' impact on women from different age groups and ethnic backgrounds. Similarly, the schedule aimed at investigating how the issues of the work–life balance and flexible working were approached by the private agencies, since their policies and programmes on these (or the lack of them) may promote or disadvantage their female clients in their career advancement. Finally, the interview schedule included a number of general questions on the operations of the agencies, for two main reasons. First, these general questions provided the research participants with an increased freedom during their narrations. Second, they helped us to contextualize the agencies' impact on the promotion of women into senior positions within the scope of their general operations and their approach to the diversity and equality issues.

8.4   Private sector recruitment agencies in the UK

In this section we begin by outlining the state of private employment and guidance agencies in the UK, as revealed by previous research evidence in terms of the types of organizations, volume and forms of employment in the sector. Then, the key operations of the private recruitment agencies, as suggested by the field research findings, are described. Lastly, a short summary of the findings and the policy implications arising from them are presented.

Overview of the private recruitment sector in the UK

Private employment agencies play a more prominent role in the UK than similar agencies in other European countries (IRS 2002). The private recruitment sector in the UK is mainly composed of small, niche organizations employing less than ten people. It has been estimated that the sector directly employs 78,000 staff (Hotopp 2001). In 1999, it was estimated that there were around 6,500 private recruitment agencies in total (Purcell and Cam 2002) with 11,950 offices across the UK (IRS 2002).

One reason for the large number of small organizations in the industry is that it has low start-up costs and weak regulation. Indeed, one of the key considerations for the REC is the lack of any licensing scheme for recruitment companies; at the moment, entry to the sector is not regulated and almost anyone with the set-up capital can start a recruitment business in the UK. As a result, the REC believes that there is a high turnover of businesses in the sector. It has suggested that the Government could introduce a licensing scheme for the recruitment industry, though this approach might not be popular with all its members; for example, when asked whether there is a need for regulation in the sector, a respondent from a large recruitment agency, which is also an REC member, said:

> My personal view is that I think there should be few barriers to entry. I think if someone wants to come into a sector and do business, I think they should be allowed to, with as little red tape as possible. But I also expect that this needs to be regulated, otherwise you get cowboys and all sorts of things.

Some private employment agencies are much larger in size and provide services nationwide. In 1999, agencies with 100 or more employees accounted only for between 8 and 14 per cent of the industry (Hotopp 2001). However, our literature and web research indicated the presence of around 80 big players in the private staffing industry in the UK. The biggest player is Manpower, which accounted for 3.7 per cent of total industry turnover in the late 1990s (Wilkinson 2000). Other key players in the sector include Adecco, Blue Arrow, Brook Street, Kelly Services UK, Reed, Robert Walters and Michael Page, all of which have offices all over the UK.

NTC Economics carries out a monthly Recruitment Industry Survey of a panel of 600 private sector recruitment agencies in the UK. According to the December 2005 and February 2006 surveys, placement of both temporary and permanent staff by the private sector agencies is increasing, and so the revenues of agencies continue to rise (NTC Economics 2006a; 2006b). The agencies themselves consider that this expansion is the result of the rising business activity of their existing clients, as well as their attraction of new clients, and that it demonstrates the employers' confidence in them. The agencies which participated in the surveys by NTC Economics reported skill shortages, with increasing demand for permanent staff in the areas of accounting and finance, engineering and construction, executive and professional jobs, IT and computing, and the secretarial and clerical sectors. Similarly, the surveys indicated a rising demand for temporary staff in the sector areas of engineering and construction, hotels and catering, secretarial and clerical, IT and computing, and accounting and finance.

Despite the steady rise in the demands put upon the private sector agencies, NTC Economics (2006b) reported that 2004 had been the recruitment industry's best year for growth since the boom year of 2000, and that 2005 had been marked by a decline in the expansion rate. This decline is interpreted as the consequence of the slowing economic growth in the UK, with a decrease of GDP growth from 3.2 per cent in 2004 to 1.8 per cent in 2005, rather than as an indication of the decline of the private recruitment sector. Similarly, several participants in our research noted that the slowing down of the growth of the sector is also coupled with the intensification of competition between recruitment firms to the advantage of their customers. As one of them put it:

> What we have is candidates having more than one offer, or interims getting snapped away really quickly, like they are available today and not available tomorrow, and before you had more time. And clients often don't understand it, they think candidates are available for four to six weeks, and they're not. They get other jobs.

What is more striking for the aims of our research is the reported increase in the private recruitment sector activity, as opposed to the steady decline in recruitment through job centres and press advertising (NTC Economics 2006a; 2006b). This trend points to the growing significance of private sector agencies within the UK recruitment sector.

Industry turnover and employment figures in the sector

As noted earlier, an estimated four per cent of the working population is employed in temporary and permanent jobs through private sector recruitment agencies. According to data from NTC Economics (2006b), 1.5 million temporary workers are registered with private sector agencies, and up to 1 million temporary workers are deployed in all sectors every day. In addition, NTC predicts that just under 400,000 people were employed in permanent positions through private agencies (NTC Economics 2006a; 2006b). However, the predictions made by different bodies about the employment figures in the sector show a considerable variation. For instance, Hotopp (2001) points out that REC's estimate of the number of temporary agency workers is significantly higher than that made by BMG research for the DTI. BMG estimated that 557,000 temporary workers were placed by the private recruitment agencies every week. The ONS estimate of the number of agency temps is 523,000, whereas the LFS estimate is less than half of this figure at 239,000 agency employees (Hotopp 2001).

Similarly, as pointed out by Hotopp, figures regarding the volume of industry turnover vary considerably according to the source of data; BMG estimates it to be £18 billion, whereas the ONS and the REC estimate the same figure to be £13.8 billion and £14 billion respectively. More recent statistics from REC's Annual Industry Report in 2004 and 2005 places this figure now at £20 billion. However, the sectoral data fails to provide a coherent picture of trends in the sector, as there is neither an authoritative study of the sector, nor an institution which collects data across the sector (for an extended discussion of the methodological shortcomings regarding the sectoral data collection see Hotopp 2001). Therefore the available data provide at best patchy insights into sectoral practices and patterns. Nevertheless, it is noted that the UK has been the first foreign market which has been entered by the largest US temporary recruitment agencies and that the sector is expanding (Hotopp 2001; Ward 2002). Although there was a large expansion of the sector from 1993 to 2003, turnover from temporary sales has decreased slightly in the last four years (REC sources).

Some research evidence suggests that agencies are less effective in finding job placements for marginalized groups in society than for other groups, and may reinforce the existing segregation patterns. Purcell and Cam (2002), for example, suggest that agency services operate less effectively in job placements for the socially excluded. They argue that one of the negative outcomes of agency placement is that the minority ethnic workers are over-represented amongst temporary job placements. Nevertheless, Battu *et al.* (2004) show that for unemployed ethnic minority workers, searching jobs through agencies, rather than by informal means, leads to better outcomes.

Research also shows that private employment and guidance agencies reinforce traditional patterns of labour market segmentation and occupational segregation, which stunt work and career prospects of disadvantaged groups in society. The results of BMG research commissioned by the DTI show that the occupational categories into which male and female temps are placed mirror the traditional gendered occupational segregation framework (Hotopp 2001). For example, Hotopp explains that 25 per cent of female agency workers, but only 4 per cent of male agency workers, held secretarial, clerical and junior office staff positions. On the other hand, 17 per cent of male agency workers worked in engineering and electronics, and 16 per cent as drivers, compared with 3 per cent and 2 per cent respectively of female workers. Thus women's employment is concentrated in secretarial, clerical, office support and nursing jobs, and men's in the areas of construction, driving, engineering and electronics. As other research shows, these male-dominated occupations tend to have better terms and conditions of employment than the female-dominated occupations (Grimshaw and Rubery 2001; Miller and Neathey 2004).

The nature of temporary employment

Although agencies may be placing more and more people in employment, research evidence suggests that most of the job placements are temporary. A survey of 99 employers by IRS (2002) shows that both public and private organizations predominantly use private agencies for the selection and recruitment of their temporary staff. To be precise, 97 per cent of the public employers and 85 per cent of the private employers in the IRS sample reported that they recruit their temporary clerical and secretarial staff through private agencies. Furthermore, Ward *et al.* (2001) point to the increasing share of private agencies in the placement of temporary workers in the UK. However, regarding permanent recruitment to similar jobs, use of agency service declines to 65 per cent in the case of private sector organizations, and to a remarkably low 12 per cent in the case of public sector organizations (IRS 2002: 1).

It is frequently stated in the literature that, compared with permanent jobs, temporary jobs often lead to less desirable terms and conditions of employment, such as lower levels of security and pay for the jobseekers (Dale and Bamford 1988; Gottfried 1992). Similarly, research by the Trades Union Congress (1994) revealed that the growth of private agency work led to a deterioration in employment rights, pay and benefits, and training opportunities provided through collective bargaining and agreements.

Nevertheless, there were improvements to the legal standing of temporary workers since the mid 1990s. Furthermore, some research studies argue that agency employment provides women with opportunities to enter the labour market without having to make a permanent commitment; it also enables the unemployed to gain skills and experience in preparation for permanent employment in the future (Hayghe and Bianchi 1994; Purcell and Cam 2002). Another benefit of temporary agency employment is said to be its potential to enhance lifestyles through increased opportunities of flexible working (Bronstein 1991). Furthermore, a recent study by Guest and Clinton (2006) claims that temporary work enhances the employees' well-being and health, as well as their positive work attitudes and behaviour. Similarly, research conducted by BMG Research for the REC found that satisfaction levels between the temporary agency workers were high, with four-fifths of them being satisfied overall with temporary work, whereas only one-fifth reported dissatisfaction (Wiseman and Dent 2005).

These two last reports are frequently cited by the REC. However, it may be misleading to conceptualize temporary workers as a single category, since temporary exists across significantly different types of occupations and posts. For example, the BMG study was based mainly on research amongst highly skilled temporary workers, with 56 per cent of the respondents holding NVQ Level 3 or higher level qualifications, while 29 per cent were working in senior and professional positions. The BMG research findings also reveal that the gender distribution in different occupational categories in highly skilled temporary jobs reflects the gendered occupational differences in the UK, with female workers concentrated in administrative and secretarial occupations. Furthermore, the highly skilled temporary worker profile is predominantly male, and the under-representation of female workers is particularly evident amongst the youngest and oldest respondents of the BMG study. More specifically 79 per cent of 16–19-year-old highly skilled temporary workers, who participated in the study, were male. Similar male bias was evident for the older age groups, with 72 per cent of those aged 45–54, and 68 per cent of those aged 55+, being male.

Moreover, considering the fact that highly skilled workers (i.e. higher managerial and professional status, currently standing at 15.3 per cent) form only a minority of the overall temporary workforce, these more positive research findings about temporary workers should be interpreted with caution, with particular attention being paid to the occupation type and skill levels of the groups analysed. Indeed, some authors have pointed out that the benefits of temporary work are mostly accrued by the highly skilled professionals, while at the other end of the spectrum, agency workers with lower educational and vocational qualifications feel themselves involuntarily confined to 'flexible' agency jobs (Wilkinson 2000; Purcell and Cam 2002).

Operations of private sector recruitment agencies

The private recruitment agency sector is characterized by a three-way employment relationship involving candidates (job seekers), clients (firms with vacant posts) and recruitment agencies, which are placed firmly between the candidates and the clients. What is unique about the recruitment agencies is that they essentially have two sets of clients and thus work to match the demands of both. Therefore, the recruitment agencies apparently have divided loyalties. However, it would be naive to suggest that each of these three parties in the recruitment business enjoy similar levels of power and influence in negotiating their terms of work and pay.

Clearly, in times of economic growth and skills shortages, the candidates may enjoy periods of increased negotiation power. However, this is often unique to certain pockets of jobs, or sectors of employment. In the main, the clients have the dominant power in this three-way relationship, often dictating the terms and conditions of employment for the candidates, as well as the recruitment processes of the agencies. Nevertheless, there is still scope for agency power to materialize in the context of labour market dynamics: placed at the intersection of supply and demand of labour, progressive recruitment agencies can shape expectations, mould jobs and negotiate terms and conditions of work with both clients and candidates. In other words, some agencies are not passive agents which simply react to the pressures of supply and demand in the labour market. Indeed, they shape both factors through their recruitment practices. They offer advice to clients and candidates, provide them with diverse contractual choices, and shape their expectations.

Hotopp (2001) argues that there are three distinct types of operations that private agencies undertake. These are to:

- identify and supply candidates with particular skills to clients within particular sectors;
- supply all kinds of workers within a given locality;
- cover functionally specialist operations concerned with headhunting, outplacement or information provision.

On the other hand, regarding contractual arrangements, BMG data show that the majority of agencies (63 per cent) provide both temporary and permanent job placements, whereas 23 per cent specialize in permanent recruitment and the remaining 14 per cent provide temporary services (Hotopp 2001).

Clearly, the majority of the operations of the private sector recruitment agencies are related to temporary or permanent job placements rather than advice and guidance activities. As Watts (1996) points out, advice and guidance activities in the field of employment are generally seen as a responsibility of the public sector, as part of welfare provision. Watts *et al.* (2005: 2) argue that the association of career advice and guidance with other services, such as education, and the difficulty of standardizing career advice, are among the reasons why the private sector is significantly lagging behind the public sector in terms of advice and guidance activities.

Recruitment

Private recruitment agencies use various methods during the recruitment and selection process. To begin with, the methods of creating a candidate pool largely depend on the group targeted by the agency. Most agencies use several methods to reach out to the potential candidates, including advertising the vacancies in the newspapers and on job-search websites. In addition, most provide online application on these websites. Hence, for the majority of the agencies, it is the prospective candidate who has to approach them for a vacancy. The exception to this in our research was some of the executive recruitment agencies, the so-called headhunters. Although some of these agencies also advertise vacancies through different media, headhunting generally involves the agency approaching the candidate, rather than the candidate having to apply for a vacancy. Most of the executive recruitment agencies which participated in our research reported that they created their client pool through networks, rather than through advertisement via different channels, the method which is most commonly used by the other agencies. For instance, some executive recruitment agencies rely on repeat business and sometimes use the executives that they place in work, as contacts in new workplaces, to broaden their candidate pool. The predominant method of acquiring new clients among the executive recruitment firms that we have studied is by word of mouth. In the context of male-dominated executive elites, such inward-looking practices are not likely to generate egalitarian outcomes.

Once the candidate pool is created and, in some cases, the candidates have filled in the application forms, agencies use several methods to make the recruitment decision. All agencies in our sample said that they conducted interviews with the candidates. Alongside the interview, some agencies reported using psychometric tests to assess the skills, abilities and competencies of the candidates. Indeed, what appears worrying is the abundance of discredited psychometric tests, as well as behavioural and body language assessments that may entertain discriminatory biases. Regarding the psychometric tests, one participant cautiously explained:

> We do quite a lot of assessment as in tests and personality profiling, and there is a school of thought (nothing to do with our firm) that some of the test in itself might sometimes disadvantage some people of an ethnic minority, for example. Obviously you don't want any part of the assessment to discriminate at all, and you take that into account when you interpret the results.

There are three key concerns about the use of psychometric and personality tests. First, the usefulness of personality testing as a predictor of job–person fit has been debated. Such tests have been criticized for being underpinned by a belief that a single personality type would provide a perfect fit for each job. This is a very weak approach considering the complex and relational nature of personality (Barrett 1967). Second, the psychometric and personality tests require expertise in design and delivery (Bartram 2004). Thirdly, the tests are likely to suffer from gender, ethnicity and other forms of bias should they be adopted from other organizational and cultural contexts. Therefore, the tests require a level of adaptation when implemented in new settings and need to be sensitive to equality and diversity concerns (Wood 1992).

On the other hand, another respondent argued that the most decisive factor in the final decision is the interviewing process between the recruitment consultant and the candidate: 'The matching comes from the listening and the judgement and the interpretation, it's a lot about experience and a lot about judgement'. Hence, the recruitment consultant's judgement regarding the candidate is what eventually determines the recruitment decision. This situation renders the process of recruitment and selection open to the influence of subjective values and beliefs held by the consultant. Thus, the equal opportunities and diversity awareness levels of recruitment consultants may have a significant impact upon the recruitment activities in the agencies and therefore the sector's potential to open up opportunities for women and other disadvantaged groups.

Advice and guidance

The core business function of the agencies we interviewed was staffing activities rather than the provision of advice and guidance. Nevertheless, advice and guidance activities are essentially integrated in the selection and recruitment processes in the agencies that participated in the research. Agencies adopt different strategies to offer guidance to their clients and job candidates, before, during and after the recruitment process. Recruitment agencies work in multistakeholder environments that place different demands on them.

The two most important stakeholders are the clients and the candidates. Their clients place demands on the firms in terms of the desirable and required attributes of the job candidates, as well as the spatial and temporal requirements of the job. Job candidates also have demands and expectations in terms of their work terms, conditions and spatial and temporal requirements. At the outset, the recruitment agencies' role is to match the client and candidate expectations. However, our interviews suggest that the agencies also play a role in moderating the expectations of their clients and candidates based on labour market conditions. This involves a whole range of activities from running seminars, workshops, educational events, face-to-face discussions and trial offers, to extended negotiations with clients and candidates. Whilst the larger agencies may opt for the former and more formal methods for shaping client and customer demands, the smaller agencies adopt more interactive and face-to-face methods. Thus they engage in extended discussions with their clients and customers in order to understand their needs and to offer guidance if there are alternative means of assessing or restructuring those needs.

Some organizations offer specific training programmes on discrimination law for their client firms. For example, good practice agencies in our sample actively sought to raise the awareness of their clients through regular forums and work-shops, as well as through their interaction with the client, when they mediated the recruitment and selection process. During the research, we came across some very creative educational activities offered to the clients by the agencies. For instance, the respondent from one of the medium-sized agencies in our sample said that they ran employment law forums three times a year to update their clients about equality legislation. Then she went on to describe the last one they had where they had organized a mock tribunal on a sexual discrimination case:

> We had one last Thursday which was a mock tribunal showing people what happens in a tribunal if . . . a sexual discrimination case comes up. We set it up just like a courtroom and the claimant was in fact one of our consult-ants here and she did a wonderful [job]. It was so life-like, she was brilliant and they were so horrible to her and the liars came this side. It was literally like playing out a whole drama. It was showing all the people in the audi-ence that these men who had treated her unfairly what would happen to them and how they would be [dealt with]. The questions would be asked and they [got into a] mess because they didn't keep their paperwork in order and they didn't deal with the situations with best practice and they were going to lose. The company ended up in our tribunal coming out los-ing out quite substantially to the plaintiff for not having kept paperwork in order, for not having put an equal opportunities policy into practice and for the fact that they hadn't trained any of their staff. So it's a very useful and dramatic way of getting that message across. If they had only trained their staff in equal opportunities, they would have not lost that case and that lost them a lot of money. And bad publicity and a good employee.

The same respondent also pointed out that they not only target the human resource managers in their client companies, but other senior and middle managers:

> The HR person knows jolly well best practices, its about educating other people and the mock tribunal is a very good way of showing that, showing what fools they make of themselves for using incorrect practice and how

the law will then interpret it and deal with them and how companies will be seriously out of pocket if they don't do this because somebody is going to bring [a] case quite simply.

As this example clearly demonstrates, recruitment agencies may play a crucial role in delivering equality and diversity issues on to the agenda of the other actors with whom they interact. Hence, the agency's commitment to equality of opportunity will not only open up opportunities for their candidates from disadvantaged segments of the labour force, but will also positively impact upon the levels of awareness of their clients from different sectors and in different sizes of organization.

Summary and policy implications

The private recruitment sector in the UK is an expanding sector dominated by small- and medium-sized enterprises. Currently, the sector is marked by the absence of any strong regulation in the field of equality or a licensing scheme which regulates the new entries into the sector and the equality monitoring activities of the existing agencies. Neither is there robust and consistent statistical data available regarding the volume of business and operations of the private sector recruitment agencies.

Private sector agencies act as brokers in the three-way relationship between job seekers, employers and themselves. They have two major sets of operations: recruitment and guidance. The former establishes the key business function of the private recruitment agencies, whereas the latter is, most of the time, integrated into the recruitment and selection process. Private sector recruitment agencies place their candidates (jobseekers) into both temporary and permanent, and both part-time and full-time, jobs across all sectors and industries in the UK.

Private sector recruitment agencies, through their recruitment and selection decisions, and through their advice and guidance activities targeting both their candidates and clients, may potentially play a crucial role in promoting equality opportunities in the field of employment. However, their recruitment and guidance activities are also prone to discriminatory practices, since they are not specifically regulated in terms of equality, and most of the time recruitment and guidance decisions are left to the subjective judgement of the recruitment consultant.

A number of policy implications arise out of the evidence presented in this section. First, despite the key role that recruitment agencies play in providing access to employment, studies on equal opportunities in the private sector recruitment agencies should recognize the vast heterogeneity of agency work across the diversity of contractual arrangements as well as the sectoral, functional and hierarchical niches in which the agencies operate. Accordingly, research and policy on equal opportunities in private sector recruitment agencies should recognize the significance of firm size and the type of services provided by the agencies.

Second, as recruitment agencies are not passive agents at the intersection of labour supply and demand, and as they play a significant role in shaping the supply of and demand for labour, it is important that their role is recognized and regulated in terms of its impact upon equality of opportunity in access to employment. For instance, agencies should be encouraged to provide their own staff, particularly their recruitment consultants, with diversity and equality training. Moreover, regulation of the private recruitment sector in terms of equality could enhance agencies' accountability in this regard by allowing for public, professional and legal scrutiny of their practices.

Lastly, although advice and guidance are not viewed as the most obvious activities of the agencies, they indeed are an integral part of their recruitment activities. Therefore, any policy on their recruitment activities should also consider the advice and guidance activities that precede and support their recruitment processes.

8.5 The REC's role in shaping the equality and diversity agenda

As noted earlier, the Recruitment and Employment Confederation (REC) is the umbrella organization of the private sector recruitment and guidance agencies in the UK. It was established in 2000 by the merger of the Institute of Employment Consultants, which was the professional association of individual members of the recruitment industry, and the Federation of Recruitment and Employment Services, which was a trade association for the corporate industry. The other two key associations in the recruitment sector at present are the Interim Management Association (IMA) and the Association of Executive Recruitment (AER). Both function under the aegis of the REC. This section explores the structure and functions of the REC, as well as its equality perspective and activities. We conclude the section with a short summary and an outline of the policy implications which arise from the evidence presented here.

Structure and functions

One of the research participants from the REC told us that currently the Confederation represents around 70 per cent of the UK private recruitment sector, with over 7,000 recruitment agencies and 6,000 recruitment consultants as its members. However, according to the DTI research in 1999, only 48 per cent of the agencies surveyed by BMG reported that they were REC members (Hotopp 2001). Commenting on this an REC representative explained that the Confederation has increased its membership by 52 per cent since 2002, and that a third of employment businesses are less than three years old. The discrepancy between these figures either points to an increase in REC membership in the sector between 1999 and 2006, or again to the inconsistency of the sectoral estimates made by different bodies. Nevertheless, our respondent from the REC stated that the majority (90 per cent) of the Confederation's members are small- and medium-sized organizations which have one or two branches in specialized industries. REC members cover all sectors and industries of the UK economy and place employees into jobs with all types of contracts, including into temporary and permanent, and part-time and full-time, work.

The Confederation operates 11 specialist sector groups. These are in the areas of childcare; construction; drivers; executive recruitment; education; hospitality; IT and communication; the medical sector; nursing and social care; the technical, construction and engineering sector; and interim recruitment. It gathers and holds extensive sectoral data and publishes these periodically. It also has a number of schemes and a professional code of practice in place to monitor its members within different sector groups. However, the data are partial with regards to equal opportunities concerns, due to the lack of regulation on equality monitoring in the sector, which makes it impossible for it to monitor equality issues in the sector.

The REC also provides its members with legal advice, specialist lobbying, PR campaigns and networking opportunities. Its representative pointed out that it received 40–50,000 calls from its members during 2005. The Confederation also offers workshops around the UK on legislation and gives documents covering legislation to its members. Indeed, these membership organizations play an important role in educating and informing their members regarding their legal requirements concerning gender equality, as well as possible discretionary activities towards promoting diversity. However, as the IRS (2002) research reveals, only a small number of client organizations (22 per cent) take into account the REC membership of an agency when they are making their decisions about which agency to work with. This may have a negative impact on the ability of the REC's policies and initiatives to promote the equality and diversity agenda in the sector, since the indifference of clients may discourage the agencies from committing resources to the diversity and equality initiatives of the REC. Nevertheless, the REC provides the sector with a number of equality and diversity initiatives and policies, as we explain in the following sections.

Diversity and equality perspective and activities

In its 2006 Code of Professional Practice, the Confederation informs its members that it is 'uniquely placed, as the conduit between work seeker and client, to promote diversity and challenge discriminatory practice'. The 'respect for diversity', which is one of the ten principles of the code, reads:

- Members should adhere to the spirit of all applicable human rights, employment laws and regulations and will treat work seekers, clients and others without prejudice or unjustified discrimination. Members should not act on an instruction from a client that is discriminatory and should, wherever possible, provide guidance to clients in respect of good diversity practice.
- Members and their staff will treat all work seekers and clients with dignity and respect and aim to provide equity of employment opportunities based on objective business related criteria.
- Members should establish working practices that safeguard against unlawful or unethical discrimination in the operation of their business.

Its inclusion as one of the principles of the code may potentially promote diversity among REC members, because in order to gain the highly respected 'REC Audited' status, members need to demonstrate to the independent auditors that they comply with the code. To assist their members to develop good practice in the field of equality and diversity, the Confederation also offers them a model diversity policy and a model equal-opportunities and diversity-monitoring form.

Diversity Forum

The confederation also runs a Diversity Forum. It currently has 40 members, which include both small- and medium-sized enterprises and large organizations from different parts of the UK. Among the forum's priorities for 2006 were promotion of the Diversity Pledge (see below); supporting the pilot and finalization of the DiverCity Audit (also see below); preparing the REC members for the introduction of age discrimination legislation in October 2006; and inviting new members to join the forum.

During our research, we observed the Diversity Forum meeting which took place in March 2006. In total, ten small, medium and large organizations were represented, as well as the REC. The forum started with two presentations given by the guest speakers from the Probation Service and Business Action on Homelessness. Such an approach helps to promote potential collaborations between the private sector recruitment agencies and voluntary and public sector organizations, in order to open up opportunities for disadvantaged segments of the society, such as ex-offenders and the homeless. Such exchanges are also significant in terms of knowledge and information transfer between the parties, which will potentially raise their awareness in terms of diversity.

Diversity Pledge

In 2005, the REC and Jobcentre Plus jointly launched a Diversity Pledge, which sets out their shared commitment to promote together the diversity agenda in the industry. The pledge is open to all private recruitment agencies, whether they are REC members or not, as well as to public sector recruitment and guidance organizations. The pledge thus benefits from best practice in the public sector, in terms of the sophistication of policy-making, and from the private sector, in terms of the development of business case arguments.

The pledge document starts by stating the business case for diversity in the recruitment sector:

> By 2010, only 20 per cent of the labour market will be white, non-disabled men under 45. In addition, we face short, medium and long-term skills shortages and must recruit talent from every possible source. Diversity is about harnessing the talent and potential of everyone to achieve business success. To succeed in recruiting in the 21st century, diversity is a necessity, not a choice. To achieve performance, employers must have a mixture of background, cultures, approaches and thinking. Diversity is not just about 'doing good' but 'doing good for business'.

By signing the pledge, organizations commit themselves to:

- value and harness the differences between people, and the benefits that can be gained from those differences;
- seek actively to identify diverse candidate pools and promote their engagement;
- review all aspects of the employment process to eradicate unjustifiable discrimination;
- promote recruitment and selection best practice in accordance with our agreed standards, as set out in the support pack that accompanies this pledge;
- work with others to challenge discrimination where we find it.

However, signing up to the pledge is a voluntary measure, and the take-up of the pledge among the REC members was not very high at the time of research. Only around 220 agencies out of 6,500 had signed the pledge. Nevertheless, the REC is actively encouraging its members to sign, and promoting the pledge is stated to be one of the priorities of its Diversity Forum.

Diversity Diagnostic

The REC also offers a diversity diagnostic check, which is a voluntary measure that is available via its website (http://www.4mat.com/diversitytoolkit/survey/

form.asp). The diagnostic check is open to all organizations and accessible to agencies of all sizes, including small ones. Organizations can freely turn to this page to assess their current practices in terms of diversity. The diagnostic aims to help recruitment agencies 'to become more inclusive organizations' and investigates the levels at which equality and diversity issues are addressed throughout their different operations. The areas covered are advertising, selection, monitoring and training. Upon the completion of the diagnostic, a corresponding action plan is provided for the organization.

The Diversity Diagnostic also includes a business case for equality and diversity. The business benefits of diversity as given by the diagnostic are:

- increased customer satisfaction;
- more effective marketing strategies;
- increased market share;
- being an employer of choice;
- lower staff turnover;
- enhanced PR;
- increased productivity;
- increased creativity and innovation;
- enhanced ability of problem solving;
- being a best practice organization;
- operating within the law.

The diagnostic also points out the changing demographics of the labour market, highlighting, for example, the ageing population and the increasing number of women, migrant workers and people from diverse cultural backgrounds in the labour market. It concludes that, in these times of skill shortages in many sectors and regions in the UK, the recruitment agencies should look at diverse sources of labour. It is also stated that reaching a diverse pool of candidates will help them to meet the needs of their clients whose workforces are becoming more diverse. Interestingly, the business case benefits in the diagnostic do not mention enhancing flexibility and the work–life balance to secure best use of the widest talent pool. Nevertheless, our interviews reveal that there is wide recognition of the diversity diagnostic tool and the diversity pledge offered by the REC. Indeed, the REC provides a good source of inspiration for industrial practices in the field of equality and diversity.

DiverCity Audit

The REC is also planning to start auditing its members against the Diversity Pledge by 2007. At the time of research, it was finalizing and piloting its DiverCity Audit, which will require agencies to demonstrate their compliance with equality legislation. REC members are already aware of the Confederation's plans to audit its members in the area of equality and diversity. One member explained that they were waiting for the audit and also hinted that these audits were also adding to their work load:

> Discrimination and equality audit is another audit that they have not started yet, they will do that in the middle of this year. So we will probably try to get that also because it would not be a big thing for us. It's just . . . one more policy. In the end, there are so many policies that they don't really make sense any more . . . One organization with seven people, we have like a whole batch of policies: health and safety, data protection, etc., etc.

The comments of this respondent suggest that the policy should be tailored to capture the size of the organization. This has been recognized by the REC and the draft DiverCity Audit is already tailored to the size of the agency, with its levels becoming more demanding depending on the size of the company. Hence the agencies with less than 50 employees need to demonstrate that they meet minimum requirements (Level 1), whereas agencies with 50 or more employees are required to meet more comprehensive criteria (Level 2).

At both levels, the DiverCity Audit covers religion and belief, gender, sexuality, disability, ethnicity, age and ex-offenders, and also investigates the integration of diversity and equality issues throughout the various processes and policies of the agencies. The areas that are assessed by the audit include: the equal opportunities policy; recruitment, selection, training, promotion, discipline and dismissal; the anti-harassment policy; adjustment and accommodation for candidates with disabilities; equality training for managers and any staff responsible for recruitment and selection; vacancy advertisements; communication of the equal opportunities policy; monitoring; and record keeping during the recruitment and selection process.

Additionally, there is a third level for the 'diversity champions', that is for the companies of all sizes who wish to mainstream DiverCity within their overall corporate strategy. At this level, the audit aims to identify the business case for diversity for the individual agency in question and to provide it with practical recommendations and an action plan tailored to its needs and circumstances. The third level of the DiverCity Audit covers: management and leadership; resourcing the commitment; policy, planning and strategy; recruitment, retention and work–life balance; training and development; internal communications; marketing and community engagement; procurement and supplier diversity; monitoring; and evaluating the impact. One of the potential weaknesses of the DiverCity Audit is that flexible working and work–life balance issues only feature in the third level of the audit, which is the highest level. Hence, inclusion of flexible working and work–life balance related targets at the first two levels of the audit may enhance its capability to promote the opening up of opportunities for the disadvantaged segments of the labour market through private recruitment agencies.

Summary and policy implications

The private recruitment sector in the UK has an umbrella organization which was established in 2000 and has 8,000 recruitment agencies as its members: the REC. The Confederation assists its members through the provision of information, advice and guidance, as well as a professional code of practice scheme. One of the principles in this code is 'respect for diversity'. The REC plays a crucial role in delivering the equality and diversity agenda in the private recruitment sector through educating and informing its members regarding their legal requirements concerning equal opportunities, as well as possible discretionary activities towards promoting equality and diversity. Within that framework, the REC provides private recruitment sector in the UK with a Diversity Forum, the Diversity Pledge which was launched in association with Jobcentre Plus, and the online Diversity Diagnostic. In addition, the Confederation is currently piloting its DiverCity Audit, which was launched in 2007.

The REC members cover all sectors and industries of the UK economy and place employees into jobs with all types of contracts. The Confederation acknowledges that it is important to recognize the diversity of private recruitment agencies throughout the provision of equality initiatives and programmes for the sector. For instance, the forthcoming DiverCity Audit will be tailored to organizational size.

A number of policy implications arise out of the evidence presented in this section. First, it is clear that the work of equalities initiatives amongst recruitment and guidance agencies will become more effective if the diversity of the sector is recognized. For example, some equalities initiatives will be effective in larger firms, but will have much less impact in smaller agencies; others will be more effective in some sectors than in others.

Second, professional networks on equality and diversity have a significant role to play in raising awareness and setting industrial benchmarks in the private recruitment sector. Equality policy in the sector should emphasize sector-wide initiatives, including networks, audits, badging and accreditation systems. Such initiatives, which currently operate on a voluntary basis, would benefit from institutional support.

More specifically, it is evident that the REC is leading the way in promoting equality and diversity in the sector through its Diversity Forum, Diversity Pledge, Diversity Diagnostic and the forthcoming DiverCity Audit. However, this role could be made more effective through the empowerment of REC as the key professional association in the sector. Thus, the impact of the Diversity Pledge, DiverCity Audit and the Diversity Diagnostic on promoting the equality agenda in the sector could be supported through national policy. Furthermore, the REC's diversity and equality perspective may be enhanced through a more comprehensive and explicit inclusion of flexible working and work–life balance issues in its diversity and equality initiatives and policies. In other words, the REC, as a leader in the field, needs to address work–life balance issues more rigorously and require this also of its members.

8.6   The state of equal opportunities in the sector

In this section we will examine the state of equal opportunities among the private sector recruitment agencies. First, barriers to equality in the private recruitment sector are discussed. Then the key factors predicting the equality perspectives of the agencies are explored. Lastly, a short summary of research findings are presented and the policy implications arising from these are stated.

Barriers to equality in the sector

Our interviews identified that the recruitment sector suffers from five ailments in terms of its equal opportunities approach and the promotion of gender equality: a focus on gender neutrality and a gender-blind discourse; gender bias; occupational segregation; a 'passing the buck culture'; and a lack of equality awareness and information.

Focus on gender neutrality and gender-blind discourse

Our interviews suggest that the processes of job placement in the private sector recruitment agencies were built on the premise of gender neutrality. For example, when asked if the organization did anything to attract women candidates specifically, a participant from a firm which specializes on temporary placements explained: 'we OBVIOUSLY accept women onto the database without discrimination'.

Although such an approach will do little to tackle the gender segregation in job placements noted earlier, a standardized system which disregarded gender was, nevertheless, often seen as a measure of an equality stance in the sector. This meant that the recruitment agencies failed to attempt to transform work practices which were structurally more conducive to the employment of women or men. For more critical participants in our study, their experience of the recruitment sector was not very positive in terms of equal opportunities.

Several participants identified that despite a facade of legal compliance, more subtle forms of discrimination were entrenched in the sector:

> I was influenced by having spent some informative years in the US, where legislation around sex and age discrimination was far ahead of the UK. So when I came to university in this country and started to work in this country, I was appalled, I was really horrified. Women were called girls. Even women would call themselves girls! Women would take less than men. That some people positively would not hire a woman into a senior role, as soon as the woman would become pregnant [shocked me] . . . Anyway, to answer your question, do I find people are disadvantaged by [the process]? I think people still hold their prejudices. Definitely. I've come across clients that say 'Oh, I think this person is too old'. Or they won't say too old, they'll say 'I think this person could be too set in their ways'. Or 'They've worked in this company so long, they wouldn't be able to make the transition into our company'.

Nevertheless, removing gender biases from systems of recruitment is seen as fully sufficient to ensure gender equality by the majority of our respondents. This assumption results in a gender-blind approach throughout the recruitment and guidance operations in the sector. The statement that the 'best person for the job' should be chosen is a reflection of the gender-blind discourse in the sector. Although, at first sight, this appears to be a gender-neutral approach, in practice, it does little to challenge inequalities that emanate from the gendered structuring of the jobs themselves. The following participant's account epitomizes the predominance of this approach and its assumed gender neutrality:

> In the selection process, I don't think women are disadvantaged. I don't give different advice to men and women about securing a job. If your question is loaded towards the fact that less women make it to senior positions, I'm aware of that, but I don't have the magic answer why it happens. From my point of view, I want to fill as many of the positions I have with the right people. And in the more senior positions, the hope is that . . . more [of] the right women get the jobs. But no, I don't give special advice. That's discrimination in its own way.

Claims of gender and ethnicity blindness were even more pronounced in the interim management firms:

> Interim management doesn't really work with that [approach]. It's rather different to permanent recruitment and so interim management is colour

blind, gender blind, whatever. People want to know what's the skill set, who can do it, who's the most appropriate person.

Another participant explained that, indeed, there is a more complex dynamic. The clients, the supply of labour and the particular approach of the recruitment agencies predict the outcome of who are selected. In this analysis, the 'best person for the job' is presented more cautiously and other intervening factors have a greater impact:

> It's interesting because for many, many years – I've been in search for over twenty years – I think every [year] since I began, a client would always say things like 'it would be really nice to have a woman in the job'. It started when I started recruiting accountants and finance officials. At that time there were women in the profession, but they were still very much outnumbered by the men, particularly in the senior levels, so right from the beginning people were asking for these things. An early experience I had in search in '89 when the Berlin Wall went down, people were asking me for 'Hungarian-speaking candidates' to work in Budapest, so I was having to find people with very particular skills. In some cases, I've done work for the NHS it really is very much required, to have a diverse range of candidates. But ultimately, the matrix, the measurement is by who are the best qualified people for the job and no allowances, no concessions are made on the person's background and diversity. I think that's a thread that's pretty much followed through. I am personally biased of course, I'm always delighted that my shortlist and my track record is pretty much fifty/fifty between men and women.

Indeed, further probing on gender equality issues were sometimes met with confused responses. The overwhelming feeling amongst respondents that discrimination did not occur because the systems for dealing with different groups were the same was evident in the following account of a participant:

> That 'women's question' – an organization like us doesn't discriminate against men or women, so a client would never say 'I want a woman for the job' so I'm not sure it's a question I can answer. I'm not trying to get men or women.

If a job is structured in such a way that it suits the experiences of a man, 'the best person for the job' is most likely to be a man in each case. Despite this widespread discourse, we have also noted that some recruitment agencies have sought to educate both their candidates and clients, not only in terms of gender equality issues (including the legislation), but also regarding how they structure and construct their job requirements to make them more accessible for both women and men.

Gender bias

There was evidence from our interviews of some gender bias occurring in the recruitment agencies. The predominant belief was that the liberal functioning of the labour market will deliver gender equality. This belief manifested itself in statements that women 'chose' certain areas of work and that there was little, if anything, that the agencies could do to change their choices of patterns and fields of work. Furthermore, different skills and abilities were attributed to women and men by some participants and there was a belief that essential differences existed in terms of the performance of women and men in different job roles. One participant stated that such gendered assumptions may also come from their clients:

> Actually, you know sometimes it happens with call centre managers. Sometimes they request a female because they think they are better managers – in that environment.

Coupled with the discourse of 'best person for the job', which accepts recruitment processes that are based on gender-blind notions of meritocracy, more subtle forms of gender bias, which relate directly to the structuring of jobs, workplaces and temporal and spatial arrangements of work, remain unchallenged. For example, a participant explained how their organization cares about merit only:

> We get 1000 CVs a month, of these 1000, we keep maybe 100 or 150 of them . . . that go into our network. I would never look at the name, you just really look at the profile, the education, then if they're good, they go in and if not, they go out. I wouldn't look [at the name] . . . actually, this is maybe a good thing to say: we have a list of criteria, when I check CVs, when I say good or bad, suitable or unsuitable. I have a list of criteria that just really says education, job progression, blue chip company name, etc. . . . no job-hopping, you know. Having a clearly defined specialism. So we have criteria that everyone can pick up. Not really discriminating, it's just according to strengths.

Recruitment agencies play a significant role in remoulding jobs, shaping expectations and negotiating terms and conditions on behalf of their clients and candidates. Therefore, they can also play a role in combating more subtle forms of gender bias by reflecting on how the structuring of jobs may have gendered impacts. This could be a step forward from the current liberal and 'voluntary' stance that the sector adopts in terms of gender equality. One participant explained that the discrimination is not direct, but rather indirect and subtle. This quote also raises the issue of flexibility for whom:

> I have men that would say 'I only want to work like 50 miles from Bristol', let's say, and I have women that say 'I only want to work like 50 miles from Bristol'. And I have women that if I say go tomorrow to Glasgow to work for six months, they just go tomorrow to Glasgow for six months. So it's the same, really. I don't see a big difference. Again, maybe people that have more restrictions wouldn't apply at all, they wouldn't put their CV through to us because we work on this kind of project where you have to be very flexible. So there is this kind of discrimination, but it isn't active, it's passive or however you would call it.

Occupational segregation

Recruitment agencies serve all sectors and all configurations of part-time, full-time, temporary, permanent and flexible work arrangements. Our interviews have revealed that occupational sex segregation is widespread across all sectors. However, participants have noted that occupational segregation is often predicted by the sector in which the recruitment agency operates. Whilst some sectors (such as services) have lower levels of gender segregation, others have stronger barriers to women's employment in senior posts. Some participants provided anecdotal evidence for variation between the sectors:

> I feel that the public sector is more female friendly. This is just my feeling, it's not statistical . . . I have many more female applicants for managing directors [in the public sector].

While certain occupational categories such as marketing, human resource management and secretarial work are dominated by female workers and candidates, others such as IT, engineering and corporate finance are male-dominated. The interviews also suggested that despite an increase in the number of female executives, executive recruitment continues to be a preserve of men. One participant from an interim recruitment firm explained:

> We happen to have a lot of women, because we work a lot with HR. Even in the public sector, there are many more women managers. If I just think about it, most of my public sector [clients] other than two, were all women clients, but I would not do anything specifically to attract them. HR managers are more often women. It also depends on how the organization is structured. If I get someone that is looking for a supply chain manager, or otherwise not in the HR department, then it might often more likely be a man.

Executive recruitment agencies could be more influential than other main-stream agencies in terms of promoting women into the male-dominated echelons of executive management. However, they are the least sophisticated of all agencies in terms of their attention to recruitment women. Indeed, the predominant discourse across the executive recruitment agencies involved a conception of meritocracy in conflict with gender equality. Representatives of executive recruitment firms often referred to a lack of women with sufficient skills and expertise and to the significance of merit and expertise in their selection systems. These two arguments suggested that women's absence was due to a lack of their perceived expertise in different aspects of managerial competence. However, missing from this belief was a problematization of the notion of merit which so firmly excluded women managers. Furthermore, the executive recruitment agencies did not see it as their prerogative to seek out suitable women candidates when there is a clear gender balance, unless this is explicitly required by their clients.

Another participant elaborated that horizontal and vertical occupational segregation is evident by gender and ethnicity:

CEOs and Managing Directors tend to be more men than women, like 75 per cent to 25 per cent. In some cases like HR they are more women than men at the middle management level, but at the executive management level there are more men than women. More ethnicity within HR and marketing, than sales and general management.

Similarly, another participant also noted the strong form of gender segregation across functional departments at the organizational level:

To be honest when you have lower level HR positions, you have mostly women. If you have a lower level marketing position, you have mostly women applying. If you have the higher level, international, really juicy projects, you have more men applying. It's just really the cliché. It's true, unfortunately . . . It's really sad but a lot of our jobs, like the traditional jobs, like managing directors, international finance directors, manufacturing supply chain [jobs], operations directors, etc. would all be male. It's just very cliché, like what you would expect, unfortunately. Even though we all think that we are very advanced in the company but at the end of the day, we place women in HR positions and marketing or call centre managers – typical women's positions. But I don't know of any women MDs. Other than xxx, she was in the change management, but she was at a very high level. I have placed women at very high levels but more in HR and marketing.

So, our findings suggest that job placement activities in the private recruitment sector reflect the occupational segregation patterns in the labour market in general. In summary, female candidates tend to be placed in female-dominated areas, such as human resources and marketing, by the private recruitment agencies, while male candidates tend to be placed in the traditionally male-dominated areas, such as accounting and finance. This was also the case across different levels of hierarchy within the same profession: non-managerial, secretarial work is dominated by women and there are more men in executive PA posts. Some participants noted that the recruitment agencies can play a role in challenging these imbalances between labour supply and demand, should the employers require more diverse pools of employment and if the public procurement requirements consider equality as a precondition for tendering, or if there was a stronger legal regulation in the field of equality in the sector. Stronger legislation may help focus the agencies' attention to issues of equality and diversity.

'Passing the buck' culture

The research participants rarely considered recruitment agencies to be responsible for addressing imbalances in the labour market supply and demand beyond their legal requirements. It was often argued that the responsibility lay either with individual women and men to make balanced occupational choices, or that the responsibility rested with employers to make reasoned selections from the pool of candidates that the recruitment agencies provided them. Accordingly our interviews reveal that some recruitment agencies simply reflect the demands of their clients:

> We work on behalf of our clients, and there are times when our client is unrepresented in a particular group, we do advertising to attract unrepresented groups. I've never done [an] advertisement that's been particularly aimed at men or women. I think on one occasion one of our clients decided to advertise in a magazine mainly read by women.

Similarly, another participant suggested that their agency serves as a mirror of client needs:

> We do things like we often offer guaranteed interview schemes, you know for disabled people. Where they meet the minimum criteria, they're guaranteed an interview. A lot of it is driven by the clients. We try and mirror our clients' policies. If their policies have a particular way of helping disabled people (for example) through the recruitment process, we do that . . . By using us to recruit, they often want to sell their own equal opportunities. So they need their recruitment partners to operate in a similar fashion.

An absence of explicit demands for gender-balanced candidate pools from the clients means that little attention is paid to the business case for gender-balanced recruitment. Client attitudes can often discourage recruitment firms from pursuing any initiatives further than those legally required. One participant explained how client demands can shape the equal opportunities outcomes and how this worked in a positive way in their case:

> Some recruitment companies don't care a whole lot, not because they're breaking any rules but it's just not a priority of theirs. It's a priority of ours because of our client base.

As made clear by the above words, client firms' attitudes and expectations in terms of equality of opportunities have a crucial impact on the diversity and equality perspective of the recruitment agencies and constitutes an important business rationale. However, a survey by IRS (2002) demonstrates that agencies' equal opportunities policies are taken into account only by a small number of public and private sector employers when they are choosing an agency. Only 22 per cent of survey respondents reported that they considered an agency's commitment to equal opportunities an important factor that impacted on their choice of a particular recruitment agency. As a result, the *transactional rather than transformative* role adopted by recruitment agencies presents itself as a barrier to greater gender equality. Although there were exceptions, where recruitment agencies acted as catalysts for gender equality in the labour market, they generally had what we would term a 'passing the buck culture' that epitomized this general stance of indifference towards gendered patterns and trends of supply and demand in the labour market.

Lack of equality awareness and information

In terms of their overall awareness about gender equality and diversity, most of the recruitment firms that we have studied demonstrate a level of legal compliance. Most of those in our sample were aware of their legal obligations and pursued compliance with the law. This meant that they would turn down any requests by employers for gender-typed candidates (e.g. requests for a female secretary). The pursuit of legal obligation, however, does not necessarily come with progressive approaches to gender equality. It often means that overtly discriminatory practices are eliminated from the processes of recruitment. On the other hand, interviews revealed that there is a lack of awareness in the sector regarding the spirit of the equal opportunities legislation, since being anti-discriminatory was equated with 'disregarding' the gender, ethnicity, age, religion, sexual orientation and disability status of the candidates. For instance, although the Sex Discrimination Act permits positive action advertising, many respondents emphasized that they do not particularly encourage women in their job advertisements. Ironically, these respondents believed this to be a confirmation of the anti-discriminatory nature of their procedures. Hence, the research findings reveal that the equal opportunities legislation is not interpreted competently in the sector. This suggests that there is a need for a wide-reaching awareness-raising campaign on positive action and positive discrimination. The REC offers a training programme which includes this issue. However, our findings suggest that the overall understanding on this issue was rather weak across the firms.

Moreover, there was a general feeling of confusion when it came to the recruitment firms' responsibilities for monitoring equality and diversity between their job candidates. At one extreme, some participants surprisingly thought that they could not have a monitoring system, because they wished to avoid discriminating against any group, including by gender, ethnicity, age, disability and sexual orientation. These participants have clearly misunderstood the purpose of monitoring. Indeed, only three participants out of 19 stated that they had equal opportunities monitoring forms.

Some respondents were confused about the implications of the age discrimination legislation. They explained that they no longer asked about the candidate's age. However, two participants noted that the age of the candidate would be revealed when the other aspects of their CV, such as their schooling, were scrutinized. The level of confusion was even greater for the monitoring of sexual orientation and religious belief. There was also little understanding of what the organization might do once such data had been monitored.

There was a general feeling that mainstream recruitment agencies did not come across many cases involving ethnicity and sexual orientation: 'Race? We don't know. We don't really come across race as an issue at all, and sexual orientation. No, there isn't anything like that unfortunately'. The only time religion and belief became an issue was when a recruitment company was looking on behalf of a religious authority that required members of a certain religion. Lack of experience in the fields of sexual orientation, ethnicity and also religious belief adds to the confusion that the recruitment firms experienced in terms of their efforts towards monitoring equal opportunities.

As noted earlier, there is an absence of legislative controls over the establishment, market entry and exit of recruitment firms in the UK. The practical implication of this is that there is a general lack of statistical data about the sector. There is of course labour market data that can be obtained from multiple sources in the UK. Nevertheless, there is little information on the size and scope of the private sector recruitment agencies. As Hotopp (2001: 8) argues, the absence of robust data 'makes it difficult for both industry and policy makers to estimate the effects of outside changes on the industry'. Furthermore, recruiters also fail to collect substantial market data on their candidates and clients. In instances where such data are collected, there is little evidence that the data were considered in relation to their implications for equality and diversity.

The majority of the agencies which participated in the research do not hold data on the sex, age, ethnicity, sexual orientation and disability attributes of the job candidates. The absence of statistical data means that there are only the observations of participants as evidence for the widening of the candidate pool. Even then, the evidence was patchy and contradictory. Whilst some participants noted that their candidate pool was becoming more diverse, others suggested that there was little change, or that their candidate pool remained the same in terms of the heterogeneity of candidate attributes. The ease of entry and exit of recruitment firms to the sector, coupled with the absence of regulation of the equal opportunities practices of recruitment firms, means that the majority do not consider equal opportunities monitoring activities as integral to their work processes. Except when clients demand equal opportunities statistics, these are not collected voluntarily. One participant explained in the case of their organization that equal opportunities monitoring activities were adopted to the client needs:

> Our clients . . . apply to us with their equal ops form, and it automatically downloads onto our system. People apply online now. And for each campaign we can demonstrate equal opportunity stats.

There were only a few recruitment agencies in our sample with formal monitoring systems in place which were independent of client request. More importantly, the agencies which systematically monitor diversity of their candidates tended to be the larger ones. Considering the fact that the majority of the recruitment agencies in the UK are small companies with ten or less employees or are sole traders, the issue of diversity and equality monitoring becomes a significant challenge that requires serious attention by policy-makers.

The reasons for the approach that individual firms adopted were also complex. Some participants considered equal opportunities irrelevant for their work, others thought of it solely as a legal obligation, and only very few participants (5 out of 19) suggested that there was a business case for equality in the sector.

8.7 Key factors predicting equality perspectives of agencies

Our research revealed that the levels of awareness regarding equality and diversity and the existence of associated diversity and equality policies, programmes and activities in the recruitment sector vary considerably. At one end of the spectrum, some organizations adopt a reactive compliance approach; at the other end of the spectrum, some adopt a sophisticated proactive approach. We found that four factors, in particular, help to predict an agency's diversity and equality perspective: the size of the agency; the senior management's level of diversity and equality commitment; membership of external networks; and the presence of a business case argument.

Organizational size

Only the large- and medium-sized agencies in our sample had formal equality and diversity policies and strategies which they shared with their clients, their candidates and their own staff. These firms also tended to have a harassment and bullying policy and the associated complaint mechanisms.

In contrast, when asked about their diversity and equality policies, small recruitment firms reported that they did not have a written policy. They also stated that they did not need one because of their size, but that equality and diversity was part of their organizational culture. Furthermore, as explained earlier, it was evident in the interviews that large agencies tended to have more formalized structures of equality monitoring, whereas in small agencies, monitoring activities were limited to informal and unsystematic mechanisms such as note-taking. Moreover, the issue of monitoring equal opportunities for candidates becomes even more complex for sole trading recruitment agents:

> I monitor them only inasmuch as I keep notes about who I speak to and who I get CVs from, of course their data is protected in the normal way under the data protection act. But again, because I'm a sole trader, I don't necessarily keep a lot of . . . these things to try and make use of them as marketing documents. The one thing I do track, though, is . . . people that I have introduced to my clients and who are subsequently hired into the company, I do keep in touch with them and keep track how soon they are promoted or given facilities in the company.

As stated in the secondary literature, keeping monitoring data is crucial for promoting equal opportunities (Tatlı *et al.* 2006). On the other hand, the evidence from our research demonstrates that organizational size is an important determinant of monitoring activity in the private recruitment sector. In the absence of regulation which requires formal equality monitoring activities in the sector, small-sized agencies are less likely to collect systematic monitoring data; in particular, they tend to use less formalized systems and procedures throughout the recruitment and selection process.

Furthermore, our research findings suggest that large- and middle-sized agencies are more likely than small recruitment agencies to offer specific training programmes on discrimination law for their staff. The REC is an important source of training for smaller firms in this field. In the case of medium and large firms, in-house training programmes cover the whole spectrum of issues.

Staff training is of particular import in terms of opening up opportunities for disadvantaged segments of the labour force. This is because the knowledge and awareness of the individual recruitment consultant predicted their approach to offering guidance services by gender, age, ethnicity and disability. One of the respondents from a middle-sized recruitment agency pointed out that the provision of equal opportunities training for the staff was crucial because they were the ones who would deliver the agency's equality and diversity policy as part of their daily practice – starting from their first telephone conversation with a candidate.

Commitment of senior management

However, the existence of a formal equal opportunities and diversity policy does not necessarily mean that an agency assumes a progressive and proactive equality and diversity approach. The implementation and delivery of the policy can vary even when a written policy is in place. Our interviews showed that the commitment to equality and diversity by the senior management, especially the chief executive officer (CEO), the managing director, or the owner of the agency, has a decisive impact on an agency's actions. This was the case both in the small-sized agencies and in the medium and large ones.

One of our participants was from a non-specialized large agency which is one of the leading recruitment organizations in the UK. The agency had a sophisticated equality and diversity approach, as well as a separate equality and diversity office. Moreover, it had developed an informed business case for diversity and equality on the basis of accessing new talent pools, changing labour market demographics and an understanding of the business and legal case for equality. However, our respondent suggested that a strong business case alone would not ensure an organizational commitment to diversity and equality. Senior management support and ownership was crucial, since it was said to be a long journey which requires a culture change and where there would not be an immediate payback. In other words, our respondent argued, the most important internal barrier for equality and diversity in a recruitment agency is that it is a long-term investment, whereas the sector predominantly relies on short-term profit making. In this agency, it was possible to overcome this barrier only through the support of the chief executive and the board. Our respondent said that the CEO's passion and commitment for equal opportunities and diversity had been decisive in engaging others in the organization with the equality and diversity agenda:

> What we wanted to do in terms of diversity, that was really important because it's everyone hearing from the chief executive, how passionate he was about this.

Sometimes the CEO's commitment may be directly related to his or her own life experiences. The example of a medium-sized agency which participated in the research is illustrative in this respect. The decision of its CEO to establish an agency that specialized in flexible job placement was the result of the conflicts she had experienced when trying to balance the demands of her domestic life and her career. The respondent from the company narrated the inspiring story of their founder as follows:

> Our founder xxx was a high achieving business woman . . . who was pregnant with her first child. She wanted to return to her career in marketing, but didn't want to go straight back into doing exactly what she was doing before, [nor] . . . to compromise on her career objectives. But she recognised that her life was going to be different after the baby, and that she would want to find a different way of working. She was working at the time for an American company and she recognised that the working day was very long and it was very much the norm, [whereas a shorter working day] was frowned upon, and it was going to get in the way of career objectives, she wasn't seen to be committed, she couldn't hold down a senior job. And xxx essentially felt that that wasn't right. There must be a way around it, must be more creative ways. So she decided to use that as her dissertation subject for her MBA, and she went and interviewed a thousand female managers to get their views on whether she was alone or whether there [were] other people out there thinking the same as her. And the very strong feedback she got . . . was, 'no you are not alone, yes this is a huge issue, something needs to be done about this'. And she decided . . . that if no one was doing it, she would do it herself. So she created a recruitment company where she could try to place people in a more creative and innovative way, whereby it was affording greater choice and flexibility in the ways in which people worked.

The above respondent also argued that offering alternative ways of working gained them a broader pool of candidates, since by offering flexible working options they were able to reach a more diverse and broader set of candidates. She summarized the business benefits of the offer of flexible working in the following words:

> And the flip side for the recruitment company was that it was offering greater access to broader talent, so not turning your back to a huge talent pool just because it didn't fit into a conventional way of delivering work. That's what we do. That's the traditional recruitment model, but its working with a very diverse candidate base and it's helping candidates and clients think a little more creatively about hard to fill vacancies.

Consequently, the agency not only has a very developed approach in terms of flexible working, but it also has a very sophisticated diversity and equality perspective. The agency's equal opportunities policy relates to both its candidates and its own staff, and covers gender, sexual orientation, marital status, age, disability, age, race, ethnic or national origin, religion, political beliefs and membership or non-membership of a trade union. To deliver this policy, the agency provides equality and diversity training for its staff. The respondent from the agency said:

> Xxx has at its core an expertise in and a commitment to diversity. Our promotion and communication delivers a uniquely diverse candidate network in terms of age and gender. In addition our work on remote working helps to deliver a greater diversity in terms of disability.

However, not all agencies in our sample had such a sophisticated equal opportunities and diversity approach. At the other end of the spectrum were the agencies with uninformed and underdeveloped equality perspectives. The case of a small executive recruitment company illustrates the extent to which some agencies might be devoid of any equality and diversity agenda, and here again the attitude of the owner was critical.

The company employed seven staff, all of whom were male. This was unusual in itself, since the recruitment sector has a significantly female-dominated employee profile. We interviewed one of the owners of the company who reported that they did not have a formal diversity or equal opportunities policy. He also said that the vast majority of their candidates were male because of the demanding nature of the executive posts. According to him, the ideal candidate for such a senior-level post with an extremely high workload would be a male candidate whose wife was not working in paid employment. He also claimed that one of the reasons why women are under-represented in senior-level posts in general, and in the agency's candidate pool in particular, might be related to the fact that some skills are gendered. He went on to illustrate his point by arguing that women tend to have better communication skills than men, whereas men have better analytical skills, and expressed other stereotypical views about the abilities and roles of men and women. Given these comments, it is very probable that these stereotypes would negatively impact upon the recruitment and selection process in this small-sized agency in terms of discouraging and disadvantaging female candidates.

Membership of external networks

The subjective nature of the selection and guidance operations in the private sector agencies, as well as the absence of strong regulation, means that the agency's operations may allow for discriminatory practices. However, there was also evidence of some progressive gender equality approaches and initiatives in the case of several participants. What separated progressive firms from others was the level of their awareness in terms of equal opportunities. As we have pointed out above, organizational size and senior management commitment were among the key factors that affected an agency's equal opportunities perspective, policy and activities. The other factor that predicts the state of an agency in terms of equality and diversity was membership of external networks. We found that the firms which engaged with networks of equality and diversity in the sector professed more progressive attitudes towards these issues.

The most important of these networks was the REC's Diversity Forum. The REC Diagnostic Check and Diversity Pledge have also helped raise awareness between members. The firms which have not engaged with these networks displayed very little understanding of equality and diversity issues. The levels of participation in, and the impact of, such initiatives are likely to be greater if membership of such networks are recognized and credited by the clients as well, since client expectations is a major driving force for the private recruitment agencies. However, the IRS (2002) research found that only 13 per cent of the employers take into account an agency's membership of a professional association such as the REC.

Nevertheless, our study reveals the importance of networks, audits and diagnostic checks in engaging the firms in the sector with the equality and diversity agenda. Guidance and training activities, which are sponsored by the membership organizations, are sometimes supported and supplemented by training offered through their broad networks (e.g. REC training). Furthermore, there are various diversity and equality networks that some recruitment agencies join. Such networks are instrumental in disseminating best practice and equipping diversity and equal opportunities officers with workplaces tools and discourses which can help them support structural and cultural change.

The business case for equality and diversity

In the academic and practitioner literature, it is frequently stated that there is a business case for equality and diversity in the current business environment because of changing labour market demographics. It is argued that skill shortages and the ageing population, as well as the changing needs of employees in terms of their working patterns, require employers to tap into the previously underutilized talent which is concentrated in the disadvantaged segments of the labour market, and to provide their employees with alternative, creative and flexible working arrangements (Shaw 1993; Schoenberger 1997; Gilbert and Stead 1999; Schneider and Northcraft 1999; Gilbert and Ivancevich 2000; Procter and Mueller 2000). During our interviews, we explored the extent to which business case arguments are adopted by the private recruitment agencies.

Changing labour market demographics

Our study has generated anecdotal evidence that there are significant changes in labour market demographics at the firm level. Recruitment agencies report increased levels of attention to issues of flexibility at more levels in organizations compared with the past. They also note that temporary work and flexible work are becoming life choices. This is an important departure from the traditional image, whereby workers opted for temporary and flexible work due to constraints. Our findings point to changes also in the psychological context, particularly in the highly skilled worker category. It is reported that such workers are less concerned about job security and that they trade this off for job quality and better terms and conditions. Several participants have also noted cultural developments which have engendered changes in women's participation in the labour market:

> I think it is the whole structure of working that has changed. I mean the role of a woman staying at home and looking after children has changed so more women work . . . and men obviously help, hopefully a bit more as well.

The underutilized potential of disadvantaged groups

Although many participants boasted about the currency of the business case arguments in the sector (i.e. that it takes up any initiative that will generate income), making good use of the underutilized potential of disadvantaged groups is not part of the mainstream business case. Only two large agencies out of the 19 agencies which participated in the research mentioned the business benefits of diversity and equality in terms of overcoming the challenge of skill shortages through tapping into a wider talent pool. Otherwise, the sector is characterized in the main by short-term business interests and a strong drive for profit making. Therefore, equality concerns do not appear to be on the agenda of many of the firms in the sector. The short-term orientation of the sector means that equality and diversity initiatives, which will yield benefits in the longer term, are marginalized in business agendas and priorities. Although the REC provides sophisticated business case arguments, individual firms do not fully understand and subscribe to this agenda. Indeed, business case arguments for gender equality and diversity that we have collected through our interviews were poorly developed when compared with other private sector services.

Summary and policy implications

Our research findings suggest that there are five key barriers to equality in the private recruitment sector in the UK. First, the discourse of gender neutrality which results in gender blindness is dominant in the sector. Second, it was evident from the interviews that subtle forms of gender bias and associated gendered prejudices do exist throughout the various operations of the agencies. Third, job placement patterns in the sector reflect and reproduce the existing occupational sex segregation, both vertical and horizontal. Fourth, there is a vacuum of responsibility in terms of promoting equal opportunities in the sector – what we called a 'passing the buck culture' – in that recruitment agencies perceive addressing inequalities as a responsibility of either their clients or their candidates. Fifth, despite the existence of a level of legal compliance, it was evident throughout the interviews that there was a general confusion among most of the participants about the agencies' responsibilities in terms of equal opportunities, that is equal opportunities monitoring. There was also general confusion about the implications of some pieces of anti-discrimination legislation, that is age legislation, which reflected the lack of equality awareness and information in the private recruitment sector.

However, the research findings suggest that the levels of awareness and the proactive stance regarding equality and diversity vary considerably in the sector. In the main, four factors predicted the sophistication level of the equality perspective of the private recruitment agencies. First, large- and medium-sized agencies are more likely to have formalized equal opportunities approaches, policies and practices. Second, senior management ownership proved to have a key impact on agencies' commitment to equal opportunities for all sizes of organization. Third, agencies which are progressive in terms of equality and diversity tend to be members of external networks such as the REC, IMA and AER. Lastly, the presence of a business case argument for diversity and equality is important in terms of delivering the equal opportunities agenda in the sector.

Interestingly, although there were some signs of a business case argument in terms of flexible working, it was rather underdeveloped in relation to changing labour market demographics, including skill shortages and the ageing population in the UK, and the tapping into the underutilized talent pool.

There are a number of policy implications arising out of the research findings outlined in this section. First of all, there is a need for an understanding of the implications of private sector recruitment practices on equality and diversity in employment. This could be achieved if an organization is tasked to collect regular equal opportunities monitoring data. However, this will also require the regulation of the entry, operation and exit of firms in the industry and the implications of these in terms of equality and diversity issues in the sector.

Second, in order to overcome the current vacuum of responsibility in the sector in terms of promoting equality and diversity, equal opportunities policy on recruitment agencies should recognize the multistakeholder and tripartite nature of the employment relations in the sector. This means that there should be different equal opportunities considerations for clients, the staff and the candidates in terms of advice and guidance activities. A more progressive and active role should be assigned to recruitment agencies through government policy and legislation in the pursuit of equality of opportunity. Within that framework, regulation and policy on equal opportunities in the sector should seek to give recruitment agencies a more active role in upholding equality on behalf of their candidates and in monitoring their recruitment processes in terms of their diversity and equality impact. In addition, agencies of all sizes need to develop formal diversity and equal opportunities policies which should also include an anti-harassment and anti-bullying policy. They should be encouraged to share their diversity and equality policies with their clients, their candidates and their own staff. Furthermore, the public, private and voluntary sector organizations which use recruitment agencies in the selection and recruitment of their workforces should be assigned more informed and active roles in encouraging the agencies to assume a progressive equality and diversity approach.

Third, our findings point to the importance of awareness-raising activities in the sector. These include awareness raising in terms of legal obligations and the business case for equality and diversity. To start with, a greater proportion of private sector recruitment agencies need to be provided with training and education activities on equal opportunities and best practice. Awareness raising and equal opportunities training activities in the sector should not only focus on documenting evidence of discrimination, but also offer instruction on how the recruitment agencies may play more progressive and transformative roles in upholding values of equality and diversity. Thus, there is scope for awareness raising, not only in terms of changes in the legal frameworks, but also in terms of the spirit of these legal changes. For instance, awareness-raising activities should specifically illuminate the differences between positive action and positive discrimination. Similarly, equal opportunities training activities in the sector should seek to dispel the myths of gender neutrality in the processes of the labour market. In other words, there is a need for awareness raising which brings in a more critical perspective that jobs and conditions of work are essentially gendered and that it is naive to assume that a standardized recruitment system can deliver gender equality if it is not checked also for gender bias.

Fourth, our findings suggest that most progressive firms in terms of equal opportunities have leaders who are personally committed to equality and diversity. These firms could be used as industry champions and promoted as examples of good practice. There is also a need for financial support to help their self-organized initiatives in equality and diversity, particularly in the case of small-sized agencies. Furthermore, senior management in the recruitment agencies should be encouraged to champion the cause of diversity and equality in the sector and within their companies. Awareness raising and networking activities targeting the senior managers should be organized.

According to our research results, in addition to senior management ownership, external networks play a crucial role in delivering the equality agenda in the private recruitment sector. The three professional bodies in the sector (REC, IMA and AER) should be assigned a stronger monitoring and regulatory power in terms of equal opportunities in the sector. Additionally, the ongoing activity in equality and diversity should be levered into becoming an industry standard and supported through regulation in the sector. However, it should be acknowledged that setting industry standards, with the expectation that recruitment agencies should provide more balanced pools of candidates, will require both regulation of the industry and voluntary collaborative activities between the firms in the sector.

Lastly, there is a need for a sophisticated business case argument to draw attention to equality and diversity issues in the sector, and to encourage monitoring and managing across all strands of equality and diversity. A sophisticated business case argument should demonstrate linkages between performance improvements through elimination of discrimination and disadvantage.

8.8   Equality initiatives and trends

During the interviews, we asked our respondents questions about their actions to support women candidates and candidates from the disadvantaged segments of the labour market; the general ways in which their placement of candidates into jobs in different sectors, posts and levels of seniority might be gendered; their activities in terms of encouraging their candidates into non-traditional areas of work; and their approaches and activities regarding the work–life balance and flexible working. The responses from the participant agencies reveal a complex picture. In some cases, agencies intentionally or unintentionally play a positive role in terms of tackling gender discrimination in the field of employment. In other cases, they reproduce the existing practice and discourse that disadvantages women. In one of the firms (although this was not a deliberate policy) the participant recalled examples of women entering non-traditional areas of work:

> I can think particularly [of] one very experienced woman project manager in telecommunication. She has worked for us, for a number of assignments in India, in the UK, and in other overseas companies. She was female, and she was extremely competent.

Thus, although specific programmes that target disadvantage are rare, nevertheless, the current work of most of the agencies involves the recruitment of women candidates at different levels and sectors. Furthermore, our interviews suggest the presence of progressive equal opportunities initiatives and approaches in place in the case of some agencies. In discussions of gender equality, flexibility is adopted as an item of central discourse in the private sector recruitment agencies. Indeed, all firms in the sector were sensitive to the demands for a flexible workforce from clients. However, there were three progressive firms which had communicated various agendas of flexibility to their clients even when the clients were reluctant to employ workers on flexible terms. Therefore, these firms were more innovative in their approach and practices.

Some firms solely base their marketing of candidates around flexibility and even undertake activities to inform and educate their clients about the alternative forms it can take. Most firms in our study noted that they would view flexible work as an investment for the future, both for themselves and for their clients. Legal changes also seem to have a significant impact on recruitment agency practices. An increase in the number of protected categories to include age, religion, belief, sexual orientation and nationality, amongst other factors, has prompted firms to run training programmes on equal opportunities and diversity management. These updates are very instrumental in improving the practice of recruitment agencies at the level of contact with clients and candidates.

In this section, we outline the current initiatives and trends in the sector that impact upon equality of opportunity. Within that framework, we firstly explore in detail the advantages and disadvantages brought in by flexible working. Then we explore the specific initiatives in terms of staffing and guidance to non-traditional areas of work through public–private sector collaboration, and the support programmes and mechanisms provided by the agencies to help disadvantaged people into work. Lastly, a summary of findings and policy implications arising out of them are presented.

Flexible working

Our interviews suggest that flexibility is indeed a boom area for the sector. In terms of contractual arrangements, several participants identified that, in the past, full-time employment was the preferred choice for skilled workers. Now this is slowly changing in favour of flexible working arrangements across the contractual spectrum. Indeed, several recruitment agencies were established in the late 1990s with the specific intention of catering for the flexible labour market. Flexibility manifests itself in various ways: interim work, temporary contracts, flexible-time arrangements of arriving and leaving work, three- or four-day weeks, job share, and so on.

Demand for flexible work not only emanates from both client firms and candidates, the agencies also offer flexible work conditions to their own staff to an even greater extent than for their clients and candidates. One participant explained:

> Within our company, there is a lot of flexibility because we have many mothers who are able to work from home two to four days a week (this is within the company. They are all set up to work from home, and they work 80 per cent or 60 per cent jobs) but it's not with a client company.

One of our interview participants noted that the types of flexibility requested by clients and candidates do not always match. Therefore, the agency plays a role to renegotiate demands for flexibility by going between the client and the candidate until an agreement is reached:

> A client, who owned their own company, would approach me and had a problem. Now the problem wasn't necessarily a bad thing. We always think problems are the company going bust or something, but sometimes it can be a challenge. They needed to develop an expanded market or cope with a merger or acquisition. So what they would approach me with is a requirement for a job and it was up to me to find the right candidate and work with the client about how we would fulfil that objective, and often we would look and say actually so and so would like to work four days a week not at home and one day a week at home, and as long as we were clear about delivering to the objective, it wasn't a problem.

Some recruitment agencies did not take the expectations of their clients for granted. Instead, they sought to understand the nature of the job vacancy and fill this by offering the client a range of options including high levels of flexibility:

> We go back to clients because of the nature of what we do. We do go back to them sometimes with something that they are not expecting to see, because not every brief that comes to us has any forms of flexibility by any means, and very often they don't think it can, and it's our job to try and put something in, if we think it can be done. So if we've listened carefully and understood and we've found someone who we think is very, very good, we can go back with a short list and say 'here are two CVs that look like that, but here's a CV that is a little bit different, and the reason I'm putting this person forward is because I think they have this, this and this to bring to the party in addition to what you've asked they've got this, this and this, but be aware they want to be doing this on a four day week not a

five day week'. So I don't take a full time job and only fill it with a full-time person, I try and find the right candidate to do it and if I can offer some sort of diversity to the individual at the time and an opportunity for them I will do it. If I sat and waited for part-time jobs then I wouldn't be making any placements because there are not that many good quality part-time job opportunities, so we have to make them flexible.

The same respondent also argued that they had a similar negotiation process with their candidates as well in order to find the best match between the job and the candidate. Thus advice and guidance about different flexibility options were an integral part of the interviewing process:

We would also be advising them (candidates) about what forms of flexibility might work with what sort of jobs, because sometimes they do have an unrealistic expectation. Sometimes they do say but I want to work in this sort of a job and I want to do it two days a week. And it's like, the only way you are going to achieve that, really, probably is by a job share. Because the job, that sort of a job, doesn't exist on a two-day week, it can only exist on a five-day week, so you are only going to achieve that sort of opportunity, if you find a partner. They can register online and see if they can find other people look-ing for part-time work and go together for a full-time job. So we give all that sort of advice through the interview. And sometimes you find someone ideal for a job, but there has to be a compromise, because this one is slightly more days but it's on your doorstop, so the commute is very easy, and that one is a tough commute so there's no way you can do that three days a week.

Our research findings reveal that there was growing recognition of two important issues regarding flexible working between participants. First, increased flexibility is accepted as an important mechanism by which gender equality can be promoted. It is recognized, for example, that people with domestic responsibilities, caring roles and career breaks benefit from flexible working arrangements. In a way, flexibility allows for the better accommodation of work and life demands for workers. However, in order to reap such benefits, the recruitment agencies should recognize the relevance of flexibility to equal-ity of opportunity. However, such awareness remains at a very basic level in general. Whilst some firms which specialize in flexibility recognize this essen-tial link, others consider flexibility only in terms of business opportunities.

Second, there is increased recognition that flexibility is not only desirable for women, but has appeal to a wider range of workers. Our interviews suggest that there has been a very slight extension of flexible working arrangements from unskilled and non-managerial work to senior posts. One participant explained the dynamic nature of negotiating flexibility and how flexibility has become more prevalent in senior posts over the years:

> Sadly I have to tell you . . . that at the senior level there isn't much oppor-tunity for people to be given senior and executive level job share or jobs on a part-time basis. I will come across candidates who have been with their company already for a few years and they may have already negotiated a four-day a week or part-time or some home-working, so I definitely come across people who have different ways of working. I don't come across many clients offering such work. Not in the first instance. In my experi-ence, what I find is that people tend to start with a company first full-time, and then after they've proven themselves and got to their own track records in that organization, if they're in a situation where they would like to nego-tiate a different way of working, then they can do [so]. Some people negoti-ate time off to do an MBA, to do a loan programme, people take time off to make families, some take time off to do trips around the world – at [a] senior level that happens more than at the junior and middle management level.

Flexibility for all

Flexibility is often considered a preserve of women, or a way of organizing work that caters for women's patterns of work and life. Indeed, there was increasing recognition that flexibility is becoming a life-style choice for a wider segment of society. Interviewees have suggested that flexible work is now demanded by non-traditional segments of the workforce, including senior managers, technical staff and professional workers. The respondent from the agency which specialized in flexible recruitment pointed out:

> This [flexible working] isn't just only about women but also for men, for their families. It's about career choices. So we don't want to make it a gender issue.

She then argued that flexible working should not be seen as an option only for those with caring responsibilities, but should be perceived as a life-style choice:

> We do see it broader than that because when I'm talking to candidates, which I'm doing daily, there are so many reasons people want this flexibil-ity, and actually there is a bit of a kickback in companies if you think its exclusively female and you think its exclusively about childcare. Then you get the person who is 28 years old, who is thinking, 'hang on, why am I on the receiving end of all of these policies? Because she's got her daughter and so has she, and [I] haven't. And I want to go home and I'm being allowed to, but you are not'. So why is it? Why don't you have an opportunity for

flexibility, because you might actually just want to play golf and may want [to] leave early.

The respondent complained about the narrow-minded understanding in the business environment around the issue of flexibility and explained how her agency tries to raise the awareness of their clients on the issue:

And you'd be amazed the number of companies we've sat in [and heard people] saying, 'I don't have children but why doesn't that allow me a right to flexible working? Because I want to write a book or I want to do further study'. It should be reason neutral and gender neutral. So nobody needs to have a conversation about why they want it. It's about can it work? Does it work for the business? Does it commercially still allow them to deliver their role to their internal and external customers? And they don't need to say why. Because that involves the line manager making some subjective decision about whether your rationale for asking for flexible working [is] greater than mine, and that makes it very difficult because when he has a team of three he's thinking 'I can't have three of you all working flexibly, and its like, hey yours is about golf, hers is about a child and hers is about an elderly mother, so I'll let her have it and yours is a no'.

The agency clearly stands out in our sample as a good practice example of flexible working. It not only offers creative and alternative solutions to both its clients and candidates in terms of work arrangements, but, as explained above, is actively involved in helping its clients regarding the aspects of flexible working that they might find challenging, that is training programmes on managing a flexible workforce. When we asked about an example of creative good practice, where it delivered support for a client in relation to flexible working, our respondent gave the following example:

Xxx did some research amongst their employees and discovered that there was a high level of dissatisfaction about the level of employee control and engagement. So we went in and [did] a number of test groups and piloted flexible working in two of their very, very different bits of the business, one distribution, one marketing team, and the teams created their own solutions with some help from us, and they put in flexible working practices and tried them in those two departments, and learnt a lot. And the flexibility has been in all manners. On one end of the spectrum you have someone's who says 'well what I've always wanted to do is work three days a week', at the other end you have someone who says, 'well can I start at 9.30 and finish at 5.30 rather than be here until 8.30'. So it's a whole team. And it's worked on the basis that if we were a team of people and you wanted one form of flexibility and I wanted another and you wanted another, we can still deliver the objectives of the business. And then what they've done is rolling it out across the business, and they've seen very real improvement in employee engagement and motivation.

Some participants have clearly noted that flexibility is mostly the preferred option for women rather than for men in their current experience:

Fewer men ask for flexible working hours than women; you wouldn't be surprised by that. For example here, I have more women working flexible hours. Not many men ask for it.

Interim management

In most agencies, the availability of flexible working options for the candidates indirectly provided help and support for the employment of women in general, and for women returners in particular, as well as for older workers and male carers and parents. Within that framework, interim management, a specialism for some agencies, emerged during the research as one of the most important routeways into senior-level jobs for women returners, older workers and people with caring responsibilities.

There are many firms which specialize in interim management work. The difference between full-time, long-term, contracted work and interim management work is the nature of the work. Interim managers are expected to start on the first day and complete a project during their stay in a company. This means that at the end of the project, interim managers are released from work. One of our participants explained why there is rarely repeat custom in interim work: 'Because interim is a "distress purchase", you don't plan it long ahead. You rarely have established providers'. Thus, recruitment agencies which specialize in interim management look for candidates who are highly skilled and can deliver a temporary management project to the client firms. Normally, interim management appointments are made at the highly skilled end of the spectrum and the interim managers are expected to take on the responsibility for their appointment on their first day at work, without there being much provision for induction or career progress at work:

In this business, these people all really want to go out and work and want to do their next job. I don't need to try to convince them to do it, you see. Because they are free agents, freelancers, they are dying to do the next job. They are much less choosy than a permanent employee would be, and much less demanding, because they say 'this is my job. For six months or nine months I do this really highly intense job, then I take two or three months off and then I do the next one'. So it's a different pattern . . . There is no progress; it's interim. So they go in and do a project, they progress from one job to the next, they can maybe work with a bigger company or [on] a more complex project or [in a] . . . more complex situation.

Some informants argued that interim management is a good alternative for women returners, as the CVs of interim managers include career breaks by definition:

This is ideal for women, to do interim work, because you don't really look so much at what they have done in the past six months, or [if] there is a gap. I never get a client who calls me back and says 'There is a gap of four months in the CV!', because they are not interested in that. What they are interested only is, can they get the job done? Are they the best person to get the job done? So background only as an indication of being able to do the job, rather than having a flaw in the CV.

As career breaks are not negatively viewed in interim management jobs, women returners, if they are highly skilled, can benefit from this as a route for their careers. One informant noted that some candidates use interim management as a way to acquire full-time posts. This suggests that, despite the growth of flexible work arrangements, more often than not flexible work is seen as a temporary arrangement or a route into more prestigious forms of full-time work. Therefore, the expansion of flexible work has not brought about a feeling of equality between flexible and full-time workers, as the former group continue to enjoy limited financial, job-security and status benefits.

One of the striking findings of our research, however, has been the lack of similar flexible working options for permanent senior-level jobs. Most of our respondents argued that flexibility conflicts with the nature of the jobs at senior management levels. When flexibility was mentioned for permanent senior management jobs, it was rather in the form of 'flexibility' of the candidates, in terms of working long hours and travelling, rather than giving them the opportunity to manage their work–life balance. The outcome of the absence of flexible working for permanent senior management roles was the high level of underrepresentation of women in jobs of this type. One of the respondents from a small executive recruitment company even argued that very senior-level jobs are most suitable for the male candidates with wives who are not working, since the job brings a very high workload.

In short, the upside of interim management for equal opportunities, particularly for people on career breaks or with caring responsibilities, is that the number of completed projects and skill sets of the candidates, rather than their long service record, helps them get interim management posts. The respondent from an agency that specializes in interim recruitment argued that interim management is a beneficial career path for women at senior levels, since it provides them with the opportunity to resume their careers after a break and gives them the flexibility to reconcile the demands of their work and family lives:

> And also the thing with interim management . . . Women if they have children for example or need a bit more work/life balance because . . . a lot of women who do have, you know, very senior level roles up to board level, when they have children, find it very difficult to slot back into their career where they left off. Working on a project-focus basis can often mean that they can maintain the same level of seniority and responsibility in their job, keep the challenge going, but also have that flexibility to not work during school holidays for example or perhaps work three or four days a week and in it help with child care.

The downside of the interim management posts is that they require intensive periods of work with little, if any, training. Although some interim managers are reportedly working only six months a year and taking up to six months off for domestic work or leisure, the periods of work are more intensive than for full-time workers. One participant elaborated on the possible implications of interim work on equality from the firm's perspective:

> We don't take on people that are under 35. And no one over 60, also. We wouldn't discriminate against them, but interim – for example, if there is a female caretaker with three young children, you know they would probably not even apply for jobs, because an interim job is such that you have to go within a day's notice anywhere in the country to work on six or nine month projects. I think there is no discrimination from our side but maybe no applications to these kinds of jobs. It's a different type of discrimination I would think.

Impact of flexible working on different groups of employees

However, growth in flexibility should be viewed with caution. Flexibility does not happen in a vacuum of values and ideology. Indeed, it can present both opportunities and constraints in terms of equality of opportunity. As one of our participants explained, it is important to recognize that there are a wide range of flexible forms and ways of work, and what the clients and the candidates mean by flexibility often differs extensively. Therefore, it is important to recognize that different forms of flexibility have a different impact upon equality of opportunity for the workers.

Thus, regarding the advancement of women in the field of employment, flexible working displays an ambivalent role, acting both as a constraint and as an opportunity. It is a very well-documented fact that flexible working, atypical contracts and part-time working are among the major causes of the gender pay gap, particularly in the cases of low-skilled female workers. On the other hand, they may open up opportunities for women who are disadvantaged by the unequal burden of domestic and childcare commitments from entering the labour market. Flexible working may help highly skilled professional female employees to resume and advance their career while at the same time accommodating their family and childcare 'responsibilities'. On the other hand, it may deteriorate the pay and work conditions of low-skilled female workers, hence it may function as a discriminatory mechanism against female candidates. In other words, whilst this is a promising trend, flexibility does not herald better conditions of work for flexible workers at the lower echelons of the hierarchy. Indeed, flexibility may happen at the expense of job security. For example, the study participants have provided anecdotal evidence that most flexible job placements are at the less secure and lower ranks of organizational hierarchies and that they are dominated by women, mirroring the occupational segregation patterns in the UK labour market.

Furthermore, there are cases in which atypical, temporary and flexible working contracts seriously deteriorate the pay and work conditions of the agency workers. Clearly, recruitment agencies have an important role to play in the determination of the pay and work conditions of their candidates. One of our respondents from a large international agency said that, despite the high levels of competition in the sector, they try to get the best deals for their candidates, while on the other hand providing their clients with high quality staff:

> Obviously, the client is looking to drive down the pay rate, so that his or her overall bill rate is lower. But we will always engage with them to recommend the best pay-rate for that appropriate level of staff. And there's no point [in] us promising a low pay-rate, when we know we're not going to get the quality of staff at the end of the day, in that environment. So I guess it is a bit of juggling, and we need to condition ourselves as the best person in the marketplace would suggest the rate, as appropriate to skill and qualification. And at the end of the day, most clients will want the skill and the experience, above the lowest cost. They're willing to pay.

On the other hand, the respondent pointed out that competition in the sector is intensifying, and he told us that one of the most recent and worrying trends in the sector is the increasing popularity of e-auctions:

> We went through quite an interesting scenario recently, where a major public sector employer was looking via an e-auction, I'm not sure if you're aware how an e-auction works? It's one mechanism for them to drive down the price. So they get a number of agencies in, electronically, and generally you drive down

the margin by having them bid against each other. I've only been involved in a number, and again most people look to drive down the margin. But this particular one was looking to drive down the pay-rate and the margin.

Our respondent was responsible for the staffing for the public sector in his agency and involved in the e-auctions opened up by the public sector organizations. He found the most recent e-auction he attended significantly disturbing and worrying:

It is awful. That's the point – it is awful. For stationery, pencils and pens, it's fine, but we're talking about people here, you know? But this major public sector body [was] actually driving down the pay-rate. Well they were doing the margin. But they were doing the pay-rate up front. So you actually had a situation where, again, lots of agencies were sitting and bidding at the same time in this e-auction, and driving down the pay-rate, which is a ludicrous scenario. And you actually had organizations bidding at below the minimum wage. They were discounted, they were knocked out of the e-auction, because it was against legislation. But it just shows you what people are willing to do. What that sort of environment, the e-auction environment is.

When we were more interested in learning about the process and mechanisms of e-auctions, he said that they were organized by some private companies and were becoming an increasingly common and prominent tool to drive down the labour cost for both public and private sector organizations. Unfortunately, these e-auctions were only available to the recruitment industry, hence not to us for observation. However, it is clearly an important research area in terms of understanding the private sector agencies' impact upon equality of opportunity and diversity in recruitment and selection, particularly in terms of pay and conditions of work.

Staffing and guidance to non-traditional areas of work through public–private sector collaboration

In our study of recruitment firms, we have not come across any explicit attempts at guidance offered for encouraging women and men into non-traditional areas of work. However, there were several cases where this has happened, even when this was not an outcome of an intentional effort on behalf of the recruitment company:

I don't know about measures, but we have that quite a bit, yes – atypical women. Like we have women as facilities managers, which would be maybe atypical. Big programme management. I have a super-smart woman right now in a programme management for an outsourcing consulting company.

Apart from such unintentional outcomes, our interviews suggest that the private recruitment agencies' contribution to staffing and guidance of women into non-traditional areas of work is most of the time realized through their collaboration with public sector bodies. Thus, there is scope for equality- and diversity-related bodies, and relevant public and voluntary sector organizations, to collaborate with private sector firms in order to set up such initiatives. Despite the general sense of there being a lack of attention given to challenging traditional norms of gender segregation at work, there are several European and UK initiatives which seek to encourage women into non-traditional areas of work. These include construction (currently in collaboration with the REC) and IT (funded by the DTI and the ESF). Participation of these agencies, as well as the public sector organizations as discussed earlier, in the employment relationship in the sector offers the possibility of progress. One participant explained that their involvement with Aurora, a business women's network, and the EOC has helped them focus on gender issues in recruitment:

> We've done an odd number of things, we've been involved . . . with Aurora, are you familiar with Aurora: the women's forum? We've had dealings with them . . . our CEO has actually been involved with the Equal Opportunities Commission, they have done a report last year and she sat on a committee there. We've been involved in women in IT with another [project] . . . we've worked with them to do a piece of research.

Some other joint initiatives between the public sector and private recruitment agencies were also reported during our fieldwork. For example, one of our respondents from a large recruitment agency told us that they had worked with a public body to train and recruit women as construction workers. Our respondent argued that this partnership was also beneficial for the agency, since it helped them to overcome the challenges of skill shortages in the construction sector:

> We worked closely with them and that helped because you know there was clear skill shortage, and it was in everyone's interest to get involved in the project.

Clearly, such partnerships have the potential of both benefiting the parties involved and of opening up opportunities for the disadvantaged groups in the labour market.

Support programmes and mechanisms to help disadvantaged people into work

Although it is not a sectoral standard, several recruitment agencies, particularly the ones in the voluntary sector, specialized in dealing with various aspects of equality. For instance, there are voluntary sector agencies which specifically cater for workers with disabilities or workers from BME backgrounds. Although we have identified agencies which specialize in ethnicity and disability issues, similar agencies which specialize in gender were absent. The REC representative noted that there may, indeed, be a gap in the market for agencies that specialize on gender equality. Our interviews with participants revealed that the absence of explicit requests from employers for gender-balanced recruitment pools may be responsible for the sectoral inattention to issues of gender inequality in recruitment, above and beyond the requirements of the law.

Nevertheless, some programmes, which are supported by key government agencies, such as the London Development Agency and the European Union (ESF), seek to tackle gender inequality and offer training, education and awareness-raising activities for the areas of work where imbalances are identified. For instance, a respondent from a large recruitment agency gave the example of a partnership between his organization and the Department for Education and Skills in a project targeting low-skilled candidates:

> We looked at some very serious kinds of projects, whereby we would work together, to identify low skilled candidates and do a sort of sandwich arrangements whereby we would place them in a role. And when they would not be working, they would be getting training and they would get some sort of state subsidy for that. That was really quite an exciting work, because the advantage that recruitment agencies have, which trainers don't have, is that agencies have very good relationships . . . not only with the candidates, but also with the employers, so they are the ideal brokers.

Thus, again we found that close collaboration between the government and the EU programmes, and voluntary sector organizations and the private sector recruitment agencies, may prove useful in helping disadvantaged people into work. The Diversity Pledge is a good example of collaboration between public and private recruitment sectors where the REC and Jobcentre Plus have jointly launched the initiative. The public recruitment sector has also New Deal schemes which target disadvantaged segments of the UK population; and the private recruitment agencies' involvement in these schemes may open up opportunities for a larger number of job seekers. However, the investigation of public recruitment sector undertaken by Rolfe and Nadeem (2006) suggests that while there are progressive New Deal schemes, there has been no mainstreaming of good equality policy and practice across the sector. Within that framework, public–private collaboration may lead to positive outcomes and practice if Government-led schemes set standards for levels of engagement and delivery on equality issues by both public and private recruitment sectors.

Similarly, collaboration alone may not be the answer. Indeed, this may lead to a functional division where the public and voluntary sector organizations once again are viewed as the sole route of access to employment by members of disadvantaged groups. The risk of polarization between public, private and voluntary sector organizations on equal opportunities issues can be avoided if there is also an expectation from the private sector firms to mainstream equal opportunities issues through knowledge transfers in these collaborative activities. But this is not likely to happen without regulation of the industry. If this is to be pursued on a voluntary basis, there should be better and more widespread recognition of the sophisticated business case and legal compliance arguments for equality.

However, none of the agencies participating in this research had activities which targeted the disadvantaged segments of the labour market specifically, with the exception of the small female-owned agency. This agency provided an excellent example of good practice in terms of helping disadvantaged people into work. The agency proactively searches and recruits candidates from minority ethnic and religious backgrounds, from discouraged and unemployed groups, and from single parents and returners. The owner of the company said that her own background and life experience had been crucial in her decision to open such an agency, and for her commitment to equality and diversity:

> We're a small organization but the reason I'm passionate about it is because I'm an Asian woman, I'm a single parent and I know how hard it was for me, so I'd be stupid, or silly not to give these young women the opportunity or tell other companies to wise up because you can get a really good member of staff if you just look beyond them doing you know 9 to 5.

The respondent had a very comprehensive diversity approach, which also included the generally ignored categories of diversity such as sexual orientation and ex-offenders, and she saw educating her clients regarding equality and diversity as one of the main parts of her role:

> Diversity is a big issue. People don't understand that it is not just about the colour of your skin and your ethnic background. It is about recruiting people that are gay, who have criminal records and its about educating people. Guys, this is what it is.

The agency follows several strategies to reach and place candidates from disadvantaged backgrounds. These include going to communities, schools, centres, mosques and temples. The owner of the agency said that going into the communities is a particularly effective way of reaching female candidates because some women might not be aware of either the vacancies or the ways in which they can get information. The agency also provides advice and guidance for unemployed people who are discouraged for different reasons:

> We try and motivate them. Because sometimes they've been to so many interviews with other organizations that they've got really fed up and de-motivated.

Moreover, the agency proactively seeks to present a diverse shortlist of candidates, even when this is not requested by the client:

> We make sure we send them a mix . . . like women, men, single parents, people that are working, people that are currently unemployed and are looking to get back into work.

Unfortunately, this agency was an exception among those we interviewed. For other participants, concealed behind a facade of the business case discourse of 'best person for the job' is the reality that the support programmes and mechanisms to help disadvantaged people into work are few and far between. In particular, the agencies which deal with gender equality are rare. One participant explained that if there is a market-driven need for such an agency, it will happen. If there is not a market specifically for women in management, it is unlikely that any recruitment agency will champion this cause.

Summary and policy implications

Our interviews suggest that offering flexible working options is one of the key mechanisms through which private recruitment agencies may open up opportunities for disadvantaged segments of the labour market. The agencies may play a crucial role in terms of negotiating the terms and conditions of flexibility, both with their candidates and clients, and raising the awareness of both parties regarding different flexible working options. However, for such a progressive role by the agencies to materialize, there is a need to develop an awareness regarding the business benefits of flexibility, which was evident only in a few progressive agencies in our sample. Nevertheless, our findings demonstrate that flexibility might be preferred by the job seekers, since it allows for the better accommodation of work and life demands. Flexible and atypical working arrangements, such as interim management, part-time or home work, and job share, may provide viable and effective alternatives to traditional forms of full-time work for those returning to employment after a career break or seeking to balance the needs of their work and domestic lives. This may be particularly the case for highly skilled women. Within that framework, our interviews reveal that flexibility may appeal not only to women, but to a wider range of workers.

However, it should be noted that there is an extensive diversity in the forms of flexibility, and each form of flexibility comes with a set of benefits and costs to employers, workers and other constituent groups. Similarly, flexible working has different outcomes for different groups of female workers. Thus, flexibility can present both opportunities and constraints in terms of equality of opportunity. Furthermore, the tendency in the sector to equalize the work–life balance with flexible working should be viewed with caution, since this may prevent any real discussion of hard measures such as the provision of childcare facilities.

Next, we found that most of the agencies do not have any autonomous programmes designed for staffing and guiding female candidates into non-traditional areas of work. However, there was evidence of collaborative activities between private recruitment agencies or organizations and public sector bodies in that respect. Clearly, such collaborations may potentially contribute to tackling occupational sex segregation. Lastly, with the exception of one, none of the agencies which participated in the research had any specific support programmes or mechanisms to help disadvantaged people into work.

Once again, a number of policy implications arise out of these research findings. Regarding flexible working, the role of recruitment agencies in negotiating terms and conditions of work with both clients and candidates should be recognized and this should be levered in support of equal opportunities. There is scope for awareness-raising activities that will help recruitment agencies recognize the essential linkages between flexibility and equal opportunities as well as the business case for flexibility. Additionally, work–life balance policies should capture both soft and hard measures and should relate to both women and men. Also, good practice in the sector in terms of flexible work should be promoted and disseminated across the sector.

However, a policy on flexible working should recognize the diversity of flexible work patterns as well as the different equality and diversity implications of each form of it. Thus, a policy on flexible and temporary work may be mobilized to encourage the unusual union of atypical work with job security, preventing a polarization of the transformation of work across these two dimensions. More specifically, the ambivalent nature of flexible work and gender equality needs to be addressed by regulative frameworks which protect flexible workers from commercial exploitation. Within that framework, there is need for awareness raising, as well as for lobbying activities, in terms of equal pay and the interlinkages between pay equality and flexible working. Similarly, developing a business case for improving the terms and conditions for temporary workers, and ultimately equalizing the status of flexible and full-time work, should be a policy aim. In particular, there is a need to broaden the scope of flexibility to a wider range of jobs, including senior management and better paid ones, which have reportedly retained their ways of work over time, if flexible work is to gain the same prestige as full-time work.

Lastly, our research findings suggest that public–private sector collaboration is crucial for the delivering of equality of opportunity in recruitment. There is scope for further collaborative provision through professional networks between public and private sector employment and guidance agencies. In particular, in areas where there is clear absence of activity, collaboration in multistakeholder networks across industries and sectors may prove useful. In this regard, recruitment agencies should be encouraged to work in such multistakeholder environments in order to address equality issues more effectively. Similarly, there is a role for agencies to reach out to communities to search for their candidates.

8.9   Policy implications

Below, as informed by our analysis, we summarize the possible policy recommendations to tackle discrimination and open up opportunities for disadvantaged segments of the labour market through private sector recruitment and guidance agencies. This is followed by a good practice guide for equality and diversity for these agencies.

Policy implications for recruitment and guidance operations

The UK recruitment sector is regulated by the EAA and others, but there is not a general licensing system. Thus, there is no standard by which the private agencies enter the industry or operate. The absence of regulation means that equality monitoring, and the provision of advice and guidance, as well as standards of recruitment activities, are solely left to the discretion of the individual agencies. First, most of the agencies which participated in our research do not monitor the statistical composition of their candidate pool in terms of gender, age, ethnicity, sexual orientation and disability attributes. Similarly, there is no hard data on the ways in which traditional occupational segregation patterns, both horizontal and vertical, are mirrored or tackled by the agencies when they match their candidates with the clients. Hence, an absence of data leads to the invisibility of issues of equality and diversity as areas of action.

Second, provision of guidance mostly takes place in the form of informal advice and guidance provided to the candidates by the individual recruitment consultant during the interviewing process. There are no standardized formal systems of advice and guidance. Accordingly, the scope and nature of the advice and guidance largely depends on the discretion of the individual consultant. Hence, the level at which issues of equality and flexible working are addressed throughout the recruitment process is affected by the recruitment consultants' perspectives and awareness regarding these issues. This suggests that equality and diversity training may be an important medium to combat discrimination and inequality in recruitment.

Third, our interviews revealed that only some of the recruitment agencies provide their recruiters with equality and diversity training which may enhance their awareness of, and commitment towards, equality. We observed that in the cases of agencies with such training programmes, the individual consultants are more likely to provide the female candidates with advice and guidance to help them into senior posts and to return to work after a career break. Moreover, the role of recruitment agencies not only involves advice and guidance for the candidates, but also for their clients. Recruitment agencies are key brokers in negotiating terms and conditions between their clients and candidates. Thus, they play a significant role in educating their clients and candidates in terms of legal, social, economic and broad demographic shifts in the labour market with a view to reshaping their expectations of work. In this context, our interviews suggest that some of the agencies provide education to their clients in terms of changes in equality and diversity legislation as well as practices based on the business case.

Informed by these findings, we propose the following policy implications:

- The government needs to consider the introduction of a stronger regulatory framework which promotes equality and diversity for the private sector recruitment agencies. This framework should include an obligation that an equality monitoring system for the candidates is established.
- Private sector recruitment agencies should be encouraged to formalize and monitor their advice and guidance procedures. A good practice guide could be developed to help the agencies address the issues of equality, diversity and the work–life balance during the provision of guidance, both for their candidates and their clients.
- Private sector recruitment agencies should be encouraged to provide their recruitment consultants with a diversity and equality training programme.

Policy implications of the impact on disadvantaged populations

Our research revealed that the level of equality and diversity awareness of private sector agencies can be summarized as gender blindness as well as blindness to other strands of diversity. The outcome of this is an unintentional gender bias and indirect and covert discrimination. Coupled with the discourse of 'best person for the job', which accepts that jobs are unquestioningly gender blind, more subtle forms of gender bias, which relate directly to the structuring of jobs, workplaces and temporal and spatial arrangements of work, remain unchallenged by the private recruitment agencies. Moreover, the discourse of 'best person for the job' is also used as a justification for the lack of any proactive initiatives by the agencies to encourage women into non-traditional areas of work, and to provide support programmes and mechanisms to help disadvantaged people into work.

Informed by these findings, we propose the following policy implications:

- An awareness raising campaign about different forms and types of inequality and discrimination, as well as about the work–life balance and flexible working issues, should be launched.
- Awareness raising in terms of equal opportunities legislation should be undertaken. Such activities should particularly include raising awareness around positive action advertising.
- Good practice regarding general equal opportunities and diversity issues, as well as the work–life balance and flexible working issues, should be promoted and disseminated.
- Good practice, where women and men are encouraged into non-traditional areas of work by the recruitment agencies, should be promoted and disseminated. In addition, recruitment agencies should actively provide support programmes and mechanisms to help disadvantaged people into work.
- Support for the initiatives that actively seek to encourage women into non-traditional areas of work, and for the programmes and mechanisms to help disadvantaged people into work, should be provided.
- A multistakeholder approach to encourage both agencies and clients to assume a role and responsibility in tackling discrimination and segregation throughout the recruitment process should be encouraged.

Policy implications of awareness of recent trends in the labour market

Our interviews identified that the private sector recruitment agencies mainly focus on the flexible working demands, both of their clients and candidates, within the framework of changing trends in the labour market. The respondents reported increased levels of attention to issues of atypical working arrangements, noting that temporary and flexible work are becoming life choices. In addition, most of the respondents argued that they experience difficulties in finding candidates in certain sectors due to the skill shortages.

Interestingly, only a few respondents thought that people from disadvantaged groups whose talents are underutilized can be an important source to widen their candidate pool and to overcome the challenge brought in by the skill shortages. This finding is crucial because 'tapping into the talent pool' and 'utilizing the previously underutilized potential of disadvantaged groups' are among the most frequently uttered business rationales behind diversity and equality initiatives in the private services and manufacturing sectors in the UK. Although many research participants insisted that the sector takes up any initiative that will generate income, making good use of the underutilized potential of disadvantaged groups is not part of the mainstream discourse of the business case in the sector. In other words, business case arguments for gender equality and diversity are not fully developed in the private sector recruitment industry, compared with other private sector industries. This may be partially due to the fact that private recruitment agencies do not collect data on their candidates and clients. Furthermore, none of the agencies in our research reported that their work processes are informed by substantial market data on candidate pools, clients or the local labour market. Combined with the absence of explicit demands for gender balanced or diverse candidate pools from the clients, the outcome is that the business case arguments for gender balanced recruitment are virtually non-existent.

Informed by these findings, we propose the following policy implications:

- a sound business case argument for equality and diversity to enable strong commitment and proactive action by the private sector recruitment agencies should be developed;
- a business case argument for equality and diversity should be communicated and disseminated through different channels and media across the sector;
- employers and recruiters should be engaged through networks on equality and diversity.

Good practice guidance for equality and diversity

It is not possible to offer a single set of prescriptions that transcend variations by size, industry and contractual diversity in the private recruitment sector. Nevertheless, we have identified a number of good practices in the sector. We identify these good practices in a relational framework:

Agencies' relationships with candidates

There were progressive firms in the sector which championed equality, diversity and flexible work arrangements. There were also pockets of progressive practice in each organization that we studied. Our depiction of progressive firms therefore summarizes both these firms and the progressive practices that we have identified through our interviews. It is evident that progressive recruitment agencies, irrespective of size, carry out monitoring activities in order to assess the equality and diversity implications of their recruitment processes. Small firms tend to attend to these activities in a less structured manner, through observations, and through less formalized record keeping. Large and progressive firms, however, develop sophisticated methods of monitoring, including equal opportunities forms which seek information on strands of diversity.

Progressive agencies recognize a need actively to seek candidates from disadvantaged and marginalized groups in order to widen their candidate pools. They also do not see these positive action initiatives in conflict with the notions of meritocracy, often voiced as 'the best person for the job' in the sector. Some of the ways of engaging with these positive action initiatives are to utilize links with specialist press, communities, networks and collaborations with public and voluntary sector organizations.

Training and development activities that some firms offer to their candidates to improve their employability is also a marker of their progressive attitudes towards equality and diversity, should these programmes seek to serve these ends. Such activities include confidence-building sessions for returners, directing candidates to reskilling programmes and engaging discouraged workers with possible ways to return to work.

It was also evident that the progressive firms did not simply bow to the client expectations. Indeed, they negotiate better terms and conditions for their workers, prevent discriminatory requests being realized in the process of recruitment and offer guidance and advice to their candidates as well as their clients on equality and diversity issues.

Progressive firms also concentrate on the skills, abilities and talents of their candidates, rather than their stereotypes associated with gender, ethnicity, age, disability, sexual orientation, and so on. They also lobby their clients for change of behaviour in this regard.

Agencies' relationships with clients

We have extensive evidence from the field study to suggest that progressive firms use different methods to raise the awareness of their clients in issues of equality and diversity. For example, if a client makes a request for a female candidate, a progressive firm would explain to the client the legal and business case why this is not a legitimate and lawful request. Some firms also hold formal seminars and workshops, as well as a mock tribunal in one case, to demonstrate the significance of equality concerns.

Some firms champion flexible working as well as interim management as a way of overcoming gender disadvantage and also to facilitate the return to work for members of marginalized groups. These firms also talk to the clients who are looking for standard candidates for full-time posts and try to explore if these posts can indeed be filled through flexible work and by non-traditional candidates. Therefore, the recruitment agency adopts a transformative role in the process of negotiation.

It is also a marker of good practice that a recruitment agency offers a diverse pool of candidates to their clients, even when they do not receive an explicit request along these lines. This means that the progressive firm does not act as a passive agent of recruitment transaction, but plays a more proactive role in the process. More importantly, progressive firms develop sophisticated discourses and business case arguments so that they can convince their clients of the benefits of diversity and equality.

Progressive firms also share good practice with their clients. This can take the form of advising them of their own equal opportunities policies, helping the client firm to establish similar systems and put in place equality and diversity initiatives.

Agencies' relationships with their own staff

Progressive firms issue policies not only for their clients and candidates, but also for their own staff. They also adopt progressive approaches that mainstream equality and diversity in all processes of employment and business management.

There is, of course, a significant role for leadership in diversity and equality. Progressive firms have leaders who take the challenge of diversity and equality and cascade the message down the hierarchies in their organizations. Flexible work is not only seen as something that the firm offers externally, but something that is practised by its own staff. This also helps them lead the business case of flexible working by example as they develop very sophisticated ways of offering their staff flexible options.

Recruitment agencies can also ensure that their staff profiles reflect a diverse selection. That also helps them support their claims for diversity when they are negotiating with their clients and approaching their candidates.

Some firms also offer equality and diversity training to their customer-facing staff. This ensures that the subjective element of a recruitment agency's work is cleared of any discriminatory bias and instead promotes best practice.

Agencies' relationships with other actors

The significance of networks, external contacts and professional forums cannot be overstated in upholding values of equality and diversity. It is through these external and sectoral networks that the firms acquire knowledge on best practice and ways of monitoring, managing and reaping the benefits of equality and diversity. Networks like the REC's Diversity Forum serve this purpose. However, the firms can also interact with other public sector organizations and charities in pursuit of equality initiatives.

8.10   Conclusions

In the current business environment, equality and diversity is a prerogative for organizational competitiveness. However, this can be only achieved in global diversity management practice if the formulations of policy are sensitive to sectoral demands. Intensified process of globalization and growth of service-orientated economies, coupled with changing labour market demographics, have brought issues of equality and diversity to the forefront of the corporate business agenda. The legislative-driven approaches to equality are slowly replaced by inclusive diversity approaches which are underpinned by a recognition of the business benefits of equality and diversity. Recruitment agencies are at the heart of these developments, as the key brokers in the employment relationship in today's economy. They are destined to play more significant roles in carving out future jobs and offer different ways of working. Therefore, the employment agencies' role in promoting the essential linkages between equality and flexible working cannot be overstated. There is also a growing recognition among the recruitment agencies that equality, diversity and flexible working do not only make business sense for employers, but also enable the agencies themselves to reach a wider pool of candidates.

Our analysis suggests that private sector recruitment agencies may play a crucial role in tackling discrimination and segregation in the field of employment on the basis of gender, ethnic and religious background, age, sexual orientation and disability. However, this role in not fulfilled due to their low levels of awareness and commitment regarding diversity and equality issues. What we observed in most of our interviews is the avoidance of responsibility on these issues – what we termed as 'passing the buck'. In other words, most of our respondents argued that they respond to the requests and priorities of their clients which, they implicitly assumed, immunize them against taking any responsibility in combating the indirect discriminatory practices throughout the recruitment process. On the other hand, human resource departments of the public and private sector clients increasingly transfer their role in the recruitment and selection of their workforce to the agencies. In some cases, recruitment agencies even take over the function of not only recruiting, but also managing, the workers on behalf of their clients (Ward, 2002). Under these circumstances, a vacuum of responsibility is created where neither the agency, nor the client, assumes a role in the provision of equality and diversity.

Still, some activities of the agencies unintentionally open up opportunities for some groups of female workers, while others reproduce the existing discriminatory patterns and mechanisms. Furthermore, the REC plays a crucial role in raising the diversity and equality awareness in the sector through its Diversity Diagnostic and the Diversity Pledge.

Appendix A: Diversity interview schedule

Exercise: Use the below interview schedule in order to interview one or more private sector recruitment agents. These interviews should then be thematically analysed by being based on the framework described in this chapter.

Explanation:

The aim of this research is to understand the equality and diversity approaches of the private sector recruitment agencies and to explore the support that is provided to women and men by the agencies with a particular attention to the advice and guidance available to help women progress into more senior positions in organisations. We will ask you questions about the operations of your organisations; advice and guidance programmes provided by your organisation particularly to your female candidates; the demographic composition of candidates; and your organisation's approach regarding the issues of equality and diversity. No individual names will be revealed and they will be kept strictly confidential.

1. **Could you shortly tell me about the operations of your organisation?**
   Probe: What are the key guidance and employment programmes provided by your company?
   Probe: Which fields of employment do you cover?

2. **How do you create a candidate pool?**
   Probe: Advertise, internet, TV, newspaper?

3. **Do you do anything to attract women candidates specifically?**
   Probe: Could you explain?

4. **When a prospective candidate comes to register what do you do?**
   Probe: Could you explain the process a bit?
   Probe: May I have a sample of application forms?

5. **How do you find the firms with vacancies?**

6. **Could you tell us about the firms you are working with?**
   Probe: Which sectors?
   Probe: Large, small or medium sized?

7. **Do the firms ever request a gender balance in recruitment?**
   Probe: Could you explain?
   Probe: The reasons?
   Probe: What kind of firms?

8. **How do you match the clients with candidates?**
   Probe: Do you carry out recruitment and selection activities?

Probe: Do you have equality/diversity training programmes for your recruiters?

Probe: Do you address equality, work life balance and flexible working issues in the selection and recruitment process? How?

9. **Could you tell us if in your opinion particular groups of women or men might be disadvantaged by the requirements of some or all of these programmes?** (i.e. having an age limit?)

10. **What is your overall equality and diversity approach?**
    Probe: Do you have an equality and diversity strategy? Could you explain?
    Probe: Do you have any equality and diversity programme or activity? Could you explain?
    Probe: Is there an overall culture of equality and diversity?

11. **Do you have an equal opportunities or diversity policy?**
    Probe: Could we see it?
    Probe: How did you formulate it?
    Probe: Do you give this to staff? How?

12. **Could you tell us how gender, age, ethnicity and disability issues are addressed in your operations?**

13. **Do you have an anti-harassment and bullying policy?**
    Probe: For your staff? For your candidates?
    Probe: Do you have a grievance procedure?

14. **Do you have an equality monitoring system?**
    Probe: For the staff, for the candidates?
    Probe: How do you monitor?
    Probe: What aspects of your candidates and staff do you monitor? (gender, ethnicity, age, disability etc.)

15. **What is the gender composition of your staff?**
    Probe: Do you breakdown the gender statistics of your staff by age and ethnicity?
    Probe: Could you tell me about the gender composition of your staff by age and ethnicity?

16. **What is the gender composition of your candidates?**
    Probe: Do you breakdown the gender statistics of your candidates by age and ethnicity?
    Probe: Could you tell me about the gender composition of your candidates by age and ethnicity?

17. **Is there a different pattern in terms of recruitment of women and men in different sectors, posts, levels of authority? Could you explain?**
    Probe: In terms of occupational categories, part-time/full-time, temporary/permanent contract?

Probe: How do you see the recruitment of young, middle aged and older women in your company?

Probe: How do you see the recruitment of women from BME backgrounds in your company?

Probe: Do you see a change in this pattern over the last years?

18. **Do female and male candidates have different requests and interests in terms of their preferred conditions of work?**
    Probe: What are they? (space, time, geography)
    Probe: How do you address them?

19. **Do you take any measures to encourage women into atypical (non-traditional) forms of employment and occupation?**
    Probe: Are there any ways in which traditional occupational segregation patterns are reinforced or combated through your programmes and procedures?
    Probe: In what ways are traditional working patterns reinforced or flexible working and work life balance promoted by your organisation?

20. **Do you offer flexible working options for your candidates? Could you explain?**
    Probe: If yes, what is the main reason for implementing flexible working?
    Probe: If no, if you offered flexible options, do you think that you could gain new customers? Why not?
    Probe: Are the graduates and non-graduates different or similar in terms of their pursuit of flexible working patterns later in their careers? Women and men?

21. **How would you evaluate the demands and perspectives of your candidates in terms of flexible working?**
    Probe: The individual candidates?
    Probe: The firms?

22. **Do you see flexible working as an investment for the future?**
    Probe: Is the offer of flexibility now and in the future a key recruitment selling point?
    Probe: Can the lack of flexible working options lead to failure to recruit certain groups?

23. **Do you have any advice and guidance provided to professional women to help them progress into more senior positions in organisations?**
    Probe: Do you have any specific initiatives that seek to promote women into managerial posts?
    Probe: Do you have any guidance and employment programmes on encouraging women into senior posts?
    Probe: What are they?

24. **Do you have any advice and guidance provided to professional women to help them return to work after a career break and resume their career?**
    Probe: What are they?
    Probe: How effective are they?

25. **Do you have any examples of good practice or examples of cases in terms of encouraging women into senior posts?**
    Probe: Could you explain?

26. **How do you evaluate the changes in the labour market trends in the last decades with regard to supply and demand of labour?**
    Probe: Do you experience any difficulties in recruiting for certain posts and positions or in certain sectors of work? Can you explain?
    Probe: Lack of enough skilled people for certain areas, posts, jobs? What do you do to overcome this?
    Probe: With regard to supply and demand of labour for women (and professional women)?
    Probe: Difficulties in recruiting women for certain posts and positions or in certain sectors of work? How do you deal with that challenge?

27. **How do you evaluate the changes in the labour market trends in the last decades with regard to changes in the needs of female and male employees (i.e. caring responsibilities)?**
    Probe: What kind of actions do you take to meet this new challenge?

28. **Are you a member of REC?**
    Probe: Are you aware of the equality and diversity policies of your competitors in this market? How would you compare your organisation?
    Probe: Are you aware of REC's diversity policy? What do you think of it?

29. **Could you please tell me any additional comments you feel are relevant to our understanding of your organisation's approach to equality and diversity particularly in relation to encouraging and helping women into senior positions?**

30. **Do you know any other recruitment agencies that may be interested in participating in our research?**
    Probe: May I have their contact details?
    Probe: Could you introduce me to them?

31. **Do you know any agency that specialises in business services, such as accounting and other financial investment services; legal and advisory services; health; education and hi-tech manufacturing?**

Thank you very much for your time and support.

Further reading

Battu, H., Seaman, P. and Zenou, Y. (2004) 'Job Contact Networks and the Ethnic Minorities', Working Paper no. 628, The Research Institute of Industrial Economics.

Böheim, R. and Taylor, M.P. (2002) 'Job Search Methods, Intensity and Success in Britain in the 1990s', Working Paper no. 0206, Department of Economics Johannes Kepler, University of Linz.

Mayrhofer, W. (1997) 'Warning: Flexibility Can Damage your Organizational Health', *Employee Relations*, vol. 19, pp. 519–34.

Michielsens, E., Shackleton, L. and Urwin, P. (2000) 'PPPs and the Jobless: Can Private Employment Agencies help Deliver the New Deals?', *New Economy*, vol. 7, pp. 168–71.

Powell, G.N. (1987) 'The Effects of Sex and Gender on Recruitment', *Academy of Management Review*, vol. 12, pp. 731–43.

Purcell, K. and Cam, S. (2002) 'Employment Intermediaries in the UK: Who Uses them?', ESRU Working Paper no.7, The Research Institute of Industrial Economics.

Rolfe, H. and Nadeem, S. (2006) 'Opening up Opportunities through Advice and Guidance', Equal Opportunities Commission Working Paper Series no. 49, Manchester: EOC.

Ward, K., Grimshaw, D., Rubery, J. and Beynon, H. (2001) 'Dilemmas in the Management of Temporary Work Agency Staff', *Human Resource Management Journal*, vol. 11, no. 4, pp. 3–21.

Watts, A.G. (1996) 'Careers Guidance and Public Policy', in A.G. Watts, B. Law, J. Killeen, J.M. Kidd and R. Hawthorn (eds), *Rethinking Careers Education and Guidance: Theory, Policy and Practice*. London: Routledge, pp. 380–91.

The Case of Work Placements in the Creative and Cultural Industries

9.1 Introduction

We have discussed the implications of sector on global diversity management in the previous chapter. In this chapter, we focus on the creative and cultural industry, which reveals a different set of issues. We present the findings of a scoping study of London-based higher education organizations' work placement practices within the creative and cultural industries. The project was commissioned by the London Centre for Arts and Cultural Enterprise (LCACE), with the funding of Arts Council England. Within that framework, this research project involved documentary reviews and interviews with representatives from higher education institutions and organizations in the creative and cultural industry, as well as students who are undertaking their placement projects through these institutions and organizations.

In Section 9.2 we will explain the key aims as well as the methods of the research project. There is a literature review in Section 9.3, which explores work placement practices in the creative and cultural industries. In Section 9.4 we will provide an overview and analysis of the findings of the field research and, in section 9.5, we present our conclusions. In the appendices, we offer a sectoral review of the creative and cultural industry, and supply the three sets of interview schedules used for studying equality and diversity practices for work placement students, institutions and higher education organizations in the sector.

9.2   Conducting research in the creative and cultural industries

The work was conducted in three phases. The first stage involved a systematic review of the relevant academic and practitioner literature on work placement in general and work placement practices within the creative and cultural industries in particular, in order to situate the practice of work placement within the creative and cultural industries in the London-based Higher Education Institutions (HEIs). The systematic literature review was drawn from academic and practitioner sources, as well as publications produced by relevant Government departments.

The second stage involved a detailed exploration of the work placement practice in creative and cultural industries in London. At this stage the investigation was informed by four sources: (i) the existing documentation (institutional documents and grey literature collected from the HEIs participating in the project, as well as from the host institutions) on work placement practices and models; (ii) interviews with the persons who are responsible for the work placement exercise in the arts and humanities departments in their institutions; (iii) interviews with arts and humanities students who have an experience of work placement; and (iv) interviews with London-based host institutions which offer work placements.

Firstly, documentation made available by the HEIs was collected and reviewed to scope different models of work placement utilized by them. This documentation included guidelines and handbooks for students and host institutions, and work placement handbooks for students and course module outlines. In addition, documentary evidence was collected and reviewed from the organizations that host the work placements.

Secondly, telephone interviews were conducted with the key persons who were responsible for the work placement in their organization, in order to further identify the models of work placement and to investigate the way in which the effectiveness of these models are evaluated by the institutions. In addition to the seven LCACE partners (Birkbeck University of London; City University; the Courtauld Institute; Goldsmiths College, University of London; King's College London; Queen Mary, University of London; and Royal Holloway, University of London), we contacted 13 other London-based HEIs with arts and humanities departments to request interviews. Research access was granted by 10 of those 20 HEIs. In total, 11 interviews were conducted. In-line with tender specifications, LCACE partners were directly included in the study. The selection criteria for the other HEIs was (i) representation of different institutional configurations, such as old and new university sector institutions and ones with and without dedicated placement facilities for cultural industries; and (ii) a high level of representation of students from BME backgrounds, since we aimed to acquire a sample that would be sufficient to allow us to investigate the work placement experiences of such students.

Throughout the interviews, we used a semi-structured schedule which was constructed subsequent to the systematic literature review in the first stage of the project, and which was revised in-line with the suggestions of the steering committee. During the interviews with the HEIs we aimed to address the following issues:

- the range of work placement practices in the institution;
- the communication with the host organization;
- the process of matching the students with the host organization;
- good practices/examples of work placement;
- models of evaluation for work placement practices;
- opinions about the impact of work placement on host organizations;
- mechanisms of feedback from the host organizations;
- opinions about the impact of work placement on students;
- mechanisms of feedback from the students;
- barriers to successful placements;
- opinions about the impact of work placement practices on the collaboration and knowledge transfer between HEIs and the arts and cultural industries;
- opinions on the impact of students' demographic background on the success of the work placement.

Thirdly, telephone interviews were conducted with students who had completed their work placement or who were currently engaged in one. In total we limited the number of student interviews to ten due to the limited budget of the project. We aimed to reach a balanced sample for these interviews with respect to participant students' genders and ethnic backgrounds. Throughout the interviews, we used a semi-structured schedule (see Appendix D) which aimed to explore the students' feelings and opinions on the following issues:

- impacts of work-based placements on students in terms of employment opportunities;
- impacts of work-based placements on students' knowledge of the creative and culture industry;

- impacts of work-based placements on students' understanding of the world of work and the skills they require for the careers they wish to pursue;
- impacts of work-based placements on students in terms of their future career plans;
- impacts of work-based placements on students' academic work in their schools;
- students' personal assessments of different models of placement;
- students' criticisms about the practice of work placement in their institution;
- students' recommendations for improving the work placement practice in their institutions;
- students' levels of satisfaction from the work placement experience;
- students' general feelings about the work placement experience;
- the ways in which experiences of students from different gender and ethnic backgrounds differ regarding the above.

Lastly, five interviews were conducted with four host organizations in the creative and cultural industries which offer work placement. A semi-structured interview schedule was designed. During the interviews we aimed to address the following issues:

- range of work placement programmes offered by the organization;
- the communication with the HEIs;
- the process of matching the students with their work placement role;
- good practices/examples of work placement;
- models of evaluation for work placement practices;
- opinions about the impact of work placement on the organization;
- mechanisms of feedback to the students and HEIs;
- opinions about the impact of work placement on students;
- mechanisms of feedback from the students;
- barriers to successful placements;
- opinions about the impact of work placement practices on the collaboration and knowledge transfer between HEI and the arts and cultural industries;
- opinions on the impact on students' demographic background on the success of the work placement.

All interviews, except one, were tape-recorded and fully transcribed for the purposes of qualitative analysis. Confidentiality concerns were sensitively addressed and anonymity will be ensured for all interviews. In order to secure informed consent, the aims, purposes, processes and expected outcomes, as well as deliverables of the research project, were communicated to the partici-pants through a cover letter. The interviews and the documentary evidence were fully anonymized. No participant details are disclosed as a consequence of interviews. The researchers safeguard the confidentiality of any data supplied for the purposes of this research.

Stage Three of the project was built upon the conceptual framework drawn in the first two phases, combining the systematic literature review in the field and evidence from existing documents and interviews. The interview transcripts and documentary evidence were subject to axial and open coding and analysed using thematic analysis techniques.

This chapter provides a full account and discussion of the findings, implications for policy and methods. It also includes an indication of the problem areas and recommendations for improvement.

9.3   Work placement practices within the creative and cultural industries

Much of the literature on work placements comes from disciplines of study which have strong traditions of work placements in industry and from countries where work placement is common practice within the higher education sector. We have reflected best practice examples, drawing on interdisciplinary as well as international studies of work placement.

There are a wide range of terms used to refer to work placements. The National Council of Work Experience (NCWE 2006) provides definitions of the various terms, revealing their slight differences from work placements:

Sandwich and industrial placements: a fixed term period of assessed, paid work that forms part of a university degree. It often lasts for a full year.

Work-based project: A specific piece of assessed work for a university course, undertaken at an employer's premises.

Work placement: A period of work experience, which can be paid or unpaid, and is part of a course of study. This can be arranged through the university with an employer or by the student and is for an agreed period of time.

Internship: A phrase that is increasingly used by large companies and refers to a placement within their organization, usually over 6–12 weeks during the summer holiday.

The NCWE also lists other forms of work experiences:

Voluntary work: Any type of work undertaken for no payment, usually outside of the university course in a student's spare time.

Part-time work: Paid or unpaid work, undertaken either during term-time, in the holidays or both, for less than 35 hours per week. For a project that is providing assessment and accreditation of part-time work, see the CRAC Insight Plus programme at www.insightplus.co.uk.

Work shadowing: Where a student observes a member of staff working in an organization, and so gains an understanding of what a particular job entails.

Shell step: Vacation work experience where students undertake a specific project within a small- to medium-sized business for eight weeks during the summer. See www.shellstep.org.uk.

In this chapter, the term work placement is used as a period of work in industry and which is recognized as a structured period of learning by the respective higher education and host institution of the student.

Any scholarly attempt at describing industrial practices in any sector of work or occupation would start with defining the boundaries and content of the sector which is about to be brought under public scrutiny. In keeping with this tradition, we would like to start our review by defining 'creative and cultural industries'. The Creative Industries Task Force, in their national mapping exercise in 1998, defined 'creative industries' as (British Council 2006):

> Those industries that have their origin in individual creativity, skill and talent and which have a potential for wealth and job creation through the generation and exploitation of intellectual property.

The Department for Culture, Media and Sport (DCMS 2006) offer a similar definition:

> We define the creative industries as those industries which have their origin in individual creativity, skill and talent and which have a potential for wealth and job creation through the generation and exploitation of intellectual property. This includes advertising, architecture, the art and antiques market, crafts, design, designer fashion, film and video, interactive leisure software, music, the performing arts, publishing, software and computer games, television and radio.

UNESCO (2006) defines 'cultural industries' in a way which overlaps with the definition of 'creative industries':

> It is generally agreed that this term applies to those industries that combine the creation, production and commercialisation of contents which are

intangible and cultural in nature. These contents are typically protected by copyright and they can take the form of goods or services. Depending on the context, cultural industries may also be referred to as 'creative industries', sunrise or 'future oriented industries' in the economic jargon, or content industries in the technological jargon. The notion of cultural industries generally includes printing, publishing and multimedia, audio-visual, phono-graphic and cinematographic productions, as well as crafts and design. For some countries, this concept also embraces architecture, visual and per-forming arts, sports, manufacturing of musical instruments, advertising and cultural tourism. Cultural industries add value to contents and generate val-ues for individuals and societies. They are knowledge and labour-intensive, create employment and wealth, nurture creativity – the 'raw material' they are made from – and foster innovation in production and commercialisation processes. At the same time, cultural industries are central in promoting and maintaining cultural diversity and in ensuring democratic access to culture. This twofold nature – both cultural and economic – builds up a distinctive profile for cultural industries. During the 90s they grew exponentially, both in terms of employment creation and contribution to GNP. Today, global-isation offers new challenges and opportunities for their development.

The issue of definition is an important one within the creative and cultural industries. There remains much debate about where the boundaries of the cre-ative industries might cross with the cultural industries. Although the purpose of this chapter is not to engage in a deep semantic debate about the origins and boundaries of cultural and creative industries, it is nevertheless important to note that the definitions above indicate the significance of the role that cre-ative and cultural industries provide in terms of wealth and job creation as well as economic regeneration. Furthermore, creativity is the 'golden thread' that draws together all the different elements of the creative and cultural industries (Hall and Bewick 2006).

The Rt Hon. Tessa Jowell MP (2006), Secretary of State for Culture, Media and Sport, made a speech on 14 March about the importance of the creative industries. The below excerpts from this speech highlight the economic sig-nificance of the creative and cultural industries in the UK:

The global market value of the creative industries has increased from $831 billion in 2000 to $1.3 trillion in 2005; more than 7 per cent of global GDP. In the UK, KPMG predicts 46 per cent employment growth and 136 per cent output growth in the Creative Industries between 1995 and 2015 . . . Many of you may remember the Creative Industries mapping document published by my predecessor Chris Smith eight years ago. A useful bench-mark, but just look at what has occurred since then. In 1998, employment in the UK's creative economy stood at around one and a half million people. Today they employ almost 2 million people. These sectors now produce almost £1 in £12 of our total Gross Value Added (GVA) – a higher proportion than in any other country, and they contribute £11.4billion to our balance of trade, well ahead of economic sectors such as construction and insurance, and twice as much as the widely praised pharmaceutical sector.

Tessa Jowell continues her speech by noting how the above economic success can be cultivated by schools and universities:

Of course, the infrastructure for the creative industries is already supported by public policy at national, regional and local level. A schools system and University sector that nurtures the creative *and* entrepreneurial talent of all our young people is essential to providing the highly skilled labour force needed by business. And our HE sector can act as a magnet for talent from all over the world.

The size and scope of creative and cultural industries in the UK and London are explored through several reports by the CCS consultation papers and reports from the Arts Council England (see Appendix A).

What are the drivers for university–industry collaboration in training and work?

The issue of workplace training is highly politicized in the UK. The current government agenda aims to close the training gap that scholars such as Finegold and Soskice (1988) have identified. However, the training gap is a contested issue. For example, Wolf (2002) demonstrates that there is not a training gap to be filled in the UK and that the UK economy is not driven by a low-skilled workforce as suggested by the proponents of the training gap hypothesis. Any conclusion as to the ongoing political debate on this training gap has implications as to how work placements are treated by the state, universities and the industry. Under the current Labour Government, the drive is towards supporting workplace learning through structured mechanisms of university–industry collaboration.

Despite wide spread support for university–industry collaboration, the evidence for the success of current initiatives in the UK is only partial. This raises concerns about a possible gap between the discourse and reality of placement initiatives. For example, Duignan's study (2002) reveals no difference in terms of academic achievement of students who took work placements and who did not. Similarly, Westhead *et al.* (2001) argue that in their study of students who have taken up a programme offered by Shell plc did not perform in a way which is significantly different from their counterparts who have not partici-pated in the programme.

Under its various guises as industrial or professional placements, or sandwich courses, work experience is now a familiar feature of higher and further educa-tion in Britain. However, Uzzell argued in 1986 that much of the literature in the field is highly descriptive and largely a theoretical. Since the 1980s, owing to the strength of the university–industry collaboration drives of the respective UK gov-ernments, there have been major developments in the field of work placements, although the literature in the field has remained fragmented and largely a critical.

Hutton (2006: 23) reviews the current situation of work-based learning in the creative and cultural industries. He explains that there were drastic improve-ments to the quantity of workplace learning initiatives in the last couple of years:

By 2001 it was clear that the number of young people taking up work-based learning had not increased. In fact between 2000 and 2003 the number of young people starting apprenticeships fell from 76,800 to 47,300. However, things have turned around more recently. By 2004–05, about a quarter of a million young people were pursuing an apprenticeship and some 130,000 employers were involved. The Government has hit its target of 175,000 under-22-year-olds starting an apprenticeship by July 2005, which is a major improvement. The new target is that 35 per cent should start an apprenticeship by 2010 – taking the UK to the North West European average.

These developments should be seen in the context of the sizeable contri-bution that creative and cultural industries make to the UK economy. In recent years, awareness of the significance of the industry to the economic and social well-being of the UK has become the major driver for reform in terms of work-based learning in the sector. However, reflecting on the eco-nomic success of the sector, Hall (2006: 4) cautions against complacency:

While the UK's creative and cultural sector is at the heart of the knowledge economy, there is no room for complacency. The competition is already snapping at our heels. But for many of the people working in our area, deal-ing with these challenges is difficult. Over 25 per cent of the workforce are freelance or working as individuals. Organizations are small. We are a sector characterised as freelance and micro, where people's skills are too often under-capitalised or not recognised, and where the sector as a whole is under-managed. People are also motivated to enter or work in this sector for differ-ent reasons and at different times, hence the large number of volunteers.

The porous and fragmented nature of the sector with domination of micro- , self-employed and small businesses means that job security, relative stability in pay and conditions of work do not prevail in the creative and cultural industries. So, what can be done to improve the conditions of work and structural fragmentation in the sector? It is naive to assume that self-regulation of the current situation will lead to better outcomes. However, it is also possible to argue that a very managerialist model may stifle creativity and innovation which are essential ingredients of this sector. However, this debate is futile in the light of the fact that it is still possible to provide policies, support structures and management perspectives that foster rather than constrain innovation and creativity.

What is the role of the state in the creative and cultural industries?

There have been state-level initiatives to boost support for the creative and cultural industries. The Creative Industries Task Force was established by the Prime Minister in 1997 and led by Government Ministers and leaders from the creative industries sectors. Between 1997 and 2000 the Task Force advised on policy development. The work of the Task Force is continued by an interdepartmental government committee, the Ministerial Creative Industries Strategy Group. Furthermore, there are other state agencies which focus on creative and cultural industries: the Creative Industries Export Promotion Advisory Group (CIEPAG), with a joint secretariat from the Department for Culture, Media and Sport (DCMS) and UK Trade and Investment (TPUK) serves as an interesting example. This group had four subgroups: Content, Design, Heritage and Tourism, and Performing Arts. However, CIEPAG ceased operation in 2002, leaving the four subgroups to be re-established as Creative Export, Design Partners, Cultural Heritage and Tourism (CH&T) and Performing Arts International Development (PAID). DCMS and TPUK continue to provide the secretariat for these four groups.

The Creative Industries Higher and Further Education Forum is an organized group made up of representatives of higher education, further education, creative industries, education and research. It aims to investigate how to strengthen the collaborative activities between higher education, further education and the creative industries (DCMS 2006), as a follow up to the Lambert Review of Business–University Collaboration (2003).

At the nexus of state policy and involvement of young people in arts also resides the Arts Council England (2005: 11), which commits itself to the following strategies for involving young people in the arts:

- support activity that broadens young people's experience of different art forms, practices and traditions;
- support activity that provides young people with routes for progression through their arts experiences;
- adapt the ways we work to allow for more coherent planning and direct engagement with children and young people and their services;

- identify organizations with the skills and commitment to pioneer new ways of working with and for children and young people;
- review our portfolio of regularly funded organizations to ensure that we are supporting a wide range of high-quality provision for children and young people.

These objectives are congruent with and relevant to a drive towards improving work placement experiences of students, most of whom are young, in creative and cultural industries.

What are the likely problems associated with work placements?

Recent moves by universities to embrace industry-based learning has implications for support made available to students undertaking this type of education. This is particularly important in order for universities and host institutions to foresee and address proactively any problems due to the organization of their workplace arrangements.

There are studies that suggest that work placement programmes may involve some difficulties for institutions as well as students. Among a group of social work students, Maidment (2003) investigated problems that students face during their work placement in the industry. She noted that workplace stress and conflict are considerable concerns for students, as they often lack skills and organizational status in order to resolve conflicts in work experiences. Furthermore, there are financial pressures on placement students, who are underpaid by their institutions and fall out of the normal higher education funding nets. It is clear that the problems experienced by this group of social work students require pedagogical strategies in order to transfer skills to deal with workplace stress and conflict, and to identify strategies for financial survival. Maidment argues that these skills should be offered as part of the curriculum before the students embark on their placement experience in the industry.

In a study of work experience in the hospitality, leisure and tourism industries, Kelley-Patterson and George (2001) found that divergent expectations of employers and lack of strong collaborative ties between workplaces, HEIs and students are the main barriers in the way of a successful placement experience. The authors also identified that the nature of the contract also changes from relational to transactional between work placement and graduate employment. Therefore, the authors call for attention to the nature of the psychological contract, as well as the written contract, in order to understand both the subjective and the objective realities of work experience.

Ashworth and Saxton (1992) note that assessment of work placement outcomes may suffer from various forms of assessment bias. The authors argue that these could be eliminated with careful investigation of assessment systems for bias.

What are the issues of equality and diversity in work placements?

Higher education institutions as well as host institutions have both legal, moral and business reasons to consider equal opportunities practice across all strands of equality and diversity. The Arts Council England (2005:10) also highlights its desire to extend support to individuals in priority groups including:

- low-income families;
- those living in areas of London with few, or no, appropriate cultural facilities or opportunities;
- those with disabilities;
- those who are vulnerable or at risk.

Skill (National Bureau for Students with Disabilities) has issued some guidelines for students, HEIs and employers to consider in addressing issues of disability during study and work experience. Skill (2006) offers information and an information phone line to help students with disabilities to achieve their full potential. Blankfield (2001) argues that the provision of work placement should be designed in a way which makes the experience more welcoming for students with disabilities. Blankfield examined the experiences of a group of students with dyslexia. Her findings suggest that students, except for one, found it difficult to disclose their conditions to their employers. This requires the workplaces and the HEIs to recognize the unique requirements of the whole spectrum of disabilities. Treating all disabilities the same would not yield positive outcomes, the author argues.

One of the important issues of equality and diversity in work placements is the place of minority ethnic students, as well as students who are non-native speakers of the English language. Through a case study of placement students at Surrey University, Mandilaras (2004) identifies a gap between the performance of British and international students subsequent to their placement year. A study of international students' placement outcomes in the US (Shen and Herr 2004) also demonstrates that the international students find the counselling and placement services offered by the centralized university administration as ill-fitting their requirements. This gap is of importance in terms of the equal opportunities that universities profess to commit themselves to: although the UK higher education system accepts a large number of fee-paying international students, there is a growing resentment about their arrival in such numbers and a widening of the divide between the treatment of home and foreign students. Samway and McKeon (1999) seek to debunk some of the myths associated with the education of language-minority students. The authors identify that the HEIs have a responsibility and major role to play in the successful delivery of higher education curricula and placement of students to workplaces. Furthermore, Beard *et al.* (2001) demonstrate how an employer of international students can provide an environment in which the student achieves personal and professional growth. The authors argue that professional and personal growth for the student can be predicted by the negotiated placement objectives between student and employer and on-going support from stakeholders during the placement.

What makes a successful work placement?

Research on work placements and what contributes to the success of work placement experience in the creative and cultural industries has been sparse. However, there are some examples and case studies from the UK, and more widely internationally, which highlight the need to consider the multiple constituents, as well as the multidimensional nature, of work placement experience (Neill and Mulholland 2003). The main institutional constituents of the student experience in work placements are the institutions which host the student and their university programmes which prepare them for the experience and monitor their progress. The number of individuals involved in the process from these key organizations may vary depending on institutional arrangements. Student experience is also multidimensional, involving both subjective and objective experiences of work placement. Research from work placements in Australia (Smith *et al.* 2001) suggests that the students' social backgrounds, previous work experience, family, financial and employment commitments influence their choice of work placements. This suggests that work placement experience is not an outcome of only a tripartite relationship between the HEI, the host institution and the student. Indeed there is a wider array of institutions and individuals in a student's social and work network that shapes the choice and quality of the student placement experience. Therefore, a successful work placement design should encourage better ties between these diverse constituent groups and across the multiple dimensions of the work placement experience.

There is a general agreement that a number of benefits can accrue from the students' placement year (Richardson and Blakeney 1998). However, reaping these benefits requires the host institutions and the HEIs to consider a number of factors that influence the success of work placements. Several authors have attempted to develop models and reveal factors that contribute to the success of student placements: Leslie (1994) offers a total quality management model for organizing work experience. The model suggests that quality should be considered at every phase and by all constituent groups, including individuals who are involved in the work placement experience of students. The model suggests that through small and gradual quality improvements, the work placement experience can be radically improved in the long term. The longer term perspective, however, may conflict with the short-term expectations of the line management in the industry, the author contends. Drawing on a case study, Barthorpe and Hall (2000) elaborate on a collaborative placement and careers preparation programme. This model involves students being prepared for their placement experience through a set of training programmes which aims to improve their employability and survival skills in industrial placements.

The studies which focus on success factors for work placements are more widely available across a wide range of sectors, industries and national contexts: Crebert *et al.* (2004) have studied student perceptions of three learning contexts: university, work placement and post-graduation employment in the US. Their study reveals that although students value their university education, they rate their learning in work placement and subsequent employment very highly. It is interesting to note that the study shows that teamwork, being given responsibility, and collaborative learning are the most important factors for effective learning in the three contexts under consideration.

Drawing on a study of medical placements, Maurana *et al.* (2000) explain that partnerships between the HEI and the host institution are crucial for the success of the placement experience. They identify four stages in which the work placement can be fostered: (i) establish and build relationships between the HEIs and host institutions; (ii) develop common goals; (iii) develop and implement programmes; and (iv) maintain and expand progress. Such a stepwise approach to work placements is important as different stages of setting up a work placement programme requires different considerations.

Support for better coordination between host institutions and HEIs comes from Nolan's study (1998) of a group of Australian work placements, which identifies that a strategic approach should be adopted in order to strengthen the ties between these two parties. Similarly, Mulraney and Turner (2001) present a learning partnership model which recognizes the multiconstituent nature of relationships in work placements. The model suggests that the HEIs, host organizations and the students agree on a set of learning activities and then monitor and assess these with a view to generate benefits for all parties involved. The authors also argue that any preparatory training for work placement should consider unique sectoral and organizational configurations. They focus on the case of SMEs and work placements and effectively demonstrate that the absence of the SME sector in academic curricula does disservice to students who may opt for placement experience in that sector.

In their study of student work placements in hospitality management, McMahon and Quinn (1995) explain that there is a need for HEIs to build up successful relationships with individual companies for mutually beneficial outcomes in student learning. They also suggest that the HEIs must invest the necessary resources in the placement function in order to reap the suggested benefits. They also argue that the organizations must develop a more considered approach towards placements. In the same vein, the students should be positive and forthright in their attitude in order to benefit from the whole process.

Ashworth and Saxton (1992) explore the interpersonal dynamics of placement experience as possible source of success. They explain that the educational purpose of the placements should be supported by tutors from HEIs who are responsible for placement projects as well as workplace mentors who are assigned to assess student performance. Cahill's (1996) research on students' experiences of mentorship suggests that students perceive mentorship more as a mechanism of control and less as a mechanism of support. The support function of mentoring activities is as vital as the control aspect of it for adding value to a student's experience of work placement.

Measurement is often considered an important precondition to manage any process, and the student placement experience is no exception. Whilst some occupational groups and certain industries incorporate elaborate assessment techniques in work placements, other industries adopt a more liberal laissez-faire approach to such assessment and management. One of the sectors where work placements are monitored and assessed is the health services sector (Nolan and Chung 1999; Drennan 2002) or in civil engineering (Majewski *et al.* 2000). Intersectoral transfer of knowledge may be a useful means of adopting monitoring and measurement tools in the cultural and creative industries, which appears in the literature to have little structured methods of engaging with such assessment mechanisms.

Although there may be some human errors in this interactive design, possible biases could be eliminated through careful design which makes assessment an integral part of the placement experience. Huntington *et al.* (1999) argue that successful assessment also relies on careful briefing and preparation of students prior to placement and close liaison between placement tutor, employer and student during the their work placement term.

The role of placement coordinators in students' experiences of work placements cannot be overstated. The placement coordinator role can be outlined in three different models: (1) a purely administrative model, in which a placement tutor is solely responsible for the placement function; (2) as part of a centralized administrative team in which the placement coordinator is a member at the HEI; and (3) a mixed role where the placement tutor is also an academic member of staff. Coll and Eames (2000) argue that the third model presents better prospects for students to combine their academic learning with work placement experience. Furthermore, the combined role allows for placement considerations to be integrated into the academic curriculum, should the placement coordinators champion such a cause. Newton and Smith (1998) argue that the role of the personal tutor is to help the students to develop both professionally and academically. To facilitate this, a good interpersonal relationship between student and personal tutor is essential. However, such a relationship requires time and effort on both student and tutor's part. Indeed, Saxton and Ashforth (1990) note that the supervisor is the most important factor in ensuring the success of the work placement. Schaafsma (1996) explains that the university and the workplace offer contested venues of learning. Work-based mentors should serve as trainers in order to engender more effective learning experiences for students. This may in most cases require the mentors in the host institutions to be trained.

In the same vein, based on a study of work placement experience of a set of Australian students, Cope *et al.* (2000) argue that the placement is a complex social and cognitive experience in which there are elements of situated learning. They also demonstrate that acceptance into the community of practice is an important aspect of this situated learning experience. This acceptance can be separated into a social acceptance which might be extended to any student and a professional acceptance which relies on the display of appropriate competence. In the former case, issues of diversity and equality are important considerations for the host institutions and the HEIs in order to ensure that the students receive fair and decent treatment in their social encounters as well as professional work in the host institution. The authors also argue that any mentoring, monitoring and assessment schemes which are organized by the host and HEIs should take into consideration both social and professional aspects of the student workplace experience.

Research by Misko (1998) in an Australian setting revealed that there is a correlation between student expectations and outcomes of workplace experience. The research suggests that if the student expectations are set high regarding workplace experience, they can make better and fuller use of the available opportunities. This suggests that the HEIs and the host institutions can facilitate induction programmes which set realistic and positive expectations of the workplace experience in order to ensure that the students can make full use of possible options. Furthermore, Drever and Cope (1999) demonstrate that students may also be equipped with skills to relate their theoretical and conceptual understanding to their work placement experiences. This will require the prework placement curriculum to introduce students to the ideas of communities of practice and situated learning. This may then be supported by monitoring of student learning through a placement report.

Hislop *et al.* (1996) note that in order to foster a culture of knowledgeable practice, HEIs should consider various aspects of work placement and proactively integrate these considerations into their curriculum design. This means that the teaching should be phased in synchrony with their placement experiences.

Neill *et al.* (2004) argue that part-time working has not been studied as a possible route into later work placement and a way of gaining students work-related experience. The authors argue that part-time student work can be brought into considerations of a student's learning in situated settings, and that this can help students acquire better placement experiences by drawing on their part-time work.

Morgan and Turner (2000) investigated the role of professional accreditation on the work placement experience of students, revealing that accreditation positively impacts on the placement experiences of students.

As the work placement experience takes place outside the university environment, university education during placement year displays similarities with distance learning. Hall *et al.* (2000) explore the possibilities of using Information Technology (IT) in order to improve student experience during work placement. Despite initial set-up costs being relatively high, the authors explain that the IT systems can help universities keep better track of student placements, whilst helping improve collaboration between different constituent groups. Gammie *et al.* (2002) also identify that distance learning systems help facilitate communication between stakeholders, and that such initial communication between the representatives of the host institution and the HEIs and the student is very crucial for the success of the placement experience. However, the authors point to the difficulties of ensuring equity in the adequate use of distance learning systems by all stakeholders.

There have been some national attempts in the UK to establish what constitutes a successful work placement. The National Council of Work Experience (2006) presents a checklist for ensuring work placement success. The list has been drawn up through a consultation with practitioners:

1 the student should be trained by the higher education institution (HEI) to identify potential learning outcomes;
2 learning and work objectives should be set by HEI, employer and student;
3 a supervisor trained in the objectives and learning outcomes of work experience should provide academic supervision and visit(s) to the host institution should take place;
4 regular feedback should be offered;
5 an appraisal should be planned during the work experience and at the end;
6 the work placement should involve a structured project when appropriate;
7 students should articulate their learning and achievements in written form;
8 an assessment is made, including an assessment of development of skills, by the HEI, employer and student;
9 the HEI and the host institution should offer recognition, credit or a certificate.

The literature suggests that successful planning and delivery of work placements require multiparty and multifaceted approaches. This can be achieved if work placements are designed with unique recognition of labour market dynamics, social and economic circumstances, unique institutional arrangements and requirements in both universities and host institutions, as well as the particular conditions, expectations and career ambitions of students who take up these work placements. The cycles of design with multiparty involvement, delivery, monitoring and revaluation and redesign activities are key requirements for a successful work placement process. These requirements suggest that a process approach to work placement design is of importance for successful delivery as well as progressive development of work placement projects.

9.4   Work placement practice within the creative and cultural industries in London-based HEIs: analysis of the study findings

The study has focused on three constituent groups involved in work placement practices in the creative and cultural industries in London: the Higher Education Institutions (HEIs), the host institutions and the students.

Work placement models and practices of the London-based HEIs

We have conducted 11 interviews with representatives of ten HEIs. Except for two LCACE partners, all of the HEIs that participated in this research had formal work placement programmes in place. However, the structure and nature of the work placement, and the associated requirements as well as the target student group, displayed variation.

To begin with, in all of the HEIs with formal placement programmes, work placement was a part of students' postgraduate studies at diploma or MA level. However, only three of the participating HEIs had work placement programmes for their undergraduate students. In four of the participant organizations work placement was a compulsory part of students' studies. In addition, one of the them had a work placement requirement as a part of one compulsory and one elective course module. Minimum required duration of the work placement varied from 30 hours to 30 working days. However, all HEIs reported that the students can do a longer placement if they wish so. Most of the participants also reported that they are flexible in terms of the type and location of the host institution, and gave the student the option to do their work placement in overseas organizations as well as in the UK-based ones.

The types of organizations that students can do their work placement in displayed a wide spectrum. All respondents reported that their students undertake their work placements in various kinds of organizations in the creative and cultural industry in terms of size and sector of the host. It is reported that students do their work placements with small- and medium-sized organizations as well as very large ones. Some of the respondents argued that their students sometimes do work placements even with individual artists or curators. In addition, host organizations mentioned by the respondents included both public and private sectors organizations in the creative and cultural industries. The host organizations named by the respondents included galleries, museums, libraries, performing arts organizations, festivals, media organizations and funding organizations.

The HEIs used several methods to reach and communicate with the host organizations that may offer work placements for their students. All of the participant HEIs kept a list of host organizations which was then made available to the students. In addition they actively sought work placement offers from their alumni. Moreover, in most of the cases the module tutors and work placement administrators exploited their personal contacts to widen their pool of host organization.

Work placement opportunities were communicated to the students through distributing the list of host organizations. Different work placement opportunities were also advertised through email and the school website. With the exception of two cases, tutors as well as the work placement administrators were involved in reaching out to and communicating with the host organizations, and in providing the students with the information regarding work placement opportunities. However, the level of involvement and support by the tutors and placement administrators to the students during the search for and application to a work placement position varied extensively from one HEI to another. In some of the participating HEIs, the school offered a minimal support to the student by only letting them know the names of different host organizations at which they could do their work placement. These HEIs also strongly encouraged their students to take a proactive role, to look for other work placement opportunities and to find their own placements. In other cases, the students were offered extensive guidance and advice to find a work placement. In these cases the tutors and administrators were actively involved in the communication between the student and the host organization as mediators, and took into account the student's needs and interests throughout the process.

In terms of formal structures of advice and guidance, only five of the participating HEIs provided their students with handbooks or guidelines and only two of them had formal documents that they sent out to the host organizations. Moreover, in only two of the HEIs there were formal sessions during the work placement to support and guide the student throughout the placement experience. As explained in the next sections, the absence of guidance from the school during the work placement led many students to feel left alone without support from time to time. Nevertheless, most of the HEIs offered some support and training sessions before the beginning of the work placement.

Our interviews revealed that structured and formal evaluation mechanisms regarding the impacts and success of the work placement was not available in most of the HEIs. The most common evaluation method was through the assessment of the students' reports or placement diaries in addition to the course evaluation forms. More active and objective evaluation methods are only used by a few of the participant HEIs. One of these was formal visits by the course tutor during the work placement where both the students and his/her line manager in the host organization were interviewed by the tutor. Unfortunately, only three of the participant HEIs had reported active involvement in the evaluation process through such formal visits. Nevertheless, two of the remaining respondents mentioned that they had informal telephone conversations with the host organizations regarding students' performance throughout the placement. Another HEI stated that they had a short feedback form that they sent out to the host organizations at the end of the work placement.

Overall, evaluation of the work placement was largely based on students' feedback in terms of their placement reports and diaries. This situation makes it impossible to assess the impact of work placement on the host organization. Interestingly, all of the respondents agreed that work placement may be an important medium for knowledge transfer between academia and industry. However, absence of effective techniques of evaluation and feedback from the host institutions renders it very hard to understand whether work placements fulfil such a role in the process of knowledge transfer and collaboration between the universities and industry.

Furthermore, the research findings suggested that feedback received from the students and assessment of their work placement performance were insufficient in terms of evaluating the satisfaction levels of the students and the impact of work placement experience on students' future employability. In general, most of the respondents stated that it was very uncommon for the students to be employed by the organization where they undertook their work placement. However, it is argued, the work placement contributes to students' employment prospects more indirectly through gaining them work experience, skills, knowledge of the industry and more importantly personal networks and contacts. Although, all respondents argued that work placement practice contributes to the future career of the students through providing them with skills, networks, contacts and work experience in the creative and cultural industry, most of the respondents failed to display any evidence to qualify this assertion. In other words, none of the HEIs monitored their work placement model in terms of its impact on the students' future employability.

The assessment of the performance of the host organization in terms of managing the work placement seemed to be even less significant. As we explain later many students complained about the lack of involvement of their school in terms of monitoring and controlling the host organizations' attitude towards work placement. In our interviews, only one of the respondents reported that they asked the host organization to sign an agreement at the start of his or her work placement. Obviously, the absence of any control mechanism by the HEI may lead to the exploitation of the student and to a dysfunctional work placement practice.

Similarly, the impact of work placement on the level of satisfaction of students from different demographic backgrounds were not monitored by the HEIs. In general, interviews suggested that the issues of equality and diversity were not high on the agenda of the participant HEIs within the scope of work placement practices. When we asked the respondents whether they believed that their work placements may have different impacts by gender, ethnicity, age, disability, sexual orientation and religion of the students, all said that the success of the work placement depends on the personality of the student rather than their demographic characteristic. Most of them also argued that creative and cultural industries are female dominated and much more open to gay men and lesbians compared to other industries.

Many respondents noted that their students are very diverse in terms of their nationality, with many students from Europe, North America and South Asia. Interestingly, it is also reported that they do not have many black and ethnic minority students. Nevertheless, it was generally argued that the race and ethnicity of the student would not affect the success of the work placement. However, it was noted by many respondents that the linguistic skills of the students may be a barrier to a successful work placement. Seven respondents argued that the students whose first language is not English may perform poorly during their work placement particularly in the cases in which quick response is required, such as answering the telephone or making conversation. This demonstrates a general lack of self-critical thinking, as well as full awareness of equal opportunities, on the part of the research participants. However, this gap in terms of equal opportunities in the higher education sector is not peculiar to the arts and humanities fields, but rather is a feature of work placement practices in other fields as well. The paradox is that although the universities self-regulate in terms of their linguistic requirements in admissions, there is a continued resentment against international students about their perceived levels of English.

Models and practices of work placement in host institutions

In total we have conducted five interviews in four host institutions. Only one of the host institutions had a clear set of guidelines for placement experience. It offers a clear job description, an induction programme, and monitoring and appraisal structure. Furthermore, it provides opportunities for placement students to gain professional experience and join various important professional networks. It also professes to offer employment to a select number of placement students. There was evidence of supportive training and provision of feedback from host mentors, which aim to build students' personal and professional skills. These structures are offered in a contractual manner, covering both a transparent employment contract outlining expectations and responsibilities of the host institution and the student, as well as a strong sense of psychological contract, of expectations and responsibilities, which are fostered through mechanisms of acculturation and induction at work.

In the context of both contracts, trust between host and students is an aspect of work placement, absence of which is considered a serious barrier to successful work placement experience. All respondents argued that realistic expectations by students are key to the success of work placement. A respondent from the large host institution explained that students' narrow focus on furthering their own careers and network ties, as well as their disinterest in the vision and values of the organization, can also be detrimental to the building of trust between the parties. However, only two of the organizations mentioned the importance of reasonable expectations by the host institution. Treatment of students as 'free resources', in a city like London where living costs are prohibitive, may be perceived as exploitation, and this can clearly breach any trust that may be built between the host and the students.

It is interesting to note that the host institutions always refer to trust as a dual system between a student and themselves. This approach disregards the role of the HEIs in the tripartite relationships that characterize placements in the sector. Host institutions in our study failed to identify any meaningful relationships with HEIs in supervision and mentoring of the students. They would, for example, not offer feedback to the HEIs regarding the placement performance of the student, unless it was explicitly requested. One of the respondents argued that such minimum involvement by the HEIs during the work placement is desirable for the host institutions. This may not be a wise strategy as there are also expectations placed on students by the HEIs, which will directly or indirectly affect their attitude and patterns of work placement. Moreover, the HEIs have a duty to protect their students with regards to workplace risk, involving issues of health and safety, and exploitation. Furthermore, they have a stake in ensuring that the work placement contributes to students' professional and personal development.

However, this level of sophistication and formality was not in evidence in the other three host institutions. It is important to note that it is still possible for host institutions to provide a similar experience to students with less sophisticated and formalized approaches. Indeed, this was the case in one of the small host institutions, in which both the student experience and the host institution discourse suggested a very productive and mutually beneficial relationship.

The attitude of the host institution seems to be the most important factor in delivery of effective placement programmes. These attitudes include the way students are treated when they join the organization, the voice of the placement students within the processes of decision-making in the organization and the perception of staff in host institutions of the work placement in terms of its value and worth for the organization.

In order to develop these positive attitudes and perceptions, host institutions need to invest in creating and disseminating a positive discourse surrounding placements. This was done through formalized newsletters and policy statements in the large institution (as explained above) and through informal means of integrating students to the work in the smaller organization.

However, two of the institutions that we have included in our study failed to offer a positive environment in which placements are experienced. The reasons for this are complex. Our interview with a representative of one of the institutions revealed that the students are perceived as low-level administrative and secretarial resources. They are expected, for example, to carry out an extensive range of mundane tasks such as photocopying and running errands. Their suitability for the placement is measured against their willingness and resilience to cope with such low-level administrative tasks. Therefore, their work in the host institution stretched beyond the expected scope of creative and cultural industry work.

Another participant from a host institution in this study also revealed that the students are employed as free or cheap resources to carry out work in roles which simply seek to reduce the low-level administrative burden of the full-time staff. When compared to the guidelines for successful placement experience in the literature review, these two work placement experiences suggest that there is little scope for students to develop their skills in those two host institutions.

One of the problems that appear to be common across the industry is the treatment of placement students as free or cheap labour. All of the host institutions in this study only paid for essential travel expenses. In the best paid case, the daily gratuity was £8. The institutions have suggested that the absence of pay was due to the sectoral difficulties in financing. The respondents also noted that there were many institutions that would not even pay this meagre amount towards the travels costs of students.

The sectoral excuse for low pay for placements is not legitimate when placed in the context of growth and economic development that has characterized the industry. Furthermore, the absence of pay means that students are self-selecting placement experience, based on their own financial conditions. It would be therefore naive to expect students from disadvantaged socio-economic backgrounds to be able to survive their placement experiences. This in itself has a strong explanatory power in terms of the current absence of heterogeneity in employment and student and consumer profiles of the cultural and creative industries.

Similar to higher education institutions in our study, the host organizations do not sufficiently attend to diversity and equality issues in work placements. However, two of them do realize that they should pay more attention to this in the context of placements. They are aware, for example, of local community diversity and its implications for recruitment of placement students.

However, diversity issues cannot be addressed simply through statements of intent and commitment. Diversity and equality are not only processes but also outcomes. The large host institution in our case stated that only 14 per cent of their placement students are from black and minority ethnic backgrounds. However, they would like to increase this number. Effective management of equality and diversity in placements would require funds and resources to be made available if this target is to be achieved. For example, the issue of free labour will have implications across race and class.

It is also important to note that religious belief is not considered by host institutions to be of relevance as an issue of equality and diversity. However, this is not a wise approach, as religion crosses many significant fault lines of race and class. An effective understanding of race and ethnicity in London surely requires an attention to issues of belief and religion, or the lack of them.

Another strand of equality and diversity that is problematic in placements is age. Three out of four of the host institutions said that they prefer to recruit experienced and mature students for their work placement programmes. This clearly disadvantages younger students in terms of finding a work placement. This also indicates unwillingness on the part of host institutions to offer adequate training and development activities to students.

The issue of disability was not discussed by any of the host institutions. This means that disability issues remain invisible and that the institutions are ill prepared to offer reasonable accommodation should the need arise.

The issue of sexual orientation diversity was interesting in this sector. All host institutions suggested that the sexual orientation of students would not disadvantage their prospects for securing a placement. Indeed, it is possible to identify a unique gay male advantage in the sector, which is highly female dominated.

Students' perceptions of work placement practices

Within the scope of the field research ten interviews were conducted with the students who had completed their work placement or who were currently still doing it. The host organizations in which the participant students had their work placements displayed a variation in terms of size and sector, including both large and small organizations, museums, libraries, exhibition centres, funding bodies and festivals.

Students' applications for work placements generally involved sending a CV to the host organization and sometimes writing a proposal about the project that they would like to undertake during their placement. In the latter case, writing a work placement project proposal was, most of the time, a part of their module requirements as well. This initial contact with the host organization was followed by an interview where the host makes a decision about offering a work placement to the student or not. Some students reported that they did not receive a sufficient level of guidance and support from their tutors or work placement administrators throughout the process of application. These students argued that should there be better guidance from their schools, their decisions and selection of the host organization would have been more informed; hence the work placement experience would have contributed to their personal and career development more as they had expected.

The role of the student within the host organization during the work placement showed variation in the case of different students. In all of the cases it involved some low-level administrative work, such as data entry, answering the telephone and photocopying. However, in the case of some students, the job placement role did not go beyond such tasks, whereas in other cases students carried out a specific project, were involved in decision-making and took higher levels of responsibility. In their evaluation of the contribution of the work placement, participant students put a strong emphasis on the types of work they did and their role in the host organization. Our research findings suggest that the students whose placement roles were more or less limited to mundane administrative tasks were unsatisfied with their work placement experience. On the other hand, the students who took higher levels of responsibility, who were situated in clearly defined project roles and were given a part in the decision-making process in the host organization, displayed higher levels of satisfaction regarding their practice. It was also pointed out by eight of the students that having a work placement in smaller organizations is more advantageous for the students, since small organizations tend to assign more responsibility and industry-related tasks to their placement students, unlike the large organizations that tend to see the placement students as a source of extra labour for undertaking mundane administrative tasks.

All of the students who participated in the research thought that potentially work placement may be a very important opportunity for them in terms of contributing both to their academic studies and to their career. There was a very direct link between work placement and academic study. In the case of seven students, work placement was neither a compulsory nor an optional part of their studies. In some cases the students were also expected to integrate their learning from the work placement into their MA dissertations. On the other hand, the impact of work placement on students' future career was more indirect. Only one of the students in our sample was employed by the host institution after her work placement. Similarly, our respondents from host organizations and HEIs also pointed out that it is very rare that the students are employed by the organization where they did their placements. Nevertheless, all students in our sample thought that work placement may potentially contribute to their future career in other ways than being employed by the host organization. For instance, all students pointed out that they expected that they would gain new skills, enhance their knowledge of the world of work and creative and cultural industries, and hence understand how the sector actually works in real life, as well as establishing contacts and networks in the industry which would be helpful for them later in their career.

However, these expectations were not fulfilled in the case of some participant students. One of our respondents in particular was very negative regarding her work placement experience. She told us that all she did during her placement was photocopying, that she did not gain any skills and did not even make any contacts. The students who rated their work placement experience as poor, generally argued that they were ill-prepared for the placement due to lack of guidance and support from their HEIs. They also pointed out that it is very important for the tutors or placement administrators to have genuine contacts in the creative and cultural industries. In addition, it was argued that the work placement model in the HEIs should require students to submit a proposal listing clearly what they would like to achieve during their placements. All students argued that the tutors should be sensitive to students' needs and aims regarding the work placement and provide them with tailored advice and guidance.

All students believed that in the tripartite relationship involving the HEI, student and the host within the scope of work placement practice, the HEIs had an important role to play in terms of supporting and guiding their students. It was suggested that the guidance and support should not be limited to the placement application stage, but should be available throughout the work placement. Moreover, eight out of ten students also argued that the HEIs had a role to play in terms of monitoring how the host organizations manage the work placement and in ensuring that the attitudes of the host institutions to the placement conform to the work placement objectives put forward by the HEIs.

Within that framework, all of the students argued that the way the work placement is managed by the host institutions is crucial for the success of the placement. It is argued that the host institutions should have a clear understanding of the objectives of the HEIs and students regarding the work placement and that they should take these into account when deciding on the placement role of the student. It was also argued that if the work placement was to be a positive and beneficial experience to the students, the host needs to have a positive attitude towards the work placement practice and the placement student. Such a positive attitude on the side of the host is defined by the students in terms of showing respect to the placement student, understanding and taking into account the students' needs and priorities regarding the placement, and assigning creative and cultural industry related responsibilities to the students.

Another issue raised by all students was related to the financial difficulties around doing unpaid work placement. Seven out of ten students reported that the host organizations covered their travel expenses. However, it was emphasized that the lack of any other payment caused financial difficulty for them, since they were students and did not have any income. Moreover, the students argued that doing work placement prevented them taking part-time jobs to improve their financial situation. Some students also pointed out that they would like to do work placement for a longer period of time but that this was not feasible due to the lack of any payment during the placement. So it was apparent from the interviews that at least payment of a minimum wage salary is crucial for a successful, satisfying and efficient work placement experience.

Lastly, we asked students whether they thought that the impact of work placement on a student's career and the work placement experience itself, may be different for students from different demographical backgrounds. Some of the respondents pointed out that age and lack of experience may be important barriers for younger students. For instance, it was argued that it is much easier for mature students to find a work placement. Another issue raised by the black student in our sample was the potential race and class bias in work placement. She argued that cultural and creative industries in general are dominated by the white middle class and that the same situation holds true for the HEIs in the sector. She put forward that because of the white middle-class orientation of the sector, black people and people from lower class backgrounds do not feel welcome in either the organizations or the HEIs in the sector. She argued that although there are some attempts to increase the representation of minority ethnic students in the work placements in the sector, this remains at a very superficial level. As an example, she told us about her work placement in a large institution. She suggested that the organization recruited minority ethnic students as placements to fulfil the criteria of a funding body, but did not spend real effort to contribute to the personal development of these students. She thought that these students from ethnic minority backgrounds were only recruited for 'ticking the boxes' and were seen as 'numbers' representing their ethnic origin rather than as individuals with skills and abilities. She explained to us the reason why she thought in that way. She said that there was a position opened during their work placement and the only white student out of five placement students was offered the job.

9.5 Policy recommendations

Our study has generated the following policy recommendations for work placement practices across the creative and cultural industries.

Recommendations for work placement models and practices of HEIs

- The HEIs should sustain and strengthen their provision of supporting students in the process of applying for and securing work placements in the industry.
- This requires HEIs to exploit opportunities to identify suitable work places through all possible networks, inspect their requirements, get involved in matching students with placement vacancies, and assessing the running and completion of placement work.
- Work placement opportunities should be communicated to the students via formal channels.
- Module tutors and work placement administrators should be offered adequate temporal and financial resources in order to play a more significant and responsible role in monitoring and guiding the work placement experience of students.
- The HEIs should provide formal structures of advice and guidance both for students and host organizations, including handbooks or guidelines as well as statements of ground rules and standards that they sent out to the host organizations.
- The HEIs should offer structured and formal evaluation mechanisms regarding the impacts and success of the work placement.
- This evaluation should be based on feedback from students and host institutions.
- The HEIs should monitor their work placement model in terms of its impact on the students' future employability.
- The impact of work placement on the level of satisfaction of students from different demographic backgrounds should be monitored by the HEIs.
- The issues of equality and diversity monitoring activities should be integrated in the process of work placement design in the HEIs.

Recommendations for models and practices of work placement in host institutions

- Host institutions should be encouraged to provide a clear set of guidelines for placement experience with a clear job description, an induction programme, and a monitoring and appraisal structure. A sample could be provided by the HEIs in order to help the host institution with such documentation.
- Realistic expectations should be set between host institutions, placement students and HEIs. This is important in establishing parameters of trust in this tripartite relationship.
- Placement students should not be treated as free or cheap labour. Funding bodies should consider part funding, with the host institutions and the HEIs, a decent living wage for students.

- A formal and meaningful relationship should be established between the HEIs and the host institutions for the supervision and mentoring of placement students.
- The host institutions should be encouraged to play a positive role in the effective operation of placement programmes by supporting the students' personal and professional development.
- The host organizations should also attend to diversity and equality issues in work placements through an effective monitoring system. This requires attention to all strands of equality and diversity, including age, gender, race and ethnicity, disability, sexual orientation and religious belief, amongst others.

Recommendations for students' experiences of work placement practices

- Students should be offered guidance in preparation for their placement work. This would include practical sessions from CV writing skills to interviewing and other personal and professional skills that may be expected of them in the process of their work placements.
- Students should be encouraged to write project proposals outlining their expectations and plans for the project. This can help them set realistic expectations.
- The role of the student within the host organizations should be specified as clearly as possible.
- The work placement should facilitate the professional and personal development of students. Therefore, an assessment of work placement experience should be constructed along these lines.
- Varied, meaningful and purposeful work placement roles should be negotiated for students.
- Students should be encouraged to gain new skills, enhance their knowledge of the world of work and the creative and cultural industries, and establish contacts and networks in the industry which would be helpful for them later in their career.
- The students should be well prepared for the placement through continuous guidance and support from their HEIs.
- The way the work placement is managed by the host institutions should be assessed by the students, and their feedback should be seriously considered by the HEIs.
- A formal mechanism should be introduced in order to ensure adequate health and safety conditions and to protect students against all forms of exploitation, bias and discrimination in the workplace.

9.6 **Conclusions**

Global diversity managers should take note of sectoral requirements. The creative and cultural industry provides a useful example, due to the international nature of its work and employees. Our study has revealed that there is a body of academic writing in the field of work placements and the design and delivery requirements for successful work placement practices. The studies that we have drawn on to frame our approach has been interdisciplinary in nature, due to the relative absence of literature on work placements in the field of creative and cultural enterprises. Nevertheless, our field study findings provide fresh evidence to demonstrate the current state of play in the sector, drawing on interviews with representatives from universities and host institutions as well as placement students.

Our study has revealed that despite evidence of some examples of good practice in work placement programmes offered by universities in the sector, there is certainly room for progress. The main strength of the work placement design and implementation in the higher education sector is the hands-off and organic approach, which is characterized by flexibility in arrangements of work placements. This flexible approach means that the students have a role to play in searching, identifying and approaching the host institutions and deciding on the content of their work placement projects. Provided that the university link, the academic tutor of the student, is supportive, this arrangement may provide work placement opportunities which are tailored to the student's needs.

However, the liberal arrangement of work placements, as well as the inherent flexibility involved in this design, are also at the same time the key weaknesses of the work placement programmes offered by the HEIs. Flexibility in itself is not a weakness at all. However, absence of robust and standardized procedures for monitoring and evaluating student performance, as well as the management of the work placement by the host institution, exposes the student and the work placement experience to several undue risks. For example, any form of exploitation, misuse of student time, as well as discriminatory practices in the host institution may be left unchecked and unaddressed. Considering that all universities in London subscribe to high levels of service delivery standards in terms of their academic programmes and employment practices, the work placement experience needs also to be considered.

HEIs need to provide clear and assessable criteria for successful work placements, as well as for the aims and objectives of the work placement projects. This also requires that the HEIs provide a budget through which these systems of monitoring and assessment can be formalized. Institutions of best practice do help students identify work placements, continuously monitor student experience and learning during work placements, and require constructive feedback from host institutions.

Our study revealed that host institutions do not always consider work placement as a developmental tool for the students, using them as cheap or free resources, often for low-level administrative, monotonous and repetitive tasks. The practice of not paying the students for their work placement has a dual impact, which both undermines and devalues students' work. This clearly conflicts with the logic and spirit of the work placement arrangements, which should aim to provide students with an experience that they can reflect on in terms of their academic learning and their future careers. In this context, there is scope for universities to recognize potential pitfalls and to promote better procedures for work placement which will benefit all constituent parties.

Lastly, our research findings revealed that the cultural and creative sector has a strong white, middle-class bias. This manifests itself as various forms of tacit exclusion of certain groups of students or devaluing their work and performance. The issue of linguistic ability is a key concern in the sector. This is often used to justify exclusion or demarcation of international students from work placement experience. Similarly, racial and ethnic discrimination also have a negative impact on the student experience of work placement. Universities have a major role to play in promoting the agenda of equality and diversity in the sector as well as inside their organization.

Appendix A: State of the creative and cultural industries in the UK (from CCS Consultation Paper 2006)

Exercise: Reflecting on the below characteristics of the creative and cultural industries in the UK, identify groups which may find it difficult to seek inclusion in the sector as employees, customers, students or business owners.

In brief, the creative and cultural industries sector:

- employs 459,200 people in the UK;
- which is a rise of 38,400 between 1998 and 2002. This equates to a growth of 9.1 per cent, or roughly twice the overall growth in UK employment in the same period;
- it contributes £16.5 billion to total output;
- which is approximately 2 per cent;
- it has 130,000 self-employed freelancers. This is around 29 per cent of the sector's total workforce;
- which rises to 64 per cent in the performing, visual and literary arts;
- in the overall UK labour force just 13 per cent are self-employed;

- it has 312,000 people in managerial, professional, technical and associated professional roles, many with high-level qualifications. This represents 68 per cent of the sector's workforce, compared to 42 per cent of the overall UK workforce;
- it is over-represented in London and the South, and under-represented elsewhere;
- it has 450,000 volunteers contributing to the sector's success;
- it experiences relatively few skills shortages and gaps compared to the rest of the economy;
- 'creative and cultural industries' does not have an agreed definition in the UK;
- the sector is economically successful;
- the growth is fast;
- the sector enjoys a highly qualified workforce and labour market;
- there are flexible structures of employment in the sector;
- success requires responding to opportunities of freelance and short-term work;
- there is need for leadership and management competencies in the sector.

The arts in London – some useful facts

London's creative and cultural sector:

- generates an estimated total annual revenue of £25–£29 billion (second only to business industries);
- represents 33 per cent of the UK's total creative industries sector;
- employs over 500,000 – representing London's third largest employment sector;
- is responsible for one in four of all new jobs in London created between 1995 and 2000;
- represents 25 per cent of people working in the creative and cultural sectors in the UK;
- is expected to be the fastest growing sector in London's expanding economy to 2016 (with the business industries).

London is home to:

- two opera houses;
- five orchestras;
- seven purpose-built concert halls;
- 125 dance companies;
- 167 galleries and museums;
- 205 theatres;

- 1,500 theatre companies;
- 1,700 visual arts and crafts groups;
- 2,500 amateur groups;
- 2,650 music businesses;
- 19 national museums;
- numerous events in schools, community centres, youth clubs, parks and public spaces;
- more than 33 per cent of the UK's 1,600 performing arts companies supported by public investment;
- 70 per cent of the UK's recording studios;
- 90 per cent of the UK's music business activity;
- 75 per cent of the UK's film and broadcasting industry revenues;
- 33 per cent of the UK's arts and antiques dealerships;
- 46 per cent of advertising employment;
- 30 per cent of the UK's visual artists and photographers;
- 27.5 per cent of the UK's architects;
- 80–85 per cent of the UK's fashion designers;
- all the major UK auction houses;
- the majority of UK-based multinational leisure software HQs;
- three world heritage sites – Greenwich, Westminster Abbey and the Tower of London.

London attracts:

- 13.2 million overseas visitors each year (56 per cent of the UK's total);
- 14.8 million domestic visitors each year;
- 30 per cent of all visitors say that arts and culture are an important reason for their visit;
- 22 million visits to performances of music, theatre and dance each year;
- 30 million visits to museums and galleries each year.

Sources:
Mayor's Draft Cultural Strategy (June 2003)
London Analytical Report (No. 10 Policy Unit, 2003)
Case for London (London Arts, 2000)

Londoners:

- see the arts, culture and nightlife as among the top five reasons for living in London;
- attend more arts events than people in other regions;
- 82 per cent attended at least one arts event in the last 12 months;

- have the most eclectic taste in the arts – they are more likely than people from any other region to attend several types of event;
- are more likely to participate in the arts;
- 90 per cent took part in at least one artistic activity in the last 12 months;
- appreciate the arts;
- 79 per cent think that the arts play a valuable role in the life of the country;
- appreciate cultural diversity in the arts;
- 80 per cent think that arts from different cultures contribute a lot to the cultural life of the country.

Sources:

Arts in England: Attendance, Participation and Attitudes in 2001, commissioned by Arts Council England from the Social Survey Division of the Office for National Statistics (ONS) in 2001. The report is supported by *Resource: The Council for Museums, Archives and Libraries* and is based on interviews with over 6,000 adults across the country.

Appendix B: Interview schedule – higher education institutions

Exercise: The three interview schedules in Appendices B, C and D are designed to explore equality and employability issues in work placements in the creative and cultural industry. The interview schedules are specifically designed for higher education institutions, employers and workplace students. The schedules can be used for further research, that is replicating the study which was explored in this chapter. They can be also used in order to assess equality and employability in the sector in the classroom. In order to achieve this, students should bring with them transcripts with one or several participants from these constituent groups.

Explanation:

This interview is conducted as part of a research project funded by the London Centre for Arts and Cultural Enterprise. This research project aims to undertake a scoping exercise of work placement practices in London based HEIs. We will ask you questions about the operations of your organization with particular reference to the placement programmes provided by your organization in the arts and cultural industries: the demographic composition of candidates; and your organization's approach regarding the issues of work placement. No individual names will be revealed and they will be kept strictly confidential.

1. **Could you briefly tell me about the range of work placement practices in your institution?**

   Probe: What are the key programmes provided by your institution?

   Probe: Which fields of employment do you cover?

   Probe: What is the nature of these work placements? Are they part of the students' programme of study? Are they voluntary or compulsory elements of study?

   Probe: Could we please obtain the forms and documents relating to work placement practices and models in your institution?

2. **How do you create a candidate pool of students for work placements?**

   Probe: newsletters, email, speeches, etc.?

3. **How do you reach and communicate with the host organizations?**

   Probe: Could you explain?

   Probe: Do you have any standards documents that you use for this? Could we see these?

4. **What is the process of matching the student with the host organization?**

   Probe: Could you explain the process a bit?

   Probe: May I have a sample of application forms?

5. **Could you please tell us any examples of good practice in work placements in your organization?**

6. **What methods do you use in order to evaluate your work placements?**

   Probe: Do you use any documents?

   Probe: Who are involved in evaluation?

7. **What do you think are the impact of work placements that you organise in the host organizations?**

   Probe: How do you find out?

   Probe: The reasons?

8. **Do you have any feedback mechanisms from host institutions for work placements?**

   Probe: Do you carry out monitoring and feedback activities?

   Probe: Could we have any feedback reports?

   Probe: What form of action do you take once you receive feedback?

9. **What are your opinions regarding the impact of work placement on students?**

   Probe: In terms of students' future career?

   Probe: In terms of students' current study?

10. **Do you have any feedback mechanisms from students on work placements?**
    Probe: Do you carry out monitoring and feedback activities?
    Probe: Could we have any feedback reports?
    Probe: What form of action do you take once you receive feedback?

11. **Are there any barriers to successful placement?**
    Probe: What are they?
    Probe: Why?
    Probe: How can they be overcome?

12. **What is your view on the impact of work placement practices on the collaboration and knowledge transfer between HEIs and arts and cultural industries?**
    Probe: Does such a knowledge transfer take place?
    Probe: Is this part of the objectives for the placement programme?

13. **Do you plan to modify your work placement model in the future?**
    Probe: Why?
    Probe: How?

14. **Do work placement projects in arts and cultural industries differ from work placements in other industries?**
    Probe: How?
    Probe: Why?

15. **Do you think that your work placements have different impacts by gender, ethnicity, age, disability, sexual orientation and religion of the students?**
    Probe: Please explain

16. **Could you please tell me any additional comments you feel are relevant to our understanding of your organization's approach to work placements particularly in relation to arts and cultural industries?**

17. **Do you know any other higher education institutions that may be interested in participating in our research?**
    Probe: May I have their contact details?
    Probe: Could you introduce me to them?

Thank you very much for your time and support.

Appendix C: Interview schedule – host institutions

Explanation:

This interview is conducted as a part of a research project funded by the London Centre for Arts and Cultural Enterprise. This research project aims to undertake a scoping exercise of work placement practices in a range of organizations in the cultural and creative industry in London. We will ask you questions about the operations of your organization with particular reference to the placement programmes provided by your organization in the arts and cultural industries: the demographic composition of candidates; and your organization's approach regarding the issues of work placement. No individual names will be revealed and they will be kept strictly confidential.

1. **Could you briefly tell me about range of work placement practices in your institution?**
   Probe: What are the key programmes provided by your organization?
   Probe: Which fields of employment do you cover?
   Probe: What is the nature of these work placements?
   Probe: Could we please obtain the forms and documents relating to work placement practices in your organization?

2. **How do you create a candidate pool of students for work placements?**
   Probe: newsletters, email, speeches, word of mouth, etc.?

3. **Do you reach and communicate with the higher education institution where your placement students come from?**
   Probe: Could you explain?
   Probe: Do you have any standards documents that you use for this? Could we see these?

4. **What is the process of matching the student with their placement roles?**
   Probe: Could you explain the process a bit?
   Probe: May I have a sample of application forms?

5. **Could you please tell us any examples of good practice in work placements in your organization?**

6. **What methods do you use in order to evaluate your work placements?**
   Probe: Do you use any documents?
   Probe: Who are involved in evaluation?

7. **What do you think are the impact of work placements on the host organisations?**
   Probe: How do you find out?
   Probe: The reasons?

8. **Do you have any feedback mechanisms from students for work placements?**
   Probe: Do you carry out monitoring and feedback activities?
   Probe: Could we have any feedback reports?
   Probe: What form of action do you take once you receive feedback?

9. **What are your opinions regarding the impact of work placement on students?**
   Probe: In terms of students' future career?
   Probe: In terms of students' current study?

10. **Are there any barriers to successful placement?**
    Probe: What are they?
    Probe: Why?
    Probe: How can they be overcome?

11. **What is your view on the impact of work placement practices on the collaboration and knowledge transfer between HEIs and arts and cultural industries?**
    Probe: Does such a knowledge transfer take place?
    Probe: Is this part of the objectives for the placement programme?

12. **Do you plan to modify your work placement programme in the future?**
    Probe: Why?
    Probe: How?

13. **Do work placement projects in arts and cultural industries differ from work placements in other industries?**
    Probe: How?
    Probe: Why?

14. **Do you think that your work placements have different impacts by gender, ethnicity, age, disability, sexual orientation and religion of the students?**
    Probe: Please explain

15. Could you please tell me any additional comments you feel are relevant to our understanding of your organization's approach to work placements particularly in relation to arts and cultural industries?

16. Do you know any other organizations in the creative and cultural industry that may be interested in participating in our research? Do you know any higher education institutions with placement programmes in the sector that we can contact?
    Probe: May I have their contact details?
    Probe: Could you introduce me to them?

Thank you very much for your time and support.

Appendix D: **Interview schedule – students**

Explanation:

This interview is conducted as a part of a research project funded by the London Centre for Arts and Cultural Enterprise. This research project aims to undertake a scoping exercise of work placement practices in London based HEIs. We will ask you questions about the experiences and opinions with particular reference to the placement programmes provided by your university. No individual names will be revealed and they will be kept strictly confidential.

1. Could you briefly tell me about your work placement experience?
   Probe: When? How long?
   Probe: Where?
   Probe: What was the nature of the work placement project?
   Probe: Why did you do a work placement?

2. Do you think that your work placement had an impact on your future employment opportunities?
   Probe: If yes, how?
   Probe: Why not?

3. Do you think that your work placement had an impact on your knowledge of the creative and cultural industry?
   Probe: If yes, how?
   Probe: Why not?

4. Do you think that your work placement had an impact on your understanding of the world of work and the skills you require for the career you wish to pursue?
   Probe: If yes, how?
   Probe: Why not?

5. Do you think that your work placement had an impact on your future career plans?
   Probe: If yes, how?
   Probe: Why not?

6. Do you think that your work placement had an impact on your academic work in your school?
   Probe: If yes, how?
   Probe: Why not?

7. How do you assess the currently available model of work placement in your university?
   Probe: How do you rate it?
   Probe: What are its key characteristics, strengths and weaknesses?

8. Do you have any recommendations for improving the work placement practice in your university?
   Probe: What are they?
   Probe: Explain

9. How do you rate your level of satisfaction from your work placement experience?
   Probe: Areas with which you are satisfied? Reasons?
   Probe: Areas with which you are dissatisfied? Reasons?

10. What is your general feeling about your experience of work placement?
    Probe: Please explain?

11. Do you think that your institution's work placement model has different impacts by gender, ethnicity, age, disability, sexual orientation and religion of the students?
    Probe: Please explain

12. Could you please tell me any additional comments you feel are relevant to our understanding of your institution's approach to work placements and your experience of it?

Thank you very much for your time and support.

Further reading

Barthorpe, S. and Hall, M. (2000) 'A Collaborative Approach to Placement Preparation and Career Planning for University Students: A Case Study', *Journal of Vocational Education and Training*, vol. 52, no. 2, pp. 165–75.

Maidment, J. (2003) 'Problems Experienced by Students on Field Placement: Using Research Findings to Inform Curriculum Design and Content', *Australian Social Work*, vol. 56, no. 1, pp. 50–60.

Mandilaras, A. (2004) 'Industrial Placement and Degree Performance: Evidence from a British Higher Institution', *International Review of Education Economics*, vol. 3, no. 1, pp. 39–51.

McMahon, U. and Quinn, U. (1995) 'Maximizing the Hospitality Management Student Work Placement Experience: A Case Study', *Education and Training*, vol. 37, no. 4, pp. 13–17.

Morgan, A. and Turner, D. (2000) 'Adding Value to the Work Placement: Working towards a Professional Qualification in an Undergraduate Degree Programme', *Education and Training*, vol. 42, no. 8, pp. 453–60.

Neill, N.T. and Mulholland, G.E. (2003) 'Student Placement: Structure, Skills and e-support', *Education and Training*, vol. 45, no. 2, pp. 89–99.

Neill, A.N., Mulholland, G.A., Ross, A.V. and Leckey, A.J. (2004) 'The Influence of Part-time Work on Student Placement', *Journal of Further and Higher Education*, vol. 28, no. 2, pp. 123–37.

Newton, A. and Smith, L.N. (1998) 'Practice Placement Supervision: The Role of the Personal Tutor', *Nurse Education Today*, vol. 18, no. 6, pp. 496–504.

Richardson, S. and Blakeney, C. (1998) 'The Undergraduate Placement System: An Empirical Study', *Accounting Education*, vol. 7, no. 2, pp. 101–21.

Saxton, J. and Ashworth, P. (1990) 'The Workplace Supervision of Sandwich Degree Placement Students', *Management Education and Development*, vol. 21, no. 2, pp. 133–49.

Schaafsma, H. (1996) 'Back to the Real World: Work Placements Revisited', *Education and Training*, vol. 38, no. 1, pp. 5–13.

Uzzell, D.L. (1986) 'The Professional Placement for Students: Some Theoretical Considerations', *Oxford Review of Education*, vol. 12, no. 1, pp. 67–75.

Organizational and Individual Effects

The Organizational Level: **10** The Case of a Global Automobile Manufacturing Company

10.1   Introduction

In a multilevel framework, understanding the parameters of global diversity management requires the investigation of the organizational-level dynamics. The organizational level has two main dimensions: objective structures and formal rules; and culture and informal rules impacting on the everyday life in the organization.

This chapter focuses on the exploration of the organizational-level dynamics of diversity management prevalent in the case study company. The analysis is informed by the documentary evidence and semi-structured interview data collected through a case study of a global automobile manufacturing company. The chapter starts with a brief description of the company to set out the context, then explores the characteristic objective and subjective structures shaping the diversity management policies and practices in the company.

10.2 **Description of the company**

Bourdieu (1990: 54) stated that temporal aspects of the *habitus* should be carefully studied, since without the historical dimension it would be impossible to understand the nature of *habitus*:

> The habitus, a product of history, produces individual and collective practices – more history – in accordance with the schemes generated by history. It ensures the active presence of past experiences, which, deposited in each organism in the form of schemes of perception, thought and action, tend to guarantee the 'correctness' of practices and their constancy over time, more reliably than all formal rules and explicit norms.

The historical legacy of organizational *habitus* is what makes diversity management a challenging and long-term process. Hence, it is crucial to situate the diversity management framework within the context of organizational history. For that reason we start the chapter with a brief historical description of the company.

The case study company was established in the early 20th century in the United States. The introduction of the assembly line in the company's plants, accompanied by Taylorist scientific management, led to rapid expansion of the company. Thanks to the moving assembly line, the company's annual production boomed from the thousands in the 1900s to the billions in the 1920s. In the post-second World War years the company experienced a vast global expansion with the establishment of European and North American branches. Currently, the company employs over 300,000 workers in around a hundred plants across six continents. In Europe alone there are around 35 sites, including the United Kingdom, Germany, Russia, Turkey, Belgium, Norway, Spain and the Netherlands. As we explain further in the next chapter, the nature of the organization of the work process makes the case study company a very valuable example for diversity management research.

Organizational culture

Regarding its culture, the company presents a curious case for the study of diversity management, since its founding principles are in deep conflict with the so-called pillars of diversity. To start with, assembly line production rests uneasily with the concepts of diversity management due to its reliance upon Taylorist scientific management, which is strongly associated with mass production through a highly planned and standardized organization of labour process. In the literature, one of the arguments put forward by the advocates of diversity management suggests that, in order to be competitive, organizations of the post-industrial era need to overcome organizational rigidities by developing higher levels of adaptiveness and responsiveness to change, by improving flexibility and fostering team work through a flatter network type of work organization (Schoenberger 1997; Schneider and Northcraft 1999; Procter and Mueller 2000; Boxall and Purcell 2003). Hence, the argument goes that workforce diversity, if utilized and managed effectively, is the key to the requirements of 21st-century organizations which need to attain high levels of productivity, efficiency, innovative capacity, adaptability and flexibility, and to meet diverse consumer demands in order to survive (Carroll and Hannan 2000; Blazevic and Lievens 2002; Allard 2002; Ashkanasy *et al.* 2002; Chevrier 2003). In their work on the competencies in UK business, Kandola and Pearn (1992: 66) point out the shift from a 'parochial outlook' and 'procedure-bound' approach to 'company commitment' and 'innovative/open-minded' thinking, which are considered the positive outcomes of flexible forms of work organization. Others argue that diversity culture is more likely to be achieved in flexible organizations than bureaucratic ones (Golembiewski 1995; Thomas and Ely 2002). Still, other research shows that diversity provides a competitive advantage when performance of novel and complex work tasks, which require high levels of creative thinking, innovation and problem solving skills, are at stake (Cordero *et al.* 1997; Dwyer *et al.* 2003).

However, what is generally ignored in that literature is the fact that the new saga of flexible organizations does not sit comfortably within the framework of assembly-line production, which leaves little room for any sort of flexibility due to the very nature of its logistics and organization of work. Moreover, in the literature, the positive association between diversity and creativity is implicitly made with professional employees in mind, rather than blue-collar workers. Being an automobile manufacturing company, the dominant type of production in the case study organization is mass production based on Taylorism, and 90 per cent of its employees are blue-collar workers who spend their working hours at the assembly line, subject to rigid standardization and control.

Taylorist scientific management is based on the detailed calculations of timing, speed and use of space to attain the most efficient and productive arrangements on the assembly line. Accordingly every minute of work and each body movement of the workers are calculated and planned to achieve greatest time efficiency. Principles of Taylorism and mass production posit challenges for diversity management which is celebrated in both the academic literature and company documents alike as an approach for harnessing the differences between employees to 'create a productive environment in which everyone feels valued, where their talents are being fully utilised and in which organizational goals are met' (Kandola and Fullerton 1998: 7). At the unforgiving pace of the assembly line, it is hardly possible for the blue-collar workers to think at all, let alone take initiative and be creative. Furthermore, previous research on automobile company workers demonstrates that assembly-line workers do not think that they are part of their organizations as much as the white-collar employees do (Beynon 1973).

Such studies debase the credibility of the arguments made for the connection between diversity and enhanced feelings of organizational attachment and belonging in the manufacturing environment (Fernandez 1991; Morrison 1992; Cox 1993) unless the white–collar/blue-collar divide is taken into account in the diversity management process. For blue-collar workers their difference from the rest of the employees, in terms of the nature of their work and working conditions, forms an important dimension of their diversity and that impacts upon their attachment to their company. Interestingly enough, in a stark contrast with the celebration of a wide range of differences between the employees, diversity management literature keeps silent about social-class differences in the workplace (Thomas 1990; Cox and Blake 1991; Kandola and Fullerton 1998; Gilbert and Ivancevich 2000). Not surprisingly, this silence can be depicted also in the case study company's diversity policies and documents, as will be shown later in the chapter. Hence, studying the possibilities of diversity management in a manufacturing company also brings about a critical engagement with the mainstream diversity management literature and sheds light on the blind spots in this discourse. To sum up, reading the diversity literature with a critical eye reveals that business case arguments that are presented as the main justification for managing diversity implicitly exclude some categories of employees. In other words, the rhetoric of the business case for diversity management is implicitly based on the idea of professional employees as the 'norm', with the assumption that employees who benefit from diversity management policies will add value to their organizations through increased organizational attachment, flexibility, problem solving capacity, creativity and innovation. However, business case arguments may fail to present any justification to employers for workforce diversity in the case of non-professional employees or manual workers, since their job may not add value to the organization by being 'creative' or 'innovative', in which case diversity will cease to be an 'asset'. So, it seems, diversity rhetoric leaves the manual workers out in the cold, without admitting this serious flaw in the arguments for bottom-line benefits of diversity. The question that then comes to mind is whether the adoption of a diversity management approach by the case study company comes at the expense of an equal opportunities perspective but which will be detrimental or disadvantageous for the majority of its employees, while offering advanced working conditions and opportunities for the few.

Nevertheless, the company claims that their diversity policy is based on 'inclusion of every person and every perspective', which means 'an opportunity for everyone in the organization, not just minorities', and on understanding diversity as 'all the differences that make us unique individuals'. Within that framework, the company's definition of diversity includes a wide range of differences regarding culture, religion, education, experience, opinions, beliefs, language, nationality, as well as race, ethnicity, gender, age, disability, and sexual orientation. This perspective is in conformity with mainstream diversity management theory, which argues that such a wide ranging definition of diversity, as opposed to one based solely on gender and ethnicity, is preferable, since it overcomes the risk of a backlash by the majority group members in the organizations, and prevents stereotyping of individuals as members of some demographic groups (Thomas 1990; Locke 1992).

However, the case study company has issues of racial and ethnic discrimination, as demonstrated by the lawsuits that the British branch of the company had to face in the 1990s. Under these circumstances, reducing the workforce diversity to individually based difference may potentially undermine anti-discriminatory measures. Equating difference with individual preferences and choices, which reveals itself in the uniqueness of each individual, entails the risk of blindness towards the historically and socially constructed and deeply rooted stereotypes, particularly regarding gender, ethnicity, sexuality, disability and age. For that reason, at least in the case of the case study company, it seems important to explicitly acknowledge the most crucial and urgent problem areas working against equality and diversity, and to prioritize some categories of difference over the others within the scope of diversity management policy and strategy. An ambiguous definition of diversity, like the one preferred by the company, as the backbone of the company's strategy in the field, will not promote a serious and sustainable diversity management programme unless the aim is to pay lip service to the idea rather than initiating an organizational change. As Elmes and Connelley (1997: 164) state, 'neglecting to recognise and deal with these more subtle and difficult aspects of diversity management dooms structuralist initiatives to failure'.

Both company documents and interviews conducted with the diversity managers of the company demonstrate that the diversity management process is associated with cultural change. Ironically there is a huge lack of clarity about what lies behind that rhetoric of change, such as what is actually meant by 'change', which aspects of organizational culture are targeted for change and in what ways. On the other hand, all interview respondents have pointed out that the company has a very established organizational culture which is primarily orientated around white male values and that the majority of company employees are white, male and middle-aged. Research shows that white males react more negatively to diverse work groups, whereas females or minorities are more favourable of them (Wharton and Baron 1987; Tsui *et al.* 1992; DiTomaso *et al.* 1996; Cordero *et al.* 1997). This implies that some groups of employees may be more receptive and supportive of the diversity management process, while others may display resistance and opposition (Knouse and Dansby 2000). However, if the fundamental impact of group-based differences on organizational culture is blurred through an individualistic definition of diversity, as in the case of the case study company, the scope and the nature of the so-called change targeted through diversity management efforts becomes even more ambiguous.

10.3 Organizational structures of diversity management

In this section we analyse the objective systems and structures governing the diversity efforts in the case study company. After providing an overview of the general diversity management approach of the company, we explore the diversity structure of the company, and its diversity management activities and programmes.

To start with, the global diversity policy statement of the company is 'to build a diverse and inclusive culture that drives business results'. In the company documents one of the core values of the company is claimed to be 'an inspired, diverse team' which 'respect and value everyone's contribution'. It is stated that diversity is essential to the company's mission, which is 'to become the world's leading consumer company for automotive products and services'. Then this is justified as follows: 'We need many unique skills, talents and ways of thinking and looking at the world to help us succeed'. All these extracts from the company website and diversity documents make it clear that the company's global diversity approach is based on the business case.

It is argued in the diversity management literature that the positive impact of diversity management on the business outcomes is one of the most important motivations for the integration of diversity principles into the mission and vision of a company at all levels, and for attracting necessary resources for the diversity management programmes (Cox and Blake 1991; Dobbs 1996; McDougall 1996). The company documentation demonstrates that the need for managing diversity at both global and European levels is predominantly justified on the basis of the argument that diversity contributes to the bottom line.

The *2005 Diversity Brochure* of the company goes on to explain how the company values the diversity of its customers, through capitalizing on women and the minority ethnic, gay, lesbian, bisexual and transgender markets; the diversity of its dealers and suppliers; and the diversity of its cross-functional teams that aims to build and sell 'best-selling cars and trucks'. In the company documents and the website, it is frequently emphasized that 'diversity is a competitive advantage in a global economy'. The points made in the company documentation regarding the benefits of diversity are (i) increased customer satisfaction, enhanced customer relationships and being appealing to the women and minority customers whose purchasing power as car buyers is rising; and (ii) increased organizational innovation, creativity and production. Thus, the explanation of the association between diversity and competitiveness in the company documents is the blueprint of the business case arguments in the diversity management literature, and remains at a rhetorical level since no company or country specific data is presented to qualify these statements or to demonstrate the benefits of diversity in real terms.

Diversity managers of the company made similar points also during the interviews and emphasized the importance of using the 'business rationale' for diversity management as a strategy for convincing different organizational members. However, when they were asked about how they measured and monitored the impact of diversity on factors such as customer satisfaction, increased market share, organizational innovation, creativity and production they said that measuring the association between these factors and diversity was not easy and that they did not monitor the impact of diversity on these factors. Ironically, there is another strand of academic research on workforce diversity that claims that low morale, ambiguity, conflict/tension, confusion and communication problems associated with diversity may undermine organizational attachment and reduce the effectiveness and cohesion of the workforce (Wharton and Baron 1987; O'Reilly *et al.* 1989; Tsui *et al.* 1992; Nemetz and Christensen 1996; Thomas and Ely 2002; Robbins 2001). In the face of these conflicting findings, and the fact that the business case discourse of a company's diversity managers relies on rhetoric rather than evidence and measurement, the question then comes to mind as to how sustainable and long-lasting could be the company's diversity management efforts if they solely rely on business case motivation. Although the bottom-line arguments offer an effective strategy for introducing and gaining commitment for the diversity management process in the present situation in the case study company, in the long run the question is: how would diversity management programmes and policies be affected when diversity proves to be not-so-profitable for the company or that bottom-line considerations conflict with diversity and equality goals?

Interestingly enough, the most important business motive for the company, at least in the case of its British branch, to adopt its current diversity management policy was the discrimination lawsuits it had faced, and the possible economic loss and bad publicity associated with it, rather than the other benefits of diversity. However, oblivious to that fact, the objectives on which diversity strategy of the British branch of the company is based read as follows:

- being an employer of choice in the war of talent by recruiting, retaining and developing the best people from the widest pool of talent available;

- being a brand of choice by serving a diverse customer base;
- promoting community involvement and corporate image by linking diversity into the corporate citizenship and the grant-giving programme across Britain.

Hence, although the new diversity programme of the British branch has been initiated in the aftermath of a discrimination lawsuit, the style and tone of the company documents still continue to imply that the main motivation for the diversity management programme is not legal compliance or ethical consider-ations, but the 'fact' that 'it makes business sense'. In a way, business case argu-ments are used to de-emphasize the fact that the company's current diversity programme in Britain was launched only in the aftermath of the employment tribunal cases that the company had to face over the last decade.

Diversity structure of the company

The global diversity strategy and policy of the company are designed and coordinated by the Diversity Office that is situated in the headquarters of the company in the United States. The Office was established under the Human Resource Department in the 1980s. As stated in the literature, establishing a clear management structure for managing diversity has a crucial impact on the effect-iveness of diversity and equality policies (Lawrence 2000). At the case study com-pany, thanks to the traditionally system-driven nature of all work organization, there is a very clear structure for diversity management. At the top of the hierar-chy is the Global Diversity Council, which is comprised of top executives and officers from all functional areas, and which is chaired by the CEO of the com-pany. The role of the Council is to set the tone and strategies for diversity efforts throughout the company. The five areas for action that are identified by the council to establish the framework of diversity policies and programmes are:

1 leadership within the corporation;
2 valuing a diverse workforce;
3 building a respectful and inclusive work environment;
4 valuing work–life integration;
5 developing external partnerships.

Under the Global Diversity Council are the National and Functional Diversity Councils, which exist in all areas of the company's operations. Finally, the company has Local Diversity Councils located in its plants which primarily deal with diversity training and organize educational and cultural-awareness events and local corporate citizenship efforts.

Integration of diversity goals into different functional areas of organization, and senior management support and ownership, are emphasized in the literature as being crucial for the clout of both diversity office and diversity policy (Cox and Blake 1991; Dobbs 1996; Muir 1996; Joplin and Daus 1997; Brimm and Arora 2001: 119). The case study company documents claim that through global, functional and local diversity councils, whose role is described in detail later in the chapter, diversity objectives are integrated to all areas of their business and are reinforced by a visible top-management commitment.

However, this structure proves that the company adopts a top-down approach when dealing with equality, and situates employees mainly as the receivers of the policies that are initiated, designed and approved by the senior management. As company documents reveal, the most crucial part of the employee involvement in the diversity management process takes place through the medium of Employee Groups (EGs) which are defined as 'company-sanctioned organizations formed by employees with common interests, backgrounds, or lifestyles'. The company has around ten such groups formed by female employees, gay, lesbian and bisexual employees, ethnic minority employees, parents, disabled employees and faith groups.

However, there is no mechanism for investing the EGs with formal power or authority to influence the company's diversity strategy and policy. They are rather perceived as helpers or supporters of the company's diversity programmes. Within that framework, company documents indicate that the activities of EGs involve helping the company in recruiting and retaining diverse employees and in getting involved in community events and projects; and in supporting diversity education in the company. Most important of all, EGs are seen by the company as important resources providing insights to diverse markets and supporting the marketing of the company's brands among diverse segments of the population. Accordingly, the company's diversity publications are full of narrations of success stories about EGs helping the company to achieve a greater market share among ethnic minority, female, gay, lesbian, bisexual and transgender consumers. Both interviews and company documentation state that EGs are not identity or pressure groups in the traditional sense but they are company-sanctioned organizations with 'clear aims in terms of their business impact in making [the company] an Employer and Brand of Choice for diverse communities'. This statement clearly attempts to hide the potentially political principle that brings these employees together in the EGs, that is, their identities in terms of being members of disadvantaged demographic groups. What is striking in the business case rhetoric for diversity management is the focus on the employers' interest. So, it seems that within the diversity management framework employees' interests are issues of consideration as long as they contribute to business outcomes. And this focus on profit is very well illustrated in the case of this company's perception of the

EGs as mediums with which to exploit the diversity of its employees in order to sell more cars to minority customers.

In addition to senior management and employees, line management establishes the other organizational group that exerts an important influence on diversity managers' agency and on the diversity management process. As Acker (2000) points out, despite the fact that implementation of diversity management and programmes is associated with an organizational change process, the diversity and equality officers most of the time lack the direct authority to control the different functions of the organization. This brings out the importance of the investigation of the mechanisms in place in the organization to provide diversity managers with power and authority to control and influence line managers regarding the implementation of diversity management policies. Interestingly, there are important differences between the American and British branches of the company regarding the structure and organization of diversity management, hence the levels of power and authority of diversity managers on the line managers.

These differences are largely due to the motivation behind the diversity management programme. In the US, the introduction of the global diversity programme was the result of the proactive stance taken by the company's CEO on the basis of the business case for workforce diversity. Hence, the global diversity efforts display a loosely connected and voluntary characteristic, and diversity objectives are required to be part of only the senior managers' scorecards and not of line managers, who are key actors for the implementation. On the other hand, in Britain, the company suffered from a series of race discrimination allegations in the 1990s. Following these incidents, the company signed an agreement with the unions on equality and diversity in the British branch of the company. Subsequently, the branch launched a diversity review process and introduced a comprehensive diversity policy, which seeks to initiate a process of organizational change. As opposed to the American branch of the company, in the British case diversity objectives are linked to team, individual and line management objectives and appraisal and pay/performance systems. The British branch has established diversity as a key objective in the Balanced Scorecard for all functional areas and line management across the organization. Line managers are required to submit regular reports at all levels on their diversity objectives to the National Diversity Council. In effect, unlike the American case, there is a very structured and systematic diversity and equality audit process in Britain, where diversity objectives and responsibility is cascaded down through all levels of the organization.

This difference in the diversity management structure between two country branches of the company also reflects itself in the status, position and background of the diversity managers in each case. Diversity managers in the United

States are reported to be part-time, meaning that they are doing the diversity work as a part of their main job, whereas they hold a full-time office in the European and British context. Furthermore, different routes followed for the recruitment of diversity managers in the UK and the US proves to be an interesting case. All of the diversity managers in the United States have been recruited from within the company, whereas in Britain most senior diversity staff have been externally recruited and have a long career history in the public and private sector organizations as diversity managers or equality officers. Clearly there is a stark contrast between the recruitment strategies for diversity managers in the cases of American and British branches of the company, as well as the mechanisms that are available for the diversity managers to exert influence on different organizational actors, such as line managers. These differences in the diversity management practice between the two countries show that despite the fact that the business case rhetoric dominates the company documents, in practice the legal sanctions continue to be more motivating than the possible positive business outcomes of diversity for the establishment of sound diversity management programmes.

Diversity management activities and programmes

The diversity activities and programmes of the case study company can be summarized under six categories: diversity training, work–life balance programme, anti-harassment policy, HRM operations, community involvement and diversity monitoring. One of the interesting findings from the analysis of the company's diversity activities is that, despite the emphasis of individually based differences in the policies, the actual diversity activities created to implement the policies are most of the time founded on group-based differences. A similar tendency is also to characterize the diversity of the management programmes of other organizations in the UK. As Liff (1996: 22) notes, commenting on the review of the diversity policies of 300 organizations in the UK by Kandola and Fullerton, 'of their list of the ten most frequently implemented diversity initiatives, the top three include the words of equal opportunities and four others are explicitly targeted at social groups'. When asked who are in the target groups of the company's diversity programmes, one of the diversity managers of the company replied:

> It's everybody. I think it's an important issue that if you're going to get an embracement of this issue, yes it's everybody. But at the same time you need to acknowledge that there are certain people that need different types of support. But you can't assume that all people in that group need that type of support.

Still, most of the actual programmes are targeted to specific groups of employees or focus on specific demographic categories, although policy regarding each programme states that it is 'open to everyone' or 'for everyone in the organization'.

Training

One of the diversity managers in the Global Diversity Council states that they see the training first and foremost as 'a communication vehicle or a way of showing your priorities'. Hence, the Council has designed several training programmes for different groups of employees. Among these, four hours of Diversity Awareness training is mandatory for all salaried employees. Parallel to this is a training programme designed in partnership with the trade unions for the hourly employees. Unlike the British case, in the United States the company's Diversity Office handles diversity only for the salaried employees. There is a separate diversity and equality office which works closely with the trade unions and deals with diversity management for the unionized employees of the company. Our study revealed that the main diversity management activity for the unionized employees focuses on training, whereas different types of diversity activities and programmes, in addition to training, are in place for the salaried employees. This focus of diversity management programmes on the salaried employees evokes questions about whether managing the diversity perspective is suitable for all employees or fits better with the demands and conditions of professional employees and office workers. As Liff (1996) suggests, unlike the association of the equal opportunities approach with the traditional industrial relations framework, the diversity management approach sits more comfortably with the human resource management perspective. The industrial relations perspective of managing labour is based on the conception of the workforce as a collective, and stresses the role of trade unions for representing workers' interests. Conversely, the human resource management perspective treats employees as individuals rather than as part of a collective and emphasizes involvement, commitment and loyalty. It is clear that in the American branch of the case study company, division of labour regarding diversity management is based on a distinction between salaried employees and hourly workers. Although one of the diversity managers of the company replied that 'that's how we do the things here', when asked about the reason for this separation, it is not hard to guess that what lies behind it is the different employee management methods the company is using for its salaried employees, who are not unionized, and its hourly workers, who are union members. However, diversity training for the hourly employees is very similar to the Diversity Awareness training for the salaried employees in terms of its coverage, that is definition of diversity; the business case; prejudices, biases and stereotypes; the organizational environment; the meaning of inclusion; personal responsibility and behaviour awareness.

On the other hand, there are various other diversity training courses offered for specific groups of salaried employees such as groups like purchasing, HR personnel, managers, people in local diversity councils and diversity managers. In addition to these diversity training programmes, the company has Affirmative Action, Equal Employment Opportunity and Anti-Harassment training open to all of its employees. The first Diversity Awareness training in the company dates back to the 1990s. It was designed by the Global Diversity Office and initiated in the United States. Later, it was sent over to European branches of the company. However, this strategy of importing the training programme, which had been developed according to the US framework, did not work out since the European counterparts found the training 'too American', in other words, ethnocentric.

Accordingly, the European branch of the company developed its own diversity training courses. One of the members of the European Diversity Team of the company stated that they devised the training programmes with a focus on inclusion, unlike the traditional equal opportunities training programmes that are primarily based on gender, ethnicity and race. He argued that the majority of people react negatively to training based on legislation and perceive that training as unrelated to them:

> And people have been attending diversity trainings since the 70s. But unfortunately what you tend to get from people is that diversity is nothing to do with me, it's about ethnic minorities. People would come and say 'because I've been a naughty boy, I've been sent to diversity' or 'I'm not a racist what am I doing here. This is a total waste of time because you're not gonna change me. Nothing to do with me. I'm just being forced to sit here'. It's not uncommon to get those reactions. And then you do get people who will say I want to do good things for people. So it comes very socially oriented or responsible whatever you want to call it, or caring for somebody else. So both sides see it from, you know, it's nothing to do with them. So if you do a piece of research and look at how many courses start from a legal perspective, from a conflict perspective. Now after eight hours of that there's nothing in it for me because what all I see is that everybody has got a piece of legislation to cover them, everybody is protected, chances of me getting the job is going to be less, because they're going to be given more chances. That's wrong, that's wrong, race, race, race, race, disability, disability, disability.

Hence, he argues, his training approach is an inclusive one and aims to encourage people to relate the concepts in the training to their experiences.

From my training perspective, I felt very strongly that we need a totally different approach. I think where people were getting stuck is they could not see how it connected with them personally. To be able to understand what diversity is you need to understand your own diversity, where you're coming from and what impact does this have on others in a safe environment and what options you have. So what you've now got is these people discussing from the position of where they are in the company, their age, their life cycle. But you don't push them too hard, you just warm them to start thinking. Because once you put them on that road they can't stop. So they actually engage and start discovering. And then you tell them what the law is. But you don't start with the law, you finish with the law. It's quite different.

Accordingly, an extensive training programme has been designed to raise the awareness of the employees and managers at all levels, in the issues of diversity. This is themed in-line with the competencies relevant to the different groups of employees' roles and responsibilities in the organization. This framework includes four levels: acquiring the basic knowledge for the employees who have just started and who do not manage anybody; applying the knowledge the supervisors or managers who just manage one person; guiding the people who apply the knowledge for the team leaders and line managers; and finally creating the knowledge for investigators and HR professionals. One-day Diversity Awareness Workshop and the Dignity at Work training are compulsory for everybody in the British branch of the company. In addition to these two courses, team leaders and line managers undertake a more in-depth two-day workshop on diversity. Lastly, there is a two-day programme which merges harassment and bullying with diversity for the people who investigate the complaints, and a three-day programme on recruitment, retention and diversity for the HR professionals.

Work–life balance

The diversity managers from the British branch and the European Diversity Team stated that the practice and policies regarding the worklife balance is more developed and sophisticated in the United States, so they follow their example in Europe by introducing similar programmes.

The work–life integration programme of the company includes three categories: childcare leave, parental leave and alternative work practices. Only the traditional work–life programmes regarding childcare and parental leave are available for the hourly workers of the company. In partnership with the trade unions, the company introduced centres to offer support to working families. The 40 such centres throughout the United States offer services including childcare, family and adult education programmes and health services.

On the other hand, alternative work programmes are designed for salaried employees. In one of the company documents it is admitted that work–life balance is a challenge for the company, particularly regarding manufacturing, since 'Plant schedules are more rigid. Night, weekend and holiday shifts are often the rule'. Similarly, a member of the Global Diversity Team argued:

> Work life is not something easy to do in a manufacturing environment as it is in high-tech environment. When you're working in manufacturing environment, you have people who are tied to getting production on the line. Flexible working is not so easy in manufacturing. It's not so easy to telecommute, those kinds of things.

Hence, the alternative work programmes primarily aim 'to attract and retain top professional talent'. These programmes cover transitional work arrangements (such as part-time work), job sharing, Alternative Work Schedule (flexitime) and telecommuting. When asked about the beneficiaries of these programmes, one of the diversity managers in the Global Diversity Team said:

> None of our programmes are specifically for one gender or another. We have more women than men working part-time, telecommuting is fifty–fifty. In terms of leave people get their eight weeks as a physical or medical leave and they can take up to a year. Men can take leave for paternity. But then the higher percentages of men are taking educational leave. Women take maternity leave. So I would say that it's programme specific.

Similarly, a member of the European Diversity Team of the company stated:

> And we try to make all our policies inclusive. So the whole issue of inclusion is important. Because we have an employee profile where the majority of our employees are men. So everything we've done we've tried to relate them as well. If you look at the work–life issues, it is about work and life, it is about caring, it is about carers; it is about your whole life outside the work. So a man who wants to be a football referee outside, or play in an orchestra or you know the other things, the issues just as important to him as somebody who is a mother, who wants to take time off, or somebody who has an elderly relative to look after. It depends on the need, but it is inclusive of everyone.

Hence, the company strongly emphasizes the inclusive nature of the work–life balance policies and that they are not targeted to any specific demographic group but are for everyone in the company with the exception of manufacturing employees who are tied to the assembly line.

Anti-harassment policy

The senior management of the company displays a serious commitment in communicating the company's anti-harassment policy to the employees. In one of his weekly notes to the employees the CEO of the company states his concern that all company personnel may not be conducting themselves with the highest standards of professional behaviour and ethics, and stressed that harassment will not be tolerated, instructing employees to report any such incidents immediately. Similarly, in 1997, one of the company's senior managers sent all hourly and salaried employees a letter stating the company's commitment to zero tolerance of harassment. This commitment is hardly surprising since the company had serious problems regarding racial harassment, and had to pay large sums of money to its harassed employees as a result of industrial tribunal decisions. However, the rhetoric regarding the justification of the anti-harassment policy continues to be business focused. The letter mentioned above reads: 'All of us have a role to play in creating and sustaining a work environment which is inclusive and which allows all people to fully contribute to the business success of (the company)'.

Hence, harassment is defined in this policy as in terms of its effect on work performance and the working environment. It means, as the company's global anti-harassment policy document states, 'conduct of a harassing nature, whether in the workplace or off-site, which has the effect of interfering with someone's work performance, or which creates an intimidating, hostile and offensive working environment'. Then, it is said, the company has a zero tolerance for 'sexual harassment; racial or national origin harassment; harassment based on sex, race, colour, religion, age, national origin, disability, sexual orientation, or veteran status; retaliation against anyone for making a good-faith complaint of such harassment or for cooperating in company investigations of such complaints'.

However, this policy did not seem to work very effectively, at least in the case of the British branch of the company. When this branch had been shaken in the late 1990s by the news of a tribunal decision regarding a racial harassment case, the company already had an Anti-Harassment Policy in place, but which had not prevented the harassment. So, the British branch developed the Dignity at Work Policy in partnership with the trade unions. The guide explaining the policy still emphasizes the business case for anti-harassment:

> Dignity at work means that as a Company we are committed to providing a healthy working environment where we all feel valued and respected so that we can make full use of our abilities, skills and experiences and contribute fully to the success of the company.

The policy includes not only harassment but bullying and victimization. Although the definitions of the concepts emphasize the individual-based understanding of diversity, differences based on demographic categories are particularly stated. Three points are important with regard to this policy, which seems to be an improvement over the global anti-harassment policy. First, it explicitly puts forward that in the case of a complaint, the recipient's perception is what counts rather than the perpetrator's intention. Second, abuse of power is included in the harassment clause. And lastly, under bullying, more covert types of discriminatory treatment are covered such as 'unfair work assignments', 'continual unjustifiable criticism', 'non-cooperation, isolation or exclusion by other employees'.

Employees can fill in a complaint formally or informally through talking to their line manager, a union representative, a member of the HR team, a member of a local diversity council or the occupational health department. In addition, an employment harassment helpline has been introduced all over the company to provide employees with confidential advice. With the Dignity at Work Policy, handling of complaints is speeded up as well. Parallel to the introduction of the new policy, a compulsory training course has been developed to explain the company's Dignity at Work policy to all employees.

Human resource management operations

The company's diversity-related HRM operations largely focus on recruitment of ethnic minority employees. Although one of the diversity managers in the Global Diversity Team claims that their diversity recruitment efforts are not 'just about ethnicity', most of the activities and programmes that are mentioned in the interviews and the company documents are specifically targeted at ethnic minority recruitment. She further explained that they do quarterly reviews of recruiting and then 'if it appears that there is any group that we are not recruiting appropriate numbers for, then we will talk about that function about concentrating in that area for the following quarter'. However, she also admitted that they do not have specific targets and goals for diversity recruitment. Absence of targets may well mean that the level of recruitment from diverse groups depends on personal attitudes and interpretations of the diversity managers and functional managers who are in charge of recruiting.

In reaching the prospective recruits the company uses a variety of methods, such as ethnic minority recruitment fairs, partnership with ethnic minority professional organizations, a mentoring scheme and summer internship for undergraduate students, partnership with universities with a high population of ethnic minority students, and advertising vacancies in local newspapers with a high ethnic minority population. The company's diversity-based recruitment efforts are supported to a large extent by the EGs, whose members volunteer for mentoring, attending careers fairs, and so on.

In the case of the British branch of the company it is claimed that diversity and equality objectives are an integral part of recruitment and selection procedures. All line management and Human Resources Departments who participate in recruitment and selection in the British branch are trained and made aware of company diversity policies, practices and procedures. National, regional and local demographic information is used to compare the company's workforce profile with the local population. Accordingly, it is stated that all recruitment and selection processes, assessment centres, training in fair selection techniques for all recruiters/selectors, testing, and the manner in which interviews are conducted are systematically reviewed. However, since the company statistics were not made available for this research, it is hard to reach any conclusion about the impact of these diversity activities in relation to recruitment on the actual workforce figures of the company.

Community involvement

Another area of the company's diversity management activities is community involvement. External partnership, and, as a part of that, community outreach, is one of the five strategic areas of focus of the Global Diversity Policy. The company encourages its salaried employees to become involved in community activities by giving them the option of two full days per year to devote to volunteer not-for-profit organizations. Consequently, company employees are reported to participate in community projects and charity walks, raise money for charities, and so on. One of the diversity managers of the company said:

> We try to influence a lot of public opinion, we sponsor, give money and support a lot of community organizations. And we mention diversity as part of our corporate citizenship and living where our employees are involved in mentoring and supportive programmes in schools and so on.

In addition, the company documents advertise the company's partnership with its EGs, who are said to be very active in community outreach. However, the company's community involvement activities are not at all as altruistic as they sound. In particular, one of the examples of EG community involvement activity, given by one of the respondents, was very clear in terms of the profit motive behind the company's community involvement efforts:

> Our . . . Asian Indian Group for example brought in a number of Asian Indian doctors and we had a programme for them and then we let them drive cars around the track, because we wanted to sell them cars.

Accordingly, the company corporately sponsors several diversity activities and events, and financially supports various ethnic minority and women's groups /organizations, as a part of its marketing strategy both globally and in Britain. For instance, the British branch's diversity documents say: 'We have proactively sought opportunities to be involved in events which target ethnic minority communities and customers. It raises the profile of . . . as a company and a brand amongst those customers'.

Other groups that are included in the company's community outreach framework are suppliers and dealers. The company states that in the United States it purchased goods and services from minority- and women-owned businesses more than any other automobile company in the country. Regarding the dealers, the company documents suggest that the company has a greater percentage of minority dealers than any other major automaker in the US. In addition the company offers a training programme for minority dealers in the United States. The diversity strategy manager for the company's Minority Dealer operations says: 'We see the demographics and the purchasing power, a recent study found that more than one out of every 10 new car buyers is a minority. . . Company wants the dealerships to reflect the customers'. In order to sell more cars to diverse groups of customers, the company does not only support minority dealers, but also tries to raise awareness of all its dealers regarding diversity through seminars, guides and web-based training. Hence, the company's 2005 Diversity Brochure explains that the company aims to help its dealers to 'better understand and serve African–Americans, Asian–Americans, gay, lesbian, bisexual and transgender customers, Hispanics, women and young adults'.

Diversity monitoring and impact assessment

At the global level, diversity is monitored in three areas. First, representation of women and people of colour at all salary levels is measured quarterly. Second, diversity objectives are monitored as a part of senior managers' scorecards. Senior executive bonuses are tied to diversity management, along with traditional performance measures. However, global diversity policy does not require cascading diversity goals down to the performance reviews of middle managers. Third, the company has an annual employee attitude survey distributed to all employees globally. This survey includes 55 questions, six of which are related to diversity. Interestingly, in the 1996 survey results the lowest score (42 per cent) came from ratings for the statement 'Diversity issues are a priority for top management'. The survey results of 2003 showed that scores regarding the items on various aspects of workplace diversity, along with the scores of items on training and development and overall job satisfaction, has declined compared to previous years.

In the British branch of the company there is a much more systematic monitoring and impact assessment process. In addition to the employee attitude survey, the company conducts women only, men only, minorities only and mixed focus groups to elicit employee perceptions and opinions on diversity. Additionally, data on recruitment, retention, rate of return to work after maternity leave, access and development opportunities, internal promotions, grievances, complaints of discrimination, harassment and bullying cases, sickness/absence rates and take–up of internal training programmes are collected regularly with consideration of employee diversity.

In the British branch of the company all this process of monitoring and impact assessment is systematically conducted through a baseline diversity and equality audit. The audit is based on the CRE's racial equality standard, and it establishes the ground for the diversity policy development in the British branch of the company. Throughout the audit process, diversity is measured against six areas of business activity at five levels: policy and planning; selection; developing and retaining staff; communication and corporate image; corporate citizenship; and auditing for diversity and equality. The audit is conducted by trained auditors. These internal auditors were verified by an independent auditor. The company uses its diversity and equality audit process to deliver long-term sustainable change and share best practice in Britain. As a member of the European diversity team explained, the systematic and process-driven nature of the audit fits very comfortably with the long-established organizational culture of the company:

> I think that is driving change through because there is a systematic process . . . is a very systematic process driven company. So that process drives change, clearly outlining what line management responsibility is, what we need to do from one step to the next and how we measure that change. And there is a robust independent auditing process annually monitoring the implementation of the Action Plans for each area.

Hence, the company's traditional command and control culture is being utilized as an advantage to design, implement and monitor diversity policies and programmes. The European Diversity Team plans to launch the diversity and equality audit process in other European branches of the company as well. However, there is no hint showing that the Global Diversity Office is willing to transfer the audit to the company's other branches outside Europe. Although not admitted by the diversity managers or in the company documents this unwillingness is largely due to the fact that European legislation in the field of diversity and equality is more advanced than the legislation in the other parts of the world, and this puts pressure on the companies in Europe to develop sophisticated and well-grounded diversity management policies.

10.4 Conclusion

In this chapter, we have explored global diversity management at the level of organizational policy and practice. In doing so, we examined the different dimensions of the organizational level dynamics of diversity management. Although the case study company had a global diversity management policy, we have explained that the implementation of this policy displayed cross-national variation. This shows the necessity of multilevel attention to the global diversity management practices. The chapter has been largely based on the analysis of the company's grey literature, and is limited to the company website and documentation that was made available by the company. In addition to this documentation, semi-structured interviews conducted with the diversity managers of the company have informed our analysis.

The chapter has demonstrated that even in a single company, which has a global diversity management policy, structures and practices of managing diversity vary across national contexts. Furthermore, the macro-social and macro-institutional structures at the national level, such as legislation and institutions, which enforce legislation, are key determinants of these national variations, which, in turn, provide diversity managers in different countries with different configurations of resources and constraints. One of the important insights that can be drawn from the influence of macro-social dynamics on organizational practices of diversity management is that diversity management practices materialize in a multilevelled context, and the scholarship in the field needs to acknowledge and account for the multiple sources of influence on processes of diversity management at the social, organizational and individual levels. National-level factors, such as legislation and labour market characteristics, impact upon the translation of global diversity policies in different national settings and across the branch network of multinational companies.

Further reading

Aldefer, C.P. and Smith, K.K. (1982) 'Studying Intergroup Relations Embedded in Organizations', *Administrative Science Quarterly*, vol. 27, pp. 35–65.

Ashkanasy N.M., Hartel, C.E.J. and Daus, C.S. (2002) 'Diversity and Emotion: The New Frontiers in Organizational Behaviour Research', *Journal of Management*, vol. 28, no. 3, pp. 307–38.

Bacharach, S.B., Bamberger, P.A. and Vashdi, D. (2005) 'Diversity and Homophily at Work: Supportive Relations among White and African–American Peers', *Academy of Management Journal*, vol. 48, pp. 619–44.

Barak, M.E.M. (2000) 'The Inclusive Workplace: An Ecosystems Approach to Diversity Management', *Social Work*, vol. 45, no. 4, pp. 339–52.

Chatman, J.A., Polzer, J.T., Barsade, S.G. and Neale, M.A. (1988) 'Being Different yet Feeling Similar: The Influence of Demographic Composition and Organizational Culture on Work Processes and Outcomes', *Administrative Science Quarterly*, vol. 43, no. 4, pp. 749–80.

Larkey, L.K. (1996) 'Toward a Theory of Communicative Interactions in Culturally Diverse Workgroups', *Academy of Management Review*, vol. 21, pp. 463–91.

Lau, D.C. and Murnighan, J.K. (1998) 'Demographic Diversity and Faultlines: The Compositional Dynamics of Organizational Groups', *Academy of Management Review*, vol. 23, pp. 325–40.

Milliken, F.J. and Martin, L.L. (1996) 'Searching for Common Threads: Understanding the Multiple Effects of Diversity in Organizational Groups', *Academy of Management Review*, vol. 21, pp. 402–33.

Moore, S. (1999) 'Understanding and Managing Diversity among Groups at Work: Key Issues for Organizational Training and Development', *Journal of European Industrial Training*, vol. 23, pp. 208–17.

Mor Barak, M.E. (2000) 'The Inclusive Workplace: An Ecosystems Approach to Diversity Management', *Social Work*, vol. 45, pp. 339–52.

Muir, C. (1996) 'Workplace Readiness for Communicating Diversity', *The Journal of Business Communication*, vol. 33, no. 4, pp. 475–86.

Richard, O.C. (2000) 'Racial Diversity, Business Strategy, and Firm Performance: A Resource Based View', *Academy of Management Journal*, vol. 43, pp. 164–77.

Smith, W.J., Wokutch, R.E., Harrington, K.V. and Dennis, B.S. (2004) 'Organizational Attractiveness and Corporate Social Orientation: Do Our Values Influence Our Preference for Affirmative Action and Managing Diversity?', *Business and Society*, vol. 43, pp. 69–96.

Tsui, A.S., Egan, T.D. and O'Reilly, C.A. III (1992) 'Being Different: Relational Demography and Organizational Attachment', *Administrative Science Quarterly*, vol. 37, pp. 549–79.

Watson, W.E., Kumar, K. and Michaelsen, L.K. (1993) 'Cultural Diversity's Impact on Interaction Process and Performance: Comparing Homogenous and Diverse Task Groups', *Academy of Management Journal*, vol. 36, pp. 590–602.

Welch, D. and Welch, L. (1997) 'Being Flexible and Accommodating Diversity: The Challenge for Multinational Management', *European Management Journal*, vol. 15, pp. 677–85.

Individual Effects: **11**
The Agency of the
Diversity Manager

11.1 Introduction

Global diversity management is often examined as an organizational phenomenon. Throughout this book, we demonstrate that multilevel influences shape global diversity management policies and practices. What remains unattended in the current literature is the role of diversity managers in the diversity management process. In this chapter, we will address this issue. Following the publication of *Workforce 2000: Work and Workers for the 21st Century* by the Hudson Institute (Johnston and Packer 1987), 'diversity management' has become one of the most uttered words in both business and academic circles alike (see Hays-Thomas 2003). Despite the rising popularity of the subject, coupled with an increasing amount of management research on the issue, a review of the literature suggests that diversity managers as professional workers and agents of organizational change have remained a largely neglected topic of research. Diversity managers are the most visible, if not the most effective, actors in the process of managing diversity due to their professed role in the design and implementation of diversity management policies and programmes. In this chapter we will seek to understand the agency of diversity managers in organizational change; in other words, to find some clues for answering the question: can diversity managers engender the organizational change which they envision? Seeking to answer this question and fill the gap in the diversity management literature, we examine the role and impact of diversity managers as organizational change agents. We then turn to the literatures on change agents and diversity managers with a view to offering a three-dimensional analytical framework of situatedness, relationality and performativity, which situates the agency of diversity managers within the relational scope of organizational change as triggered by diversity management policies and programmes or the person of the diversity manager.

11.2   Diversity managers as professionals

Since the diversity management process is associated with organizational change in the literature (Cox and Blake 1991; Mighty 1991; Dobbs 1996; Gilbert and Ivancevich 2000), we argue that diversity managers should assume the role of change agents in their organizations. There can be a spectrum of organizational approaches to equality and diversity, ranging from rejection of any relevance or concern to legal compliance to more sophisticated diversity management perspectives. Unsurprisingly, the agentic role of change of diversity managers may also vary: the role may be devolved to the level of line management, it can be centralized in a unit or assumed by a single person. Our aim is not to unpack the interplay between the various configurations of organizational approaches and personal interventions in the process of diversity management, but to explore the scope and content of the diversity manager's agentic power, resources and strategies which manifest in their efforts to achieve organizational change. It is well documented that in the field of diversity research there is a wide lack of interest in the agency of diversity managers, as the few available references on diversity managers (e.g. Jones *et al.* 1989; DiTomaso and Hooijberg 1996; Brimm and Arora 2001; Todd 2002) are in the form of personal accounts and anecdotes. Ironically, this situation holds true also for the equal opportunities field, which is a longer established area of research, and in which there has been little interest in investigation of individual officers and managers of equal opportunities and their individual role in transforming organizations. There is one book specifically on equal opportunities officers by Kandola *et al.* (1991) which reveals that equal opportunities officers suffer greater levels of job-related stress than their peers, and another study on the impact of equal opportunities officers on the culture of universities in Australia (Burrett 2002). In her research, Burrett found that organizational change is a highly political process. Accordingly, the impact of equal opportunities officers on organizational culture depends on a number of factors ranging from their individual communication and interpersonal skills, and the seniority of their position in the university system and societal context.

In addition to these two studies, which are directly related to equal opportunities officers, it is possible to pinpoint other remarkable works in the field of equal opportunities that may provide important insights into the nature of the job of these officers. However, the focus of these studies is not necessarily on equality and diversity officers as agents of change either. For instance, Jewson and Mason (1986) distinguish between liberal and radical approaches to change, where the scope of the former is limited to equality of opportunity, while the latter aims for equality and fairness in outcomes. The distinction between these two approaches may be very instrumental when investigating the equality values and ethics of diversity managers as well as their strategic planning and implementation of change programmes. On the other hand, Cockburn (1989: 214–15) has criticized the liberal–radical dichotomy posited by these authors and has put forward the terms 'short' and 'long transformational agenda'. She states that 'short' and 'long agendas' should not be understood as contradictory but complementary within the equal opportunities framework, where the short agenda focuses on minimizing the bias in human resource management (HRM) procedures, and the long agenda targets the transformation of the field of employment and organizations to radically dissolve the discrimination and inequality in the workplace (Cockburn, 1989: 218). In her monograph, *In the Way of Women: Men's Resistance to Sex Equality in Organizations*, Cockburn (1991) includes some accounts of the equality officers in her case study organizations. These stories reveal how the job of equal opportunities officers is embedded in the organizational politics. Against the backdrop of heterosexist, patriarchal and capitalist culture in society and organizations, the role of equality officers involves a great deal of strategic manipulation of the organizational rules and the power relations that exist among organizational actors, such as minority and majority group employees, unions, and middle and senior management.

In addition to the works mentioned above, our literature survey revealed that there are two empirically based published research articles focusing specifically on equal employment opportunities officers. The first one of these is the study by Lawrence (2000) which reports on interviews conducted with 30 equal opportunities officers from different sectors in the UK. The interviews generated data on the process of recruitment, knowledge and expertise, individual and organizational approaches towards equal opportunities, and individual strategies for tackling organizational change. Lawrence found that the concept of human rights underpins the perspectives of equal opportunities officers and that they have a long agenda for organizational change. The study also revealed that senior management support for equality objectives and the seniority of equality officers, as well as their personal traits such as patience, persistence and resilience, and their knowledge of legislation, industrial relations and human resource management procedures, are among the decisive factors for the legitimacy and influence of the officers in engendering change within their organizations. The author concludes by pointing out the need for further research on equal opportunities officers as an occupational group to examine their role and effectiveness in implementing policy changes.

The second study (Parker 1999) is based on interviews with 12 equal opportunities officers who produced 'best practice' sexual harassment policies in Australia's financial services sector. The article presents insights into the dual strategies used and the dual identities held by the best practice equal opportunities officers to initiate or support change initiatives in their organizations. Parker reports that the majority of the equal opportunities officers she interviewed described their role as 'weaving external EEO (*Equal Employment Opportunity*) principles, as institutionalized in anti-discrimination law, with management practices' (1999: 29). Hence, she claims that as 'double dealers', equal opportunities officers based their strategies on comfortably slipping between public values of equality and justice, and private concerns of business and profits, as well as between their own dual personal commitment to public ethical norms and private corporate duties (1999: 34).

Unfortunately, similar research on diversity managers is lacking. In the absence of such research, it seemed appropriate to consult the literature on change agents, and their role in transforming organizations, since diversity managers are expected to act as change agents within the framework of diversity management initiatives that seek to transform organizations (Dobbs 1996). We turn to the literature on change management in pursuit of clues to the scope of a diversity manager's role in organizational change. Review of the change agency literature shows that there is no authoritative evaluation of diversity managers or equality officers as change agents. Another point that became apparent after the review is that change agency literature is not without its own flaws and contradictions, and that it displays important deficiencies in some respects. In the next section, the suitability of change agency literature to offering a formula for understanding the change agency role of diversity managers is discussed.

11.3   Models of change agency

Our survey of the literature on change agency has revealed an over-fragmented research area, crowded with various disconnected works, each piece focusing on a specific aspect of the phenomenon without articulating it within the totality of the subject or situating it in a wider theoretical framework of change agency. In addition to the lack of theoretical rigour, the works in the field also suffer from a lack of empirical grounding. As noted by Huy (2001), most of the works are examples of predominantly prescriptive models of change agents, established on scientifically vulnerable theoretical and empirical bases. In addition to this general flaw in the literature, there are three other problematic areas: (i) a rational, autonomous and individualistic conceptualization of change agency; (ii) an acontextual and disembodied focus on change agents' competencies and traits; and (iii) a lack of consideration for the power dynamics in the change process.

First, there are several competing models of change agency that treat the concept as an individualized phenomenon. Until the 1980s, the work on change agency was confined to organizational development (OD) research, inspired by the works of Lewin (1951). Within the OD tradition, the conception of change was that of a linear and rational process of planned change in relatively stable organizations, and an understanding of the role of the change agent was that of unbiased external or internal consultant as facilitator armed with counselling, consensus building, listening and coaching skills (Beckhard 1969; Tichy 1974). These rationalized and individualized understandings of the change process and change agency were later identified as main weaknesses of the OD perspective (Dawson 1994; 2003; Caldwell 2003).

Another strand in the literature that presents such a linear process of change focuses on the tempo of change for understanding change agency. Weick and Quinn (1999: 375) define two types of change corresponding to different tempos of the process: (i) episodic or radical change, which is discontinuous and intermittent; and (ii) continuous change, which is incremental and evolving. Drawing on that typology of organizational change, change agents are associated with different types of roles and competencies. In episodic change, change agents assume a proactive role as 'prime movers' in the process which is governed by the 'logic of replacement' (*ibid.*). On the other hand, the basis of continuous change is described with reference to the 'logic of attraction' and the role of the change agent is that of a facilitator, where she or he acts as a 'sense-maker'(Weick and Quinn 1999: 380). These two distinct logics, which epitomize change agents' roles and strategies, correspond to two different types of leadership conceptualized by Bass (1995, cited in Munduate and Gravenhorst 2003: 4): transactional leadership (logic of replacement) and transformational leadership (logic of attraction). The common vulnerability of these contributions is their tendency to analyse the strategies and activities of change agents as linear processes which are coordinated by autonomous individuals, who act on their rational calculations by drawing on 'perfect' information on organizational resources for change. Indeed this approach is insufficiently detailed to capture the reality of organizational processes of change, which is characterized with layers of negotiated and politicized forms of access to resources.

Our second concern is over a decontextualized and disembodied understanding of change agency in the literature. In the 1980s, associated with the rhetoric of the flexible, competitive and innovative organization (Atkinson 1985;

Volberda, 1998), a new stream of literature, which is fed by leadership research and which primarily focuses on the role of senior managers and organizational leaders throughout the change process, had begun to grow outside of the OD tradition (Kanter 1984; 1999). In this literature, the role and skills of change agents – such as personal drive, energy, courage and vision, the desire to lead, honesty and integrity, cognitive ability, self-confidence and knowledge of business, flexibility and risk-taking – have become almost identical with those of effective leaders (Kirkpatrick and Locke 1991; Dulewicz and Herbert 2000). Due to its reliance on a single individual as the focus of the change process, that is the extraordinary qualities of a charismatic leader, this approach was criticized by many change agency scholars (Nadler and Tushman 1990; Caldwell 2003).

Posing a challenge to the 'change leader' approach, the 'contingency perspective' claims that there is not a universal, standard formula for change agency; rather it is contingent upon business and organizational environment (Dunphy and Stace 1993: 305). Nadler and Tushman (1990) argued that there is not a single type of organizational change and an associated style of leadership. They proposed a typology of four different change types based on the pace of and motivation for change, each requiring different types of leadership styles. Ironically, although the contingency perspective is based upon a critique of the 'charismatic leader' approach, it is also centred on the idea of the individual leader as the focal point of organizational change process (Westley and Mintzberg 1989).

However, in both 'change leader' and 'contingency' perspectives, change agents are ontologically situated as disembodied and acontextual individuals. Correspondingly, the level of exploration of change agency is overwhelmingly reduced to that of individual psychology. Caldwell (2003: 132), in his critical review of change agent literature, asserts that the inclination to associate change agents with extraordinary qualities, traits and attributes endures in different models of change agency alike. This ontological attribution leads to the omission of a contextual analysis of change and to an excessive focus on change agents' competency and traits which essentially results in inflation of prescriptions regarding the necessary competencies for change agents and recipes for success. Consequently, the change agency literature is packed with a series of presumably universal lists of competencies and skills required by change agents. These lists sometimes include skills in specific areas such as forecasting, anticipating, counselling, consensus-building, listening, coaching and facilitating (e.g. Beckhard 1969; Bass 1995; Weick and Quinn 1999) or more professional competencies such as being trained in work process analysis, process consultancy or organizational development training (e.g. Tichy 1974; Huy 2001). At other times, some personal traits, such as the desire to lead, honesty and integrity, cognitive ability, problem solving, self-confidence, expertise, information and flexibility and risk taking, are also included in these lists (e.g. Kanter 1984; 1999; Kirkpatrick and Locke 1991; Buchanan and Boddy 1992; Dulewicz and Herbert 2000; Munduate and Gravenhorst 2003). Still, some others (e.g. Buchanan and Boddy 1992; Muir 1996; Huy 2001) include interpersonal skills, such as team-building, negotiation, authority, effective communication, building trust, being sympathetic and competency, in inter-personal inquiry in their list of requirements. Hence, most of the works attempt to present blueprint models of change agency in the form of advice and guidelines. Although these may be considered useful from the practition-ers' point of view, as they specify possible individual strategies that may be employed by the change agents, they add up to an unsatisfactory attempt at scientific inquiry due to the lack of a robust multilayered analysis of the con-ditions in which change agency takes place.

Lastly, although there are models of change agency that seek to contextualize the role of change agents within the organizational framework, these works overlook the power dynamics involved in the change process. An example of this is the model of change agency which is proposed by Huy (2001). Focusing on the planned change process, he constructs a model exploring two dimensions of organizational change: time and content. Four ideal types of intervention that come out of the time–content matrix of change are commanding, engi-neering, teaching and socializing, each corresponding to a change in different spheres of organization, that is in formal structures, work processes, beliefs and social relationships respectively (Huy, 2001: 604). Accordingly, Huy argues that corresponding to these four ideal types, change agents will be different organizational actors in each intervention. Namely, the people from the higher echelons of organizations assisted by external consultants will be change agents in commanding the type of intervention. The professional task analysts will be change agents in engineering the type of intervention. The process consultants and psychoanalysts will act as change agents in teaching the type of intervention. Finally, the organizational members themselves will adopt change agent roles in socializing the type of intervention. Huy's model of ideal types furthers the debate on the role of change agents by pointing out the various personal competencies and styles of leadership required for inter-vening in different aspects of organization. However, the model still shares the myopic tendency of the mainstream tradition of change agency to limit the study of the subject to the construction of 'ideal types' and to the assign-ment of some trait and competency requirements to change agents.

Another work on change agency that deserves to be mentioned in this con-text is Muir's 'system readiness approach' (1996: 478). Here, the author attempts to situate the change process in the external macro-environmental situation and internal organizational context, such as formal and informal networks and procedures, as well as pointing to the importance of assessing the impact of different ranks of organization on the process. Muir's work presents a valuable contribution by including external and internal contextual factors as the factors affecting the success of the change process. However, after the discussion of the contextual nature of change, change agents are again depicted as apolitical individuals with some skill and ability requirements.

Alternatively, Munduate and Gravenhorst (2003) draw a model for exploring the power bases of change agents within the organizational change process, which is based on a dual typology of episodic and continuous change. Focusing on the continuous change process, and relying on the social psychology tradition, they note that the individuals who are targeted through change programmes display three possible reactions to the change process: public compliance, private acceptance or identification, and internalization. Munduate and Gravenhorst (2003: 6) state that change agents have six bases of power, and that each will elicit different reactions by organizational members: reward, coercion, legitimacy, expertise, reference and information. Use of reward and coercion as the power bases by the change agent leads only to public compliance, leaving the value systems of the targets of change intact. On the other hand use of legitimacy (belief in the legitimate right of the change agent to exert influence on the target), reference (the situation where targets identify themselves with the change agent) and expertise (targets perceive the change agent as having expertise in the area), as power bases, induce private acceptance on behalf of the target. The only base of power which creates a sustained change independent of surveillance by and presence of the change agent is noted by the authors as information which will lead to a cognitive change in the target's beliefs, attitudes or values (Munduate and Gravenhorst 2003: 7).

The model of power bases of change agents proposed by Munduate and Gravenhorst offers an original approach for understanding the impact of leadership style on the organizational members during the change process. However, overemphasis of the interpersonal relationship between the change agents and change targets, as the basis of the evaluation of the success of the change process, renders the model deficient in explaining the change at the organizational level and the associated role of the change agent. Change of interpersonal relations corresponds to the micro-level of organizational change, while, for instance, organizational culture establishes the mesolevel of the change process. Neglecting any reference to organizational culture which is more than the sum of the actions, values, attitudes or beliefs that are held by the individual organizational members, and of the interpersonal relationships, the model proposes an oversimplified notion of the potential power bases of change agency and the impact of their use on change process. Moreover, the rather implicit assumption of change agent as a rational decision maker in the previous research on change agency here becomes explicit with the presentation of change agent as the leader who utilizes the power bases he or she has, on the basis of rational cost–benefit calculations.

The role of change agents is not limited to the publicly visible activities associated with seemingly rational and linear change processes on which the prescriptive models in the literature are based; but, more importantly, it involves what Buchanan and Boddy (1992: 27) call 'backstage activities', where the activities of the change agent are focused on bargaining and negotiation with different interest groups in the organization. Unfortunately, this publicly covert and inherently political dimension of change management is often ignored in the change agency research. Meyerson and Scully point to the depoliticized nature of change and change agents in the organizational studies literature as follows:

> Change agents in organizational literature generally do not have broader visions of change in mind. Although terms like 'revolutionary' and 'deep' are sometimes used to describe change, those terms rarely refer to system change that challenges the embedded assumptions of the status quo. (1995: 594–5)

In the final analysis, owing to all these implicit assumptions on change agents, which reduce them to apolitical, disembodied, decontexualized, autonomous and rational actors, the main thrust of the literature is on the key traits of change agents. An exception to this attitude to overlook power relations, as well as other embedded processes taking place throughout the change process, is offered by Agocs (1997). She maintains that organizational change is political, in that the exercise of power and control by different parties involved is central in the process. This, in turn, means that change agents may need to confront institutionalized resistance by the power holders in the organization. However, prescriptive models of change agency or 'guidelines' for success, which dominate the literature, are designated as tools for dealing with the resistance from middle or lower ranks, not from the higher echelons of the organization. The lack of consideration for potential resistance by power holders, it can be argued, is largely due to the blindness towards the organizational power dynamics. Others (Collinson *et al.* 1990; Acker 2000; Lawrence 2000; Dawson 2003) also point to the contradictory status of change agents in the organization, which stems from the friction between their job responsibilities and organizational position when they, as a part of their job, need to monitor and control the persons who hold higher ranks than themselves. In stark contrast with other literature on change agency, which focuses on necessary skills and competencies of change agents, Agocs claims that:

> It is not the knowledge or expertise in itself that is the source of power and a resource for organizational change: it is the knowledge upon which authorities have conferred legitimacy and assimilated into the organization's ideological framework. Whether a change message will be accorded legitimacy is the choice and decision of authorities. (1997: 925)

Hence Agocs incorporates the micro-politics of interpersonal relations to her framework of the potential power sources for the change agents. Accordingly, six potential strategies that change agents may make use of are: (1) to resist; (2) to create allies; (3) to make a case for change; (4) to make effective use of existing resources; (5) to mobilize politically; and (6) to build new parallel organizations (Agocs 1997: 929). With Agocs's contribution, the field gains a politicized notion of change agency as opposed to the abstract idea of agency dominating the mainstream literature. However, in that article where she aims to 'assist change advocates' by offering strategies to struggle with institutionalized resistance, Agocs (1997: 917) does not offer a comprehensive contextual analysis of change agents. Nevertheless, as Acker (2000) emphasizes, in her interpretation of the success and failure of gender equity intervention projects, competencies, capacities and strategies of the change agent are only a few among many factors that affect the outcome of the change process.

In addition to the political nature of organizational relations, change agents themselves are also political beings who strive to act according to their own personal values. For example, Tichy (1974: 164) explained change agency on the basis of the interplay between the role assumed by change agents, their personal values and life projects. Based on a survey of 91 social-change agents, he formulated what he calls the 'change agents' general change model' that covers three components: value component, cognitive component and change technologies, all of which refer to the qualities and traits of change agents. He looks at the congruence of values and actions and of cognition and action. The model that Tichy proposes makes an important contribution to the change agency research, since it is not limited to competencies of the change agents, but also takes into account the values and cognitions of the change agents. In addition, Tichy's model sheds light on some possible sites of self-contradiction that change agents may experience while they are realizing their role throughout the change process.

One of the most original contributions to change agency literature in recent years has been Meyerson's (2001a) illustrious book, *Tempered Radicals: How People Use Difference to Inspire Change at Work*. The basic contribution of the work to the organizational change literature is the introduction of a new type of change agents, 'tempered radicals', who are both the insiders and the outsiders of the organization, due to the conflict of their personal values with the dominant organizational culture (Meyerson 2001a: xi). The term is defined by Meyerson and Scully as follows:

> The individuals who identified with and are committed to their organization, and are also committed to a cause, community or ideology that is fundamentally different from, and possibly at odds with the dominant culture of their organization. (1995: 586)

Being an insider in the organization equips tempered radicals with information regarding the dynamics of the organizational system and the ability to act confidently within that familiar system (Meyerson and Scully 1995: 596). Moreover, tempered radicals are aware of the importance of gaining allies among those representing the majority perspective, which will provide them with 'a sense of legitimacy, access to resources and contacts, technical and task assistance, emotional support, and advice' (Meyerson 2001b: 99). This new understanding of change agency allows for the investigation of power relations not only to situate the role of the change agent, but also to examine the potential strategic power sources, which are shaped by their life projects and which they may exploit in order to mould and promote change.

Another work that provides an alternative perspective to organizational change and agency is an edited book by Ledwith and Colgan (1996a), *Women and Organizations: Challenging Gender Politics*, which is a collection of empirical studies from different sectors. Throughout the book, strategies used by women to challenge the status quo and gender order in their organizations are explored. Ledwith and Colgan (1996b: 30–1) argue that women as change agents need to have political skills and to be aware of organizational power relations. Neither Meyerson's study, nor Ledwith and Colgan's edited work, focus on a specific functional category in organizations, but conceptualize change agency as a quality which is rather dispersed through different levels of organization. However, within the scope of this chapter, we will limit our discussion to a particular and highly visible category of change agent, although this in no way suggests that we see organizational change as solely the property or responsibility of some more visible individuals. Conversely, being critical of such an individualistic and elitist understanding of change agency, we offer an analytical framework which can be operationalized to answer the curious question of 'can diversity managers engender the organizational change which they envision?'.

In the next section we propose a framework for understanding the phenomenon of change agency as related to diversity managers. Thus, the aim will not be to repeat the traditional practice in the literature by offering another prescriptive model of change agents, but to suggest a comprehensive analytical framework which can be employed in empirical research to reveal the change agency of diversity managers.

11.4 Diversity managers in organizational change: a proposed framework

Attending to the implicit assumptions made in both models of change agency in organizational literature, and anecdotal reference to diversity managers in the diversity management literature alike, would lead us to the notion of diversity managers as autonomous individuals who are to a large extent responsible for the success or failure of the diversity management initiatives and programmes. Moreover, within the scope of that understanding, the diversity management process in an organization would be bound up with the convenience and timing of the strategies and actions of the diversity manager, who is equipped with some abstract competencies and traits, and whose actions are assumed to be determined by the principle of rationality and free will.

We argue against such individualistic accounts of agency on the basis of the assumption that both the organizational change and the role of change agents within it are much more complicated than are depicted in the literature. Accordingly, we propose an analytical framework that embeds both agency and structure for the investigation of diversity managers as a professional group. In that respect, we find the late French sociologist Pierre Bourdieu's conceptual framework very appropriate for the study of the agency of diversity managers. The potential contribution of Bourdieu's theoretical framework to management and organizational studies is also cited elsewhere (Everett 2002; Özbilgin and Tatlı 2005). Bourdieu's whole work can be defined as one big project of developing an alternative to the analytical dualism between structure and agency which dominates the social scientific endeavour (Nash 2003). Throughout this lifetime project, Bourdieu (1977; 1990; 1998) used three concepts: *field*, *habitus* and *capital*, in addition to other notions such as *dispositions*, *doxa* and *symbolic violence*, as the building blocks of his theory of human agency, which is generated through situated relationality between different levels of social reality. His effort towards finding an 'epistemological and methodological third way' (Grenfell and James 1998: 2) to overcome the traditional dualism of agentic versus structural approaches has parallels with that of Giddens (1984) in the Anglo-Saxon tradition (see also Layder 1993; 1998; Archer 1995). Similar to Bourdieu, Giddens (1984) also proposed an alternative theoretical framework to investigate the complex and interwoven nature of social reality, presenting this through his theory of structuration, which purports that social structures and human agency and action co-evolve by reaffirming and reconstituting one another. However, we argue that Bourdieuan formulation of *habitus*, *capital* and *field* offers greater explanatory power in revealing the role of individual agency in the process of social and institutional change. Although the structuration theory suggests that structural changes result from changes in repetitive forms of individual and collective acts, Bourdieu has gone further to explain the kinds of varied resources (capitals) that individuals draw on in order to enact their strategies and how their strategies are both negotiated in and shaped by the logic of the field, that is the social structures, which in turn is altered through enactments of human agency.

We argue that there are three dimensions of diversity managers' change agency: situatedness, relationality and performativity. First, situatedness relates to the contextual nature of agency and points to how the actions of diversity managers, and the choices and constraints that generate these actions, are embedded in a historical trajectory of social and organizational becoming. Second, relationality refers to the relational character of the actions and decisions of diversity managers at seven different levels, which will be elaborated in the next section. Lastly, the dimension of performativity brings out both dynamic and stable characteristics of the agency, revealing the interplay between discourses, identities and strategies assumed by the diversity managers, as well as the total volume of *capital* under their disposition, and in the form of routinized behaviour and *habitus*. In the change agency literature only the dimension of performativity, which was studied under the banner of 'the learning approach', is explored to a limited extent, while the practice of change agents is modelled on the basis of their competencies and traits. **Figure 11.1** shows our three dimensional framework which encapsulates the agency of the diversity manager in the process of organizational change.

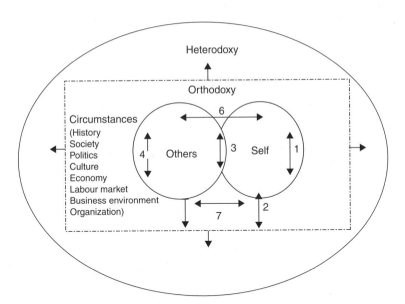

Figure 11.1   Situatedness, relationality and performativity of diversity managers' agency

Note: The list of circumstances on the left signifies the layers of situatedness.
        Key to forms of relationality:
1 the self–reflexivity and inner dialogue
2 the self and circumstances
3 the self and others
4 the other persons
5 the other persons and circumstances
6 the self, others and circumstances
7 the organizational phenomena (i.e. structures, conditions or circumstances).

Situatedness

We propose to investigate the dynamics underlying the agency of diversity managers as real individuals in their historical, economic, social and organizational settings, rather than as free-floating practitioners abstracted from their context. Hence, we argue that diversity managers' agency is situated within the context of the society and organization in which they operate. Our conception of situatedness is in-line with what Granovetter (1985: 504) has termed as 'embeddedness', which suggests 'that most behavior is closely embedded in networks of interpersonal relations'. However, in order to operationalize the situatedness of agency in the social and organizational context, we borrow one of Bourdieu's most important concepts, the *field*. Within Bourdieu's framework, *field* denotes the universe of partly preconstituted objective historical relations between positions (Bourdieu and Wacquant 1992: 16). Jenkins interprets the concept as

> a structured system of social positions – occupied either by individuals or institutions – the nature of which defines the situation for their occupants. It is also a system of forces, which exist between these positions; a field is structured internally in terms of power relations. Positions stand in relationship of domination, subordination and equivalence to each other by virtue of the access they afford to the goods and resources (capital). (1992: 85)

Hence, by utilizing the notion of *field* we aim to bring the social and organizational structures and power relations into the analysis of the agency of diversity managers.

Recognition of symbolic as well as objective power struggles in Bourdieu's formulation of the *field*, sets it aside from the original conception of the notion by Lewin (1951) and makes it more appropriate for our purposes (Özbilgin and Tatlı 2005: 967). Within that framework, social and organizational *fields*, as the defining principles of the allocation of several power positions in society and organization, draw the boundaries of individual agency. Hence, situating diversity management practice within the context of the social and organizational *fields*, both of which embed power relations at different levels and in different forms, improves our understanding of the choices and constraints that frame the actions, decisions and strategies of diversity managers.

To start with, any attempt to investigate the limit and potentials of diversity managers' agency requires the understanding of the logic of the social *field* in which their actions take place. In our framework, social *field* of diversity management refers to three historically formed structures at the social level: cultural and demographic dynamics in the labour market; institutional structures regarding diversity and equality (legislation and institutional actors), and the business environment. Firstly, the cultural and demographic dynamics in the labour market frame the diversity concerns in a society (Cavanaugh 1997). Depending on different historical trajectories of each society, some demographic groups are socially constructed as majority or mainstream, while others are pushed to the minority status or marginality. Hence, the definition of diversity that is focused throughout the diversity management process varies according to the cultural dynamics prevalent in the society and labour market (Prasad and Mills 1997). In her work, *Professions and Patriarchy*, Witz (1992) offers a clear account of how exclusion and inclusion work their way through organizations' closure and demarcation strategies. Based on the case of the medical profession, this work demonstrates that prominent gender ideologies in society will exert influence on the actual processes and relations in organizations. In addition to the cultural aspect, demographic dynamics in the labour market impact upon the diversity management practice. Composition of the labour market and contemporary trends regarding the patterns of supply and demand of labour are frequently cited as proof of the pressing need for diversity management (Thomas 1990; Shaw 1993; Gilbert and Ivancevich 2000; Allard 2002).

Secondly, the institutionalized structures that reproduce or combat inequality in the area of employment impact upon the handling of workforce diversity at the institutional level. Diversity management research needs to situate organizational diversity management policies within the context of employment and anti-discrimination legislation, and situate institutional actors in the field of employment, such as professional and legal bodies, and trade unions (Kirton and Greene 2000).

Lastly, the social *field* of diversity management is affected by the dynamics of the business environment. In the diversity management literature it is frequently stated that in addition to changing labour market demographics, the globalization of business (Adler and Ghadar 1990; Loosemore and Al Muslmani 1999; Marable 2000) and changing patterns of work organization, production and competition (Carroll and Hannan 2000; Allard 2002; Ashkanasy *et al.* 2002; Blazevic and Lievens 2002) have led to the rising need for diversity management. Furthermore, diversity management practice in an organization is affected by the interests of different stakeholders, including consumers, shareholders, employees, the state, trade unions, diversity and equality institutions, and other communities (Fernandez 1991; Morrison 1992; Cox 1993; Evenden 1993; Tyson 1995; Kirton and Greene 2000).

In addition to being embedded in the social *field*, diversity managers' agency is also situated within the organizational *field*. Katz and Kahn (1978) proposed that leadership in an organization implies working with and through formal and informal organizational structures at different levels. Simpson *et al.* (2002: 1209) refer to a range of 'negative capabilities', or the skills to manage under uncertainty, as significant in our times of increased complexity in organizational politics. Similarly, the role of diversity managers as change agents also involves working through the structures and power relations in the organizational *field* to implement diversity management policies and practices. The main constituencies of the organizational *field* of diversity management are organizational diversity policy and strategy; integration of diversity objectives throughout different functions and levels of the organization; and organizational culture.

Firstly, the limits and effectiveness of diversity managers' actions are influenced by the diversity policy and strategy of the organization. The scope and coverage of organizational diversity policy, of programmes and initiatives included in the policy, (i.e. HRM operations, the work–life balance and flexible work, harassment, corporate responsibility and community involvement), of the target and reach of the policy, of the procedures and systems for communicating, implementing and monitoring the policy, are the basic components of the diversity policy structure of the organization. Particularly, HRM systems and operations are stated as being among the most important areas of intervention throughout the diversity management process (Dobbs 1996). Despite attribution of diversity management to a wider range of functional areas, the playing field of diversity managers is strongly interrelated with the structures and procedures of HRM operations, such as selection, recruitment and retention, promotion, mentoring and career development, performance appraisal and compensation, and training and development (Fine 2003). Hence, the scope and coverage of organizational diversity policy and strategy will provide many hints regarding the choices of and constraints met by the diversity managers.

Secondly, the level of integration of diversity objectives throughout the different functions and ranks of an organization plays a crucial role in determining the power dynamics in the organizational *field* of diversity management, which, in turn, draws the boundaries of the power and effectiveness of diversity managers' actions. The status of the diversity office, and inclusion of diversity goals in overall corporate objectives, are among the most direct and visible illustrations of the level of integration (Cox and Blake 1991; Mighty 1991; Morrison 1992; Joplin and Daus 1997). In her study of equality officers, Parker (1999: 39) argues that equality officers may gain the necessary 'clout' to be effective in two ways, formally through holding a senior position and informally through having support of the senior management. The position of the diversity manager within the organizational hierarchy and the level of authority allocated to him or her also illustrate the extent of centrality of diversity management in mainstream organizational policies and strategies. Furthermore, lack of seniority can be interpreted as a reflection of a lack of commitment by the senior management (Lawrence 2000).

In addition to the individual position of the diversity or equality officer within the organizational hierarchy, the position and status of the diversity office within the organizational structure establishes a crucial source of legitimacy and power for the actions and decisions of diversity managers. Acker (2000) points out the dilemma faced by many equality and diversity officers, due to their position in the organizational hierarchy. She notes that despite the fact that implementation of diversity management and programmes is associated with an organizational change process, the diversity and equality officers, most of the time, lack the direct authority to control the different functions of the organization (Acker 2000: 627). For that reason the level of prestige and status attached to the diversity office within the organization becomes a crucial factor in the agency of the diversity managers, by either hindering the influence of their actions or encouraging it. Whilst the above depiction of diversity management applies to large corporations, in the context of small and medium enterprises, where a diversity management function or office is not in evidence, it is further problematic to talk about the power or prestige of diversity managers.

Furthermore, support for and ownership of diversity objectives by different organizational members provides an important source of legitimacy for the actions and decisions of diversity managers. Importance of senior management support for the success of diversity management programmes is frequently cited in the literature (Thomas 1990; Cox and Blake 1991; Fernandez 1991; Mighty 1991; Morrison 1992; Cox 1993; Joplin and Daus 1997). In addition, line managers' attitudes towards diversity and equality are as important as those of senior managers. In their Equal Opportunities Commission (UK) research project on recruitment and promotion, which covered 45 private sector organizations from five different industries, Collinson *et al.* (1990) found that personnel managers, who are responsible for organizational equal opportunities policies, had little influence on the recruitment and promotion decisions of the line managers, either because they were based at the corporate office, hence geographically too remote from the local branches, or because they were at a lower hierarchical level than the line managers. As a result, line managers frequently acted upon their personal ideological approaches, although these might have contradicted the corporate equal opportunities policy (Collinson *et al.* 1990: 90–1).

Lastly, analysis of organizational culture is crucial to understanding the role of diversity managers in organizational change. Organizational culture, through informal and unwritten norms and values of the organization, governs the conduct of actions of and interaction between the organizational members. Interaction between different groups and individuals is one of the most heavily researched areas in the diversity literature and is stated to be one of the most important areas of intervention throughout the diversity management process. For instance, Elmes and Connelley (1997) urge diversity managers to pay attention to intergroup relations if they are to enforce change in the organizational fabric. Moreover, it is maintained in the literature that some types of organizations associated with specific organizational cultures present a more nurturing and receptive ground for diversity management efforts, that is organizational cultures which are based on collectivist values (Chatman *et al.* 1998), 'clan culture type' and 'adhocracy culture type' (Dwyer *et al.* 2003), multicultural organization (Cox 1991), organizations with positive 'equal opportunities climate' or 'diversity climate' (Knouse and Dansby 2000). Consequently, to understand the agency of diversity managers within the organizational change process, it is necessary to analyse organizational culture for two basic reasons. First, organizational culture informs the choices, constraints and resources available to diversity managers. Second, diversity managers have to work through the organizational culture to initiate a sustainable and long-term organizational change. Diversity managers need to understand the dynamics governing the organizational culture in order to consciously enforce its change as part of the diversity management process, as well as to anticipate sites of resistance in the change process and to plan strategies to manage it (Dobbs 1996).

Relationality

We argue that the second dimension of diversity managers' agency is relationality, a concept borrowed from social psychology and structural sociology (Somers 1998; Mitchell 2000), and which refers to interdependence, intersubjectivity and interactivity of individual and organizational phenomena. Diversity managers' actions and decisions throughout the diversity management process, which aims to initiate an organizational change, gain meaning and become effective through seven levels of relationality.

The first level of relationality refers to the dimension of self-reflexivity of the diversity managers, where they reflect on their values and beliefs, and on their actions and strategies that they had taken within their organization. The importance of personal values and beliefs for understanding the actions of change agents is also stated in the literature (Tichy 1974; Meyerson and Scully 1995; DiTomaso and Hooijberg 1996). For instance, Meyerson and Scully point out that 'some individuals choose to do "diversity work" because of their commitment to social justice, their identification with a marginalized group, and their insights into the dynamics of disadvantage and privilege' (1995: 596–7). Similarly, Lawrence (2000) finds out in her research that the concept of human rights underlies the perspectives of equal opportunities officers and that they have a long agenda for organizational change. Lastly, DiTomaso and Hooijberg (1996: 170) argue that a 'political commitment . . . to a better organization, and hence to a better society' is one of the necessary skills for diversity and equality managers to be effective in their roles.

Secondly, relationality between the self and its circumstances refers to the impact of diversity managers' demographic and cultural background (macrostructural circumstances) and their organizational setting and role (organizational circumstances) on their role as a change agent. Bourdieu's concept of *habitus* has strong explanatory power for this level of relationality. In Bourdieu's framework, *habitus* functions as a bridge between structure and agency: 'Social reality exists, so to speak, twice, in things and in minds, in fields and in habitus, outside and inside social agents' (Bourdieu and Wacquant 1992: 127). *Habitus* is formed through the past experiences of agents and feeds their present perceptions and actions (Bourdieu 1977: 95). Bourdieu defines *habitus* as 'the strategy generating principle enabling agents to cope with unforeseen and ever-changing situations' (1977: 72). Within our framework *habitus* is relevant as it relates the demographic and cultural background of the diversity managers and their organizational circumstances to their present actions and decisions, hence the strategies they utilize while doing their jobs as change agents. The driving force behind the *strategies* is 'the encounter of habitus with the peculiar conjuncture of the field' (Bourdieu and Wacquant 1992: 129). This relationality between the *habitus* of diversity managers and organizational *field* is one of the key areas for understanding both their agency and success or failure of the change programme. Affiliation with or experience regarding disadvantaged groups based on religion, race, ethnicity, sexual orientation, gender, age, disability, and marital and parental status forms an important aspect of diversity managers' micro-*habituses*, which are defined as the set of dispositions formed through their past experience and socialization. Since these will have an impact upon their understanding and values of diversity, they may in turn form an advantage or disadvantage in the course of doing their job. For instance Lawrence (2000) points to the necessity of knowledge and understanding of the perspectives of the discriminated groups in the society for the equality work in the organizations.

The third level of relationality refers to the relationship between the self and others, so to speak, that is between the diversity manager and the other organizational members. At this level the amount of *social capital* (Bouty 2000; Blyler and Coff 2003) held by the diversity managers has a decisive impact on their relationship to the different organizational members, since they formally and informally work through several organizational levels and networks as a part of their role as change agents (DiTomaso and Hooijberg 1996). The sources of *social capital* for diversity managers can be both external and internal. Internal sources are relationships with organizational members from different groups and levels and inclusion in different informal organizational networks. This implicitly requires the 'interpersonal skills', the most frequently referred category of competencies in the change agency literature, such as negotiation, facilitation, communication and networking. External sources of *social capital* are related to the involvement in civil society and politics through any membership or link to formal or informal groups, networks or institutions outside the organization. Particularly, the involvement of diversity managers in networks, institutions and groups in the diversity and equality area influences the framework of their agency within the diversity management process in several ways. Firstly, this involvement provides feelings of solidarity and support through sharing experiences with other individuals in the field. Braithwaite (1992, cited in Parker 1999) in her quantitative work on Australian affirmative action officers stresses the importance of networks with the others in the profession for affirmative action officers to maintain their progressive attitudes, to retain their commitment and to get social validation of their views. Secondly, it entails the possibility of learning from the experiences of other diversity managers, gaining the knowledge of what is going on in the field and accessing different perspectives regarding equality and diversity issues, all of which may contribute to the effectiveness of the diversity manager in his or her organization through the increased ability to understand the main dynamics, to foresee the future challenges and opportunities and to produce efficient strategies for managing diversity (Meyerson and Scully 1995: 597). These processes of learning are subsumed under the title of symbolic capital of knowing, which are explored in the next section on performativity.

Internal sources of *social capital* are at least as important as external ones for diversity managers. As DiTomaso and Hooijberg (1996) emphasize, the job of managing diversity requires 'emotion work', since the sphere of intervention is a sensitive one related to deeply seated values and norms of the individuals and may invoke negative as well as positive reactions on the side of organizational members. The authors claim that leaders of diversity management 'have responsibility to understand, confront, and help address the emotional responses that people may have to diversity – whether anger, bewilderment or fear' (1996: 179). The amount of *social capital* owned by the diversity manager determines the boundaries of his or her role as a negotiator or facilitator, both between different groups and between individuals and their emotions. In the literature, involvement and buy-in regarding the diversity management policy and programmes by the organizational members and groups from different levels and functions are cited among the key pillars of successful diversity management (Dobbs 1996; Gilbert and Ivancevich 2000). A diversity manager's formal and informal networks within the organization and his or her personal skills, such as negotiation, persuasion, attracting voluntary involvement, become particularly important in the light of the budget constraints of the diversity management programmes and initiatives. For instance, Meyerson (2001a; 2001b) stresses the significance of gaining the support and involvement of various organizational actors for the organizational change agent. Newman (1995) and Itzin (1995) point to the relational dimension of organizational change and the importance of the political process of persuading the power holders in the organization regarding the necessity of change. Newman (1995: 280) argues that effectiveness of change agents relies not only on managerial activities but also on political activities which include 'making connections' with political sites and actors outside of and within the organization.

As well as the diversity managers' relationship to different organizational members, the relationship between different organizational members themselves is an important level of relationality that impacts upon the agency of diversity managers. As we previously pointed out, the vast majority of research in the diversity field focuses on intergroup relationships in the organization. The nature of the relationships between different groups in the organization can be situated in a spectrum ranging from conflict and prejudice to understanding and mutual respect (Aldefer and Smith 1982; DiTomaso and Hooijberg 1996), and those dynamics of intergroup relations to a certain extent draw the boundaries of diversity managers' agency and effectiveness in organizational change through building a matrix of choices and constraints for them. Closely connected to that, the fifth level of relationality, which impacts upon the diversity managers' agency, is the relationship between different organizational actors and their circumstances. Like diversity managers, other organizational actors also bring their *habituses* into the organizational setting, by reflecting on their different past experiences, cultural and demographic backgrounds, as well as drawing on their present situations and future aspirations. Studies analysing the impact of diversity on different groups of employees indicate that effects of and reactions to workforce diversity may show variations for different groups. For instance it is found that white males react more negatively and display lower levels of morale, job satisfaction and innovation in diverse workgroups, whereas females or minority ethnic groups are more favourable towards diverse workgroups and show evidence of increased rates of job satisfaction and participation (Wharton and Baron 1987; Tsui *et al.* 1992; DiTomaso *et al.* 1996; Cordero *et al.* 1997;). These findings, in turn, imply that some groups of organizational members will be more receptive and supportive of the diversity management process, while some others will display resistance and opposition due to their cultural and demographic backgrounds (Knouse and Dansby 2000).

Another level of relationality is the relationship between the self, others and circumstances, which connects relationality between the diversity managers' and other organizational actors' *habituses* in their organizational setting. As stated previously, the level of concurrence or conflict between the organizational *field* and different *habituses* brought in by different organizational members have an impact upon the reproduction or transformation of the organizational *field*. This level of relationality is in-line with the relational ontology adopted by Mauthner and Doucet as it 'posits the notion of "selves-in-relation". . . or "relational-being" . . . a view of human beings as embedded in a complex web of intimate and larger social relations' (2000: 125). Hence at this level of relationality, diversity managers need to relate and utilize their own values and dispositions to strategically manage and transform the sensitive balance between the dominant organizational *habitus* and micro-*habituses* brought in by different organizational actors. Elmes and Connelley's argument below binds these three aspects, the self, the other and the circumstances, together when they summarize three major implications of intergroup relations that need to be considered by change agents:

> First, change agents need to understand the impact that inter-group relations has on organizational processes. They must acknowledge that subordinate groups may not share the same normative and value systems that the organization embodies. . . . Second . . . addressing the underlying emotions and group membership issues associated with diversity is a far more important, yet difficult and complex task. . . . Finally, change agents need to differentiate diversity programs that create an impression of embracing diversity from those that acknowledge real complexities and barriers to diversity. . . . Although management's espoused theory of diversity may appear sensitive and progressive, its theory-in-action may, in fact, only patronize differences and obfuscate underlying issues rooted in status maintenance, identity conflict and ethnocentrism. . . . Neglecting to recognize and deal with these more subtle and difficult aspect of diversity management dooms structuralist initiatives to failure. (1997: 163–4)

The last level of relationality situates the organization within the macrostructural and social context. Since we conceptualize organizations as embedded in society, it is necessary to investigate the interplay between the larger societal and business environment, and the organizational dynamics regarding the diversity management framework. Hence, at the last level of relationality, analysis of diversity managers' agency should include the relationship between the wider social *field* and the organizational *field*, which have been explained in detail in the previous section. Variations in the social, economic and political structures in the social *field* are reflected in practices at the organizational *field* of diversity management.

Performativity

The last dimension of diversity managers' agency is performativity, which brings out both the dynamic and stable characteristics of agency. Performativity is a concept which was introduced by Judith Butler to denote the power of discourses in both being and doing. Butler (1997; 1999) argues that discourses are learned and continuously enacted and that these two processes of declaration and enactment reinforce each other to allow for the discourses to be reified and enacted. In the context of management, performativity is important as it combines both elements of performance and activity.

The two earlier dimensions of situatedness and relationality are constructs developed within the structuralist tradition. They are underpinned by an idea that the diversity managers' role as change agent is shaped and constrained by their embeddedness in an institutional and relational context. However, the notion of performativity is informed by a poststructuralist understanding which recognizes individual capacity to learn and exert influence through the use of relevant discourses. Therefore, performativity presents a dynamic and agentic understanding of the diversity manager's role, in the form of variability of discourses, identities and strategies assumed by the diversity managers as well as the total volume of *capital* under their disposition, and in the form of routinized behaviour and *habitus*. In the change agency literature, some aspects of performativity are explored in order to reveal the hidden influence of powerful discourses in enacting practices. One pertinent example of this is the study by Boje and Winsor (1993) which illustrates that the performative appeal of the Total Quality Management discourse conceals an enactment of a hidden agenda which simply resurrects Taylorism in organizations.

However, except for this unique example, exploration of performativity in the existing change agency literature has been to a large extent limited to the human capital tradition. Contrary to the focus of human capital theories on individual skills and qualifications obtained through education, training and experience in explaining workplace careers and agency (see Becker 1975), Bourdieu (1977; 1984; 1990; 1998) offers a relational theory of capital. The human capital approach is criticized for creating an illusion of 'free choice' and of an individual isolated from the socio-economic dynamics, thus for offering an ideological justification for sustaining the status quo (Witz 1992; Crompton and Mann 1994). Bourdieu's conception of capital goes far beyond the simplistic framing of merit-based human capital. In addition to *economic capital*, Bourdieu proposes three other forms of capital. *Symbolic capital* refers to attributes such as prestige, status and authority; *cultural capital* refers to factors such as taste, education and forms of language; and *social capital* refers to more or less institutionalized networks of relationships based on recognition (Bourdieu 1984; 1990; Bourdieu and Wacquant 1992). Only through the mediation of *habitus*, different forms of *capital* gain their value. Thus, *different forms of capital* owned by individuals should not be seen as free-floating entities which have values of their own, independent from the very framework from which they are generated and reproduced (Bourdieu and Wacquant 1992). However, this does not mean that agents, in this case diversity managers, are devoid of voluntary action and potential of performance. They utilize *strategies* to transform, allocate and distribute their *volume of capital* between different forms (Mahar *et al.* 1990), and in doing so they reproduce or transform the very structures that frame their performance. In other words, the three dimensions of agency – performativity, situatedness and relationality – are symbiotically projected onto each other and each dimension exists through its enactment in the other two dimensions. Hence, we argue that the performative aspect of diversity managers' agency becomes possible only through a relational and situational framework. Bourdieu and Wacquant (1992: 101) argue that different forms of *capital* do not exist and function except in relation to a *field* and *habitus*; rather they become efficient 'like the aces in a game of cards' only if actors know the 'rules of the game' and adhere to these rules. In order to reach their goals within the scope of diversity management policies and programmes, diversity managers have to tune their performance according to the rules embedded in the organizational *field* and relations. They learn the rules governing the organizational *field* and *habitus* by gaining an understanding of the organization through their experience of practice in the organization and by being part of formal and informal organizational networks and, thus, having access to insiders' knowledge. This learning, on the one hand, empowers diversity managers through establishing them as legitimate 'players' in the game; on the other hand, it dictates to them the 'acceptable' limits of their intervention in the organizational *field* and *habitus* within the scope of their diversity management efforts. Hence, organizational performance of diversity managers is linked to the dual character of that learning and acceptance of the formal and informal rules of the organization which simultaneously enable and constrain their agency. Only within that framework do diversity managers participate in the reproductive transformation of the organizational *field*, by virtue of the amount of different forms of *capital* they own. This implies that the volume of different forms of *capital* owned by a diversity manager has a crucial effect on the potential power bases available to them, and through employing *strategies*, they activate that potential.

As Hardy *et al.* (2000) suggest, discourse and performativity are strategic resources of organizations, as they are for the diversity managers. In the main, the diversity managers' work is to learn, disseminate, implement and enact discourses of diversity. One pertinent example of performativity of a diversity discourse is the discourse of the business case for diversity, that is the causal relationship between effective management of diversity and improved business performance (see for example Gatley and Lessem 1995; Barkema *et al.* 2002; Harrison *et al.* 2002). Another example is the discourse of inclusion. As Dutton and Ashford (1993) point out, in order to be effective, change agents need to package the change message in insiders' language. Lawrence (2000) finds that conflict strategies are identified as ineffective by equal opportunities officers.

Similarly, following the strategy of negotiation rather than opposition, diversity managers might utilize the discourse of inclusion to gain allies at different levels of the organization. Once equipped with these discourses, their legitimized ways of knowing and unique anecdotes from the organization the diversity managers may set out to enact these discourses in their organizations, by producing policy statements which affect managerial decision processes and enact the professed diversity discourses in their daily practice of work. Therefore, diversity management is enacted through the efforts of diversity managers, not only through implementation of policy across the organization, but also as individual enactments of daily performance that will generate 'small wins' (Weick 1984; Meyerson and Fletcher 2003: 230). Barak (2000) presents a negotiated framework of organizational change for diversity management which brings to our attention the primacy of individual-level enactments of diversity management.

However, although it is implicit in the above account of performativity, the emphasis on conversion of the organizational setting to an educational setting, where learning is acquired and used to effect change, is also problematic. Gunn and Gullickson (2003) argue that managers' willingness to act on their learning is constrained by performativity, that is their belief in how acceptable their approach would be in the context of the prevailing organizational setting and discourse. Garrick and Clegg question the legitimacy of such a performative design, in what they term as project-based learning, that is learning in organizational settings that create their legitimacy to enact and implement:

> The legitimacy of project based learning appears on the surface to be quite simple: does the learning lead to problem solution? But this apparently self-evident picture of learning rests upon philosophical instabilities that are not often acknowledged. Too frequently the desired corporate outcomes of learning hinge on positivistic behavioral psychology and positivism containing discredited notions of a value-free social science – an objectivist illusion. The 'true' situation is that such frameworks are saturated with the ideologies of technical-rationalism and market economics. The trick of the illusion is that by rules of inference, corporate capabilities are transformed into 'facts', social values into 'inputs' and irreducible assumptions become taken-for-granted 'givens'. (2001: 123).

Conversely, we argue that the performativity of diversity managers within the framework of diversity management programmes that seek organizational change requires uncovering the illusions that legitimize hegemony and challenging the *doxic experience* prevailing in the organization. The notion of *doxa* refers to 'the preconstructed representation of this world' and 'the cognitive schemata that underlie the construction of this image' (Bourdieu and Wacquant 1992: 247). Accordingly, the *doxic experience* as 'uncontested acceptance of the daily lifeworld' will be only possible when objective and cognitive structures coincide (Bourdieu and Wacquant 1992: 73). In organizations, the hegemonic majority culture corresponds to the domain of orthodoxy (the right opinion), whereas deviances from that constitute the domain of heterodoxy. The doxic experience is sustained by both members of majority and minority groups, and the dominant and dominated individuals in organizations. As Bourdieu suggested, dominated agents 'tend to attribute to themselves what the distribution attributes to them, refusing what they are refused ("That's not for the likes of us"), adjusting their expectations to their chances, defining themselves as the established order defines them' (1984: 471). Similarly, Lorde (2003: 274) asserts that danger and fear 'of contempt, of censure, or some judgment or recognition, of challenge, of annihilation', which are inherent in the process of transforming silence into speech and action inhibit one's acts of self-revelation. Thus, exclusion and inequality, which work against principles of successful diversity management, are reproduced in organizations through everyday utterances of *doxic experience*. Hence, diversity managers' *performativity* would include transforming the domain of orthodoxy. In other words, the awareness raising process, which is cited frequently as the learning based approach (Argyris and Schön 1978; Pedler *et al.* 1991; Senge1990; Dodgson 1993; Contu and Willmott 2003) and which constitutes an important part of most diversity managers' prescribed role (Cox 1991; Fernandez 1991; Elmes and Connelley 1997; Kirton and Greene 2000; Allard 2002), seeks to challenge the *doxic* experience to diversify and enrich the *doxic* space.

11.5 Conclusions

Diversity managers are important actors in the process of diversity management. In this chapter, we have provided a model for understanding their agency in the context of organizational change. Diversity managers are expected to serve as internal agents of organizational change. However, cultural change that is foreseen by the diversity management process cannot be achieved in the absence of multiparty engagement with and plural support from the actors outside and inside of the organization or structural conditions that are conducive to change. Furthermore, the actions and strategies of diversity managers are framed by situational and relational factors. Returning to our orientating question, can diversity managers engender the organizational change which they envision?, based on our arguments above, we contend that diversity managers' agency can only be judged through its situatedness, relationality and performativity. Our conceptual framework of three dimensions presents a number of challenges to the contemporary change agency literature, which conceives change agents as autonomous, de-contextualized and apolitical beings. Our three-pronged framework seeks to situate both the role of diversity managers as individuals and the diversity management as a change process in a social and organizational context.

First, situatedness in the context of diversity managers' change agency denotes the web of organizational and social structures and power relations that mould that agency and that resides in the social and organizational field of diversity management. The social field of diversity management refers to three historically formed structures at the society level: cultural and demographic dynamics in the labour market; institutional structures regarding diversity and equality (legislation and institutional actors); and the business environment. The main constituencies of the organizational field of diversity management are organizational diversity policy and strategy; integration of diversity objectives throughout different functions and levels of organization; and organizational culture. Our formulation of situatedness is in essence a critique of the blueprint approaches to change agency and change management articulations prevailing in the current literature. Our framework calls for an approach to managing change that is tailored to address social and organizational circumstances. In doing so, change is envisioned as an embedded process and diversity managers as resourceful, creative and strategic, but yet constrained, agents of change.

The second dimension of diversity managers' agency is relationality, which refers to seven levels of interdependence, intersubjectivity and interactivity among individuals and the organizational context. Thus, our framework provides an inclusive set of relationalities among self, others and circumstances that capture our imagination of the organizational terrain. Therefore, the diversity managers' agency in this dimension presents an understanding of individual and organization, not as autonomous rational entities, as framed in agentic literature, but as relational beings intertwined in a constant process of emergence and becoming. Thus, relationality de-emphasizes the role of the individual as conceptualized in agentic approaches to change, yet it reorientates us to focus on the individual capacity to strategically make use of material and symbolic resources in a change process.

Whilst situatedness and relationality are constructs which are developed within the structuralist tradition, and which focus on embeddedness in institutional and relational contexts, our third dimension, performativity, belongs to a poststructuralist tradition which resides at a more abstract level, at the intersection of discourse and practice. Through the lens of performativity, diversity managers' agency is viewed in a way which is true to its form, with both dynamic and static components, embodying a symbiotic relationship between the symbolic power of knowing (awareness of diversity discourses) and doing (practice of diversity management) in organizational settings. Conceptualizing performativity as a dimension of diversity managers' agency allows us to conceive organizational change as a non-linear and negotiated process, which embeds daily activities of diversity management in organizational politics, resistance and power relationships. This takes place in the iterative process at the individual and institutional levels where the logic of practice and the logic of discourse are intertwined.

In conclusion, we have demonstrated that the diversity managers' agency can be explored in a way that is true to its nature through the constructs of situatedness, relationality and performativity. This three-pronged framework advances our current understanding of diversity managers' role in the organizational change process by transcending earlier formulations which attribute this change to either the person of the diversity manager or the structural circumstances that permit such change. Furthermore, our review suggests that there is scope for the person of the diversity manager to initiate and support organizational change, alongside the drive that the diversity management initiatives and programmes may engender towards organizational change. Nevertheless, the nature and scope of the agency of diversity managers in the process of organizational change are demarcated by the situatedness, relationality and performativity of their agency.

Further reading

Buchanan, D. and Boddy, D. (1992) *The Expertise of the Change Agent*. London: Prentice Hall.

Caldwell, R. (2003) 'Models of Change Agency: A Fourfold Classification', *British Journal of Management*, vol. 14, pp. 131–42.

Cao, G., Clarke, S. and Lehaney, B. (2003) 'Diversity Management in Organizational Change: Towards a Systematic Framework', *Systems Research and Behavioural Science*, vol. 20, pp. 231–42.

Kanter, R.M. (1999) *Leading Change*. London: Simon and Schuster.

Kirkpatrick, S.A. and Locke, E.A. (1991) 'Leadership: Do Traits Matter?', *Academy of Management Executive*, vol. 5, no. 2, pp. 48–60.

Kyriakidou, O. and Özbilgin, M.F. (eds) (2005) *Relational Perspectives in Organization Studies: A Research Companion*. Cheltenham: Edward Elgar.

Meyerson, D.E. (2001) *Tempered Radicals: How People Use Difference to Inspire Change at Work*. Boston, MA: Harvard Business School Press.

Mighty, E.J. (1991) 'Valuing Workforce Diversity: A Model of Organizational Change', *Canadian Journal of Administrative Sciences*, vol. 8, no. 2, pp. 64–71.

Mitchell, S.A. (2000) *Relationality: From Attachment to Inter-subjectivity*. Hillsdale, NJ: The Analytic Press.

Munduate, L. and Gravenhorst, K.M.B. (2003) 'Power Dynamics and Organizational Change: An Introduction', *Applied Psychology: An International Review*, vol. 52, no. 1, pp. 1–13.

Nadler, D.A. and Tushman, M.L. (1990) 'Beyond the Charismatic Leader: Leadership and Organizational Change', *California Management Review*, Winter: 77–97.

Özbilgin, M.F. and Tatlı, A. (2005) 'Book Review Essay: Understanding Bourdieu's Contribution to Management and Organization Studies', *Academy of Management Review*, vol. 30, no. 4, pp. 855–69.

Weick, K.E. and Quinn, R.E. (1999) 'Organizational Change and Development', *Annual Review of Psychology*, vol. 50, pp. 361–86.

Westley, F. and Mintzberg, H. (1989) 'Visionary Leadership and Strategic Management', *Strategic Management Journal*, vol. 10, pp. 17–32.

Individual Effects: The Case of a Global Automobile Manufacturing Company

12.1 Introduction

The previous chapter offered a theoretical overview of diversity managers' agency. In this chapter we will present a case study of this phenomenon in a global organization, exploring the micro-individual level. The analysis here focuses on the investigation of *different forms of capital* at diversity manage disposal and of the different *strategies* employed by them. We will conceptualize the micro-level dynamics of the agency of diversity managers with reference to two key properties that impact upon diversity managers' actions and decisions. First, diversity managers are 'bearers of different forms of capital'. Second, they are agents who employ strategies to transform or reproduce the amount of capital they own. Such a conceptualization of diversity managers' agency at the micro-level acknowledges the active and strategic aspects of human agency.

Accordingly, we will analyse the composition of different forms of capital owned and the strategies employed by diversity managers in their organizational setting. This work is informed by the literature review and insights provided in the previous chapter. An interview schedule for studying the agency of diversity managers in a global organization is offered in Appendix A.

12.2   Researching the agency of diversity managers

The analysis in this chapter is based on the interviews conducted with the 12 diversity managers of the case study company. The demographic characteristics of the respondents are summarized in **Table 12.1**.

Cultural capital

The sources of cultural capital include the traits which are traditionally subsumed under the so-called *human capital*, that is, formal education, training and work experience, as well as cultural and demographic background. The issue of the educational, functional background and training that diversity managers need to accomplish their job deserves research of its own. The role of diversity and equality officers requires knowledge of legislation, industrial relations and human resource management procedures (Lawrence 2000). The responses of research participants display the role of their educational and functional background in their job. However, despite their mention of the importance of their education, most of the respondents emphasized the bigger role played by their previous work experience and 'on-the-job learning' for the requirements of their diversity job. Lawrence (2000: 397) asserts that diversity and equality work also requires personal traits such as patience, persistence and resilience. However, these traits are developed through previous work experience and a present role as a diversity manager, rather than being hereditary individual qualities.

Table 12.1   Demographic table of the case study company research participants

Branch	Gender	Age
Europe	Male	Middle-aged
Europe	Male	Middle-aged
Europe	Male	Middle-aged
Europe	Female	Middle-aged
Europe	Female	Middle-aged
United States	Female	Middle-aged
United States	Female	Middle-aged
North America	Female	Middle-aged
North America	Female	Middle-aged
Canada, Mexico, South America	Male	Middle-aged
United States	Male	Middle-aged
United States	Female	Middle-aged

Interview findings made clear that particularly work experience in their current organization is a valuable source of cultural capital for the respondents, since it provides them with insiders' knowledge. One of the respondents stated:

I got a lot of human resources, labour relations type of work before I moved into the diversity job. I am working for (the company) now for 27 years. I think that having worked at (the company) in a number of different assignments helped me to really get a good understanding of the company, and I think that that probably have helped more than my educational background, probably have helped the most.

Except for three, who were recruited to their diversity role externally, all of the respondents had an extensive knowledge of the structures, procedures and culture of the company due to their long work history with it. Work experience and on-the-job learning are pointed out as important sources of cultural capital by the respondents. However, interview findings show that traits associated with human capital are not sufficient for understanding the respondents' cultural capital in its totality. On the contrary, respondents' demographic and cultural backgrounds form an important source of cultural capital.

Respondents frequently emphasized the value-based nature of the diversity managers' job. The theme of relating personal values and job requirements has been repeated in different ways and places in most of the interviews. For instance, interviews reveal that the demographic background of respondents and their experience related to that have a decisive impact on their values, which in turn affect their commitment to equality and diversity. Moreover, respondents explicitly point out to the connection between their demographic background and their decision to pursue their career in the diversity field. One of the diversity managers of the company said:

I mean I am an African American woman and I think that that's one of the reasons why I gravitated towards this job because I felt that I can really work to make a difference. You know it's not just my own passion, but even personal experience of that I have had. So I think that it plays a role in how I perceive things.

The demographic background of the respondents shows that tendency towards working in the diversity field is connected to respondent's gender and ethnicity. Only one of the 12 respondents is a white male, while seven of them are female and seven are from minority ethnic groups. Interview findings reveal that affiliation with or experience regarding disadvantaged groups, particularly based on ethnicity and gender, forms an important aspect of cultural capital for at least two reasons. First, a diversity manager's experience of being from a minority group, or relating his/her experiences to different minority groups and people, impacts upon the micro-*habitus* of the diversity manager as defined as the set of dispositions formed through his/her past experience and socialization, which may in turn form an advantage or disadvantage in the course of communicating with different groups. As 'relational-beings' (Mauthner and Doucet 2000: 125), diversity managers need to relate and utilize their own values and dispositions to strategically manage and transform the sensitive balance between the dominant organizational *habitus* and micro-*habituses* brought in by different organizational actors. Lawrence's (2000) study on equal opportunities officers also displays the necessity of knowledge and understanding of the perspectives of the discriminated groups in the society for the equality work in the organizations.

Second, the demographic background of a diversity manager plays a decisive role in his/her values, goals and perspective regarding diversity and equality, as well as in his/her ability to relate with and understand the conditions of different groups in the organization. The importance of demographic background and personal values of diversity managers regarding equality, justice and diversity is also cited by other others. DiTomaso and Hooijberg (1996: 170) in their theoretical work on the demands of leadership and diversity note the necessary skills for the organizational leaders in the context of diversity:

> It means not only understanding the reactions to categorisation, but acting to shape and transform those categories, to make (or reengineer) the relationships of people in various categories to resources, power and opportunity. It requires a substantively informed vision and a political commitment, not to a programme of the moment, but to a better organization, and hence to a better society.

In a similar vein, Meyerson and Scully (1995: 596–7) point out that 'some individuals choose to do "diversity work" because of their commitment to social justice, their identification with a marginalized group, and their insights into the dynamics of disadvantage and privilege'. For instance, Lawrence (2000) finds out in her research that the concept of human rights underlies the perspectives of equal opportunities officers and that they have a long agenda for organizational change.

Similarly, throughout the interviewing process, all of our respondents have referred to their personal commitment to diversity and belief in equality. In some instances, they have referred to the contribution of their personal experiences of being from a disadvantaged demographic on their understanding of diversity and equality issues.

Hence, a diversity manager's demographic background, as well as his/her educational background and experience, determine the amount of cultural capital that is at his/her disposal to mobilize during the design and implementation of diversity management policies.

Symbolic capital

The amount of *symbolic capital* owned by the diversity managers has a major role in terms of effectiveness of their actions and decisions on the organizational *habitus* and on the members of the organization. Level of *symbolic capital* in the organizational *field* is the function of the individual's status and authority within the organizational hierarchy. In the case of diversity managers, this is reflected in their level of responsibility and their role in decision-making processes, where they sit in the organizational structure, who are their superiors and subordinates, and where the prestige and status of the diversity office lies in relation to the other functions of the organization.

Acker (2000) points out the dilemma faced by many equality and diversity officers, due to their position in the organizational hierarchy. Despite the fact that implementation of diversity management and programmes is associated with an organizational change process, the diversity and equality officers most of the time lack the direct authority to control the different functions of the organization. As noted by Acker (2000: 627):

> The staff positions were relatively powerless to achieve the changes that were sought. Many studies have shown that staff positions do not have the direct control of work organization and practices that line positions routinely involve. Thus, staff could not themselves implement changes but would have to work through others to reach their goals.

For that reason the level of prestige and status attached to the diversity office within the organization become a crucial factor in the agency of the diversity managers by either hindering the influence of their actions or encouraging it. Parker (1999: 39) suggests:

> EEO officers should also have enough formal and informal 'clout' within the corporation to ensure their message is not overwhelmed by inconsistent management discourse or corporate culture.

She argues that they may gain the necessary 'clout' in two ways, formally through holding a senior position and informally through having support of the senior management.

Similarly, in the research, all of the respondents emphasized the importance of support, commitment and ownership at the level of senior management, and of an established diversity strategy that ensures the sustainability of the programmes and policies. One of the diversity managers in the company's European Diversity Team commented on the importance of senior management support as follows:

> Senior management involvement, role modelling and senior management buy-in, senior management leadership on this issue are crucial. Otherwise management and employees don't take it seriously. Our leadership is on the board, our leadership is willing to take decisions and our leadership is showing that it is serious about diversity has a major impact on the organization.

Senior management support and ownership is an important determinant of the status and authority of the diversity manager in the organization, and so of the amount of symbolic capital that he or she would hold. However, as argued by all respondents, formal structures of diversity management are as important as the senior management commitment for diversity managers to gain the necessary status and authority to realize their roles. These formal structures include the status of diversity office and integration of diversity management objectives in the different functions and levels of the organization, which in turn establish the legitimacy of diversity managers' actions in intervening and controlling the processes in other functions to meet the goals of diversity management policy. As Acker (2000) points out, the diversity and equality officers most of the time do not have the direct authority to control the different functions of the organization. This brings out the importance of the investigation of relative power and authority of diversity managers compared to the line managers in the company on whom they need to exert influence in order to implement the diversity management policies.

Comparison of the diversity management structure in the UK and the US provides an interesting illustration of the link between organizational-level commitment to diversity management and positioning of the diversity managers and the diversity offices within the organizational hierarchy, and hence to their influence on the different functional areas of the organization. Our interviews revealed that at the case study company there are differences between the United States and Europe with respect to the structure and organization of diversity management. In the US, the Diversity Office which was established in the 1980s, is under the Human Resource Department, whereas in Europe the Diversity Office has a separate status. Furthermore, diversity managers in the United States are reported to be part-time, which means they are doing the diversity work as a part of their main job, whereas they hold a full-time office in the European context. These differences are largely due to the motivation behind the diversity management programme. In the US the programme was the result of the proactive stance taken by the company on the basis of the business case for workforce diversity, whereas in Britain the diversity programme was started as a result of the discrimination lawsuits facing the company. In effect there is a very structured and systematic diversity and equality audit process in Britain, where diversity objectives and responsibility is cascaded down through all levels of the organization, in contrast to the loosely connected and voluntary characteristics of the diversity management programme in the US, where diversity objectives are a part of only the senior managers' scorecards. This situation shows that legal sanctions continue to be more motivating than the possible positive business outcomes of diversity for the establishment of sound diversity management programmes.

So the amount of symbolic capital owned by the diversity managers is closely related to the organizational and societal positioning of diversity management. Their status and authority are shaped by the legislative and institutional structure regarding the issues of discrimination and inequality in the field of employment, as well as the position of the diversity office and the integration of diversity management policies across different levels and functions of the organization.

Social capital

Diversity managers have to formally and informally work through several organizational agents and networks as a part of their role within the process of diversity management. Their success in doing this is clearly associated with the amount of *social capital* they own within the context of the *habitus* of their organization, and externally in terms of their membership to various networks and work and social groups. The sources of *social capital* can be external and internal. External sources of *social capital* are related to the involvement in civil society and politics through any membership or link to formal or informal groups, networks or institutions outside the organization.

For the case of diversity managers, the most important is their involvement in networks, institutions and groups in the diversity and equality area. Most of the respondents indicated that they are members of several diversity and equality networks and groups outside of the company. Such outside affiliations act as a source of both solidarity and information for the diversity managers who took part in this study. During the interviews, the respondents have provided several examples of the cases where they turn to their external networks for support and recommendations about new diversity management initiatives and programmes in their organization. Other studies also point out the importance of membership in external networks and groups. For instance, Braithwaite (1992, cited in Parker 1999), in her quantitative work on Australian affirmative action officers, stresses the importance of networking with others in the profession for affirmative action officers to maintain their progressive attitudes, to retain their commitment and to get social validation of their views. Similarly, Meyerson and Scully assert that 'importance of maintaining strong ties with individuals, communities or groups outside of their organization' is emphasized frequently by tempered radicals. They conclude that 'these outside affiliations act as sources of information, resources, emotional support, and perhaps most important, empathy' (Meyerson and Scully 1995: 597).

Involvement in external equality and diversity networks also entails the possibility of learning from the experiences of other diversity managers, being up to date with the developments in the field and accessing different perspectives regarding equality and diversity issues. Clearly, all of these contribute to the effectiveness of the diversity manager in his or her organization through the increased ability to understand the main dynamics, to foresee the future challenges and opportunities, and to produce efficient strategies for managing diversity. In addition, the majority of the research participants pointed out that being active members of local, national and international equality and diversity networks increases their professional credibility in the organization, particularly in the eyes of their senior managers and other diversity colleagues.

Internal sources of *social capital* are at least as important as the external ones for diversity managers. These include relationships with organizational members from different groups and ranks, and inclusion in different informal organizational networks. This area implicitly includes the *interpersonal skills*, the most frequently referred to category of competencies in the change agency literature, such as negotiation, facilitation, communication and networking. One of the diversity managers in the European Diversity Team argued that interpersonal skills are critical in his job and stressed the importance of establishing relationships with as many organizational members as possible, from secretary or cleaner to the chairman.

As DiTomaso and Hooijberg emphasize, the job of managing diversity requires 'emotion work', since the sphere of intervention is a sensitive one related to deeply seated values and norms of the individuals and may invoke negative as well as positive reaction on the side of organizational members. The authors claim that leaders of diversity management 'have responsibility to understand, confront, and help address the emotional responses that people may have to diversity – whether anger, bewilderment or fear' (1996: 179). The amount of social capital owned by the diversity manager determines the boundaries of his/her capacity as a negotiator or facilitator both between different groups and between individuals and their emotions. Most of the respondents mentioned that the role of enabler and facilitator, and support of different organizational actors such as employees, trade unions and line managers, is crucial for the implementation of diversity management policies.

Hence, the diversity manager's formal and informal networks within the organization and his/her personal skills, such as negotiation, persuasion and attracting voluntary involvement, are crucial for him/her to realize his/her role. The amount of social capital owned by the diversity manager has a crucial impact upon his/her capacity or ability to gain more allies within the organization and to ensure further involvement of different organizational actors within the diversity management process. Gaining allies can be through informal ways as well as formal ways within an organization. One of the research participants emphasized the informal dimension of the issue as follows:

> You have to find out who your champions are in your organization not formally but informally, who makes things happen, who are the people who really have either formal or informal power. And a lot of this isn't done in formal meetings, a lot of this is done in informal meetings as well.

The above words echo the argument made by Meyerson in relation to the significance of gaining the support and involvement of various organizational actors for tempered radicals:

> In navigating the course between their desire to undo the status quo and the organizational requirements to uphold it, tempered radicals benefit from the advice of insiders who know just how hard to push. (2001b: 100)

In summary, the interview findings display the importance of social capital gained through both internal and external networks. The higher the amount of their social capital, the higher is their professional credibility and authority within their organizations. Furthermore, social capital provides them with the necessary channels into the insider's perspectives in their organization and with an up-to-date overview of the wider diversity management field. Consequently, armed with credibility, authority and information, diversity managers have more chances to gain support and involvement for the diversity management policies and programmes that they design and implement.

Strategies

As we discussed in the previous sections, for diversity managers, knowledge of organization and membership in formal and informal organizational networks function as valuable sources of cultural and social capital, of which they can then transform to symbolic capital that will provide them with a legitimate basis of status and power. Bourdieu and Wacquant (1992: 101) argue that different forms of capital do not exist and function except in relation to a field and *habitus*; rather, they become efficient 'like the aces in a game of cards', but only if the actors know the 'rules of the game' and register these rules.

In order to reach their goals within the scope of diversity management policies and programmes, diversity managers have to play the 'game' according to the rules embedded in the organizational subfield and *habitus*. They learn the rules governing the organizational subfield and *habitus* by gaining an understanding of the organization through their work experience in the organization and by being part of formal and informal organizational networks and, thus, having access to insiders' knowledge. However, this learning should not be conceived as a kind of educational process in the organizational setting which will then lead to straightforward action and decisions to effect organizational change. As Gunn and Gullickson (2003) argue, managers' willingness to act on their learning is constrained by their belief in how acceptable their approach would be in the context of the prevailing organizational setting and discourse. Hence, the process of learning the formal and informal rules prevalent in the organization, on the one hand empowers diversity managers, through establishing them as legitimate 'players' in the game, and, on the other hand, dictates to them the 'acceptable' limits of their intervention in the organizational subfield and *habitus* within the scope of their diversity management efforts.

Thus, the organizational performance of diversity managers is linked to the dual character of that learning and acceptance of the formal and informal rules of the organization which simultaneously enable and constrain their agency. Only within that framework can diversity managers participate in the reproductive transformation of the organizational *field*, by virtue of the amount of different forms of *capital* they own. As Bourdieu and Wacquant (1992: 129) propose, the driving force behind the *strategies* is 'the encounter of habitus with the peculiar conjuncture of the field'. Through the investigation of strategies employed by diversity managers, we explore in this section the dual character of that learning and acceptance process as it relates to the strategies utilized by diversity managers.

Meyerson and Scully (1995: 587) say that 'tempered radical alignment and change are flip sides of the same coin'. Accordingly, the positioning of tempered radicals in the organizational structure leads to three interrelated forms of ambivalence:

> First, and most fundamentally, tempered radicals are 'outsiders within' . . . while insider status provide access to opportunities for change, outsider status provides the detachment to recognise that there even is an issue or problem to work on . . . Second, tempered radicals can act as critics of the status quo and as critics of untempered radical change . . . Tempered radicals have chosen to work for change from within organizations . . . Because of their location, they may critique some forms of radical change for provoking fear, resistance and backlash . . . Third, in addition to being critics of status quo and critics of radical change, tempered radicals can be advocates for both. Their situation is therefore more complex than that of change agents who act strictly as critics of status quo. As advocates for the

status quo, tempered radicals earn the rewards and resources that come with commitment and (tempered) complicity and these become their tools for change (Meyerson and Scully 1995: 589).

Tempered radicals need to be able to deal with the disadvantages of ambivalence and to utilize the advantages that are brought by their ambivalent position.

Similar to Meyerson's tempered radicals, those interviewed in this research occupy an antithetical position in their organization due to their job role as, in their own words, 'change agents'. The diversity management process is associated with cultural change in the case study company's diversity policy documents. However, all respondents have pointed out that the company has a very established organizational culture which is primarily orientated around white-male values. Assuming the role of change agents within that framework, in turn, leads diversity managers to experience ambivalences. They use several *strategies* to turn the ambivalences into advantages that will provide them with the resources, support, authority, power or influence required throughout the diversity management process.

One of the strategies proposed in the literature for use of change agents is packaging the change message in insiders' language (Dutton and Ashford 1993). One of the diversity managers of the case study company very clearly describes the impact of the way in which the change message is packaged and delivered on its effectiveness:

> You learn how to adapt your message and the style of your message. The essence is the same, but the delivery of the message is slightly different. You make it appropriate for that culture, for that organization; but the end result is the same. So that you know it will hit whom better with different stakeholders in the company to get them to move on things. We also use different people in the company to deliver that message. Sometimes the chairman is relevant, sometimes the HR director is relevant, sometimes the marketing director.

He continued to explain the different messages that they use within the company to 'sell' diversity:

> There are different drivers for different people. Legislation or case law would be drivers for some managers and some people. Secondly, it could be the social and moral case. Thirdly, it is around the business strategy. But really at the end of the day, unless diversity becomes a business issue, and you can relate it to people's objectives, it doesn't happen.

As has been clear in these words, in the field of diversity management, the message is dominantly packaged with business case rhetoric: workforce diversity is treated as a 'product' to be 'marketed' and 'sold' to different stakeholders in the company. Even in the cases where respondents refer to legislation or ethical reasons as the drivers for the diversity management efforts, they stressed the bottom line considerations regarding the compliance with legislation and the running of an ethical business, such as the economic and social cost of discrimination lawsuits and the associated 'bad publicity' and decrease in the number of cars they would sell versus the business benefits of a positive public image associated with being an 'employer working for equal opportunities and diversity'.

Several authors cited the importance of making the business case for the successful implementation and delivery of diversity management policies and programmes (Gatley and Lessem 1995; Barkema *et al.* 2002; Harrison *et al.* 2002). The literature suggests that this shift from the ethical case to the business case argument is also reflected in the discourses of diversity and equality practitioners. For instance, one of the respondents in Parker's (1999: 34) qualitative study emphasizes the necessity of the business case argument to convince the management of the need for a 'good' sexual harassment policy: 'I feel very passionately that you can't push it as a feminist issue but have to see it as a good for business issue'. Yet another officer, discussing the strategies for convincing the management, says:

> You have to move from social justice to business concerns. If you put up hard figures of how it could affect them, then they are more inclined to listen. You see them becoming more interested. That means both showing them that harassment and other problems do occur and cases do go to court and giving them the dollar figures of what it costs (quoted in Parker 1999: 37).

Similarly, the respondents of this research frequently emphasized the use of 'business rationale' for diversity management as a strategy for convincing different organizational members.

Referring to the cases of gender equity projects, Acker (2000) argues that using the business case argument may be an efficient strategy to gain organizational support for the change programme. However, she argues, this strategy simultaneously entails the risk of disappearance of gender from view. The same situation holds true for the case of diversity management as well. Bottom line arguments offer an effective strategy for introducing and gaining commitment for diversity management policies and programmes. However, they carry the risk of cancelling the message of equal opportunities and the disappearance of the understanding of structural inequalities, both of which in turn lead to elimination of the possibilities of organizational change that is addressed within the scope of the organization's diversity management policies.

Respondents in Lawrence's (2000: 385) study called for attention to be given to the paradoxical nature of relying on the profit motive to achieve equality goals by pointing out to the cases where bottom-line factors conflict with equality and diversity principles, rather than encouraging them as, for instance, in the cases of fast-food chains where the major consideration is cheap labour. Consequently, when bottom-line considerations conflict with diversity and equality goals, it is the profit motive that generally wins over. This paradox of the business case argument was pointed out by one of the respondents. She argued that when economic targets and 'soft' targets about 'how to deal with people' conflict, the latter vanishes from the agenda, particularly at 'economically difficult' times. Hence, although the employment of strategies has an important part in diversity managers' ability to actualize their role within their organizations, the success or efficiency of these strategies is bound up with the status of diversity management policies in the organization, which reflects the impact of social and organizational dynamics.

Commenting on this dilemma, Meyerson and Scully (1995: 596–7) state:

Those who work in corporations learn to speak the language of the insiders: in this case, to talk about diversity in 'bottom line' terms . . . However, tempered radicals may be most effective if they speak to each constituency in both languages. They do not channel their language so that business people hear only bottom line rationalisations, nor so that community organisers hear only the social justice reasons for proposed changes.

Furthermore, the authors argue that 'instead of stridently pressing their agendas, they start conversations. Rather than battling powerful foes, they seek powerful friends' (Meyerson 2001b: 100). Our interviews with the diversity managers of the case study company show that despite the overall emphasis on the business case, the respondents integrate ethical and legal rationales for managing diversity in their business case arguments. However, they modify and construct the balance of ethical, legal and business cases in-line with the characteristics of their audience at each situation. This balancing act also helps the respondents to avoid potential conflicts with the very organizational actors from whom the diversity managers seek support for.

Similarly, Parker claims that the strategies of best-practice equal-employment opportunities officers are based on comfortably slipping between public values of equality and justice, and private concerns of business and profits, as well as between their own dual personal commitment to public ethical norms and private corporate duties. Hence, the author states:

It does demonstrate the potential for some EEO officers in their character as double dealers in social control to become creative citizens weaving their own normative web out of the constraints of legal and corporate norms. (Parker 1999: 34).

Furthermore, she states that conflict strategies are identified as ineffective by equal opportunities officers (Lawrence 2000). Meyerson (2001b: 99) makes a similar point for the case of tempered radicals as follows:

> Tempered radicals don't allow preconceived notions about 'the opposition' to get in their way. Indeed, they understand that those who represent the majority perspective are vitally important to gaining support for their cause.

Similarly, case study interviews reveal that diversity managers also prefer to follow the strategy of negotiation rather than opposition and by doing that they aim to gain allies or supporters at different levels of the organization. Very frequently, the importance of gaining the support of the majority, which is white, male and middle-aged, is emphasized for achieving diversity goals. Yet, getting the majority population involved in the diversity management process is one of the basic challenges diversity managers experience. The use of discourse of inclusion came forth in the interviews as a widely used strategy to overcome that challenge. However, in the discourses of diversity managers, inclusion does not refer to the traditional progressive usage of the term to denote the inclusion of the previously excluded, disadvantaged social groups (Howarth 1999; Pena-Casas *et al.* 2002), but the meaning of the term is twisted to imply the inclusion of the category of white male, which is argued to be excluded within the equal opportunities framework. This rhetoric of inclusion goes hand in hand with an individualistic definition of diversity, sometimes at the expense of the recognition of the demographic groups that are historically disadvantaged. That sort of definition of diversity accommodates the danger of reducing all 'differences' to the same level of importance and emergency. A statement made by one of the respondents signals this danger:

> We say that we want to build a diverse and inclusive culture, so we look at diversity, we look at broad aspect. We say that diversity is all the things that really make us unique as individuals.

With the necessity of gaining the support of the majority groups to realize an organizational change and avoid a backlash and resistance by these groups, diversity managers tend to avoid conflict strategies and to use strategies of persuasion. The respondents argued that conflict strategies may breed negative reactions from white male employees and that it is necessary to make diversity management policies relevant to all organizational members, while at the same time stressing the need for targeted intervention for the disadvantaged groups. Although diversity managers still display the awareness about the group-based inequalities, that message is blurred within the rhetoric of inclusion. When asked about how they situate the concept of equal opportunities within diversity management, the respondents reported that the term in the company is 'diversity'. The respondent who is a member of the European Diversity Management Team of the company proposed:

> The word here is diversity. I mean there have been times it was equal opportunities. It goes through an evolution. Equal opportunities in the traditional way is about ethnic minorities and gender. I think you have to take into account that people have different experiences, they may not identify with the experience you're talking about. So about the diversity–equal opportunities debate I would like to say it's equal opportunity through acknowledgement of individual strength.

So, the discourses of diversity managers show that they try to establish a balance between the ideas of equality and diversity throughout their strategic moves along the organizational power dynamics. However, their strategies evolved around the business case for diversity, and inclusion may engender the disappearance of the debate of discrimination from the scene.

Nevertheless, use of strategies within the framework drawn by the organizational subfield and *habitus* to activate the potential power of different forms of capital presents the dynamic dimension of the diversity manager's agency. Two most pertinent examples of strategies utilized by the diversity managers are the use of business case discourse and the discourse of inclusion. Once equipped with these discourses, their legitimized ways of knowing, and unique anecdotes from the organization, the diversity managers may set out to enact these discourses in their organizations, by producing policy statements, affecting managerial decision processes and enacting the professed diversity discourses in their daily practice of work. Therefore, diversity management is enacted through the efforts of diversity managers, not only through implementation of policy across the organization but also as individual enactments of daily performance that will generate 'small wins' (Weick 1984; Meyerson and Fletcher 2003: 230).

12.3 Conclusions

In Chapter 11 we offered a model for investigating diversity managers' agency at the macro-, meso- and micro-levels. In this chapter we have presented an analysis of the micro-level dynamics of the diversity managers' agency, based on the semi-structured interviews conducted with 12 diversity managers of our case study company. To this end, firstly, different forms of capital owned by the diversity managers have been investigated as the potential power sources within the organizational context. The use of strategies by the diversity managers to enact that potential has also been explored.

In any global organization, effectiveness and success of diversity management initiatives are partly explained by the effectiveness and success of the diversity managers. We have framed the diversity managers' agency as their success and effectiveness and demonstrated that it is contingent upon the positioning of managers within the power structures of their organization, their possession of different forms of capital and their ability to act strategically, drawing on both personal and institutional resources.

Appendix A: Diversity interview schedule

Exercise: Use the below schedule to interview one or more diversity managers. These interviews should then be thematically analysed according to the framework described in this chapter.

Explanation:

The aim of this research is to investigate the impact of diversity management at organizational level. Different stakeholders will be interviewed about their experiences and opinions regarding diversity management. I will ask you questions under six headings: you and your organization; diversity and equality in your organization; mainstreaming and involvement; monitoring; appraisal, recruitment and training. No individual names will be revealed and they will be kept strictly confidential. Transcripts of the interview will be sent to the interviewees to enable them to make the necessary corrections.

You and your organization

1. **What is your responsibility or job role in relation to diversity and management in this organization?**
    Probe: Are you promoted to this position?
    Probe: If yes, what was your previous job role?
    Probe: How many years (approximately) have you been in your current role?

2. **How do you fit in the organizational structure?**
    Probe: What are you responsible for?
    Probe: To whom you are reporting?
    Probe: Who are reporting to you?

Probe: Do you have open access to the CEO of your company?

Probe: Do you sit in on strategy meetings?

Diversity and Equality in Your Organization

3. **How did your organization reach its current position in diversity and equality?**

   Probe: Who first proposed the idea of diversity management?

   Probe: Initially, what measures were parts of your diversity strategy?

   Probe: How did the scope of the effort expand over time? What precipitated these changes?

   Probe: Who were the key people in different stages of this process?

4. **Could you describe your organization's current diversity structure to me?**

   Probe: Does your organization have someone or a specialised office whose main responsibility is managing diversity?

   Probe: If yes, to what extent does this person have power and prestige within the organization?

   Probe: How do you relate equal opportunities issues to diversity management strategies?

5. **What are the specific facilities for certain group of employees?**

   Probe: Accessibility for the disabled, complaining mechanism for the cases of discrimination and harassment, child care facilities, training, mentoring, career development programs, flexible hours and work schedules etc.?

6. **What are the activities/initiatives/programs that are implemented in order to reach diversity goals?**

   Probe: Who are in the target groups of the diversity activities? (In other words who attends them?)

7. **Which initiatives do you consider more successful?**

   Probe: Why?

   Probe: Which initiatives have been meet with opposition/resistance?

   Probe: Why?

8. **In promoting diversity do you use different messages for different groups of employees?**

   Probe: What is the most pronounced/welcomed justification for the diversity policies in the organization?

   Probe: What types of justifications for the strategic imperative of managing diversity tend to be accepted by top management?

9. **Who in the company was the most avid champion of diversity?**

   Probe: Most opposed?

10. How would you describe the impact of diversity management policies and practices on organizational culture?
     Probe: How do you think diversity efforts have initiated a process of organizational change?

Mainstreaming and involvement

11. How do diversity management policies or initiatives relate to the overall corporate objectives and strategies?
     Probe: In mission statements, strategy planning, across different functions in the organization?

12. Literature suggests that it is difficult to involve line managers in diversity efforts. How do you get them to actively contribute to and take responsibility about the diversity efforts?
     Probe: Are they well informed and conscious about diversity management policy?
     Probe: What does your organization do to ensure they have the skills necessary to manage diverse employees effectively?
     Probe: Are they held accountable for their diversity efforts? How?

13. How do you get senior managers to actively contribute to and take responsibility about the diversity efforts?
     Probe: How are they informed and made conscious about diversity management policy?
     Probe: Are they held accountable for their diversity efforts? How?
     Probe: How would you define top management's attitude towards diversity?

14. How are the employees involved in the design and implementation of diversity policies and practices?
     Probe: How are employee responses included in the decisions to optimise diversity policies?

15. What would you say on the reactions of different groups of employees to diversity programmes?
     Probe: Are some groups of employees predictably more receptive to diversity efforts than others?
     Probe: Opponents?
     Probe: How do you evaluate the impact of diversity management policies and practices on employees' equal opportunities attitudes and behaviours?

Monitoring

16. How are diversity initiatives evaluated/monitored?
     Probe: By whom, measures, how often, and to whom are the results of these monitoring activities reported?

17. **Do you have employee attitude surveys to monitor the impact of diversity efforts?**
Probe: Could you please explain the coverage of them?
Probe: Can I have a copy of the survey form?
Probe: Can I have copy of the reports on the results of the surveys?

18. **What are the benefits of workforce diversity?**
Probe: Up to now, what benefits are derived from the diversity program?
Probe: How would you evaluate the impacts of diversity management policies on;

- Employees' level of commitment and belongingness; perceptions of fairness/justice
- Employees' performance and satisfaction
- Communication and interaction between employees from diverse backgrounds
- Organizational performance, creativity/innovation, problem solving and decision making
- Cost of labour turnover, absenteeism, recruitment, discrimination lawsuits
- Business success with regard to market penetration, diversification of customer base and level of customer satisfaction

Probe: How do you measure impact of diversity policies on these areas?
Probe: Can I have a copy of the reports on these?

19. **Up to now, what are the costs associated with diversity management?**
Probe: What kind of unforeseen costs are brought by diversity policies?
Probe: What kind of problems did you encounter during your diversity efforts?

20. **What is the customer base of the organization (diversity of customer base)?**

21. **How common are the incidents of sexual and ethnic harassment in your organization?**
Probe: Are they frequently reported?
Probe: Are there perceived repercussions for reporting such incidents? What are they?
Probe: To what extent is harassment tolerated?

Appraisal, recruitment and training

22. **What is the proportion of women, racial and ethnic minorities, gay men and lesbians and people with disabilities within the workforce?**
Probe: Within senior management?

Probe: Can I have a copy of employee statistics?
Probe: What is the role of diversity management efforts on these figures?

23. **Are there targeted recruitment efforts?**
Probe: What are they? (contacting the minority alumni associations, advertising jobs in minority or women's publications)

24. **Are hiring, promotion and compensation practices monitored with respect to their conformity with equal opportunities principles?**
Probe: What are the mechanisms for monitoring?

25. **How are performance appraisals related to diversity effort?**

26. **Does your organization offer diversity awareness training?**
Probe: Are they mandatory?
Probe: How is its effectiveness evaluated?
Probe: What is the focus of this training?
Probe: Who receives it?
Probe: Can I have a copy of the training guidelines?
Probe: May I observe some of the training?

Future

27. **In summary, how would you define the current state of your organization with regard to embracing diversity and supporting equality?**

28. **How would you define your role and responsibility in reaching the diversity and equality goals in the organization and as change agents?**
Probe: Are they given the necessary tools and resources for reaching these goals?
Probe: What resources are available for diversity management programs and initiatives?
Probe: What kind of problems/challenges did you yourself encounter during your diversity efforts?

29. **How do you ensure the sustainability of your diversity programmes?**

30. **How do you plan to modify the diversity program in the future?**

31. **Considering your experience what would be your recommendations to others in the field?**

Personal Details

We are trying to build a profile. May I lastly ask you some personal details?

32. **What are your educational qualifications?**
Probe: How does your education contribute to the needs of your current job?

33. **What is your functional background/training?**
    Probe: How does your functional background/training contribute to the needs of your current job?

34. **Did you have any specific training on diversity management? Could you explain some?**

35. **How does your previous employment experience contribute to the needs of your current job?**

36. **In summary, how did you gain the expertise required for your current role in diversity management?**

37. **Age:**

38. **Ethnicity:**

39. **Nationality:**

40. **Do you practise a religion?**
    Probe: Which one do you practise?

41. **Do you have a disability?**
    Probe: What is it?

42. **How do you think people will react if I ask about their sexuality?**
    Probe: Would you mind telling me about your sexuality?

43. **How do you think your demographic background i.e. gender/race/ethnicity affected your career progression?**
    Probe: Did it have any impact on your decision to pursue your career in diversity/equality field? How?
    Probe: Did it have any impact on your understanding of diversity/equality field?

44. **Are you a member of any voluntary groups/non-governmental organizations? Could you explain some?**

45. **What would you say on your interest/involvement in politics?**

46. **Are you a member of any networks or groups on diversity/equality? Could you explain some?**
    Probe: Within your organization?
    Probe: Outside your organization?

47. **Do you have regular contact with the other institutions/companies who are implementing diversity policies and programmes? Could you explain some?**

48. Could you please tell me any additional comments you feel are relevant to our understanding of the diversity management strategy of your organization?

49. Who else can I talk to about diversity management in your organization?

    Probe: May I have their contact details?

    Probe: Could you introduce me to them?

Further reading

Agocs, C. (1997) 'Institutionalized Resistance to Organizational Change: Denial, Inaction and Repression', *Journal of Business Ethics*, vol. 16, pp. 917–31.

Bass, B.M. (1995) 'From Transactional to Transformational Leadership: Learning to Share Vision', *Organizational Dynamics*, vol. 18, no. 3, pp. 19–31.

Boje, D.M. and Winsor, R.D. (1993) 'The Resurrection of Taylorism: Total Quality Management's Hidden Agenda', *Journal of Organizational Change Management*, vol. 6, no. 4, pp. 57–70.

Bourdieu, P. and Wacquant, L. (1992) *An Invitation to Reflexive Sociology.* Cambridge: Polity Press.

Lawrence, E. (2000) 'Equal Opportunities Officers and Managing Equality Changes', *Personnel Review*, vol. 29, no. 3, pp. 381–401.

Lorde, A. (2003) 'The Transformation of Silence into Language and Action', in R. J. Ely, E.G. Foldy, M.A. Scully and the Centre for Gender in Organizations, Simmons School of Management (eds), *Reader in Gender, Work and Organization*. Oxford: Blackwell, pp. 273–6.

Meyerson, D.E. (2001) 'Radical Change, the Quiet Way', *Harvard Business Review*, October, pp. 92–100.

Meyerson, D.E. and Scully, M.A. (1995) 'Tempered Radicalism and the Politics of Ambivalence and Change', *Organization Science,* vol. 6, no. 5, pp. 585–600.

Morrison, A.M. (1992) *The New Leader: Guidelines on Leadership Diversity in America.* San Francisco, CA: Jossey-Bass.

Parker, C. (1999) 'How to Win Hearts and Minds: Corporate Compliance Policies for Sexual Harassment', *Law and Policy,* vol. 21, no. 1, pp. 21–48.

Todd, S. (2002) 'Stakeholder Perspectives: A Personal Account of an Equality and Diversity Practitioner's Intervention Experience', in N. Cornelius (ed.), *Building Workplace Equality: Ethics, Diversity and Inclusion*. London: Thomson, pp. 265–95.

Zanoni, P. and Janssens, M. (2003) 'Deconstructing the Differences: The Rhetoric of Human Resources Managers' Diversity Discourse', *Organization Studies*, vol. 25, no. 1, pp. 55–74.

Summary and Conclusions

The Challenges Facing Global Diversity Management

Diversity management is no longer a new concept in business circles. In its development over two decades, diversity management theory has evolved extensively. Whilst the concept was received with some suspicion by equality scholars, it was embraced by the commercial industry as a way to combat a wider range of inequalities, and to contribute to the overall performance and longevity of organizations. Diversity management may be defined as a set of management interventions which seek to recognize and value individual and social category differences among individual workers, customers, suppliers, local and wider communities, and the other stakeholders of an organization. This definition marks a transformation in the discourse and practice of diversity management. However, global diversity management, as a concept in its infancy, offers a challenge to our conceptions of domestic diversity management. In this book, we have offered a multilevel framework through which global diversity management practice and policy can be understood.

The book provides both theoretical discussions and real life examples. In Part I we framed global diversity management by presenting a multilevel model of it. In Part II we examined its national and discourse effects, drawing on a national study of diversity management and examples of diagnostic equality checks and practices of storytelling. In Part III we presented examples of sectoral effects, with a focus on the private recruitment sector and creative and cultural industries. In Part IV we narrowed down the level of investigation and examined the organization and individual effects.

There are several challenges facing global diversity management today. The most prominent of these challenges is the realization that domestic diversity management requirements and policies are not adequate to respond to the global organizations' need to transcend nationally based policies and approaches.

There is increasing pressure on global organizations to adopt transversal policies which do not only transcend national differences but also go beyond standardization in policy-making. This requires them to consider sophisticated approaches to policy–making, which recognize the tension between local requirements for diversity management and the need to standardize international operations. The desirable outcome is neither standardized forms of globalization nor localization. The outcome is to generate policies and practices which serve as umbrellas under which sensitivity to local requirements can be addressed.

Examples of this approach are evident when one considers the promulgation of global diversity councils, which allow for communication across diversity professionals across the national branch networks. Supplemented with broadly defined terms of operation, global diversity management councils serve as platforms in which nationally specific policies are put to the test of globalization and in which domestic conditions are recognized and specifically tailored diversity policies are produced. In a global diversity council, absolute forms of localization and globalization are still not desirable, as both of these alternatives suffer from the common disadvantages of ignoring the complexities and demands of global diversity management.

The second challenge that global diversity management practices experience is the challenge of mainstreaming. Whilst some global organizations offer global diversity management policies as umbrella approaches, these are often withheld in problematic regions, where such approaches are deemed inappropriate. For example, a policy on gender equality in a country where sex segregation is legally permissible, or a policy on sexual orientation in which such discrimination is rampant. Therefore, global organizations face the challenge of dealing with some sensitive issues in progressing their efforts to deem diversity management as relevant across their branch networks.

Another significant challenge is the location of the global diversity management function within the organizational structures and functions. Traditionally, global diversity management is located uncomfortably within the human resource management departments. Since the message of global diversity management is to make a contribution to the overall organizational performance through effective and strategic use of resources, locating it within the human resource management departments means that marketing, finance, product development, innovation, creativity and customer relations issues that global diversity management can contribute to remain unaddressed. Therefore, it remains an important challenge for global organizations to mainstream their global diversity management efforts. We have argued in this book that this can be achieved through moving global diversity management to the strategic heart of the company in which it becomes a significant component of decision-making and resource allocation processes.

Domestic diversity management requires engagement at multiple levels and with multiple stakeholders of organizations. Global diversity management requires an even greater set of levels and stakeholders. In assessing the inclusion of certain groups in diversity management decisions, it is important to recognize the key actors that drive organizations and those others without whose voice the organizations may become unidimensional. Global diversity management as a practice is a process of discriminating between voice and noise in organizations. By effectively moving voices from the margins to the mainstream of organizational decision-making, global diversity management may achieve multiculturalism, inclusion and equality.

There are tools offered in this text for developing global diversity management. These tools include diagnostic checks which can help an organization assess its approaches, policies and practices of diversity management through a set of monitoring, evaluation, objective setting and impact assessment processes. Use of these tools, however, also requires the diversity managers to recognize the significance of transformative discourses and to use these tools in strategic ways to effect change.

Last, but not the least, there is a need to pay more attention to the resources and constraints of the person of diversity managers. Diversity managers as professional workers and change agents in their organizations are the most visible actors in the process of global diversity management. Global diversity management policies and practices tend to ignore the agency of diversity managers. In effect, global diversity policies are underpinned by an assumption that the resources of the diversity management projects are independent of the person of the diversity manager. In this book, we have shown that there is a necessity to bring diversity managers' agency into global diversity management policy.

Global diversity managers, most of the time, lack the necessary resources to initiate organizational change. In multinational corporations (MNCs), global diversity policies should be mainstreamed and positioned at the strategic heart of organizational policies and objectives. This should be supplemented with adequate resourcing and empowerment of the diversity manager and the diversity office. Furthermore, there is a wide lack of professionalization in the field of global diversity management. Training and education programmes available for global diversity managers are sparse, if not non-existent. Training and development of global diversity managers is important for them to gain power and legitimacy at work. Such training and development activities may be offered through government agencies, universities, consultancies and professional bodies, among others.

In terms of future academic research, there is a need for multilevel interdisciplinary research to bring together different disciplinary insights in order to study global diversity management at the cross-section of international, regional, national, sectoral, organizational and individual level effects. In addition, future research needs to acknowledge that the global diversity management process involves multiple stakeholders and plural support from the actors outside and inside of organizations. Finally, our understanding of global diversity management would greatly benefit from collaborative, cross-cultural and comparative research.

References

Acker, J. (2000) 'Gendered Contradictions in Organizational Equity Projects', *Organization* vol. 7, no. 4, pp. 625–32.

Acosta, A.S. (2004) 'A Diversity Perspective on Organizational Learning and a Learning Perspective on Organizational Diversity', *Academy of Management Best Conference Paper*, CMS: D1–D6.

Adams, L., Carter, K. and Schäfer, S. (2006) *Equal Pay Reviews Survey 2005*. EOC Working Paper Series no. 42, Equal Opportunities Commission.

Adams, S.M. (1998) 'Models of Conflict Resolution in Japanese, German and American Cultures', *Journal of Applied Psychology*, vol. 83, pp. 316–23.

Addleson, M. (2000) 'What is Good Organization?: Learning Organizations, Community and the Rhetoric of the "Bottom Line"', *European Journal of Work and Organizational Psychology*, vol. 9 no. 2, pp. 233–52.

Adler, N.J. (1986) *International Dimensions of Organizational Behaviour*. Boston: Kent Publishing Company.

Adler, N.J. and Ghadar, F. (1990) 'Strategic Human Resource Management: A Global Perspective', in R. Pieper (ed.), *Human Resource Management: An International Comparison*. Berlin, New York: Walter de Gruyter, pp. 235–60.

Agocs, C. and Burr, C. (1996) 'Employment Equity Affirmative Action Managing Diversity: Assessing the Differences', *International Journal of Manpower*, vol. 17, pp. 30–45.

Agocs, C. (1997) 'Institutionalized Resistance to Organizational Change: Denial, Inaction and Repression', *Journal of Business Ethics*, vol. 16, pp. 917–31.

Aguilera, R.V. and Jackson, G. (2003) 'The Cross-national Diversity of Corporate Governance: Dimensions and Determinants', *Academy of Management Review*, vol. 28, pp. 447–65.

Ahmed, P.K. (1998) 'Culture and Climate for Innovation', *European Journal of Innovation Management*, vol. 1, pp. 30–43.

Ahmed, P.K. and Zairi, M. (1999) 'Benchmarking for Brand Innovation', *European Journal of Innovation Management*, vol. 2, 36–48.

Aldefer, C.P. and Smith, K.K. (1982) 'Studying Intergroup Relations Embedded in Organizations', *Administrative Science Quarterly*, vol. 27, pp. 35–65.

Allard, M.J. (2002) 'Theoretical Underpinnings of Diversity', in C. Harvey and M.J. Allard (eds), *Understanding and Managing Diversity*. New Jersey: Prentice-Hall, pp. 3–27.

Andrialopolos, C. (2001) 'Determinants of Organizational Creativity: A Literature Review', *Management Decision*, vol. 39, pp. 834–40.

Annual Survey of Hours and Earnings, 2005, available at: http://www.statistics.gov.uk/StatBase/Product.asp?vlnk=14203

445

Appelbaum, S.H. and Fewster, B.M. (2002) 'Global Aviation Human Resource Management: Contemporary Recruitment and Selection and Diversity and Equal Opportunity Practices', *Equal Opportunities International*, vol. 21, pp. 66–80.

Archer, M. (1995) *Realist Social Theory: The Morphogenetic Approach*. Cambridge: Cambridge University Press.

Argyris, C. and Schön, D.A. (1978) *Organizational Learning: A Theory in Action Perspective*. Reading. MA: Addison-Wesley.

Arimura, S. (2001) 'Workforce Diversity in Japanese Companies in the U.S. and "Localization of People"', *Yamaguchi Journal of Economics, Business Administration and Law*, vol. 49, no. 2, pp. 317–42.

Arimura, S. (2004) 'Diversity Management and Foreign Companies in Japan: Based on a Questionnaire Survey to U.S. Foreign Companies in Japan', *Yamaguchi Journal of Economics, Business Administration and Laws*, vol. 53, no. 3, pp. 255–74.

Arredondo, P. (1996) *Successful Diversity Management Initiatives: A Blueprint for Planning and Implementation*. Thousand Oaks, CA: Sage.

Arts Council England (2005) *Children, Young People and the Arts: London Regional Strategy*, www.artscouncil.org.uk

Ashkanasy, N.M., Hartel, C.E.J. and Daus, C.S. (2002) 'Diversity and Emotion: The New Frontiers in Organizational Behaviour Research', *Journal of Management*, vol. 28, no. 3, pp. 307–38.

Ashworth, P. and Saxton, J. (1992) *Managing Work Experience*. Routledge: London.

Atkinson, J. (1985) *Flexibility, Uncertainty and Manpower Management*. Brighton: Institute of Manpower Studies.

Au, K. and Cheung, M.W.L. (2004) 'Intra-cultural Job Variation and Job Autonomy in 42 Countries', *Organization Studies*, vol. 25, no. 8, pp. 1339–62.

Auyero, J. (2002) 'The Judge, the Cop, and the Queen of Carnival: Ethnography, Storytelling, and the (Contested) Meanings of Protest', *Theory and Society*, vol. 31, pp. 151–87.

Avery, D.R. and Thomas, K.M. (2004) 'Blending Content and Contract: The Roles of Diversity Curriculum and Campus Heterogeneity Fostering Diversity Management Competency', *Academy of Management & Learning*, vol. 3, pp. 380–96.

Bacharach, S.B., Bamberger, P.A. and Vashdi, D. (2005) 'Diversity and Homophily at Work: Supportive Relations among White and African-American Peers', *Academy of Management Journal*, vol. 48, pp. 619–44.

Banerji, K. and Sambharya, R.B. (2004) 'Cracks in the Vertical Keiretsu: Switching the Behaviour of Suppliers in the Japanese Automobile Industry', *Academy of Management Best Conference Paper*, IM: pp. G1–G6.

Bantel, K.A. and Jackson, S.E. (1989) 'Top Management and Innovation in Banking: Does the Composition of the Top Team Make a Difference?', *Strategic Management Journal*, vol. 10, pp. 107–24.

Barak, M.E.M. (2000) 'The Inclusive Workplace: An Ecosystems Approach to Diversity Management', *Social Work*, vol. 45, no. 4, pp. 339–52.

Barkema, H.G. and Vermeulen, F. (1998) 'International Expansion through Start-up or Acquisition: A Learning Perspective', *Academy of Management Journal*, vol. 41, pp. 7–26.

Barkema, H.G., Baum, J.A.C. and Mannix, E.A. (2002) 'Management Challenges in a New Time', *Academy of Management Journal*, vol. 45, no. 5, pp. 916–30.

Barmes, L. and Ashtiany, S. (2003) 'The Diversity Approach to Achieving Equality: Potential and Pitfalls', *The Industrial Law Journal*, vol. 32, pp. 274–96.

Bar-On, D. and Kassem, F. (2004) 'Storytelling as a Way to Work through Intractable Conflicts: The German-Jewish Experience and its Relevance to the Palestinian-Israeli Conflict', *Journal of Social Issues*, vol. 60, no. 2, pp. 298–306.

Barone, T.E. (1992) 'Beyond Theory and Method: A Case of Critical Storytelling', *Theory into Practice*, vol. 31, no. 2, pp. 142–46.

Barrett, R.S. (1967) 'Guide to Using Psychological Tests', in E.A. Fleishman (ed.), *Studies in Personnel and Industrial Psychology*. Chicago: Dorsey Press.

Barry, B. and Bateman, T.S. (1996) 'A Social Trap Analysis of the Management of Diversity', *Academy of Management Review*, vol. 21, pp. 757–90.

Barthorpe, S. and Hall, M. (2000) 'A Collaborative Approach to Placement Preparation and Career Planning for University Students: A Case Study', *Journal of Vocational Education and Training*, vol. 52, no. 2, pp. 165–75.

Bartol, K.M., Evans, C.L. and Stith, M.T. (1978) 'Black versus White Leaders: A Comparative Review of the Literature', *Academy of Management Review*, April, pp. 293–304.

Bartram, D. (2004) 'Assessment in Organizations', *Applied Psychology: An International Review*, vol. 53, no. 2, pp. 237–59.

Bartunek, J.M., Bobko, P. and Venkatraman, N. (1993) 'Toward Innovation and Diversity in Management Research Methods', *Academy of Management Journals*, vol. 36, pp. 1362–73.

Bass, B.M. (1995) 'From Transactional to Transformational Leadership: Learning to Share Vision', *Organizational Dynamics*, vol. 18, no. 3, pp. 19–31.

Battu, H., Seaman, P. and Zenou, Y. (2004) 'Job Contact Networks and the Ethnic Minorities', Working Paper no. 628, The Research Institute of Industrial Economics.

Beard, S., Coll, R.K. and Harris, J. (2001) 'Student and Employer Reflections of an International Science and Technology Work Placement', *Asia-Pacific Journal of Cooperative Education*, vol. 2, no. 1, pp. 6–10.

Becker, G.S. (1975) *Human Capital*. Chicago: University of Chicago Press.

Beckhard, R. (1969) *Organizational Development: Strategies and Methods*. Reading: Addison-Wesley.

Beer, M. and Nobria, N. (2000) 'Cracking the Code of Change', *Harvard Business Review*, May–June, pp. 133–41.

Benschop, Y. (2001) 'Pride, Prejudice and Performance: Relations between HRM Diversity and Performance', *International Journal of Human Resources Management*, vol. 12, pp. 1166–81.

Berge, T. van den, Knegt, R., Schaapman, M.H. and Zaal, I. (2004) 'Policy Instruments to Enhance Compliance with Equal Treatment Rules', A Report Commissioned by the Dutch Ministry of Social Affairs and Employment, Amsterdam.

Bergen, C.W.V., Soper, B. and Foster, T. (2002) 'Unintended Negative Effects of Diversity Management', *Public Personnel Management*, vol. 31, pp. 239–51.

Beynon, H. (1973) *Working for Ford*. London: Allen Lane, Penguin Books.

Bhadury, J., Mighty, E.J. and Damar, H. (2000) 'Maximising Workforce Diversity in Project Teams: A Network Flow Approach', *The International Journal of Management Science*, vol. 28, pp. 143–53.

Bhimani, A. (1999) 'Mapping Methodological Frontiers in Cross-national Management Control Research', *Accounting, Organizational and Society*, vol. 24, pp. 413–40.

Biech, E. (2003) 'Executive Commentary', *Academy of Management Executive*, vol. 17, pp. 92–3.

Bigley, A.G. and Pearce, J.L. (1998) 'Straining for Shared Meaning in Organization Science: Problems of Trust and Distrust', *Academy of Management Review*, vol. 23, pp. 405–21.

Blankfield, S. (2001) 'Think, Problematic and Costly? The Dyslexic Student on Work Placement', *SKILL Journal*, vol. 70, pp. 23–26, July.

Blazevic, V. and Lievens, A. (2002) 'Learning During the New Financial Service Innovation Process: Antecedents and Performance Effects', *Journal of Business Research*, vol. 57, no. 4, pp. 374–91.

Blyler, M. and Coff, R.W. (2003) 'Dynamic Capabilities, Social Capital, and Rent Appropriation: Ties that Split Pies', *Strategic Management Journal*, vol. 24, no. 7, pp. 677–86.

Boeker, W. (1997) 'Strategic Change: The Influence of Managerial Characteristics and Organizational Growth', *Academy of Management Journal*, vol. 40, pp. 152–70.

Böheim, R. and Taylor, M.P. (2002) 'Job Search Methods, Intensity and Success in Britain in the 1990s', Working Paper no. 0206, Department of Economics Johannes Kepler, University of Linz.

Boje, D.M. (1991a) 'Consulting and Change in the Storytelling Organization, *Journal of Organizational Change Management*, vol. 4, no. 3, pp. 7–17.

Boje, D.M. (1991b) 'The Storytelling Organization: A Study of Story Performance in an Office-supply Firm', *Administrative Science Quarterly*, vol. 36, pp. 106–26.

Boje, D.M. (1995) 'Stories of the Storytelling Organization: A Postmodern Analysis of Disney as "Tamara-land" ', *Academy of Management Journal*, vol. 38, no. 4, pp. 997–1035.

Boje, D.M. and Winsor, R.D. (1993) 'The Resurrection of Taylorism: Total Quality Management's Hidden Agenda', *Journal of Organizational Change Management*, vol. 6, no. 4, pp. 57–70.

Boone, C., Olffen, W.V., Wittelloosuijin, A.V. and De Brabander, B. (2004) 'The Geneses of Top Management Team Diversity: Selective Turnover among Top Management Teams Dutch Newspaper Publishing 1970–94', *Academy of Management Journal*, vol. 47, pp. 633–56.

Bourdieu, P. (1977) *Outline of Theory of Practice*. Cambridge: Cambridge University Press.

Bourdieu, P. (1984) *Distinction: A Social Critique of the Judgment of Taste*. London: Routledge.

Bourdieu, P. (1990) *The Logic of Practice*. Stanford: Stanford University Press.

Bourdieu, P. and Wacquant, L. (1992) *An Invitation to Reflexive Sociology*. Cambridge: Polity Press.

Bourdieu, P. (1998) *Practical Reason: On The theory of Action*. Cambridge: Polity Press.

Bouty, I. (2000) 'Interpersonal and Interaction Influences on Informal Resource Exchanges between R&D Researchers across Organizational Boundaries', *Academy of Management Journal*, vol. 43, no. 1, pp. 50–65.

Boxall, P. and Purcell, J. (2003) *Strategy and Human Resource Management*. New York: Palgrave Macmillan.

Boyce, M.E. (1995) 'Collective Centring and Collective Sense-making in the Stories and Storytelling of one Organization', *Organization Studies*, 1995, vol. 16, no. 1, pp. 107–37.

Boyce, M.E. (1996) 'Organizational Story and Storytelling: A Critical Review', *Journal of Organizational Change Management*, vol. 9, no. 5, pp. 5–26.

Brett, S. and Milsome, S. (2004) *Monitoring Progress on Equal Pay Reviews*. EOC Research Discussion Series, Equal Opportunities Commission.

Brickson, S. (2000) 'The Impact of Identity Orientation on Individual and Organizational Outcomes in Demographically Diverse Settings', *Academy of Management Review*, vol. 25, pp. 82–101.

Bridging the Gap and Measuring the Gap, available at: http://www.cre.gov.uk/

Brief, A.P. (2004) 'Editor's Comments: AMR- It is about Diversity', *Academy of Management Review*, vol. 29, pp. 7.

Brimm, L. and Arora, M. (2001) 'Diversity Management at Hewlett-Packard, Europe', in M.A. Albrecht (ed.), *International HRM: Managing Diversity in the Workplace*. Oxford: Blackwell, pp. 108–24.

British Council (2006) http://www.britishcouncil.org/arts-creative-industries-definition.htm

Bronstein, A.S. (1991) 'Temporary Work in Western Europe: Threat or Complement to Permanent Employment?', *International Labour Review*, vol. 130, no. 3, pp. 291–311.

Brooks, W. and Trompenaars, F. (1995) 'Global Diversity Begins at Home', *People Management*, vol. 1, pp. 16–18.

Buchanan, D. and Boddy, D. (1992) *The Expertise of the Change Agent*. London: Prentice Hall.

Bunderson, J.S. and Sutcliffe, K.M. (2002) 'Comparing Alternative Conceptualisations of Functional Diversity in Management Teams: Process and Performance Effects', *Academy of Management Journal*, vol. 45, pp. 875–93.

Burke, W.W. (1998) 'From the Editor. . ., *Academy of Management Executive*, August, p. 184.

Burrett, A.J. (2002) 'Picking the Pitch: A Grounded Theory Study on the Impact of Equal Opportunity Officers on the Culture of Universities', unpublished doctoral dissertation, Southern Cross University, Australia.

Burton, D. (2000) 'Ethnicity, Identity and Marketing: A Critical Review', *Journal of Marketing Management*, vol. 16, pp. 853–77.

Butler, J. (1997) *Excitable Speech: A Politics of the Performative*. New York: Routledge.

Butler, J. (1999) 'Performativity's Social Magic', in R. Schusterman (ed.), *Bourdieu: A Critical Reader*. Oxford: Blackwell, pp. 113–28.

Cahill, H. (1996) 'A Qualitative Analysis of Student Nurses' Experiences of Mentorship', *Journal of Advanced Nursing*, vol. 24, pp. 791–9.

Caldwell, R. (2003) 'Models of Change Agency: A Fourfold Classification', *British Journal of Management*, vol. 14, pp. 131–42.

Calori, R., Steele, M. and Yoneyama, E. (1995) 'Management in Europe: Learning from Different Perspectives', *European Management Journal*, vol. 3, pp. 58–66.

Canen, A.G. and Canen, A. (1999), 'Logistic and Cultural Diversity: Hand in Hand for Organizational Success', *Cross Cultural Management*, vol. 6, pp. 3–10.

Cao, G., Clarke, S. and Lehaney, B. (2003) 'Diversity Management in Organizational Change: Towards a Systematic Framework', *Systems Research and Behavioural Science*, vol. 20, pp. 231–42.

Carroll, G.R. and Hannan, M.T. (2000) 'Why Corporate Demography Matters: Policy Implications of Organizational Diversity', *California Management Review*, vol. 42, pp. 148–63.

Cartwright, S. and Gale, A. (1995) 'Project Management: Different Gender, Different Culture? Part 2', *Leadership & Organizational Development Journal*, vol. 16, pp. 12–16.

Cassell, C. and Biswas, R. (2000) 'Managing Diversity in the New Millennium', *Personnel Review*, vol. 29, pp. 268–73.

Cavanaugh, J.M. (1997) '(In)corporating the Other? Managing the Politics of Workplace Difference', in P. Prasad, A.J. Mills, M. Elmes and A. Prasad (eds), *Managing the Organizational Melting Pot: Dilemmas of Workforce Diversity*. Thousand Oaks, CA: Sage, pp. 31–53.

CCS Consultation Paper (2006) 'Working with Partners in the English Regions', www.ccskills.org.uk

Chatman, J.A. and O'Reilly, C.A. (2004) 'Asymmetric Reactions to Work Group Sex Diversity among Men and Women', *Academy of Management Journal*, vol. 47, pp. 193–208.

Chaharbaghi, K. and Lynch, R. (1999) 'Sustainable Competitive Advantage: Towards a Dynamic Resource-based Strategy', *Management Decisions*, vol. 37, pp. 45–50.

Chakravarthy, B.S. (1990) 'Management Systems for Innovation and Productivity', *European Journal of Operational Research*, vol. 47, pp. 203–13.

Charmaz, C. (2000) 'Grounded Theory: Objectivist and Constructivist Methods', in Denzin, N. and Lincoln, Y. (eds), *Handbook of Qualitative Research*. 2nd edn, London: Sage.

Chatman, J.A., Polzer, J.T., Barsade, S.G. and Neale, M.A. (1998) 'Being Different yet Feeling Similar: The Influence of Demographic Composition and Organizational Culture on Work Processes and Outcomes', *Administrative Science Quarterly*, vol. 43, no. 4, pp. 749–80.

Cheng, C. (1997) 'A Review Essay on the Books of bell hooks: Organizational Diversity Lessons thoughtful Race and Gender Heretic', *Academy of Management Review*, vol. 22, pp. 553–74.

Chevrier, S. (2003) 'Cross-cultural Management in Multinational Project Groups', *Journal of World Business*, vol. 38, pp. 141–9.

Clair, J.A., Beatty, J.E. and Maclean, T.L. (2005) 'Out of Sight but not out of Mind: Managing Invisible Social Identities in the Workplace', *Academy of Management Review*, vol. 30, pp. 78–95.

Cockburn, C. (1989) 'Equal Opportunities: The Short and Long Agenda', *Industrial Relations Journal*, vol. 20, no. 4, pp. 213–25.

Cockburn, C. (1991) *In the Way of Women: Men's Resistance of Sex Equality in Organizations.* London: Macmillan.

Cohen, C.F., Baskin, O.W. and Harlow, D.N. (1982) 'The Effects of Manager's Sex and Attitudes toward Women', *Academy of Management Proceedings*, August pp. 395–8.

Coll, R.K. and Eames, R. (2000) 'The Role of the Placement Coordinator: An Alternative Model', *Asia-Pacific Journal of Cooperative Education*, vol. 1, no. 1, pp. 9–14.

Collinson, D.L. and Hearn, J. (eds) (1996) *Men as Managers, Managers as Men: Critical Perspectives on Men, Masculinities and Managements.* London: Sage.

Collinson, D.L., Knights, D. and Collison, M. (1990) *Managing to Discriminate.* London and New York: Routledge.

Commission Communication of 12 April 2005. *Integrated Guidelines for Growth and Jobs (2005–2008).* COM(2005) 141 (final).

Contu, A. and Willmott, H. (2003) 'Re-embedding Situatedness: The Importance of Power Relations in Learning Theory', *Organization Science*, vol. 14, no. 3, pp. 283–96.

Cope, P., Cuthbertson, P. and Stoddart, B. (2000) 'Situated Learning in the Practice Placement', *Journal of Advanced Nursing*, vol. 31, no. 4, pp. 850–56.

Cordero, R., Ditomaso, N. and Farris, G.F. (1997) 'Gender and Race/ethnic Composition of Technical Work Groups: Relationship to Creative Productivity and Morale', *Journal of Engineering and Technology Management*, vol. 13, pp. 205–21.

Cox, T.H. (1991) 'The Multicultural Organization', *Academy of Management Executive*, vol. 5, no. 2, pp. 34–47.

Cox, T.H. (1993) *Cultural Diversity in Organizations: Theory, Research and Practice.* SanFrancisco: Berrett-Koehler.

Cox, T.H. and Blake, B. (1991) 'Managing Cultural Diversity: Implications for Organizational Competitiveness', *Academy of Management Executive*, vol. 5, no. 3, pp. 45–56.

Crebert, G., Bates, M., Bell, B., Patrick, C.-J. and Cragnolini, V. (2004) 'Developing Generic Skills at University, During Work Placement and in Employment: Graduates' Perceptions', *Higher Education Research and Development*, vol. 23, no. 2, pp. 147–65.

Crompton, R. and Mann, M. (1994) *Gender and Stratification.* Oxford: Polity Press.

Cui, G. and Choudhury, P. (2002) 'Marketplace Diversity and Cost-effectiveness Marketing Strategies', *Journal of Consumer Marketing*, vol. 19, pp. 54–73.

Cummings, J.N. (2004) 'Work Groups, Structural Diversity and Knowledge Sharing in a Global Organization', *Management Science*, vol. 50, pp. 352–64.

Cutcher-Gershenfeld, J., Nitta, M., Barrett, B., Belhedi, N., Bullard, J., Couthcie, C., Inaba, T., Ishino, I., Lee, S., Lin, W.J., Mothersell, W., Rabine, S., Ramanand, S., Strolle, M., Wheaton, A. (1994) 'Japanese Team-work Based Work Systems in North America: Explaining Diversity', *California Management Review*, vol. 37, no. 1, pp. 42–64.

D'Netto, B. and Sohal, M.S. (1999) 'Human Resources Practices and Workforce Diversity: An Empirical Assessment', *International Journal of Manpower*, vol. 20, pp. 530–47.

Dadfar, H. and Gustavsson, P. (1992) 'Competition by Effective Management of Cultural Diversity', *International Studies of Management and Organization*, vol. 22, pp. 81–92.

Dale, A. and Bamford, C. (1988) 'Temporary Workers: Cause for Concern or Complacency?', *Work, Employment and Society*, vol. 2, no. 2, pp. 191–209.

Dansky, K.H., Weech-Maldonado, R., De Souza, G. and Dreachslin, J.L. (2003) 'Organizational Strategy and Diversity Management: Diversity-sensitive Orientation as a Moderating Influence', *Health Care Management Review*, vol. 28, no. 3, pp. 43–253.

Darton, D. and K. Hurrell (2005) *People Working Part-time below their Potential.* Manchester: Equal Opportunities Commission.

Dass, P. and Parker, B. (1999) 'Strategies for Managing Human Diversity: From Resistance to Learning', *Academy of Management Executive*, vol. 13, pp. 68–80.

Dawson, P. (1994) *Organizational Change: A Processual Approach.* London: Paul Chapman Publishing.

Dawson, P. (2003) *Understanding Organizational Change: The Contemporary Experience of People at Work.* London: Sage.

De Valk, S. (1993) 'Holding up a Mirror to Diversity Issues', *Training & Development*, July, pp. 11–12.

Department for Culture, Media and Sport (2006) http://www.culture.gov.uk/creative_industries/

Department of Health (2001) *National Service Framework for Older People* (report), London.

Department of Trade and Industry (DTI) (1999) *Regulation of the Private Recruitment Industry: A Consultation Document* URN: 99/774, produced by the Employment Agency Standards, Employment Relations Directorate, DTI, May.

Deshpande, R. (1999) 'What are the Contributions of Marketing to the Organizational Performance and the Societal Welfare', *Journal of Marketing Management*, vol. 63, pp. 164–7.

Desrochers, P. (2003) 'Local Diversity, Human Creativity, and Technological Innovation', *Growth and Change*, vol. 32, pp. 369–94.

Dick, P. and Cassell, C. (2002) 'Barriers to Managing Diversity in a UK Constabulary: The Role of Discourse', *Journal of Management Studies*, vol. 39, pp. 954–76.

Dickens, L. (1999) 'Beyond the Business Case: A Three-proged Approach to Equality Action', *Human Resource Management Journal*, vol. 9, no. 1, pp. 9–19.

DiTomaso, N., Cordero, R. and Farris, G.F. (1996) 'Effects of Group Diversity on Perceptions of Group and Self among Scientists and Engineers', in M.N. Ruderman, M.W. Hughes-James and S.E. Jackson (eds), *Selected Research on Work Team Diversity*. Washington, DC: APA and Center for Creative Leadership, pp. 99–119.

DiTomaso, N., Farris, G.F. and Cordero, R. (1993) 'Diversity in the Technical Workforce: Rethinking the Management of Scientists and Engineers', *Journal of Engineering and Technology Management*, vol. 10, pp. 101–27.

DiTomaso, N. and Hooijberg, R. (1996) 'Diversity and the Demand of Leadership', *Leadership Quarterly*, vol 7, no. 2, pp. 163–87.

Diversity Excellence Model (DEM). Available at: http://www.nationalschool.gov.uk/diveristy/index.asp

Dobbs, M.F. (1996) 'Managing Diversity: Lessons from the Private Sector', *Public Personnel Management.* vol. 25, no. 3, pp. 351–67.

Dodgson, M. (1993) 'Organizational Learning: A Review of some Literatures', *Organization Studies*, vol. 14, no. 3, pp. 375–94.

Doherty, L. (2004) 'Work-life Balance Initiatives: Implications for Women', *Employee Relations*, vol. 26, pp. 433–52.

Doktor, R., Tung, R.L., Fraser, S. and Von Glinow, M.A. (1991) 'Future Directions for Management Theory Development', *Academy of Management Review*, vol. 16, pp. 362–5.

Doney, P.M., Cannon, J.P. and Muller, M.R. (1998) 'Understanding the Influence of National Culture on the Development of Trust', *Academy of Management Review*, vol. 23, pp. 601–20.

Drach-Zahavy, A. and Somech, A. (2002) 'Team Heterogeneity and its Relationship with Team Support and Team Effectiveness', *Journal of Educational Administration*, vol. 40, pp. 44–66.

Drennan, J. (2002) 'An Evaluation of the Role of the Clinical Placement Coordinator in Student Nurse Support in the Clinical Area', *Journal of Advanced Nursing*, vol. 40, no. 4, pp. 475–83.

Drever, E. and Cope, P. (1999) 'Students Use of Theory in an Initial Teacher Education Programme', *Journal of Education for Teaching: International Research and Pedagogy*, vol. 2 (July): pp. 97–109.

Druker, J. and Stanworth, C. (2001) 'Partnerships and the Private Recruitment Industry', *Human Resource Management Journal*, vol. 11, no. 2, pp. 73–89.

Duignan, J. (2002) 'Undergraduate Work Placement and Academic Performance: Failing by doing', *HERDSA*, pp. 214–21.

Dulewicz, V. and Herbert, P. (2000) 'Predicting Advancement to Senior Management from Competencies and Personality Data: A Seven-year Follow up Study', *British Journal of Management*, vol. 10, no. 1, pp. 13–23.

Dunphy, D. and Stace, D. (1993) 'The Strategic Management of Corporate Change', *Human Relations*, vol. 46, no. 8, pp. 905–18.

Durgee, J.F. (1988) 'On Cezanne, Hot Buttons, and Interpreting Consumer Storytelling', *The Journal of Consumer Marketing*, vol. 5, no. 4, pp. 47–51.

Dutton, J.E. and Ashford, S.J. (1993) 'Selling Issues to Top Management', *Academy of Management Review*, vol. 18, no. 3, pp. 397–428.

Dwyer, S., Richard, O.C. and Chadwick, K. (2003) 'Gender Diversity in Management and Firm Performance: The Influence of Growth Orientation and Organizational Culture', *Journal of Business Research*, vol. 56, no. 12, pp. 1009–19.

Dyer, J.H. and Nobeoka, K. (2000) 'Creating and Managing a High-performance Knowledge–Sharing Network: The Toyota Case', *Strategic Management Journal*, vol. 21, pp. 345–67.

EC (2003) *Equality, Diversity and Enlargement*. European Commission Report, September.

Echeverri-Carroll, E.L. (1999) 'Knowledge Flows in Innovation Networks: A Comparative Analysis of Japanese and US High-technology Firms', *Journal of Knowledge Management*, vol. 3, pp. 296–303.

Egan, M.L. and Bendick, Jr., M. (2003) 'Workforce Diversity Initiatives of U.S. Multinational Corporations in Europe', *Thunderbird International Business Review*, vol. 46, pp. 701–28.

Elmes, M. and Connelley, D.L. (1997) 'Dreams of Diversity and Realities of Intergroup Relations in Organizations', in P. Prasad, A.J. Mills, M. Elmes and A. Prasad (eds), *Managing the Organizational Melting Pot: Dilemmas of Workplace Diversity*. Thousand Oaks, CA: Sage, pp. 148–67.

Elsass, P.M. and Graves, L.M. (1997) 'Demographic Diversity in Decision-making Groups: The Experiences of Women and People of Color', *Academy of Management Review*, vol. 22, pp. 946–73.

Elsbach, K.D., Sutton, R.I. and Whetten, D.A. (1999) 'Perspectives on Developing Management Theory, circa 1999: Moving from Shrill Monologues to (Relatively) Lame Dialogues', *Academy of Management Review*, vol. 24, pp. 627–33.

Equal Opportunities Commission (2004) *Facts about Women and Men in Great Britain*.

Equal Opportunities Commission (2005a) *Part-time is no Crime – So Why the Penalty?*, Interim report of the EOC's investigation into flexible and part-time working, and questions for consultation. Manchester: EOC.

Equal Opportunities Commission (2005b) *Response to Women and Work Commission, Part Two: Closing the Gender Pay Gap*.

Ettore, B. and Capowski, G. (1997) 'Value-added HR: People, Performance and the Bottom Line', *HR Focus*, July, 9–11.

European Foundation for Quality Management (EFQM) (2005) Business Excellence Model. Available at: http://www.efqm.org/

Eveline, J. and Todd, P. (2002) 'Teaching Managing Diversity via Feminist Theory', *International Journal of Inclusive Education*, vol. 6, pp. 33–46.

Evenden, R. (1993) 'The Strategic Management of Recruitment and Selection', in R. Harrison (ed.), *Human Resource Management: Issues and Strategies*, Wokingham: Addison-Wesley publishing Company, pp. 219–46.

Everett, J. (2002) 'Organizational Research and the Praxeology of Pierre Bourdieu', *Organizational Research Methods*, vol. 5, no. 1, pp. 56–80.

Fagenson, E.A. and Mason, G. (1993) 'Is what's Good for Goose also Good for the Gander? On Being White and Men on a Diverse Workforce', *Academy of Management Executive*, vol. 7, pp. 80–1.

Faludi, S. (1991) *Backlash: The Undeclared War Against American Women*. New York: Crown.

Fernandez, J.P. (1991) *Managing a Diverse Work Force*. Lexington: Lexington Books.

Ferris, G.R., Arthur, M.M., Berkson, H.M., Kaplan, D.M., Harrell-Cook, G. and Frink, D.D. (1998) 'Toward a Social Context Theory of Human Resources Management-Organizational Effectiveness Relationship', *Human Resource Management Review*, vol. 8, pp. 235–64.

Fine, M.G. (2003) 'Building Successful Multicultural Organizations: Challenges and Opportunities', in R.J. Ely, E.G. Foldy, M.A. Scully and the Centre for Gender in Organizations Simmons School of Management (eds), *Reader in gender, Work and Organization*. Oxford: Blackwell, pp. 308–17.

Finegold, D. and Soskice, D. (1988) 'The Failure of Training in Britain: Analysis and Prescription', *Oxford Review of Economic Policy*, vol. 4, pp. 21–53.

Fink, J.S., Pastore, D.L. and Riemer, H.A. (2001) 'Do Differences Make a Difference? Managing Diversity in Division LA Intercollegiate Athletics', *Journal of Sport Management*, vol. 15, pp. 10–50.

Finn, C. and Chattopadhyay, P. (2000) 'Managing Emotions in Diverse Work Teams: An Effective Events Perspective', *Academy of Management Proceedings*, MOC: D1–D6.

Fish, A. (1999) 'Cultural Diversity: Challenging Facing the Management of Cross-border Business Careers', *Career Development International*, vol. 4, pp. 96–205.

Fleury, M.T.L. (1999) 'The Management of Culture Diversity: Lessons from Brazilian Companies', *Industrial Management & Data Systems*, vol. 99, pp. 109–14.

Flood, R.L. and Romm, R.A.N. (1996) 'Contours Diversity Management and Triple Loop Learning', *Kybernetes*, vol. 25, pp. 154–64.

Forbes, L.H. (2002) 'Improving Quality through Diversity–more Critical more than even Before', *Leadership and Management in Engineering*, October, pp. 49–52.

Ford, L. (2000) 'Diversity: From Cartoons to Confrontations', *Training & Development*, Media Reviews, August 2000.

Foster, C. and Harris, L. (2005) 'Easy to Say, Difficult to Do: Diversity Management in Retail', *Human Resource Management Journal*, vol. 15, pp. 4–17.

Fox, T.L. and Spence, J.W. (1999) 'An Examination of the Decision Styles of Project Managers: Evidence of Significant Diversity', *Information & Management*, vol. 36, pp. 313–20.

Freeman-Evans, T. (1994) 'Benefiting from Multiculturalism', *Association Management*, February, 52–6.

Freire, P. (1970) *Pedagogy of the Oppressed*. New York: Continuum.

Gammie, E., Gammie, B. and Duncan F. (2002) 'Operating a Distance Learning Module within an Undergraduate Work Placement: Some Reflections', *Education and Training*, vol. 44, no. 1, pp. 11–22.

Garrick, J. and Clegg, S. (2001) 'Stressed-out Knowledge Workers in Performative Times: A Postmodern Take on Project Based Learning', *Management Learning*, vol. 32, no. 1, pp. 119–34.

Gatley, S. and Lessem, R. (1995) 'Enhancing the Competitive Advantage of Transcultural Business', *Journal of European Industrial Training*, vol. 19, pp. 3–11.

Geppert, M., Matten, D. and Williams, K. (2003) 'Change Management in MNCs: How Global Convergence Interwines with National Diversities', *Human Relations*, vol. 56, pp. 807–39.

Gershon, N. and Page, W. (2002) 'What Storytelling Can Do for Information Visualisation', *Communications of the ACM*, vol. 44, no. 8, pp. 31–7.

Ghosh, S. (2000) 'Management Implications of Ethnicity in South Africa', *Journal of International Business Studies*, vol. 31, pp. 507–19.

Giddens, A. 1984. *The Constitution of Society: Outline of the Theory of Structuration*. Cambridge: Polity Press.

Gilbert, J.A. and Ivancevich, J.M. (2000) 'Valuing Diversity: A Tale of Two Organizations', *Academy of Management Executive*, vol. 14, no. 1, pp. 93–105.

Gilbert, J.A. and Stead, B.A. (1999) 'Stigmatisation Revisited: Does Diversity Management Make a Difference in Applicant Success', *Group and Organization Management*, vol. 24, pp. 239–56.

Gilbert, J.A., Stead, B.A. and Ivancevich, J.M. (1999) 'Diversity Management: A New Organizational Paradigm', *Journal of Business Ethics*, vol. 21, pp. 61–76.

Glassner, A. (1999) 'Active Storytelling', *Eurographics*, vol. 18, no. 3, pp. 1–4.

Glastra, F., Meerman, M., Shedler, P. and De Vries, S. (2000) 'Broadening the Scope of Diversity Management: Strategic Implications in the Case of the Netherlands', *Industrial Relations*, vol. 55, pp. 698–724.

Glover, J., Rainwater, K., Jones, G. and Friedman, H. (2002) 'Adaptive Leadership (part two): Four Principles for Being Adaptive', *Organization Development Journal*, vol. 20, pp. 18–38.

Golembiewski, R.T. (1995) *Managing Diversity in Organizations*, Tuscaloosa, London: University of Alabama Press.

Goll, I. and Rasheed, A.A. (2005) 'The Relationship between Two Top Management Demographic Characteristics, Rational Decision making, Environmental Munifience, and Firm Performance', *Organization Studies*, vol. 26, no. 7, pp. 999–1023.

Goodman, P.S., Lawrence, B.S., Ancona, D.G. and Tushman, M.L. (2001) 'Introduction', *Academy of Management Review*, vol. 26, pp. 507–11.

Gooley, T.B. (2000) 'A World of Difference: Special Report', *Logistics*, June, pp. 51–4.

Gottfried, H. (1992) 'In the Margins: Flexibility as a Mode of Regulation in the Temporary Help Industry', *Work, Employment and Society* vol. 6, no. 3, pp. 443–60.

Govindarajan, V. and Gupta, A.K. (2001) 'Building an Effective Global Business Team', *MIT Sloan Management Review*, vol. 42, pp. 63–72.

Granovetter, M. (1985) 'Economic Action and Social Structure: The Problem of Embeddedness, *American Journal of Sociology*, vol. 91, no. 3, pp. 481–510.

Green, F. (2005) 'Trends in the Proportions of Over-educated and Under-educated Workers: Analysis of Skill Surveys Data', University of Kent, unpublished Women and Work Commission Paper, March 2005.

Greene, A. (2002) 'Variety May not be always the Spice of Life', *People Management*, May, p. 50.

Gregg, P. and Wadsworth, J. (1996) 'How Effective are State Employment Agencies? Jobcentre Use and Job Matching in Britain', *Oxford Bulletin of Economics and Statistics*, vol. 58, no. 3, pp. 443–67.

Grenfell, M. and James, D. (1998) *Bourdieu and Education: Acts of Practical Theory*. London Falmer Press.

Griggs, L.B. and Louw, L. (eds) (1995) *Valuing Diversity: New Tools for a New Reality*. New York: McGraw-Hill.

Grimshaw, D. and Rubery, J. (2001) *The Gender Pay Gap: A Research Review*, Equal Opportunities Commission Research Discussion Series. Manchester: EOC.

Grisham, T. (2006) 'Metaphor, Poetry, Storytelling and Cross-cultural Leadership', *Management Decision*, vol. 44, no. 4, pp. 486–503.

Groschi, S. and Doherty, L. (1999) 'Diversity Management in Practice', *International Journal of Contemporary Hospitality Management*, vol. 11, pp. 262–8.

Guest, D. and Clinton, M. (2006) *'Temporary Employment Contracts, Workers' Well-being and Behaviour: Evidence from the UK*. Department of Management Working Paper no. 38, King's College.

Gunn, B. and Gullickson, R. (2003) 'Performativity', *Strategic Finance*, vol. 85, no. 6, pp. 9–10.

Hall, L., Harris, J., Bakewell, C. and Graham, P. (2000) 'Supporting Placement based Learning using Networked Technologies', *The International Journal of Educational Management*, vol. 14, no. 4, pp. 175–9.

Hall, T. (2006) 'An Employer's Perspective', in C. Leadbeater (ed.), *Britain's Creativity Challenge*, www.ccskills.org.uk

Hall, T. and Bewick, T. (2006) *Skills for Creativity*, (a strategic plan 2005–2010), www. ccskills.org.uk

Hambrick, D.C., Cho, T. and Chen, M. (1996) 'The Influence of Top Management Team Heterogeneity on Firms' Competitive Moves'. *Administrative Science Quarterly*. vol. 41, pp. 659–684.

Hammilton, R.D. and Zimmerman, M.A. (1995) 'Lessons Learned getting Your Board to Initiative Change', *Academy of Management Executive*, vol. 9, pp. 67–8.

Hannabus, S. (2000) 'Narrative Knowledge: Eliciting Organizational Knowledge from Storytelling', *Aslib Proceedings*, vol. 52, no. 10, pp. 402–13.

Hardy, C., Palmer, I. and Phillips, N. (2000) 'Discourse as a Strategic Resource'. *Human Relations*, vol. 53, no. 9, pp. 1227–48.

Harris, E.W. and Tanner, J.R. (1996) 'Employment of Recent University Graduates: do age, Gender and Minority Status Make a Difference?', *Journal of Employment Counselling*, vol. 33, pp. 121–9.

Harrison, D.A., Price, K.H. and Bell M.P. (1998) 'Beyond Relational Demography: time and the Effects of the Surface- and deep-level Diversity on Work Group Cohesion', *Academy of Management Journal*, vol. 41, pp. 96–107.

Harrison, D.A., Price, K.H. and Gavin, J.H. (2000) 'Time, Teams and Task Performance: a Longitudinal Study of Chancing Effects of Diversity on Group Functioning', *Academy of Management Proceedings*, GDO: C1–C6.

Harrison, D.A., Price, K.H. and Gavin, J.H. (2002) 'Time, Teams and Task Performance: Chancing Effects of the Surface-and deep-level Diversity on Group Functioning', *Academy of Management Journal*, vol. 45, pp. 1029–45.

Hartel, C.E.J. (2004) 'Towards a Multicultural World: Identifying Work Systems, Practices and Employee Attitudes that Embrace Diversity', *Australian Journal of Management*, vol. 29, pp. 189–202.

Harung, H.S. and Harung, L.M. (1995) 'Enhancing the Organizational Performance by Strengthening Diversity and Unity', *The Learning Organization*, vol. 2, pp. 9–21.

Harvey, M.G. and Buckley, M.R. (1997) 'Managing Inpatriates: Building a Global Core Competency', *Journal of World Business*, vol. 32, no. 1, pp. 35–53.

Hatter, W., Vinter, L. and Williams, R. (2002) 'Equal Opportunities Commission Research Discussion Series'. *Dad on Dads: Needs and Expectations at Home and at work*, Manchester: EOC.

Hayghe, V.H. and Bianchi, S. (1994) 'Married Mothers' Work Patterns: The Job-Family Compromise', *Monthly Labor Review*, June: pp. 24–30.

Hays-Thomas, R. (2003) 'Why Now? The Contemporary Focus on Managing Diversity', in M.S. Stockdale and F.J. Crosby (eds), *The Psychology and Management of Workplace Diversity*. Malden: Blackwell, pp. 1–30.

Healy, G., Özbilgin, M. and Aliefendioglu, H. (2005) 'Academic Employment and Gender: a Turkish Challenge to Vertical sex Segregation', *European Journal of Industrial Relations*, vol. 11, pp. 247–64.

Heery, E. (2004) 'The Trade Union Response to Agency Labour in Britain', *Industrial Relations Journal*, vol. 35, no. 5, pp. 434–50.

Heijltjes, M., Olie, R. and Glunk, U. (2003) 'Internationalisation of Top Management Teams in Europe', *European Management Journal*, vol. 21, pp. 89–97.

Henley, A.B. and Price, K.H. (2002) 'Want a better team? Foster a Climate of Fairness: Research briefs', *Academy of Management Executive*, August, pp. 153–4.

Herbig, P.A. and Milam, R. (1994) 'When in Japan, do as the Japanese do; when in Rome, do as the Japanese do: the Archilles' hell of Japanese Business Philosophy', *Marketing Intelligence and Planning*, vol. 12, pp. 26–35.

Heugens, P.P.M.A.R. (2002) 'Managing Public Affairs Through Storytelling', *Journal of Public Affairs*, vol. 2, no. 2, pp. 57–70.

Hill, W.H. and Fox, W.M. (1973) 'Black and White Marine Squad Leaders' Perceptions of Racially Mixed Squads', *Academy of Management Journal*, vol. 16, pp. 680–6.

Hislop, S., Inglis, B., Cope, P., Stoddart, B. and McIntosh, C. (1996) 'Situating Theory in Practice: Student views of Theory-Practice in Project 2000 Nursing Programmes'. *Journal of Advanced Nursing*, vol. 23, no. 1, pp. 171–7.

Hoffman, L.R. (1978) 'Group Problem solving', in L. Berkowitz (ed.), *Group Processes*. New York: Academic Press.

Hofstede, G. (1989) 'Organising for Cultural Diversity', *European Management Journal*, vol. 7, pp. 390–7.

Hon, N.C. and Brunner, B. (2000) 'Diversity Issues and Public Relations', *Journal of Public Relations Research*, vol. 12, no. 4, pp. 309–40.

Hopkins, W.E. and Hopkins, S.A. (2002) 'Effects of Cultural Recomposition on Group Interaction Processes', *Academy of Management Review*, vol. 27, pp. 541–53.

Hordes, M.W., Clancy, J.A. and Baddaley, J. (1995) 'A Primer for Global Start-ups', *Academy of Management Executive*, vol. 9, no. 2, pp. 7–11.

Horwitz, F.M., Bowmaker-Falconer, A. and Searll, P. (1995) 'Employment Equity Human Resource Development and Institutional Building in South Africa', *The International Journal of Human Resource Management*, vol. 6, pp. 671–85.

Horwitz, F.M., Bowmaker-Falconer, A. and Searll, P. (1996) 'Human Resource Development and Managing Diversity in South Africa', *International Journal of Manpower*, vol. 17, pp. 134–51.

Horwitz, F.M., Browning, V., Jain, H. and Steenkamp, A.J. (2002) 'Human Resources Practices and Discrimination in South Africa: Overcoming the Apartheid Legacy', *International Journal of Human Resource Management*, vol. 13, pp. 1105–18.

Hotopp, U. (2001) *Recruitment agencies in the UK*. (Corrected version). London: Employment Relations Directorate, DTI.

Howard-Grenville, J.A. and Hoffman, A.J. (2003) 'The Importance of Cultural Framing to the Success of Social Initiatives in Business', *Academy of Management Executive*, vol. 17, pp. 70–84.

Howarth, C. (1999) *Monitoring Poverty and Social Exclusion*, York: Joseph Rowntree Foundation.

HSE (Health and Safety Executive) (2006) http://www.hse.gov.uk/

Human, L. (1996) 'Managing Workforce Diversity: A Critique and Example from South Africa', *International Journal of Manpower*, vol. 17, pp. 46–64.

Human Resources Centre of Canada. (2001) *Lessons Learned: Gender Equality in the Labour Market*. Government of Canada.

Humphries, M. and Grice, S. (1995) 'Equal Employment Opportunity and the Management of Diversity', *Journal of Organizational Change*, vol. 8, pp. 17–32.

Huntington, S., Stephen, J. and Oldfield, B.M. (1999) 'Formal Assessment of Student Placement within a Retail Sandwich Degree', *Industrial and Commercial Training*, vol. 31, no. 3, pp. 10–11.

Hurrell, K. (2006) *Facts About Women and Men in Great Britain 2006*. Manchester: Equal Opportunities Commission.

Hutton, W. (2006) *Creative Apprenticeship*, Creative and Cultural Skills (a report), www.ccskills.org.uk

Huy, Q.N. (2001) 'Time, Temporal Capability and Planned Change'. *Academy of Management Review*, vol. 26, no. 4, pp. 601–623.

Ibarra, H. (1995) 'Race, Opportunity and Diversity of Social Circles in Managerial Networks', *Academy of Management Journal*, vol. 38, pp. 673–703.

Iles, P. (1995) 'Learning to Work with Difference', *Personnel Review*, vol. 24, pp. 44–60.

Iles, P. and Hayers, P.K. (1997) 'Managing Diversity in Transnational Project Teams: A Tentative Model and Case Study', *Journal of Managerial Psychology*, vol. 12, pp. 95–117.

ILO (2006) http://www.ilo.org/public/english/employment/gems/eeo/

Industrial Relations Services (IRS) (2002) 'The go-betweens', *IRS Employment Review* 758, September.

INROADS, Diversity new capsules, www.inroadsinc.org

Itzin, C. (1995) 'Crafting Strategy to Create Women-Friendly Work', in C. Itzin, and J. Newman (eds), *Gender Culture and Organizational Change: Putting Theory into Practice*. London and New York: Routledge, pp. 127–51.

Ivancevich, J.M. and Gilbert, J.A. (2000) 'Diversity Management Time for New Approach', *Public Personnel Management*, vol. 29, pp. 75–92.

Iverson, K. (2000) 'Managing for Effective Workforce Diversity', *Cornell Hotel and Management Administration Quarterly*, April, pp. 31–8.

Jacoby, S.M. and Saguchi, K. (2003) 'The Role of the Senior HR Executive in Japan and the United States: Companies', countries, convergence, CIRJE-F-199 Discussion Papers, February, pp. 1–28.

Jain, H.C. and Verma, A. (1996) 'Managing Workforce Diversity for Competitiveness: The Canadian Experience', *International Journal of Manpower*, vol. 17, pp. 14–29.

Jam, O. (2005) 'Survey, Analysis and Action: Plan for Equal Pay – An In-depth Analysis of the Effects of the Regulations of 2001', Jamstalldhetsombudsmannen, Sweden.

James, E.H. and Wooten, L.P. (2001) 'Managing Diversity', *Executive Excellence*, August, pp. 17–18.

Jehn, K.A., Northcraft, G.B. and Neale, M.A. (1999) 'Why Differences Make a Difference: A Field Study of Diversity, Conflict and Performance in Workgroups', *Administrative Science Quarterly*, vol. 44, no. 4, pp. 741–63.

Jenkins, R. (1992) *Pierre Bourdieu*. New York: Routledge.

Jenner, L. (1994) 'Diversity Management: What Does it Mean?', *HR Focus*, vol. 71, pp. 11–15.

Jewson, N. and Mason, D. (1986) 'The Theory and Practice of Equal Opportunity Policies: Liberal and Radical Approaches', *Sociological Review*, vol. 34, no. 2, pp. 307–29.

JIL (2005) 'Japanese Working Life Profile 2004/2005 Labour Statistics', The Japan Institute for Labour Policy and Training, www.jil.go.jp/english/labourinfo/library/index.htm

Johnston, W.B. and Packer, A.H. (1987) *Workforce 2000: Work and workers for the 21st century*. Washington, DC: Hudson Institute.

Jones, D., Pringle, J. and Shepherd, D. (2000) '"Managing Diversity" meets Aotearoa/New Zealand', *Personnel Review*, vol. 29, pp. 364–380.

Jones, R.T., Jerich, B., Copeland, L. and Boyle, M. (1989) 'Four by Four: How do You Manage a Diverse Workforce', *Training and Development Journal*. vol. 43, no. 2, pp. 13–21.

Jones, S. (1989) 'Job Search Methods, Intensity and Effects', *Oxford Bulletin of Economic and Statistics*, vol. 51, pp. 277–96.

Joplin, J.R.W. and Daus, C.S. (1997) 'Challenges of Leading a Diverse Workforce', *Academy of Management Executive*, vol. 11, pp. 32–47.

Jowell, T. (2006) Tessa Jowell's Speech at Bloomberg – 14th March http://www.cep.culture.gov.uk/index.cfm?fuseaction=main.viewBlogEntry&intMTEntryID=2909

Kahan, S. (2006) 'The Power of Storytelling to Jumpstart Collaboration', *The Journal for Quality and Participation*, Spring: 23–25.

Kandola, R. and Fullerton, J. (1998), *Diversity in Action: Managing the Mosaic*. London: Institute of Personnel Development.

Kandola, R.S., Milner, D., Banerji, N.A., and Wood, R. (1991) *Equal opportunities can damage your health: Stress amongst equal opportunities personnel*. Oxford: Pearn, Kandola Downs.

Kandola, R.S. and Pearn, M.A. (1992) 'Identifying Competencies', in Boam, R. and Sparrow, P. (eds), *Designing and Achieving Competency*, London: McGraw-Hill.

Kanter, R.M. (1984) *The change masters*. London: Allen & Unwin.

Kanter, R.M. (1999) *Leading Change*. London: Simon & Schuster.

Kaplan, R. and Norton, D. 1996. *The Balanced Scorecard: Translating Strategy into Action*. Boston: Harvard Business School Press.

Kaplan, S. and Norton, D.P. (2001) 'Transforming the Balanced Scorecard from Performance Measurement to Strategic Management: Part I', *Accounting Horizons*, vol. 15, pp. 87–104.

Kase, K. and Liu, J.Y. (1996) 'Entrepreneurial Networking in Japanese Management', *International Marketing Review*, vol. 13, pp. 13–23.

Katz, D. and Kahn, R.L. (1978) *The Social Psychology of Organizations*, 2nd edn. New York: Wiley.

Keller, R.T. (2001) 'Cross-functional Project Groups in Research and New Product Development: Diversity, Communications, Job Stress and Outcomes', *Academy of Management Journal*, vol. 44, pp. 547–55.

Kelley-Patterson, D. and George, C. (2001) 'Securing Graduate Commitment: an Exploration of the Comparative Expectations of Placement Students, Graduate Recruits and

Human Resource Managers within the Hospitality, Leisure and Tourism Industries', *Hospitality Management*, vol. 20, pp. 311–23.

Kersten, A. (2000) 'Diversity Management, Dialogue, Dialects and Diversion', *Journal of Organizational Change Management*, vol. 13, pp. 235–48.

Kidder, D.L., Lankau M.J., Chrobot-Mason, D., Mollica, K.A. and Friedman, R.A. (2004) 'Backlash Towards Diversity Initiatives: Examining the Impact of Diversity Program Justification', personal and group outcomes, *International Journal of Conflict Management*, vol. 15, pp. 77–102.

Kirby, S.L. and Richard, O.C. (2000) 'Impact of Marketing Work-Place Diversity on Employee Job Involvement and Organizational Commitment', *The Journal of Social Psychology*, vol. 140, no. 3, pp. 367–77.

Kirchmeyer, C. and McLellan, J. (1991) 'Capitalising on Ethnic Diversity: An Approach to Managing the Diversity Workgroups in the 1990s', *RCSA/Canadian Journal of Administrative Sciences*, vol. 8, no. 2, pp. 72–79.

Kirkpatrick, S.A. and Locke, E.A. (1991) 'Leadership: Do Traits Matter?', *Academy of Management Executive*, vol. 5, no. 2, pp. 48–60.

Kirton, G. and Greene, A. (2000) *The Dynamics of Managing Diversity: A Critical Approach*. Oxford: Butterworth-Heinemann.

Kirton, G., Greene, A.M. and Dean, D. (2007) 'British diversity professionals as change agents – radicals, tempered radicals or liberal reformers?', *International Journal of Human Resource Management*, Vol. 18, pp. 1979–94.

Kluge, H. (1997) 'Reflections on Diversity', *Vital Speeches of The Day*, vol. 63, pp. 171–176.

Knouse, S.B. and Dansby, M.R. (2000) 'Recent diversity research at the Defence Equal Opportunity Management Institute' (DEOMI): 1991–1996, *International Journal of Intercultural Relations*, vol. 24, pp. 203–225.

Kodama, M. (2000) 'Business Innovation Through Customer-Value Creation: Case Study of a Virtual Education Business in Japan', *Journal of Management Development*, vol. 19, pp. 49–70.

Kodama, M. (2003) 'Strategic Innovation in Traditional Big Business: Case Study of Two Japanese Companies', *Organization Studies*, vol. 24, no. 2, pp. 235–68.

Kossek, E.E. and Lobel, S.A. (eds) (1996) *Managing Diversity: Human Resources Strategies for Transforming the Workplace*. Cambridge: Blackwell.

Kranias, D.S. (2000) 'Cultural Control: The Case of Japanese Multinational Companies and their Subsidiaries in the UK', *Management Decision*, vol. 38, no. 9, pp. 638–48.

Kravitz, D.A. and Klineberg, S.L. (2002) 'Affirmative Action Attitudes: Effects on Respondent Ethnicity, AAP Strength, and Anticipated Impacts', *Academy of Management Proceedings*, GDO: C1–C6.

Kumar, R. and Andersen, P.H. (2000) 'Inter Firm Diversity and the Management of Meaning in International Strategic Alliances', *International Business Review*, vol. 9, pp. 237–52.

Kurowski, L.L. (2002) 'Cloaked Culture and Veiled Diversity: Why Theorists Ignored Early US Workforce Diversity', *Journal of Academic History*, vol. 40, pp. 183–91.

Kusku, F., Özbilgin, M.F. and Özkale, L. (2007) 'Against the Tide: Gendered Prejudice and Disadvantage, in Engineering Study from a Comparative Perspective', *Gender, Work and Organization*, vol. 14, no. 2 pp. 109–29.

Labour Force Survey (2005) *Quarterly Supplement*. no. 28, January 2005. National Statistics.

Labour Force Survey, ONS (2006) http://www.statistics.gov.uk/STATBASE/Expodata/Spreadsheets/D7921.xls

Labour Market Trends (1999) *Methods of job search*, January 17–18.

Lambert Review of Business-University Collaboration (2003) *Lambert Review of Business-University Collaboration: Final Report*. HMSO, Norwich.

Lampel, J. (2001) 'The Core Competencies of Project Execution: The Challenge of Diversity', *International Journal of Project Management*, vol. 19, pp. 471–83.

Lang, J.C. (2000) 'Managing in Knowledge-based Competition', *Journal of Organizational Change Management*, vol. 14, no. 6, pp. 539–53.

Larkey, L.K. (1996) 'Toward a Theory of Communicative Interactions in Culturally Diverse Workgroups', *Academy of Management Review*, vol. 21, pp. 463–91.

Lau, D.C. and Murnighan, J.K. (1998) 'Demographic Diversity and Faultlines: The Compositional Dynamics of Organizational Groups', *Academy of Management Review*, vol. 23, pp. 325–40.

Lauring, J. and Ross, C. (2004) 'Research Notes: Cultural Diversity and Organizational Efficiency', *New Zealand Journal of Employment Relations*, vol. 29, pp. 89–103.

Lawrence, E. (2000) 'Equal Opportunities Officers and Managing Equality Changes', *Personnel Review*, vol. 29, no. 3, pp. 381–401.

Layder, D. (1993) *New Strategies in Social Research*. Cambridge: Polity Press.

Layder, D. (1998) *Sociological Practice: Linking Theory and Social Research*. London: Sage.

Learning for All. Available at: http://www.cre.gov.uk/

Ledwith, S. and Colgan, F. (eds) (1996a). *Women and Organizations: Challenging Gender Politics*. London: Macmillan.

Ledwith, S. and Colgan, F. (1996b) 'Women as Organizational Change Agents'. in S. Ledwith and F. Colgan (eds), *Women and Organizations: Challenging Gender Politics*. London: Macmillan, pp. 1–43.

Lee, H. (2001) 'Paternalistic Human Resources Practices: Their Emergence and Characteristics', *Journal of Economic Issues*, vol. 35, pp. 841–69.

Leonard, B. (2002) 'Ways to Tell if a Diversity Programme Measuring Up', *HR Magazine*, July, p. 21.

Lerner, G.H. (1992) 'Assisted Storytelling: Deploying Shared Knowledge as a Practical Matter', *Qualitative Sociology*, vol. 15, no. 3, pp. 247–71.

Leslie, D. (1994) 'TQM and Student Work Experience (SWE)', *Quality Assurance in Education*, vol. 2, no. 3, pp. 26–32.

Levy, B. (2002) 'The Competitiveness of MNCs in a Globalized and Regionalized Economy: The War for Talent and the Role of Women Executives', *Management International*, vol. 7, pp. 103–11.

Lewin, K. (1951) *Field Theory in Social Science*. New York: Harper & Row.

Liff, S. (1996) 'Two Routes to Managing Diversity: Individual Differences or Social Group Characteristics', *Employee Relations*, vol. 19, no. 1, pp. 11–26.

Lim, G.S. (2003) 'Compositional Dynamics and Interviewer Judgements in the Panel Employment Interview', *Academy of Management Best Conference Paper*, OB: N1–N6.

Lindsay, C. (1993) 'Paradoxes of Organizational Diversity: Living within the Paradoxes', *Academy of Management Proceedings*, pp. 374–37.

Linnehan, F., Chrobot-Mason, D. and Conrad, A.M. (2002) 'The Importance of Ethnic Identity to Attitudes, Norms, and Behavioural Intentions, toward Diversity', *Academy of Management Proceedings*, GDO: D1–D6.

Llewellyn, N. (2001) 'The Role of Storytelling and Narrative in a Modernisation Initiative', *Local Government Studies*, vol. 27, no. 4, pp. 35–58.

Locke, D.C. (1992) *Increasing Multicultural Understanding*. Newbury Park, CA: Sage.

Loirbecki, A. and Gavin, J. (2002) 'Critical Turns in the Evolution of the Diversity Management', *British Journal of Management*, vol. 11, pp. 17–31.

Loosemore, M. and Al Muslmani, H.S. (1999) 'Construction Project Management in the Persian Gulf: Inter-cultural Communication', *International Journal of Project Management*, vol. 17, no. 2, pp. 95–100.

Lorbiecki, A. (2001) 'Changing Views on Diversity Management: The Rise of Learning Perspective and the Need of Recognise Social and Political Contradictions', *Management Learning*, vol. 32, no. 3, pp. 345–61.

Lorbiecki, A. and Jack, G. (2000) 'Critical Turns in the Evolution of Diversity Management', *British Journal of Management*, vol. 11, no. 1, pp. 17–31.

Lorde, A. (2003) 'The Transformation of Silence into Language and Action', in R.J. Ely, E.G. Foldy, M.A. Scully and the Centre for Gender in Organizations, Simmons School of Management (eds), *Reader in Gender, Work and Organization*. Oxford: Blackwell, pp. 273–6.

Loudin, A. (2000) 'A Diversity Management Programme Should be Part of Every Company's Basic Training', *Warehousing Management*, April, pp. 31–3.

Lunt, P. (1994) 'Should You do Diversity Training?', *ABA Banking Journal*, August, pp. 53–4.

Mahar, C., Harker, R. and Wilkes, C. (1990) 'The Basic Theoretical Position', in R. Harker, C. Wilkes and C. Mahar (eds), *An Introduction to the Work of Pierre Bourdieu: The Practice of Theory*. London: Macmillan, pp. 1–25.

Maidment, J. (2003) 'Problems Experienced by Students on Field Placement: Using Research Findings to Inform Curriculum Design and Content', *Australian Social Work*, vol. 56, no. 1, pp. 50–60.

Majewski, S., Mayo, R., Mokrosz, A. and Gorski, M. (2000) 'Integrated Project System and Supervised Industrial Placement – Essential Cores of Civil Engineering Education', paper presented at *the ICEE Conference*, Taiwan.

Mandilaras, A. (2004) 'Industrial Placement and Degree Performance: Evidence from a British Higher Institution', *International Review of Education Economics*, vol. 3, no. 1, pp. 39–51.

Mannix, E. (2003) 'Editor's Comments: Conflict and Conflict Resolution – a Return to Theorising', *Academy of Management Review*, vol. 28, pp. 543–6.

Marable, M. (2000) 'We Need New and Critical Study of Race and Ethnicity', *The Chronicle of Higher Education*, vol. 25, pp. B4–7.

Mason, R.M. (2003) 'Culture-free or Culture-bound? A Boundary Spanning Perspective on Learning Knowledge Management Systems', *Journal of Global Information Management*, vol. 11, no. 4, pp. 20–36.

Mathiasen, D.G. (1999) 'The New Public Management and its Critics', *International Public Management Journal*, vol. 2, no. 1, pp. 90–111.

Maurana, C.A., Beck, B., Beversdorf, S.J. and Newton, G.L. (2000) 'Moving from Medical Student Placement to a Community-Academic Partnership with a Rural Community', *Journal of Rural Health*. vol. 16, no. 4, pp. 371–9.

Mauthner, N. and Doucet, A. (2000) 'Reflections on a Voice-Centered Relational Method: Analyzing Maternal and Domestic Voices', in J. Ribbens and R. Edwards (eds), *Feminist Dilemmas in Qualitative Research: Public Knowledge and Private Lives*. London: Sage, pp. 119–46.

Mayrhofer, W. (1997) 'Warning: Flexibility Can Damage your Organizational Health', *Employee Relations*, vol. 19, pp. 519–34.

MCCE (2005) 'A Celebration of Diversity, 2nd Multicultural Conference on Competitiveness and Enterprise', www.mcce.org.uk

McDougall, M. (1996) 'Equal Opportunities versus Managing Diversity: Another Challenge for Public Sector Management?', *International Journal of Public Sector Management*, vol. 9, no. 5/6, pp. 62–72.

McEnrue, M.P. (1993) 'Managing Diversity: Los Angeles Before and after the riots', *Organizational Dynamics*, vol. 21, no. 3, pp. 18–29.

McFadzean, E. (2000) 'What Can We Learn from Creative People?: The Story of Brian Eno', *Management Decision*, vol. 38, pp. 51–6.

McLellan, H. (2006) 'Corporate Storytelling Perspectives', *The Journal for Quality and Participation*, Spring, pp. 17–20.

McMahan, G.C., Bell, M.P. and Virick, M. (1998) 'Strategic Human Resource Management: Employee Involvement, Diversity and International Issues', *Human Resource Management Review*, vol. 8, pp. 193–214.

McMahon, U. and Quinn, U. (1995) 'Maximizing the Hospitality Management Student Work Placement Experience: A Case Study', *Education and Training*, vol. 37, no. 4, pp. 13–17.

McNerney, D. (1994) 'Competitive advantage: diverse customers and stakeholders', *HR Focus*, June, pp. 9–10.

Meyer, S. (1981) *The Five Dollar Day: Labour Management and Social Control in the Ford Motor Company, 1908–1921*. Albany: State University of New York Press.

Meyerson, D.E. (2001a) *Tempered Radicals: How People Use Difference to Inspire Change at Work*. Boston, Massachusetts: Harvard Business School Press.

Meyerson, D.E. (2001b) 'Radical Change, the Quiet Way', *Harvard Business Review*, October, pp. 92–100.

Meyerson, D.E. and Fletcher, J.K. (2003) 'A Modest Manifesto for Shattering the Glass Ceiling', in R.J. Ely, E.G. Foldy, M.A. Scully and the Centre for Gender in Organizations Simmons School of Management (eds), *Reader in gender, work and organization*. Oxford: Blackwell, pp. 230–41.

Meyerson, D.E. and Scully, M.A. (1995) 'Tempered Radicalism and the Politics of Ambivalence and Change', *Organization Science,* vol. 6, no. 5, pp. 585–600.

Michielsens, E., Shackleton, L. and Urwin, P. (2000) 'PPPs and the Jobless: Can Private Employment Agencies help Deliver the New Deals?', *New Economy*, vol. 7, pp. 168–71.

Mighty, E.J. (1991) 'Valuing Workforce Diversity: A Model of Organizational Change', *Canadian Journal of Administrative Sciences*, vol. 8, no. 2, pp. 64–71.

Miller, L. and Neathey, F. (2004) *Advancing Women in the Workplace: Case Studies*. Equal Opportunities Commission Working Paper Series no. 13, Manchester: EOC.

Milliken, F.J. and Martin, L.L. (1996) 'Searching for Common Threads: Understanding the Multiple Effects of Diversity in Organizational Groups', *Academy of Management Review*, vol. 21, pp. 402–33.

Millward, N., Bryson, A. and Forth, J. (2000) *All Change at Work?*. London: Routledge.

Milton, L.P. and Westphal, J.D. (2005) 'Identity Confirmation Networks and Cooperation in Work Groups', *Academy of Management Journal*, vol. 48, pp. 191–212.

Misko, J. (1998) *School Students in Workplaces: What Are the Benefits?* Report for the National Centre for Vocational Education Research, Australia.

Mitchell, S.A. (2000) *Relationality: From Attachment to Inter-subjectivity*. Hillsdale, NJ: The Analytic Press.

Mohammed, S. and Ringseis, E. (2001) 'Cognitive Diversity and Consensus in Group Decision Making: The Role of Inputs, Processes and Outcomes', *Organizational Behavior and Human Decision Processes*, vol. 85, pp. 310–35.

Moore, S. (1999) 'Understanding and Managing Diversity Among Groups at Work: Key Issues for Organizational Training and Development', *Journal of European Industrial Training*, vol. 23, pp. 208–17.

Mor Barak, M.E. (2000) 'The Inclusive Workplace: An Ecosystems Approach to Diversity Management', *Social Work*, vol. 45, pp. 339–52.

Morgan, A. and Turner, D. (2000) 'Adding Value to the Work Placement: Working towards a Professional Qualification in an Undergraduate Degree Programme', *Education and Training*, vol. 42, no. 8, pp. 453–60.

Morgan, S. and Dennehy, R.F. (1997) 'The Power of Organizational Storytelling: A Management Development Perspective', *Journal of Management Development*, vol. 16, no. 7, pp. 494–501.

Morrell, J., Boyland, M., Munns, G. and Astbury, L. (2001) *Gender Equality in Pay Practices*. EOC Research Discussion Series, Equal Opportunities Commission.

Morris, L. (1995) 'Research Capsules: Why Don't We Change?', *Training and Development*, October, pp. 59–61.

Morrison, A.M. (1992) *The New Leader: Guidelines on Leadership Diversity in America*. San Francisco, CA: Jossey-Bass.

Muir, C. (1996) 'Workplace Readiness for Communicating Diversity', *The Journal of Business Communication*, vol. 33, no. 4, pp. 475–86.

Mulholland G. Özbilgin, M. and Worman, D. (2005) *Managing Diversity: Linking Theory and Practice to Business Performance*. London: CIPD Publications.

Mulraney, J. and Turner, P. (2001) 'Learning from Small Enterprise Structured Work Placement', *Small Enterprise Workplace Learning – Links to School Vocational Education*, NCVER, Australia.

Munduate, L. and Gravenhorst, K.M.B. (2003) 'Power Dynamics and Organizational Change: An Introduction', *Applied Psychology: An International Review*, vol. 52, no. 1, pp. 1–13.

Nadler, D.A. and Tushman, M.L. (1990) 'Beyond the Charismatic Leader: Leadership and Organizational Change', *California Management Review*, Winter: pp. 77–97.

Nakakita, K. (2005) Personal Communication During Field Study of the Japan Institute for Labor Policy and Training Project.

Nash, R. (2003) 'Social Explanation and Socialization: On Bourdieu and the Structure, Disposition, Practice Scheme', *The Sociological Review*, vol. 51, pp. 43–62.

Naylor, D.M. (2000) 'Should Western Managers be Encouraged to Adopt JMPs?', *Employee Relations*, vol. 22, no. 2, pp. 160–178.

NCWE (The National Council of Work Experience) (2006) http://www.work-experience.org/cms/ShowPage/Home_page/Students/About_work_experience/pleaLdeeX

Neathey, F., Dench, S. and Thomson, L. (2003) *Monitoring Progress towards Pay Equality*. EOC Research Discussion Series, Equal Opportunities Commission.

Neathey, F., Willison, R., Akroyd, K., Regan, J. and Hill, D. (2005) *Equal Pay Reviews in Practice*. EOC Working Paper Series no. 33. Equal Opportunities Commission.

Neck, C.P., Smith, W.J. and Godwin, J.L. (1997) 'Thought Self-leadership: A Self-regulatory Approach to Diversity Management', *Journal of Managerial Psychology*, vol. 12, pp. 190–203.

Neill, N.T. and Mulholland, G.E. (2003) 'Student Placement: Structure, Skills and e-support', *Education and Training*, vol. 45, no. 2, pp. 89–99.

Neill, A.N., Mulholland, G.A., Ross, A.V. and Leckey, A.J. (2004) 'The Influence of Part-time Work on Student Placement', *Journal of Further and Higher Education*, vol. 28, no. 2, pp. 123–37.

Nemeth, C.J. (1986) 'Differential Contributions of Majority and Minority Influence', *Psychological Review*. vol. 93, pp. 23–32.

Nemetz, P.L. and Christensen, S.L. (1996) 'The Challenge of Cultural Diversity: Harnessing a Diversity of Views to Understand Multiculturalism', *Academy Management Review*, vol. 21, pp. 434–62.

Newman, J. 1995. 'Making Connections: Frameworks for Change', in C. Itzin and J. Newman (eds), *Gender Culture and Organizational Change: Putting Theory into Practice*. London and New York: Routledge, pp. 273–86.

Newton, A. and Smith, L.N. (1998) 'Practice Placement Supervision: The Role of the Personal Tutor', *Nurse Education Today*, vol. 18, no. 6, pp. 496–504.

Nikkeiren (2002) Position paper on 'Diversity Management', Tokyo.

Nishii, L. and Özbilgin, M.F. (2007) 'Global Diversity Management: Towards a Conceptual Framework', *International Journal of Human Resource Management*, vol. 18, no. 11, pp. 1883–94.

Nolan, C.A. (1998) 'Learning on Clinical Placement: The Experience of Six Australian Student Nurses', *Nurse Education Today*, vol. 18, no. 8, pp. 622–9.

Nolan, P.W. and Chung, M.C. (1999) 'Nursing Students' Perceptions of their First Mental Health Placement', *Nurse Education Today*, vol. 19, pp. 122-8.

NTC Economics (2006a) *Report on Jobs*, January.

NTC Economics (2006b) *Report on Jobs*, March.

Nyambegera, S.M. (2002) 'Ethnicity and Human Resources Management Practice in Sub-Sahara Africa: The Relevance of the Managing Diversity Discourse', *International Journal of Human Resources Management*, vol. 13, no. 7, pp. 1077–90.

O'Brien, M. and Shemilt, I. (2003) *Working Fathers: Earning and Caring*. Equal Opportunities Commission Research Discussion Series. Manchester: EOC.

O'hara, S.U. (1995) 'Valuing Socio-diversity', *International Journal of Social Economics*, vol. 22, pp. 31–49.

Olsen, W. and Walby, S. (2004) *Modelling Gender Pay Gaps*. EOC Working Paper Series no.17, Equal Opportunities Commission.

O'Reilly, C.A., Caldwell, D.F. and Barnett, W.P. (1989) 'Work Group Demography, Social Integration, and Turnover', *Administrative Science Quarterly*, vol. 34, pp. 21–8.

Orlitzky, M.F. and Benjmin, J.D. (2003) 'The Effects of Sex Composition on Small-group Performance in Business School Case Competition', *Academy of Management Learning and Education*, vol. 2, pp. 128–38.

Özbilgin, M.F. (2000) 'Is the Practice of Equal Opportunities Management Keeping Pace with the Theory? Management of Sex Equality in the Financial Services Sector in Britain and Turkey', *Human Resource Development International*, vol. 3, pp. 43–67.

Özbilgin, M.F. (2002) 'The Way Forward in Equal Opportunities by Sex in Employment in Turkey and Britain', *Management International*, vol. 7, pp. 55–65.

Özbilgin, M.F. (2005) 'Relational Methods in Organization Studies', in O. Kyriakidou and M.F. Özbilgin (eds), *Relational perspectives in organization studies: A research companion*. Cheltenham: Edward Elgar, pp. 390–421.

Özbilgin, M.F. and Woodward, D. (2004) "Belonging" and "Othemess": Sex Equality in Banking in Turkey and Britain', *Gender, Work and Organizations*, vol. 11, pp. 668–88.

Özbilgin, M.F. and Tatlı, A. (2005) 'Book Review Essay: Understanding Bourdieu's Contribution to Management and Organization Studies', *Academy of Management Review*, vol. 30, no. 4, pp. 855–69.

Panipucci, D. (2003) 'When Teams Devalue Diversity', *Academy of Management Best Conference Paper*, GDO: pp. D1–D6.

Parker, C. (1999) 'How to Win Hearts and Minds: Corporate Compliance Policies for Sexual Harassment', *Law and Policy*, vol. 21, no. 1, pp. 21–48.

Parkin, M. (2004) *Tales for Change: Using Storytelling to Develop People and Organizations*. London: Kogan Page.

Pay Equity Task Force Final Report. (2004) *Pay Equity: a New Approach to a Fundamental Right*. Department of Justice, Canada.

Pedler, P., Burgoyne, J. and Boydell, T. (1991) *The Learning Company: A Strategy for Sustainable Development*. London: McGraw-Hill.

Pelled, L.H. and Xin, K.R. (2000) 'Relational Demography and Relationship Quality between Two Cultures', *Organization Studies*, vol. 21, pp. 1077–94.

Pena-Casas, R., Degryse, C. and Pochet, P. (2002) 'European Strategy in the Field of Poverty and Social Exclusion', *Observatoire Social European*, http://www.ose.be, accessed July 2003.

Peng, M.W. and Heath, P.S. (1996) 'The Growth of the Firm in Planned Economies in Transition: Institutions, Organizations and Strategic Choice', *Academy of Management Review*, vol. 21, pp. 492–525.

Pfeffer, J. (1993) 'Barriers to the Advance of Organizational Science: Paradigm Development as a Dependent Variable', *Academy of Management Review*, vol. 18, pp. 599–620.

Piercy, N.F. (1995) 'Marketing and Strategy Fit together (In spite of What Some Management Educators Seem to Think!)', *Management Decision*, vol. 33, pp. 42–47.

Polzer, J.T., Milton, P. and Swann, Jr. W.B. (2001) 'Capitalizing on Diversity: Interpersonal Congruence in Small Work Groups', *Academy of Management Proceedings*, OB: pp. H1–H6.

Powell, G.N. (1987) 'The Effects of Sex and Gender on Recruitment', *Academy of Management Review*, vol. 12, pp. 731–43.

Prasad, P. and Mills, A.J. (1997) 'From Showcase to Shadow: Understanding the Dilemmas of Managing Workplace Diversity', in P. Prasad, A.J. Mills, M. Elmes, and A. Prasad (eds), *Managing the Organizational Melting Pot: Dilemmas of Workplace Diversity*. Thousand Oaks, CA: Sage, pp. 3–27.

Pratt, G.M. and Foreman, P.O. (2000) 'The Beauty of and Barriers to Organizational Theories of Identity', *Academy of Management Review*, vol. 25, pp. 141–152.

Procter, S. and Mueller, F. (eds) (2000) *Teamworking*. Basingstoke: Palgrave Macmillan.

Puffer, S.M. (2004) 'Introduction: Rosabeth Moss Kanter's Men and Women of The Corporation and The Change Masters', *Academy of Management Executive*, vol. 18, pp. 92–5.

Purcell, K. and Cam, S. (2002) *Employment Intermediaries in the UK: Who Uses them?*, ESRU Working Paper no.7, The Research Institute of Industrial Economics.

Raatikainen, P. (2002) 'Contributions of Multiculturalism to The Competitive Advantage of an Organization', *Singapore Management Review*, vol. 24, pp. 81–8.

Racial Equality Means Business. Available at: http://www.cre.gov.uk/

Ragins, B.R. (1997) 'Diversified Mentoring Relationships in Organizations: A Power Perspective', *Academy of Management Review*, vol. 22, pp. 482–521.

Ramos, R., Hernandez, L. and Ramos, S. (2003) 'The Networked Knowledge Economy in A Diversity Context: A European Framework', *Academy of Management Best Conference Paper*, TIM: K1–K6.

Randel, A.E. (2000) 'How Do Members of Groups Diverse On Multiple Dimensions Conceptualize One Another? Social Contextual Triggers and Work Group Conflict Implications of Identity Salience', *Academy of Management Proceedings*, GDO: A1–A6.

Randel, A.E. and Jaussi, K.S. (2003) 'Functional Background Identity, diversity, and individual performance in cross-functional teams', *Academy of Management Journal*, vol. 46, pp. 763–74.

Rapper, B., Webster, A. and Charles, D. (1999) 'Making Sense Of Diversity and Reluctance: Academic-Industrial Relations and Intellectual Property', *Research Policy*, vol. 28, pp. 873–90.

Ratman, C.S.V. and Chandra, V. (1996) 'Sources of Diversity and Challenges Before Human Resources Management in India', *International Journal of Manpower*, vol. 17, pp. 76–108.

Rausseau, R. (1997) 'Employing the New America', *R&I Exclusive*, March, pp. 40–52.

Ready, D.A. (2002) 'How Storytelling Builds Next-generation Leaders', *MIT Sloan Management Review*, Summer, pp. 63–9.

Recruitment and Employment Confederation (REC) (2006a) *Code of Professional Practice*.

Recruitment and Employment Confederation (REC) (2006b) *DiverCity Diagnostic/Audit, Draft*.

Recruitment and Employment Confederation (REC) (2006c) *Diversity Diagnostic*. Available at: http://www.4mat.com/diversitytoolkit/survey/form.asp.

Recruitment and Employment Confederation (REC) (2006d) *Model Diversity Policy*.

Recruitment and Employment Confederation (REC) (2006e) *Monitoring Equal Opportunities and Diversity: Model Monitoring Form*.

Recruitment and Employment Confederation (REC) and Jobcentre Plus (2005) *Diversity Pledge*. Available at: http://www.rec.uk.com/rec/about-the-rec/diversitypledge.pdf.

Reinmoeller, P. and N. Van Baardwijk, (2005) 'The link Between Diversity and Resilience', *MIT Slogan Management Review*, vol. 46, pp. 61–5.

Richard, O.C. (2000) 'Racial Diversity, Business Strategy, and Firm Performance: A Resource Based-View', *Academy of Management Journal*, vol. 43, pp. 164–77.

Richard, O.C. and Murthi, B.P.S. (2004) 'Does Race Matter Within a Multicultural Context? Alternate Modes of Theorising and Theory Testing', *Academy of Management Best Conference Paper*, GDO: C1–C6.

Richard, O.C., Barnett, T., Dwyer, S. and Chadwick, K. (2004) 'Cultural Diversity in Management, firm performance, and the moderating role of entrepreneurial orientation dimensions', *Academy of Management Review*, vol. 47, pp. 255–66.

Richardson, P. (2004) 'Discrimination Can Seriously Damage Your Corporate Health', *British Journal of Administrative Management*, no. 42, pp. 20–21.

Richardson, S. and Blakeney, C. (1998) 'The Undergraduate Placement System: An Empirical Study', *Accounting Education*, vol. 7, no. 2, pp. 101–21.

Robbins, S. (2001) *Organizational Behavior*. New Jersey: Prentice-Hall.

Roberson, Q.M. and Park, H.M. (2004) 'Diversity Reputation And Leadership Diversity as a Source Of Competitive Advantage in Organizations', *Academy of Management Best Conference Paper*, GDO: F1–F6.

Robinson, G. and Decant, K. (1997) 'Building a Business Case for Diversity', *Academy of Management Executive*, vol. 11, pp. 21–31.

Rodgers, J.O (2002) 'Diversity Management Strategies Bring Rewards', www.elp.com, November, 8.

Rolfe, H. and Nadeem, S. (2006) 'Opening up Opportunities through Advice and Guidance', Equal Opportunities Commission Working Paper Series no. x, Manchester: EOC.

Roper, A., Brookes, M. and Hampton, A. (1997) 'The Multi-National Management of International Hotel Groups', *International Journal of Hospitality Management*, vol. 16, pp. 147–59.

Saka, A. (2004) 'Cross-National Diffusion of Work Systems: Translation of Japanese Operations In The UK', *Organization Studies*, vol. 25, no. 2, pp. 209–28.

Sako, M., Sato, H. (eds) (1977) 'Japanese Labour and Management in Transition: Diversity', flexibility and participation, London, Routledge.

Samway, K.D. and McKeon, D. (1999) '*Myths and Realities: Best Practices for Language Minority Students*', Portsmouth, NH: Heinemann.

Sanchez, J.I. and Brock, P. (1996) 'Outcomes of Perceived Discrimination Among Hispanic Employees: Is Diversity Management a Luxury or Necessity?', *Academy of Management Journal*, vol. 39, pp. 704–19.

Sanches-Burks, J., Nisbett, R.E. and Ybarra, O. (2000) 'Cultural Styles, Relational Schemas And Prejudice Against Outgroups', *Academy of Management Proceedings*, OB: pp. G1–G6.

Satow, S. and Wang, Z. (1994) 'Cultural and Organizational Factors in Human Resources Management in China and Japan: A Cross-cultural Socio-economic Perspective', *Journal of Managerial Psychology*, vol. 9, pp. 3–11.

Saunders, C., Slyke, C.V. and Vogel, D.R. (2004) 'My Time or Yours? Managing Time Vision in Global Virtual Teams', *Academy of Management Executive*, vol. 18, pp. 19–31.

Saxton, J. and Ashworth, P. (1990) 'The Workplace Supervision of Sandwich Degree Placement Students', *Management Education and Development*, vol. 21, no. 2, pp. 133–49.

Schaafsma, H. (1996) 'Back to the Real World: Work Placements Revisited', *Education and Training*, vol. 38, no. 1, pp. 5–13.

Schäfer, S., Winterbotham, M. and McAndrew, F. (2005) *Equal Pay Reviews Survey 2004*. EOC Working Paper Series no. 32, Equal Opportunities Commission.

Schoenberger, E. (1997) *The Cultural Crisis of the Firm*. Oxford: Blackwell.

Schneider, S.K. and Northcraft, G.B. (1999) 'Three Social Dilemmas of Workforce Diversity in Organizations: A Social Identity Perspective', *Human Relations*, vol. 52, pp. 1445–67.

Schuler, R.S. and Jackson, S.E. (1987) 'Linking Competitive Strategies with Human Resource Management Practices', *Academy of Management Executive*, vol. 1, pp. 207–19.

Senge, P. 1990. *The fifth discipline*. New York: Double Day Press.

Shapiro, G. (2000) 'Employee Involvement: Opening The Diversity Pandora's Box?', *Personnel Review*, vol. 29, pp. 304–23.

Shaw, M. (1993) 'Achieving Equality of Treatment and Opportunity in the Workplace', in R. Harrison (ed.), *Human Resource Management: Issues and Strategies*. Wokingham: Addison-Wesley Publishing Company.

Shen, J. and Herr, E.L. (2004) 'Career Placement Concerns of International Graduate Students: A Qualitative Study', *Journal of Career Development*, vol. 31, no. 1, pp. 15–29.

Shumate, M., Bryant, J.A. and Monge, P.R. (2005) 'Storytelling and globalisation: the complex narratives of netwar', *E:CO*, vol. 7, no. 3–4, pp. 74–84.

Siemon, R. (2001) 'Top Team Characteristics and the Business Strategies of Japanese Organizations', *Corporate Governance*, vol. 1, pp. 4–12.

Simmons, J.C. (2001) 'Addressing Diversity in The Health Care Setting To Achieve Quality Care', *The Quality Letter*, December, pp. 2–9.

Simons, T., Pelled, H. and Smith K.A. (1999) 'Making use of Difference: Diversity, debate and decision comprehensiveness in top management teams', *Academy of Management Journal*, vol. 42, pp. 662–73.

Simpson, P., French, R. and Harvey, C.E. (2002) 'Leadership and Negative Capability' *Human Relations*, vol. 55, no. 10, pp. 1209–26.

Skill (National Bureau of Students with Disabilities) (2006) available at: http://www.skill.org.uk/index.asp

Skinner, D. (1999) 'The Reality of Equal Opportunities: E Expectations and The Experiences of Part-Time Staff And Their Managers', *Personnel Review*, vol. 28, pp. 425–38.

Skranefjell, A. and Tonnessen, M. (2003) 'Statistical Storytelling', *Statistical Journal of the United Nations*, vol. 20, pp. 51–4.

Smith, J. and Barnes, M. (2000) 'Developing Primary care Groups in the New NHS: Towards Diversity or Uniformity?', *Public, Money and Management*, vol. 20, no. 1, pp. 45–52.

Smith, K.G., Smith, K.A., Olian, J.D., Sims, H.P., O'Bannon, D.P. and Scully, J.A. (1994) 'Top Management Team Demography and Process: The Role of Social Integration and Communication', *Administrative Science Quarterly*. vol. 39, pp. 412–38.

Smith, W.J., Wokutch, R.E. and Harrington, K.V. and Dennis, B.S. (2004) 'Organizational Attractiveness and Corporate Social Orientation: Do Our Values Influence Our Preference for Affirmative Action and Managing Diversity?', *Business and Society*, vol. 43, pp. 69–96.

Smith, S., Edwards, H. and Courtney, M. and Finlayson, K. (2001) 'Factors Influencing Student Nurses in Their Choice of a Rural Clinical Placement Site', *Rural and Remote Health*, Retrieved from http:/rrh.deakin.edu.au

Solorzano, D.G. and Yosso, T.J. (2002) 'Critical Race Methodology: Counter-Storytelling as an Analytical Framework For Education Research', *Qualitative Inquiry*, vol. 8, no. 1, pp. 23–44.

Somers, M.R. (1998) 'We're no Angels: Realism, Rational Choice, and Rationality in Social Science', *American Journal of Sociology*, vol. 104, no. 3, pp. 722–84.

Soni, V. (2000) 'A Twenty-first-century Reception for Diversity in the Public Sector: A Case Study', *Public Administration Review*, vol. 60, pp. 395–408.

Spender, J.C. (1989) *Industrial Recipes: The Nature and Sources of Managerial Judgement.* Oxford: Blackwell.

Spich, S. (1995) 'Globalisation Folklore: Problems of Myth and Ideology in the Discourse of Globalisation', *Journal of Organizational Change Management*, vol. 8, pp. 6–29.

Srinivas, K.M. (1995) 'Globalisation of Business and the Third World: Challenge of Expanding the Mindsets', *Journal of Management Development*, vol. 14, pp. 26–49.

Stedham, Y.E. and Yamamura, J.H. (2004) 'Measuring National Culture: Does Gender Matter?', *Women in Management Review*, vol. 19, pp. 233–43.

Steingard, D.S. and Fitzgibbons, D.E. (1995) 'Challenging the Juggernaut of Globalisation: A Manifesto for Academic Praxis', *Journal of Organizational Change Management*, vol. 8, pp. 30–54.

Steward, R. and Barsoux, J. (1994) *The Diversity of Management: Twelve Managers Talking*, Basingstoke: Macmillan.

Stoner, C.R. and Russell-Chapin, A. (1997) 'Creating a Culture of Diversity Management: Moving from Awareness to Action', *Business Forum*, Spring/Fall, pp. 6–12.

Straw, J. (1990) *Equal Opportunities*. Manchester: Equal Opportunities Commission.

Streufert, S., Pogash, R., Piasecki, M. and Post, G.M. (1990) 'Age and Management: Team Performance', *Psychology and Aging*, vol. 5, pp. 551–9.

Strydom, J.B. and Erwee, R. (1998) 'Diversity Management in a Sample of African Companies', *South African Journal of Business Management*, vol. 29, pp. 14–21.

Stumpf, S.A., Watson, M.A. and Rustogi, H. (1994) 'Leadership in a Global Village: Creating Practice Fields to Develop Learning Organizations', *Journal of Management Development*, vol. 13, pp. 16–25.

Styhre, A. (2002) 'Constructing the Image of the Other: A Post-Colonial Image of the Adaptation of Japanese Human Resources Management Practices', *Management Decision*, vol. 40, pp. 257–65.

Svyantek, D.J., Mahoney, K.T. and Brown, L.L. (2002) 'Diversity and Effectiveness in the Roman and Persian Emperors', *International Journal of Organizational Analysis*, vol. 10, pp. 260–83.

Swan, J., Newell, S., Scarbrough, H. and Hislop, D. (1999) 'Knowledge Management and Innovation: Networks and Networking', *Journal of Knowledge Management*, vol. 3, pp. 262–75.

Swann, Jr., W.B., Polzer, J.T., Seyle, D.C. and Ko, S.J. (2004) 'Finding Value in Diversity: Verification of Personal and Social Self-Views in Diverse Groups', *Academy of Management Review*, vol. 29, pp. 9–27.

Swap, W., Leonard, D., Shields, M. and Abrams, L. (2001) 'Using Mentoring and Storytelling to Transfer Knowledge in the Workplace', *Journal of Management Information Systems*, vol. 18, no. 1, pp. 95–114.

Symposium Paper Abstracts (2002) 'Gender and Diversity in Organizations', pp. 1–14.

Tatlı, A. (2008) 'Understanding the Agency of Diversity Managers: A Relational and Multilevel Investigation', unpublished PhD thesis, University of London.

Tatlı, A., Özbilgin, M.F. and Küskü, F. (2008) 'Gendered Occupational Outcomes: the case of professional training and work in Turkey', in Jacquelynne Eccles and Helen Watt (eds), *Explaining Gendered Occupational Outcomes*. Michigan: American Psychological Association (APA) Press.

Tatlı, A., Özbilgin, M.F., Mulholland, G. and Worman, D. (2006) *Managing Diversity Measuring Success*. London: Chartered Institute of Personnel and Development.

Taylor, C. (1995) 'Building a business case for diversity', *Canadian Business Review*, vol. 22, no. 4–16, pp. 12–15.

Taylor, L. (2001) 'Melee Law', *People Management*, September, p. 55.

Teicher, J. and Speairtt, K. (1996) 'From Equal Employment Opportunity to Managing Diversity: The Australian Experience', *International Journal of Manpower*, vol. 17, pp. 109–33.

The Diversity Driver. 2006. Available at: http://www.fairplaypartnership.org.uk/diversity-driver.html

Thomas, A.D. (2004) 'Diversity as Strategy', *Harvard Business Review*, September, pp. 98–108.

Thomas, D.A. and Ely, R.J. (1996) 'Making Differences Matter: A New Paradigm for Managing Diversity', *Harvard Business Review*, vol. 74, no. 5, pp. 79–90.

Thomas, R.R. (1990) 'From Affirmative Action to Affirming Diversity', *Harvard Business Review*, vol. 68, no. 2, pp. 107–17.

Thomas Jr., R.R. (1996) 'Redefining Diversity', *HR Focus*, April, pp. 6–7.

Thomas Jr., R.R. (1999) 'Diversity Management', *Executive Excellence*, vol. 16, pp. 8–9.

Thorne, D. and Davig, W. (1999) 'Toppling Disciplinary Silos: One Suggestion for Accounting and Management', *Journal of Education for Business*, November/December, pp. 99–103.

Tichy, N.M. (1974) 'Agents of Planned Social Change: Congruence of Values, Cognitions and Actions', *Administrative Science Quarterly*, vol. 19, no. 2, pp. 164–82.

Todd, S. (2002) 'Stakeholder Perspectives: A Personal Account of an Equality and Diversity Practitioner's Intervention Experience', in N. Cornelius (ed.), *Building Workplace Equality: Ethics, Diversity and Inclusion*. London: Thomson, pp. 265–95.

Trades Union Congress (1994) 'Report of the 126th Annual Trades Union Congress', Blackpool, September, pp. 5–9.

Tsui, A.S. and Ashford, S.J. (1991) 'Reactions to Demographic Diversity: Similarity-Attraction or Self-Regulation', *Academy of Management Proceedings*, pp. 240–4.

Tsui, A.S., Egan, T.D. and O'Reilly, C.A., III (1992) 'Being Different: Relational Demography and Organizational Attachment', *Administrative Science Quarterly*, vol. 37, pp. 549–79.

Tyson, S. 1995. *Human Resource Strategy: Towards a General Theory of Human Resource Management*. London: Pitman Publishing.

UNESCO (2006) http://portal.unesco.org/culture/en/evphp-URL_ID=18668&URLDO=DO_TOPIC&URL_SECTION=201.html

Uran, C. (2005) 'Assimilation and Exoticisms: The Dialectic of Diversity Management', *American Quarterly*, June, pp. 583–92.

Uzzell, D.L. (1986) 'The Professional Placement for Students: Some Theoretical Considerations', *Oxford Review of Education*, vol. 12, no. 1, pp. 67–75.

Van Der Vegt, G.S. and Bunderson, J.S. (2005) 'Learning and Performance in Multidisciplinary Teams: The Importance of Collective Team Identification', *Academy of Management Journal*, vol. 48, pp. 532–47.

Van Der Vegt, G.S. and Janssen, O. (2001) 'The Joint Effects of Psychological Diversity and Interdependence on Individual Performance', *Academy of Management Proceedings*, OB: pp. J1–J5.

Vance, C.M. (1991) 'Formalising Storytelling in Organizations: A Key Agenda for the Design of Training', *Journal of Organizational Change Management*, vol. 4, no. 3, pp. 52–58.

Vechio, R.P. and Bullis R.C. (2001) 'Moderators of the Influence of Supervisor-Subordinate Similarity on Subordinate Outcomes', *Academy of Management Proceedings*, GDO: pp. B1–B6.

Vedder, G. (2005) 'Denkanstobe Zum Diversity Management', *Arbeit*, vol. 14, pp. 34–43.

Verloo, M. and Benschop, Y. (2002) 'Shifting Responsibilities: The Position of Equal Agencies in Gender Mainstreaming', *Management International*, vol. 7, pp. 93–101.

Volberda, H.W. (1998) *Building the Flexible Firm: How to Remain Competitive*. Oxford: Oxford University Press.

Wacquant, L. (2006) *Body and Soul: Notebooks of an Apprentice Boxer*. Oxford: Oxford University Press.

Walters, F.M. (1995) 'Successfully Managing Diversity', *Vital Speeches of The Day*, vol. 61, pp. 496–501.

Wanous, J.P. and Youtz, M.A. (1986) 'Solution Diversity and the Quality of Group Decision', *Academy of Management Journal*, March, pp. 149–58.

Ward, J. and Winstanley, D. (2004) 'Sexuality and the City: Exploring the Experience of Minority Sexual Identity through Storytelling', *Culture and Organization*, vol. 10, no. 3, pp. 219–36.

Ward, K. (2002) *The Changing Business of the UK Temporary Staffing Industry*, Research Programme Working Paper 1, 1. School of Geography, The University of Manchester.

Ward, K., Grimshaw, D., Rubery, J. and Beynon, H. (2001) 'Dilemmas in the Management of Temporary Work Agency Staff', *Human Resource Management Journal*, vol. 11, no. 4, pp. 3–21.

Watson, W.E., Kumar, K. and Michaelsen, L.K. (1993) 'Cultural Diversity's Impact on Interaction Process and Performance: Comparing Homogenous and Diverse Task Groups', *Academy of Management Journal*, vol. 36, pp. 590–602.

Watts, A.G. (1996) 'Careers Guidance and Public Policy', in A.G. Watts, B. Law, J. Killeen, J.M. Kidd and R. Hawthorn (eds), *Rethinking Careers Education and Guidance: Theory, Policy and Practice*. London: Routledge, pp. 380–91.

Watts, A.G., Hughes, D. and Wood, M. (2005), *A Market in Career? Evidence and Issues*. Occasional paper, University of Derby Centre for Guidance Studies.

Weech-Maldo, R. (2002) 'Racial ethnic diversity management and cultural competency: the case of Pennsylvania Hospitals', *Journal of Healthcare Management*, vol. 47, pp. 111–24.

Weick, K.E. (1984) 'Small Wins: Redefining the Scale of Social Problems'. *American Psychologist*, vol. 39, pp. 40–49.

Weick, K.E. (1998) 'Theory Construction as Disciplined Imagination', *Academy of Management Review*, vol. 14, pp. 516–31.

Weick, K.E. and Quinn, R.E. (1999) 'Organizational Change and Development', *Annual Review of Psychology*, vol. 50, pp. 361–86.

Welch, D. and Welch, L. (1997) 'Being Flexible and Accommodating Diversity: The Challenge for Multinational Management', *European Management Journal*, vol. 15, pp. 677–85.

Westhead, P., Storey, D.J. and Martin, F. (2001) 'Outcomes Reported by Students who Participated in the 1994 Shell Technology Enterprise Programme', *Entrepreneurship & Regional Development*, vol. 13, no. 2, pp. 163–85.

Westley, F. and Mintzberg, H. (1989) 'Visionary Leadership and Strategic Management', *Strategic Management Journal*, vol. 10, pp. 17–32.

Wharton, A.S. and Baron, J.N. (1987) 'So Happy Together? The Impact of Gender Segregation on Men at Work', *American Sociological Review*, vol. 52, pp. 574–87.

Wheeler, R.D. (1997) 'Managing Workforce Diversity', *Tax Executive*, vol. 49, pp. 493–96.

Whiteley, J. (2004) 'Creating Behavioural Change in Leaders', *Industrial and Commercial Training*, vol. 36, pp. 162–65.

Wilkinson, B. (2000) *Labour Market Flexibility and Employment Agencies in the UK, Japan and Korea*. Paper presented to the Conference on 'Economic Crisis and Labor Market Reform: The Case of Korea', Seoul, Korea Labor Institute, May, pp. 18–20.

Wilson, E.M. and Iles, P.A. (1999) 'Managing Diversity – an Employment and Service Delivery Challenge', *Managing Diversity*, The International Journal of Public Sector Management, vol. 12, pp. 27–48.

Wiseman, J. and Dent, R. (2005) *Satisfaction Levels amongst Temporary Agency Workers*. Research by BMG Research for the REC's Industry Research Unit, November.

Witz, A. (1992) *Professions and Patriarchy*. London and New York: Routledge.

Wolf, A. (2002) *Does Education Matter? Myths about Education and Economic Growth*. London: Penguin.

Women and Work Commission (2006) *Shaping a Fairer Future*. London: Women and Work Commission, DTI.

Wood, R. (1992) 'Psychological Testing free from Prejudice', *Personnel Management*, December, pp. 34–7.

Woods, R.H. and Scidrini, M.P. (1995) 'Diversity Programs in Chain Restaurants', *Cornell Hotel and Restaurant Administration Quarterly*, June, pp. 18–23.

Worman, D. (2001) 'Press Home the Advantage', *People Management*, November, p. 25.

Wright, P., Perris, S.P., Hiller, J.S. and Kroll, M. (1995) 'Competitiveness Through Management of Diversity: Effects on Stock Price Valuation', *Academy of Management Journal*, vol. 38, pp. 272–87.

Yin, R.K. (2002) *Case Study Research: Design and Methods*, 3rd edn. Applied Social Research Methods Series, London: Sage.

Yockelson, D. (2000) 'B2B Stategies. Banks mine customer data', *Internetweek*, September, pp. 45–46.

Zanoni, P. and Janssens, M. (2003) 'Deconstructing the Differences: The Rhetoric of Human Resources Managers' Diversity Discourse', *Organization Studies*, vol. 25, no. 1, pp. 55–74.

Zinkhan, G.M. and Balazs, A.L. (2002) 'A Stakeholder-Integrated Approach to Health Care Management', *Journal of Business Research*, vol. 57, no. 9, pp. 984–89.

Index

academic subfield   230–1, 245, 246
accessibility   181–2, 195
Acker, J.   376, 398, 405, 421, 422, 428
action plans   177–8, 179–80, 181
active ageing   114
ad hoc cross-cultural management   21, 33
adult and community learning, equality
    and diversity in   120, 143
advice   267–9
advisory committee   167
age   235
agency   *see* change agency
Agocs, C.   2, 24, 27, 230, 397–8
Aguilera, R.V.   18, 44
Akashi, Y.   54
anti-harassment policy   382–3
Appelbaum, S.H.   31
Argentina   227
Arimura, S.   48
Arts Council England   332–3, 334
Ashkanasy, N.M.   4–5, 35–6, 241
Ashtiany, S.   4
Ashworth, P.   333–4, 337, 338
assembly line   368–70
assessment   337
Association of Executive Recruiters (AER)
    257, 270
Athena Swan Charter   120, 144
attitudes of host institutions   344–5, 348

Au, K.   20
audit tools   117, 118–19, 127–40
Aurora   306
Australia   23, 121–2
automobile manufacturing   11, 12,
    367–88
  description of global auto
    manufacturer   368–72
  diversity managers *see* diversity
    managers
  Japan   41–52
  organizational structures of diversity
    management   372–87; diversity
    management activities and
    programmes   377–87; diversity
    structure   374–7
Auyero, J.   227
awareness
  lack of in recruitment sector   284–6
  raising and recruitment agencies   294,
    313
axial-coding technique   41

backlash   31
backstage activities   397
Balanced Score Card (BSC)   118, 127–8
Bar-On, D.   248
Barak, M.E.M.   10
Barkema, H.G.   18, 25